DOCTRINE IN EXPERIENCE

KINGSWOOD BOOKS

Rex D. Matthews
Director
Candler School of Theology, Emory University

EDITORIAL ADVISORY BOARD

Ted Campbell
Perkins School of Theology

Joel B. Green
Fuller Theological Seminary

Richard P. Heitzenrater
The Divinity School, Duke University

Henry Knight III
Saint Paul School of Theology

Mary Elizabeth Mullino Moore
Candler School of Theology, Emory University

Sam Powell
Point Loma Nazarene University

Karen B. Westerfield Tucker
School of Theology, Boston University

Jason Vickers
United Theological Seminary

Sondra Wheeler
Wesley Theological Seminary

Anne E. Streaty Wimberly
Interdenominational Theological Center

M. Kathryn Armistead, *ex officio*
Abingdon Press

John Kutsko, *ex officio*
Abingdon Press

Neil M. Alexander, *ex officio*
Abingdon Press

DOCTRINE IN EXPERIENCE

A Methodist Theology of Church and Ministry

Russell E. Richey

KINGSWOOD BOOKS
An Imprint of Abingdon Press
Nashville, Tennessee

**DOCTRINE IN EXPERIENCE
A METHODIST THEOLOGY OF CHURCH AND MINISTRY**

Copyright © 2009 by Abingdon Press

All rights reserved.
No part of this work may be reproduced or transmitted in any form or by any means, electronic or mechanical, including photocopying and recording, or by any information storage or retrieval system, except as may be expressly permitted by the 1976 Copyright Act or in writing from the publisher. Requests for permission should be addressed to Abingdon Press, P.O. Box 801, 201 Eighth Avenue South, Nashville, TN 37202-0801 or permissions@abingdonpress.com.

This book is printed on acid-free paper.

Library of Congress Cataloging-in-Publication Data

Richey, Russell E.
  Doctrine in experience : a Methodist theology of church and ministry / Russell E. Richey.
    p. cm.
  Includes bibliographical references.
  ISBN 978-1-4267-0010-1 (pbk. : alk. paper)
  1. Methodist Church—Doctrines. 2. Church. 3. Church work. I. Title.
  BX8331.3.R524 2009
  262'.07—dc22

2009007495

All Scripture quotations unless noted otherwise are taken from the New Revised Standard Version of the Bible, copyright 1989, Division of Christian Education of the National Council of the Churches of Christ in the United States of America. Used by permission. All rights reserved.

This project was supported by a generous grant from the Alonzo L. McDonald Family Agape Foundation to the Center for the Study of Law and Religion at Emory University, and was prepared by the author as a Senior Fellow of the Center. The author wishes to thank especially Amb. Alonzo L. McDonald, Peter McDonald, and the other McDonald Agape Foundation Trustees for their support and encouragement. The opinions in this publication are those of the author and do not necessarily reflect the views of the Foundation or the Center.

Page 65 and page 241 illustrations appear courtesy of the Methodist collections of Drew University.

Quotations from *The Story of American Methodism* (Nashville: Abingdon Press, 1974) are used by permission.

Quotations from the *Book of Discipline of The United Methodist Church* (Nashville: United Methodist Publishing House, 2004) are used by permission.

See pages vii and viii for additional credits or acknowledgments.

CONTENTS

Acknowledgments vii

Abbreviations ix

Introduction: Doctrine in Experience xi

PART 1: DOCTRINE IN EXPERIENCE

Chapter 1: Four Languages of Methodist Self-Understanding 3

Chapter 2: History as Bearer of Methodist Identity 21

PART 2: ITINERANT MINISTRY

Chapter 3: Evolving Patterns of Methodist Ministry 45

Chapter 4: District Superintendency: A Reconsideration 69

Chapter 5: The Teaching Office 93

Chapter 6: Itinerant General Superintendency 119

Chapter 7: Ministerial Formation 139

PART 3: CONFERENCE AND CONNECTION

Chapter 8: Methodist Connectionalism 159

Contents

Chapter 9: Methodist Creation of the Denomination 183

Chapter 10: Connecting through Education 201

Chapter 11: Methodist Culture Wars 225

Chapter 12: Are the Local Church and the Denominational
Bureaucracy "Twins"? 239

PART 4: CHURCH AND SACRAMENT

Chapter 13: Methodism's *Practiced* Ecclesiology 255

Appendix to Chapter 4 285

Appendix to Chapter 6 295

Appendix to Chapter 10 297

Notes 299

Bibliography of Frequently Cited Titles 339

ACKNOWLEDGMENTS

Chapter 1: "Four Languages of Methodist Self-Understanding," originally published as "The Four Languages of Early American Methodism," *Methodist History* 28 (April 1990): 155–71.

Chapter 2: "History as Bearer of Methodist Identity," originally published as "History as a Bearer of Denominational Identity: Methodism as a Case Study" in *Beyond Establishment: Protestant Identity in a Post-Protestant Age,* ed. Jackson Carroll and Wade Clark Roof (Louisville: Westminster/John Knox, 1993), 270–95.

Chapter 3: "Evolving Patterns of Methodist Ministry," originally published in *Methodist History* 22 (Oct. 1983): 20–37.

Chapter 4: "District Superintendency: A Reconsideration," an unpublished lecture delivered at the January 2004 SEJ Cabinet Consultation at St. Simon's Island.

Chapter 5: "The Teaching Office," originally published as "The Legacy of Francis Asbury: The Teaching Office in Episcopal Methodism," *Quarterly Review* 15 (Summer 1995): 145–74.

Chapter 6: "Itinerant General Superintendency," an essay drawing on portions of a draft report for the United Methodist Church Task Force to Study the Episcopacy, which was included in the 2008 General Conference delegate materials.

Chapter 7: "Ministerial Formation," originally published as "Ministerial Education: The Early Methodist Episcopal

Experience," in *Theological Education in the Evangelical Traditions*, ed. D. G. Hart and R. Albert Mohler, Jr. (Grand Rapids: Baker Books, a division of Baker Publishing group, 1997), 45–62.

Chapter 8: "Methodist Connectionalism," originally published as "Introduction" in *Connectionalism: Ecclesiology, Mission, and Identity*, primary coeditor with Dennis M. Campbell and William B. Lawrence (Nashville: Abingdon, 1997), 1–20. Used by permission.

Chapter 9: "Methodist Creation of the Denomination," originally published as "The Social Sources of Denominationalism: Methodism," in *Denominationalism*, ed. Russell E. Richey (Nashville: Abingdon, 1977), 161–79; and in *Methodist History* 15 (April 1977): 167–85. Used by permission.

Chapter 10: "Connecting through Education," originally published as "Connectionalism and College," *Quarterly Review* 18 (Winter 1998): 331–56; also in *Presidential Papers* 15 (February 1999): 12–23, 31–35.

Chapter 11: "Methodist Culture Wars," originally published as "Culture Wars and Denominational Loyalties: A Methodist Case Study," *Quarterly Review* 18 (Spring 1998): 3–17.

Chapter 12: "Are the Local Church and the Denominational Bureaucracy 'Twins'?" originally published in *Questions for the Twenty-First Century Church*, ed. Russell E. Richey et al. (Nashville: Abingdon, 1999), 232–41. Used by permission.

Chapter 13: "Methodism's *Practiced* Ecclesiology," originally published as "Understandings of Ecclesiology in United Methodism," *Orthodox and Wesleyan Ecclesiology*, ed. ST Kimbrough, Jr. (Crestwood, NY: St. Vladimir's Seminary Press, 2007), 149–71.

ABBREVIATIONS

For Denominations

AME   The African Methodist Episcopal Church (1816–)
AMEZ   The African Methodist Episcopal Church Zion (1820–)
CME   The (Colored) Christian Methodist Episcopal Church (1870–)
EA   The Evangelical Association/Church (1803–1946)
EUBC   The Evangelical United Brethren Church (1946–1968)
MC   The Methodist Church, USA (1939–1968)
MEC   The Methodist Episcopal Church (1784–1939)
MECS   The Methodist Episcopal Church, South (1844–1939)
MPC   The Methodist Protestant Church (1830–1939)
UAME   The Union American Methodist Episcopal Church (1865–)
UBC   The United Brethren Church (1800–1946)
UMC   The United Methodist Church (1968–)

For Citations of Writings of John Wesley

Letters (Telford)   *The Letters of the Rev. John Wesley, A.M.*, ed. John Telford, 8 vols. (London: Epworth, 1931).

Works   *The Works of John Wesley*; begun as "The Oxford Edition of The Works of John Wesley" (Oxford: Clarendon Press, 1975–1983); continued as "The Bicentennial

ABBREVIATIONS

	Edition of The Works of John Wesley" (Nashville: Abingdon, 1984–).
Works (Jackson)	*The Works of John Wesley*, ed. Thomas Jackson, 14 vols. (London, 1872; Grand Rapids: Zondervan, 1958).

INTRODUCTION

DOCTRINE IN EXPERIENCE

This book endeavors to contribute in two ways toward United Methodist self-understanding. *First*, it deals in substantial and fresh ways with church and ministry in the American Methodist experience. Revisiting itinerancy, district superintendency, and episcopacy historically, I find much that alters, indeed enriches, our most hoary commonplaces. We practice or have practiced ministry in ways that live out New Testament teaching, ways of scriptural and theological fidelity for which we do not take adequate credit. Similarly, our connectionalism and conference structures, when carefully assessed, turn out to embody practices and implicit understandings that stand up to the best in the Christian tradition's notions of "church." This faithfulness and richness characterizes our day-to-day behavior, institutions, policies, practices. So I look at Methodist praxis for its implicit theology. We have often affirmed practical theology as the Methodist and Wesleyan mode. This volume looks beyond the usual referent for that—hymnody—to the actualities of our exercise of ministry and of our institutional life for practiced or praxis theology.

That examination of praxis entails tracing out changes, evolution, transformation, some of it for the better, some of it for the worse. For instance, a look back at district superintendency discloses in the predecessor office, that of the presiding elder, a role more expansive than those currently exercised. The presiding elder dedicated himself to and served the connection in mission, outreach, evangelism, and strategy. Today the church burdens the district superintendent with myriad personnel, conflict-resolution, management, and tax-collection tasks, leaving the essential strategic and missional imperatives undone. Such retrospectives do not yield counsel to return to a primitive past. We cannot go back to presiding elders on horseback. But the reminder that an office or institution looked different in earlier days should empower policy makers today to change what now seems encumbered, overburdened, too complex. Several of the chapters "specialize" in that counsel for change by charting the evolution and successively distinct phases of practices or structures. For instance, our actual strategies of connection and connecting (chapters 8, 9, and 10), our exercise of the teaching office (chapters 5 and 7), our patterns of itinerancy (chapters 3 and 6), our ministries through educational institutions (chapter 10), and our structuring of religious life at the local level (chapter 12) show phases or styles that differ markedly from period to period.

Discerning and appreciating such evolutionary patterns should, I hope, permit decision makers to realize that faithfulness to our Wesleyan heritage does not lock us into one organizational or policy mode. If we cannot go "home" again to Mr. Wesley's or Mr. Asbury's day, we can proceed forward faithfully to their witness by attending to the ways our practice through successive periods institutionalized our Methodist commitments, values and beliefs. These chapters should help in that faithful policy making.

Noting the normative, policy encouraging dimension to these chapters and my use here and throughout of the personal pronouns "I," "we," and "our," should alert the reader to the ways in which this volume strays from current history-writing conventions. Namely, I offer these recoveries as exhortation—to use a good Methodist word—or as counsel. Here, I suggest, lies a *second* closely related contribution, the reintroduction, advocacy, and even celebration of a distinctively Wesleyan and Methodist way of employing history. This volume, especially its first section, attempts, as the title indicates, "Doctrine out of Methodist History," theologizing through history, doing theology by writing history.

I need to be clear here. I am not talking about looking historically at our theologians or tracing the unfolding of our doctrine or reviewing the treatment of classic Methodist beliefs (e.g., holiness). History of theology or historical theology, exhibited in the superb new surveys by Mark Noll, *America's God*, and my colleague,

Brooks Holifield, *Theology in America*, both of which offer fine assessments of Methodist theology, can adhere to the usual canons and expectations of history writing.[1] I do little Methodist historical theology here, leaving that to the aforementioned colleagues. Nor am I simply reiterating my first point here, the importance of attending to practices and especially the Methodist pattern of imbedding their doctrine and theology in practices, though that is entailed and assumed. Instead, I advocate and attempt to exhibit the theologizing out of history, letting history speak normatively and constructively, doing theological history (not historical theology).

I came to doing theological history or theologizing through history gradually out of my own research on early American Methodism and out of efforts to speak about the findings to United Methodist audiences. These two have interplayed in complex fashion. I discovered that the historical front matter in the *Discipline*, initially and for much of the nineteenth century, was theological history, salvation history, pneumatology—exactly the practice I now advocate. (Ironically, one would grasp very little sense of that earlier historical theologizing from scrutiny of recent *Disciplines* that sustain the placement of but offer a history of our movement in the convention historical mode.) By contrast, as chapter 2 shows, early American Methodist historians sustained well into the nineteenth century the *Discipline*'s perspective and practice of writing with an eye to providence and God's salvific activity through the people called Methodists.

When speaking to Methodist groups, given those insights, I have found myself increasingly restive with the self-restrictions with which we church historians function, or try to function, or pretend to function. Taught to be neutral observers, we weigh the evidence, hold our own views in abeyance, write in a manner as objective and value-free as we possibly can. We expect and encourage one another to interpret and assess, indeed theorize as much as the data will permit, but to function like and with the ground rules of our "secular" historian colleagues. To be sure, with the historical guild and postmodernism generally, we now recognize that historians always bring their subjectivity to the account. Nevertheless, the expectation, should I say temptation, remains, especially for those writing religious history, to follow positivist, empiricist, historicist, and relativist counsels. Indeed, to those counsels church historians, if anything, have overcommitted, a strategy to gain respectability. The overcompensation to positivist norms helped church history claim to be "real" history, achieve standing within the guild of historians, and earn legitimacy in a university setting. So church historians established their bonafides as real scholars, gained access for research findings with historical journals and with publishers, and differentiated themselves from their eighteenth and nineteenth century forebears who invoked providence too readily and facilely proclaimed God's blessings on America.[2] Further, the positivist stance continues to have defensive value as those writing serious history of religion want to distance themselves from sectarian counterparts who continue to skew history apologetically, proclaim divine interventions, and prophesy judgment and doom.

I trust that my lectures and these chapters do not stray into such cheap theologizing and hope that the reader will view my research and writing as historically exacting. Still, what he or she will find here and what in speaking to Methodist church groups I have found myself wanting to say is something evaluative, something normative, something *theological*.

I offer a personal example of such an effort and of its problematic character for some historians. Some years ago I lectured at a history conference at Asbury Theological Seminary on "Conference as a Means of Grace." When I announced the topic, everyone laughed. They had suffered through annual conferences and experienced them as anything but gracious. Today perhaps we would find the title and notion less risible having heard bishops and others wax eloquent about Christian conferencing and watched several quadrennia of efforts made to reshape annual conferences accordingly. I hope, by the way, that when the story is told of the recovery of that Wesleyan imperative, my little efforts, not the lecture so much as the book version, *The Methodist Conference in America*,[3] will get a footnote. Be that as it may, what the lecture and book sought to do was to register the gracious character of and to recover the rich spirituality, communal bonding, and disciplined integrity of early Methodist practice of conference. It was a theological reading of Methodist history. The story does not end there. When I readied that lecture for publication in a university press book, *Early American Methodism*,[4] the editor of the series said with respect to its theological nuances (actually the theologizing in that and other chapters), "Not in my series you won't!" At her behest, I took the theological out of the book, sanitized it, secularized it.

I do not disparage my editor's directive or the conventions of history writing or the expectations to which we as church historians hold ourselves. To the highest of those standards I have sought to adhere in my writing. And truth be told, the rewriting of that book made clearer to non-Methodists the practices and patterns that my theologizing left unexplained. However, something was lost as well. I firmly believe that rigorous scholarship permits a Methodist, a Wesleyan, way of doing history; permits, indeed needs, to read our life, our activities, our institutions, our meetings, our practices theologically. Systematics has not been our forte, as our Lutheran and Reformed "friends" are wont to remind us. At least in part, historical theologizing compensates, showing the fidelity and orthodoxy in Methodist praxis. So our early historians—like Nathan Bangs who produced a four-volume work, *A History of the Methodist Episcopal Church*[5]—also provided the movement with significant theological statements, *The Errors of Hopkinsianism Detected and Refuted* (1815), *The Reformer Reformed* (1816), *An Examination of the Doctrine of Predestination* (1817), and *A Vindication of Methodist Episcopacy* (1820).[6] In these books, Bangs explained and defended Wesleyan theology and Methodist ministry, orders, and episcopacy. In the first three, Bangs responded to Calvinists who derided its thought and in the fourth to Episcopalians who questioned its ecclesial legitimacy.[7] Bangs did his theologizing in his *History* as well, providing an apologetical and providential rendering of the Methodist story.

Bangs's spirit and style live on. I include among my own acquaintances quite a number of theologians who write history and historians who theologize: Randy Maddox, Mary Elizabeth Moore, Ted Campbell, Jean Miller Schmidt, Kenneth Rowe, James Kirby, Kenneth Collins, Thomas Frank, Scott Jones, William "Bobby" McClain, Dennis Campbell, Stephen Gunter, Ted Runyon, Leonard Sweet, Bruce Robbins, Geoffrey Wainwright, Thomas Oden, Thomas Langford, Albert Outler, and Robert Cushman (the latter three now sadly deceased). To my knowledge, they—and, to reiterate, this list numbers only acquaintances, those who came to mind, and certainly not all who should be counted—

have not wanted to "compromise" their historical work by claiming or proclaiming its theological freight. Does their work not speak for itself? I find the investment in history by our theologians to be highly instructive and the narrative they unfold to be theologically suggestive. To be sure, all confessions have their histories and historians, and we Methodists are not the only movement that goes to the historical record to make our theological case. Certainly the Orthodox do, but primarily to the very early Christian centuries. As compared with other Protestants—Lutherans, Presbyterians, Episcopalians, Baptists—we Methodists put a much higher valuation on our founding and subsequent development. We appeal to Wesley or Asbury, they to Scripture alone or to the Prayer Book.

To this theological dimension and value in Methodist history I have become more self-conscious and explicit in my own writing. Both my collaborative effort with colleague Thomas Frank, *Episcopacy in the Methodist Tradition: Perspectives and Proposals*,[8] and the earlier *The Methodist Conference in America: A History* call United Methodism to claim the rich theological resources, the richly practiced faithfulness, in these central aspects of our system. And I wrote *Marks of Methodism*,[9] guided by the conclusion that my two colleagues and I had reached that our United Methodism and American Culture project and the four volumes of historical and sociological research it had produced would be best summed up by writing in a theological-historical mode. *Marks* attempts to be constructive theology, an ecclesiology, which warrants Methodism's faithful enactment of the classic marks or notes of the church—one, holy, catholic, and apostolic. History yields ecclesiology.

That book and two of the chapters that follow, "Itinerant General Superintendency" (chapter 6), which draws on my draft report for the UMC Task Force to Study the Episcopacy and "Methodism's 'Practiced' Ecclesiology" (chapter 13), crafted for United Methodist dialogues with the Episcopal and Orthodox churches, make the case explicitly that to think and to write in a theological-historical mode is a Methodist way of theologizing. Indeed, such historical theologizing can actually put the Methodist quadrilateral (Scripture, tradition, experience, and reason) into practice, as those two chapters and *Marks* do explicitly. Too frequently I find, especially in Board of Ordained Ministry interviews, United Methodists quickly identify the parts of the quadrilateral and wax eloquent on the primacy of Scripture but do not address other questions in quadrilateral fashion, do not really think quadrilaterally. Truth be told and no matter what they have said about Scripture, their own experience really functions to warrant answers.

The quadrilateral—not as a doctrine but as a practice—entails thinking about church and ministry by appealing to

Scripture	*Scripture*
The Wesleyan charism	*Reason*
The Christian life as lived	
(with particular attention to North America)	*Experience*
The ecumenical witness	*Tradition*

It means being faithful to Scripture, the Wesleyan norms, the Constitution; instructed by our experience with itinerancy and conference; cognizant of best practices of leadership, teaching, ministry; drawn by our vision of the kingdom of God and our hope for the unity of Christ's Church; and committed to and oriented by the church's apostolic witness as ecumenically and faithfully mediated. I trust that the reader will experience my efforts at fidelity in the chapters that follow. Here tradition or history and my reasoning with it bring into focus Methodist efforts in the past to experientially and to faithfully put Scripture into practice.

In holding up earlier chapters of the Methodist experience for their instructive value, I do not suggest for a moment that we return to an earlier day. No primitivist counsel, no golden age, no return to Wesley from me. Rather, I think of the historical narrative as a kind of glass or mirror that allows us to view ourselves but to view as well what lies behind us. We get ourselves into perspective, seeing behind us practices and patterns out of which our own have emerged but that are distinctive enough to make us pause, to look at ourselves, and to register that faithful Wesleyanism has not always looked exactly like us. In the glass of history, we can see ourselves as standing in a tradition, a living, dynamic tradition in which patterns and practices have changed. The look back, then, frees us to rethink, move on, reclaim, transform.

Introduction

Methodist history requires the best of historical research and the telling of the story honoring the highest canons of balance, fairness, and, yes, objectivity, though without yielding, I would hope, to positivist, empiricist, historicist, relativist temptation to view the findings as scientific and absolute. Methodist history can also offer a Methodist, a Wesleyan, way of doing theology, history as theology, theology read out of history, theologizing by writing and speaking history. This has been our tradition—reflecting theologically and missionally—and I regard the recovery of doing theology in historical mode as vitally important to United Methodism's well-being. To that recovery—recognizing and rehabilitating Methodist historical theologizing—this book is dedicated. Thereby it explains Methodism to both insiders and outsiders.

PART 1
DOCTRINE IN EXPERIENCE

CHAPTER 1

FOUR LANGUAGES OF METHODIST SELF-UNDERSTANDING

Tuesday, 23d. [Dec. 1794]. I rode to Mr. Laine's, in Littleborough, and at 2 o'clock, I preached on John xi.3. I had a crowded congregation, and the melting presence of God was amongst us. Many of the people could hardly refrain from weeping aloud.... Some of the people then went home, but soon returned. One man being in deep distress, began to cry aloud to God to have mercy upon his poor soul.... I talked, prayed, and sung, and while I was singing a visible alteration took place in his countenance, and I was inclined to think his soul was set at liberty.... I then took my text and preached on 1 Peter v. 7. It was not long before another man was taken with a violent trembling, and crying, so that my voice was almost drowned. I was forced to stop. I then prayed for him, and he became more quiet. I then went on with my sermon. There was a great weeping in every part of the house. It appeared as if the whole neighbourhood was about to turn to God. I hope the fruit of this meeting will be seen after many days, and that the work of the Lord will revive from this time.[1]

Early Methodists were not afraid of the voice. Indeed, as this entry from Jesse Lee's journal indicates, theirs might be termed a movement of the voice—a preaching, singing, testifying, praying, shouting, crying, arguing movement. In Methodism, people found their voice. Methodists quite literally discovered ways of giving a voice—young men were pressed, one might even say in the military vernacular "impressed," into preaching. Hymnbooks virtually mandated congregational singing; love feasts made testifying into a quasi-sacrament. Class meetings permitted the most outcast of society to voice their inner concerns to God in the supporting presence of peers. Shouting became a hallmark of Methodist utterance.[2] Crying punctuated the discourse of both preacher and congregation. By arguing, Methodists stated and clarified their belief vis-à-vis prevalent, frequently Calvinist, options.[3] Methodists, then, were not afraid of the voice. When individual Methodists found theirs, they typically had a lot to say.[4] So they preached, sang, testified, prayed, shouted, cried, argued.

Their message may not have wrought a political revolution in the manner of the Puritan sermon.[5] It did produce quite remarkable conversions, built a mass movement, created a national church, and wrought a moral revolution. It produced effects that attest to the cogency and power of the Methodist voice. A vignette from 1790 records how loudly. Lee rode for a time with a man who had heard him preach but did not realize he rode with the preacher: "Ah! says he, these preachers speak louder than our ministers, and raise their heads, and spread their hands, and holler, as though they were going to frighten the people. I told him it would be well if they could frighten the people out of their sins."[6]

Methodists did not, however, speak always with a single voice. And by the turn of the nineteenth century, the careful auditor might well have heard some discordance and detected that harmony was proving difficult to sustain. The difficulty would increase with time, for Methodists spoke to the new nation with not one but four voices, four languages, four formulations of doctrine.[7] Had the four languages been so recognized and identified, Methodists would have quickly protested that the four were but parts that made one whole. The truth is that Methodist reliance on four distinguishable idioms proved both a source of great strength and surprising weakness.

THE FOUR LANGUAGES

The four languages might be individually designated as (1) popular or evangelical, (2) Wesleyan, (3) episcopal or Anglican, and (4) republican. Each offered a surprisingly coherent and self-sufficient gospel. None was unique to American Methodism. Each was an ecumenical idiom. The unities produced by the four varied. Each pulled Methodists in a slightly different direction. (1) The popular language Methodists shared with all groups who made up the revival—those who spoke an evangelical or pietist tongue. With it, all the children of the awakenings could communicate. (2) The Wesleyan language defined the trans-Atlantic Methodist movement. Its terms denoted the particular features, practices, beliefs, and rituals of Wesleyanism and bound Wesleyans together. (3) The episcopal language belonged to American Methodists because, with Wesley, they first claimed to be part of the Church of England and then in 1784 with Wesley's blessing became, in essence, a surrogate "Anglican" church.[8] However, this particular affinity, between the Methodist Episcopal Church and the Protestant Episcopal Church, produced more conflict than unity. (4) The fourth language, the republican, defined the tradition of British political dissent, of Whiggery, and became an ideological feature of the American Revolution and a constitutive feature of American political consciousness.[9] By its use, Methodists proclaimed their patriotism and merged their voice with the other Protestant bodies that sought a national Christian unity for the new nation.

The four languages together shaped American Methodism. They seemed compatible. Indeed, Methodists experienced them as constituting a unitary and unified discourse. They have apparently gone undifferentiated to this point. And yet from the earliest days they did pull the movement in different directions. They prove difficult to illustrate because they seldom occur close together (at least, until well into the nineteenth century). Several utterances from the year 1798 do show their nature and proximity to one another.[10] They also indicate the centripetal and centrifugal impulses of the four languages.

THE POPULAR OR EVANGELICAL LANGUAGE

The popular language, because it was common and a vernacular, is the least accessible today. It was the language of sermon, of class, of love feast, of camp meeting, of prayer. Such oral discourse often proves inaccessible to the historian. Fortunately, it was also the language of the journal. And there we can hear early Methodism and recover its popular voice. In the first citation from Lee, the reader has already met it. Another specifically from the year 1798 will recall its texture:

> Tuesday, 29th [May, 1798]. I rode to the Vansant's, at the head of Chester, and preached at 12 o'clock on Gal. vi.7. *Be not deceived.* I had a very crowded house. I felt great liberty in preaching. The power and presence of the Lord was with us, and most of the people were in tears. Our hearts were closely united together, and I was much blessed amongst my old friends.[11]

In the journals, the Christian life was an affectionate and expressive affair. Preachers spoke with freedom. Words uttered in great liberty produced tears. Hearts were melted. Souls found mercy and were closely knit in love. A new community of "brothers" and "sisters" defined itself over against the world and the distinctions of sex, class, position, and race that ruled therein. This new community reoriented itself toward Zion. Such terms recur throughout the journals, as this sampling of entries from Lee for 1794 should imply:

> I had life and liberty in preaching, and the people paid great attention.
>
> Sabbath I preached twice at Mr. Hutchen's, and the people were much melted under the word. I felt my soul much taken up with the things of God, and could truly say it was my meat and drink to do his blessed will. Then I went to N. Whiteirs' and met the class. The Lord was very precious to our souls and the people were much melted....
>
> Thursday, 27th. They collected the neighbours together, and at 11 o'clock I gave them a sermon, on Col. iii,14. It was a delightful season; my heart was humbled within me before God, and the people were melted into tears.
>
> I came to Mr. Bradford's at Farmington, and at 3 o'clock, I preached on John iv.14. Here the Lord was pleased to visit us again with his blessed presence. Tears flowed from many eyes, and it seemed to be a time of love.[12]

The terms with which Lee spoke (to himself as well as to the crowds) were richly biblical and doctrinally suggestive. They charted the Christian pilgrimage and the corporate life of the Christian community with words that all could understand. These terms comprise a surprisingly coherent religious worldview, a popular evangelical or pietist worldview. On Methodist tongues, they shaped themselves into Arminian tunes. But this language was not, for the most part, employed for formal doctrinal purposes.

THE WESLEYAN LANGUAGE

For doctrine, Methodists invoked Wesley and drew upon a distinctly Wesleyan idiom. If, in 1798, Lee epitomized Methodism's popular tongue, in 1798 John Dickins and Ezekiel Cooper epitomized the Wesleyan language. They were successive stewards of the Methodist Book Concern. The year 1798 saw both at this task as Dickins succumbed in that year to the yellow fever that struck Philadelphia.[13] It was the official and peculiar task of Dickins and then of Cooper to transmit the Wesleyan idiom. They did that through a rather remarkable series of publications, publications that sustained the remarkable publishing impulse of Wesley himself.

In 1798 Dickins saw that American Methodists had a *Pocket Hymn Book*, Wesley's *Explanatory Notes on the New Testament* and *Sermons*, all three of which formally defined Methodist doctrine. Dickins published or carried other works of Wesley, volumes that Wesley had edited that were descriptive of the Christian life, the current *Discipline* that transmitted and recast Wesley's *Large Minutes* for American usage, the *Minutes Taken at the Several Annual Conferences*—the record of the year's legislative gatherings—and *The Methodist Magazine*, 1798.[14] This literature prescribed an official Wesleyan language, one that the preachers had a stipulated duty to transmit. Their responsibilities included the charge, "To take care that every society be duly supplied with books."[15] With those books, Methodists spoke of classes, societies, circuits, quarterly meetings, annual conferences, stewards, local preachers, itinerancy, connection, discipline, love feasts, perfection, spiritious liquors, slavery, our hymns, sanctification and the like.

Wesley had not intended that these terms define a self-sufficient religious system. He was adamant, in fact, that they not, that Methodism not separate itself from the Church of England. Yet British Methodism gravitated in that direction even during his life. And, of course, American Methodists with his blessing became an independent church. He made provision, when they did so, for the more distinctly ecclesial, sacramental, episcopal realities that he had always sought for Methodists through the established church. I turn to those provisions, that language, momentarily. Before doing so, I should observe that until 1784, American Methodists had really gotten along without the established church. Its clergy and parish churches did not dot the colonial landscape as it did the English countryside. A very few Anglican clergy cooperated with the American Methodists. And so American Methodists were tempted from the very start to regard this Wesleyan language as self-sufficient. After Wesley's death, British Wesleyanism did. American Methodism came very close to the same policy in 1779 in the Fluvanna division, when for a time it seemed that the southern half of the movement would proceed with the resources at hand to establish a church and did, in fact, ordain and celebrate the sacraments. The northern half of the movement followed the leadership of Asbury, respected Wesley's desire that Methodism remain within the Anglican Church, disfellowshiped those who had struck for independence and awaited a dispensation from Wesley. The southern group capitulated to Asbury, but the possibility it represented, of regarding the distinctly Wesleyan idiom as a self-sufficient religious system, would remain a Methodist temptation. American Methodists would be tugged by it every time they sought to converse with their British counterparts. That conversation, in particular, required such Wesleyan terms.

THE EPISCOPAL LANGUAGE

In the same year of 1798, the episcopal language was clearly stated in a volume that was "sold by John Dickins." That year *The Doctrines and Discipline of the Methodist Episcopal Church in America* carried a striking subtitle: "With Explanatory Notes by Thomas Coke and Francis Asbury." The two bishops undertook a rather revealing, and one should add, rare exercise of the teaching office. By their annotations, undertaken at the behest of the prior General Conference, they explained and defended Methodism's episcopal claims. They did so, at least in part, to answer the criticisms levied by James O'Kelly and to staunch the hemorrhaging loss of good Methodists to his protest schism.[16]

O'Kelly had challenged the episcopacy and its power, politically, by moving that preachers injured by episcopal appointment have a right of appeal to the conference, and rhetorically, by inveighing against episcopal tyranny. Answering that latter charge proved to be a major thrust of the bishops' commentary. The first section of the *Discipline*, "Of the Origin of the Methodist Episcopal Church," lent itself to a disquisition, three times as long as the section, defending Methodism's adoption of episcopal government, explaining the nature of Wesley's own episcopal authority, repudiating the conception of *"an apostolic, uninterrupted succession,"*[17] and adducing the New Testament texts supportive of an episcopal plan. In the second section, "Articles of Religion," the bishops likewise marshaled the New Testament support for these Anglican affirmations.

The *Discipline* did not include, and so no annotations were given to, the text of the eucharistic rite or baptism. However, the comments on the specific articles devoted to the sacraments, "Of the Sacraments," "Of Baptism," "Of the Lord's Supper," and "Of Both Kinds," sections XVI to XIX, clearly called to mind that aspect of Methodism's Anglican character. Short, later sections of the *Discipline* "Of Baptism" and "Of the Lord's Supper," would have had some of the same force.[18]

In the sacraments, in the Articles, and in its episcopal government (bishop, elder, deacon) Methodists applied to themselves the terminology of Anglicanism. Theirs was not a high church language after the fashion of Archbishop Laud, the Non-Jurors, the early Wesley, or the nineteenth-century Tractarians. It was rather an Anglican terminology familiar to Americans who had known the established church in the colonies.[19] When it talked about its government, when it celebrated the sacraments, when it identified the core of its belief, and when it ordained ministers, Methodism spoke an episcopal tongue.

To be sure, Methodists understood that tongue to be an episcopal *Methodism*. The annotated *Discipline* clearly made that point. It did so by its very appearance, through the text, and in explicit commentary. The Wesleyan language and that of Anglicanism were put together. The page and a half that constituted section IV, "Of the Election and Consecration of Bishops, and of their Duty," insisted, for instance, that American Methodism's episcopacy simply gave suitable ecclesial expression to Wesley's style of leadership. We "must observe," stated the bishops, "that nothing has been introduced into Methodism by the present episcopal form of government, which was not before fully exercised by Mr. Wesley."[20] Elsewhere the notes commented on features of Methodism that rooted in the Wesleyan movement and explained distinctive practices and structures. In that sense and as should be expected, the volume transmitted the Wesleyan language as well as the episcopal. The notes functioned—particularly through the common appeal to the New Testament and the practice of the primitive church—to cement the bond of Methodist and Episcopal idioms and warrant the church's name and self-understanding. And yet the bond was not always a firm or a happy one.

THE REPUBLICAN LANGUAGE

In the year 1798, James O'Kelly epitomized the unhappiness over the episcopal character of Methodism. One of the eminent leaders of early Methodism, O'Kelly sought directions for the movement that threw him into conflict with Asbury and Coke. He criticized Asbury's experiment with a council, prompted the creation of the general conference, and at the first such, the General Conference of 1792, initiated a frontal challenge to episcopal power. He proposed, by motion, that preachers have the right to appeal to the conference the appointment made for them by the bishop. The motion eventually failed and O'Kelly walked out to form the Republican Methodist Church.[21]

It has been easy for Methodists to dismiss O'Kelly but, in fact, he spoke for many early Methodists. His cause had considerably more appeal than the numbers that rallied to his banner would suggest.[22] In 1798, O'Kelly produced *The Author's Apology for Protesting Against the Methodist Episcopal Government*.[23] A few citations will illustrate his appeal and the language that sustained it:

> If Christians are free citizens of Zion, they should prize those liberties, seeing they were purchased with the precious blood of Christ.
>
> Thomas and Francis were our Superintendents, as Presiding Elders, according to John's appointment. But they were not elected by the suffrage of conference, although it is so written in the book of discipline.
>
> Ah, Francis was born and nurtured in the land of kings and bishops, and that which is bred in the bone, is hard to be got out of the flesh.
>
> O Heavens! Are we not Americans! Did not our fathers bleed to free their sons from the British yoke? And shall we be slaves to ecclesiastical oppression? [24]

This was republican language, the rhetoric of the British Commonwealthman tradition, the worldview of radical Whiggery, the ideology of the American Revolution.[25] It described a world in which republics were rare and fragile institutions, where power ever threatened the liberties of the people, where authority transmuted itself into tyranny unless checked and vigilantly watched, where freedom's only hope lay in the collective resolve of a virtuous citizenry, where virtue easily succumbed to luxury or the inducements of power, where the fate of the republic therefore rested with the virtue or corruption of its citizens. Its recurrent terms were virtue, liberty, corruption, tyranny, republic, rights, and reason.

Here, as in the case of the other three languages, we find a coherent worldview. Republicanism offered Methodism and it clearly beckoned O'Kelly with a richly elaborated mythology, a saga that fit the present into a history of republics and of tyranny. To employ it was to adopt an historical account that situated today's perils in a narrative that recalled Israel's political experience, the republics of Greece, the Norman Yoke, the Glorious Revolution, and now the American Revolution. O'Kelly effectively claimed that mythology and conjured up its visions of tyranny and corruption.

O'Kelly also strove to claim that mythology for Methodist purposes. He did so clumsily, proclaiming Christians "free citizens of Zion," glossing the distinction between church and state, and construing Asbury as tyrant. The generality of Methodists thought that he protested too much. It is perhaps useful to distinguish his rhetorical maneuver from its political objectives. He was struggling to bring together Christian theology and the ideology of the Revolution. He wanted Methodism to make sense in relation to its political context. He reached for a public theology. In that, he was a Methodist and southern participant in an interpretive enterprise largely dominated by Calvinists and New Englanders. This national period was a time when other Protestants, particularly those from the Reformed camp, were struggling toward a theology that would embrace the new republic in the larger cause of God's redemption of the world. Behind their efforts lay a century and a half of colonial experience with a godly state and, of course, the challenges to establishments stimulated by the Revolution and new constitution making. Intent on sustaining that godly civic order despite disestablishment, Reformed theocrats fought for their own vision of the new order of the ages, fearing on the one side the popular threats represented by the O'Kellys, who embraced what seemed to them disorder in Christian and republican language and, on the other side, the elite like Jefferson, who seemingly would sacrifice Christianity to the self-evident truths of enlightenment. Reformed theologians construed these and other challenges to Christian order as conspiracies. Conspiratorial visions made sense of the pell-mell of postrevolutionary America.[26] In 1798, when O'Kelly wrote *The Author's Apology for Protesting Against the Methodist Episcopal Government*, eminent New England divines uncovered an international conspiracy that conveniently linked various enemies of the Puritan way with Jeffersonians, the zealots of the French Revolution, Bavarian Illuminati, and the Antichrist.[27] The new republic, they thought, was at risk. Eventually the crisis passed and Presbyterians and Congregationalists reworked this strident millennialism into a theology of the nation. This public theology combined republicanism with Christian and particularly Calvinist notions of order in ways that would shape both the national political culture and Protestant denominations. Under its banner, they labored for a Christian America.[28]

With these Reformed contemporaries, O'Kelly shared little more than a fear of conspiracy. His theology was Arminian not Calvinist, his political rhetoric Jeffersonian not Federalist, and his religious policy separationist not integral. Yet his rhetorical maneuver was one that would ultimately come to serve those Reformed purposes. They, like he, would eventually baptize republicanism. In that sense, O'Kelly's protest and his critique belonged to this larger effort to adapt the ideology of the Revolution to Christian use and to give Christian direction to the nation.

O'Kelly's adoption of republicanism probably produced greater resonances within Methodism than his treatment by Methodist historians would suggest. Certainly Asbury and the leadership loyal to him experienced O'Kelly as a formidable threat. And the threat he posed was at a point of great vulnerability. Methodism's linguistic structure was fluid and ill defined, its values unguarded and open to divergent interpretation, its several languages beckoning the movement in different directions. By appealing to this powerful democratic idiom, O'Kelly invoked Methodism's own sense of conspiracy and resort to order. In the trench warfare that followed, O'Kelly lost the allegiance of many who had initially rallied to his banner. But over the long haul O'Kelly's rhetorical cause, if not his movement, would prosper faithful. O'Kelly laid claim to a republican language that would increasingly become the Protestant idiom and eventually also the Methodism idiom. It gave shape to the reform impulse of the 1820s that resulted in the Methodist Protestant Church. It also found its way into mainstream episcopal Methodism. That appropriation is illustrated in the historical narratives of Nathan Bangs and his successors. They wove the American republic into the fabric of Methodist history. They also wove it into Methodist life.[29] By midcentury, the northern church would become as zealous for Christian republicanism as any of the Reformed.

BABEL OR PENTECOST?

Methodists found the four languages useful. They did not, in the manner of Calvinists or Lutherans, strive to bring the four languages into a common systematic framework. Rather they employed them as occasion demanded. At times, more than one seemed appropriate, so they juxtaposed them. Annual conferences frequently demanded several languages. The *Minutes* document the ease with which Methodists negotiated the several languages, moved between them, employed them successively. Those for 1798, for instance, reported the traditional Wesleyan questions in terms of which the church ordered itself:

Quest. 1. Who are admitted on trial?

Quest. 2. Who remain on trial?

Quest. 3. Who are admitted into full connexion?

Quest. 7. Who are under a location . . . ?

Quest. 8. Who are the supernumeraries?

Quest. 9. What Preachers, have withdrawn themselves from our order and connexion?

Quest. 10. Who have been expelled from our order and connexion?

Quest. 12. Are all the Preachers blameless in life and conversation?

Quest. 13. What numbers are in Society?

Quest. 14. Where are the Preachers stationed this year?

Quest. 15. When and where shall our next conferences be held?[30]

The *Minutes* also framed questions in episcopal terms:

Quest. 4. Who are the Deacons?

Quest. 5. Who are the Elders?

Quest. 6. Who have been elected by the unanimous suffrages of the General Conferences, to superintend the Methodist Episcopal Church in America?[31]

The Episcopal and Wesleyan terms, questions, and processes were juxtaposed but not really conceptually unified.[32]

Also in the *Minutes* appeared a question that elicited responses in the popular idiom. Question 11 read "Who have died this year?"

The entry for John Dickins recounted his considerable services to the Methodist cause and proclaimed that "His works shall praise him in the gates of Zion." An entry for James King invoked popular images, but also entered a republican note: "He was about 24 or 25 years of age.—He gave his life, his labours, and his fortune to the Church of Christ and his brethren; and was a friend to religion and liberty."[33]

Less formal accounts of conference also juxtaposed popular, Wesleyan, and episcopal motifs. Jesse Lee reported on a 1798 conference. In his rendering, the tremendous power unleashed by the Methodist movement clearly presupposes and requires three of the several languages. The Wesleyan occasion—conference—and the episcopal rituals—ordination and Eucharist—unleashed a revival that Lee could only convey with popular language.

> Wednesday, 29th [August, 1798], conference began in Readfield; we were closely engaged all day; the next day we set in conference very early, and broke up at 8 o'clock. At 9, we held lovefeast, and had a large number of Methodists together, and none else. They spoke freely, and feelingly. It was a good time. At 11 o'clock Mr. Asbury preached a good sermon. . . . Then we ordained Timothy Merritt, Robert Yellaley, and Aaron Humphrey, deacons, and Roger Searle, an elder. It was a very solemn time at the ordination; but the people were so crowded in the gallerys that were not finished, that some of the joists gave way, and frightened the people very much for a few minutes, and some were slightly hurt. Then I preached on Rom. xvi.20. My soul was much animated with the presence of the Lord. The people were melted into tears. It was a precious time to many. Then we administered the Lord's Supper. I suppose there were above two hundred communicants; it was a most solemn time at the table.[34]

In Lee's account as in the official *Minutes*, the three languages function together. But did they, do they, really cohere?

Four Distinct Languages and Literatures?

At various points this volume has suggested that Methodists adopted and used the languages without clarifying their relationships and compatibility. This point has been made frequently with respect to the Wesleyan and episcopal idioms and often illustrated with the confusion over ministry occasioned by the two sets of terms and processes by which and through which ministry was and is conceived.[35] Candidates proceeded along two tracks into Methodist ministry, one culminating in conference membership, the other in elder's orders.

This chapter extends that point to the two other Methodist languages. Each of their central concerns has been illustrated. It is worth underscoring here what has been implicitly documented, namely, that they differed sufficiently to generate separate literatures. The popular language produced journals and diaries. To it also belonged firsthand accounts of revivals and conversions, which in evangelical literature became a distinct genre of literature, "religious intelligence" or "missionary intelligence." Obituaries and correspondence frequently invoked popular terms as well. These reports and notices became regular features of *The Christian Advocate* and other "popular" literature. Popular literature stemmed from and expressed Wesley's own example, command, and instruction. Such colloquial expressiveness attested to Wesley's sense of the value of testimony and of an important, vital, and distinctive Wesleyan contribution to the literature and language that we are terming "popular."

Still, one can recognize as separate or semiseparate a Wesleyan literature. Wesley generated, and American Methodism continued to print and transmit, an array of publications designed to sustain Wesleyan practice and institutions. The Wesleyan literary standards were *Minutes*, *Discipline*, hymnbooks, Wesley's own *Works*, the normative *Sermons* and *Notes on the New Testament*, and eventually successful magazines. This Wesleyan literature—really a Wesleyan literary revolution—fueled Methodist expansion.[36] By this grammar, the movement distinguished itself and sold its wares in the free enterprise of American Protestantism.

Methodists generated "episcopal" literature for doctrinal, liturgical, and apologetical purposes—when formal self-expression was required. The first such instance was Bishop Coke's sermon at the 1784 organizing conference.[37] Among the most powerful was his episcopal colleague's 1813 Valedictory Address.[38] Apologetics produced the greatest volume. Attacked by Episcopalians and Calvinists, Methodists responded in episcopal mode. Among early spokespersons were Martin Ruter, Nathan Bangs, John Emory, and Wilbur Fisk.[39]

Within episcopal Methodism, O'Kelly's example and publications received only scorn. His production discouraged Methodist republicanism for at least a generation. Still, there were other early anticipations of Methodism's later republican output. Notable were the formal declarations of "General Fast" and "General Thanksgiving" that the church issued in 1795.[40] Republican items appeared in significant number in the succession of Methodist reform movements. The Methodist Protestants, for instance, essentially recast Methodism into a republican mode. So also did northern episcopal Methodism as it thought about the place of the church in American society. That redefinition of the mission of the movement can be readily discerned in the succession of midcentury histories of Methodism. The Civil War accented the tendency to give republican meaning to Methodism (to be sure only on the northern side). By that point, this language too had achieved full normative status within the movement.

FOUR DOCTRINES?

More significant, and troubling to Methodism, than separate literatures were the doctrinal tensions between and among the languages. It would stretch their differences to speak of separate doctrines since Methodists, after all, experienced them as compatible. The languages did, however, pull in different directions. They gave distinct answers to the fundamental questions that Methodism, with Wesley, took as its theological agenda:

1. What to teach?

2. How to teach?

3. What to do (that is how to regulate our doctrine, discipline, and practice)?[41]

Each, for instance, offered a distinct notion of what it meant to be a church. The definition most likely to come to mind was and is an episcopal one, formally rendered in the Articles and evoked in the liturgy:

XIII. Of the Church

The visible Church of Christ is a congregation of faithful men, in which the word of God is preached, and the sacraments duly administered according to Christ's ordinance, in all those things that of necessity are requisite to the same.[42]

Whether early American Methodists regarded this episcopal definition—really, Reformation definition—as adequate to their connectional and missionary sense of the church we do not fully know.

We have seen that when they spoke in popular terms about themselves, when they talked about Methodism as an ecclesial reality, they reached for a very different image. The term most frequently employed—the popular conception—was biblical. Methodists spoke of Zion, a term that evoked both historical Israel and the eschatological New Jerusalem. Asbury, for instance, rode into North Carolina in 1795 and observed:

This country improves in cultivation, wickedness, mills, and stills; a *prophet of strong drink* would be acceptable to many of these people. I believe that the Methodist preachers keep clear, both by precept and example; would to God the members did so too! Lord, have pity on weeping, bleeding Zion![43]

This popular notion lacks the formality and precision of the episcopal definition. It had compensating strengths for Methodism. It located Methodism in the economy of salvation, both historically and eschatologically. It identified Methodism with the people of God, the corporate, transcongregational reality of God's chosen ones. It legitimated a dynamic, political self-understanding and orientation to the world.

The Wesleyan contribution to ecclesiology—conference—lacks Zion's connection to salvation history. Nor was it or is it frequently given doctrinal status. However, in conference and particularly in the quarterly conference or quarterly meeting, Methodists gave vivid expression to how they thought the people of God should live and what it meant to offer grace to lost sinners.[44] Quarterly meetings dramatized Methodism's missionary conception of the church and of the gospel. Lee's report, cited above, captured the ecclesial drama. Methodism treated conference as an ecclesial reality, even if lacking the explicit historical and eschatological referent of Zion and the formal precision of the episcopal definition. Conference and quarterly meetings made up in act what they lacked in form. They satisfied the episcopal definition with explosive eucharists and met the popular eschatological hope by revival.

The republican ecclesiology focused on the nation. A Christian republic, God's New Israel, a redeemer nation, a Christian America—the terms for it are various. Early Methodists gave somewhat hesitant and tentative assent to this Calvinist doctrine.[45] Their commitment to it gradually increased so that by midcentury at least the northern Methodists had made it constitutive of their self-understanding. They came to believe in "The Nation with the Soul of a Church."[46] They viewed themselves as a national church, sometimes even *the* national church. The function of this conception was similar to Zion. Belief in a Christian America, in fact, represented the working out of a biblical, indeed Hebraic and covenantal political theology. It proved to be a compelling and powerful vision of Christian community, one that dominated American Protestantism and American society well into the twentieth century. This is not the place to offer a sustained criticism of that vision. Suffice it to say that it lured Methodists into politicizing their ecclesiology, giving their missionary sense of the church a rather limited societal referent, and fixing their purposes in national, not global, terms.

IMPLICATIONS

The different ecclesiologies offered distinct hopes, functioned with distinct notions of what constituted authority,[47] identified distinct purposes for corporate Christian life, and conceived the unity of the church in distinct fashion. The four languages produced theological multiplicity on other doctrines as well, particularly in such areas as anthropology, soteriology, and ethics. The languages functioned, then, to offer Methodists a range of theological options, various identities, and choices as to what constituted Methodism. They did so when each generated a distinct theological option, as with ecclesiology; they did so even more frequently in combinations. For the most part, however, Methodism managed to hold together and live with its four languages.

Its failures at unity had something to do with language. The different possible Methodist identities and the linguistic cacophony partially explain later fissures in the Methodist movement. There is a rough correspondence, for instance, between republicanism and the Methodist Protestant Church; between popular concerns of early Methodism and both Black Methodism and the Holiness movement; between episcopal emphases and the Methodist Episcopal Church, South; and between Wesleyan self-understandings and the Methodist Episcopal Church. It is instructive, for instance, that one of the African American Methodisms chose to imbed Zion in its name. Nevertheless, these correspondences are only rough. Each movement typically drew on all four languages. The African Methodist Episcopal Zion, Church, for instance, scrupulously maintained Wesleyan patterns and episcopal practices; in its pursuit of abolition, it also found republican values important. Still, the vitalities of popular Methodism were what made African Methodism attractive to Black Americans.

If we do not find various Methodisms breaking cleanly along these linguistic lines, we might profitably understand their peculiar appeal and dynamic by studying the internal configurations and relative priority each gave these languages.

Similarly, the debates and disputes within each movement become more intelligible when Methodism's several frames of reference are taken seriously and the consequent divergences of value and of commitment respected for what they are. Because of their plural languages, Methodists frequently talked past one another.

The problem for the historian is to make some sense of a Methodist past characterized by this complex interplay of languages. The interpreter may, at times, be tempted by the impulse (to which the movement or portions thereof occasionally succumbed), namely to take one of these languages as authentic, or controlling, or basic, and to construe Methodism in its terms alone. That lure has shaped histories as well as policy. Methodism is better understood by recognizing the place and power of all the languages. The four languages, after all, have been claimed, used, valued, and even championed. They represent for the historian rich intellectual resources, symbol systems in terms of which to understand the movement. The question raised, but not solved, by this volume is the relation these languages had to one another: was it Babel or Pentecost?

CHAPTER 2

HISTORY AS BEARER OF METHODIST IDENTITY

> So it was that Methodism, with a system more mobile than that of any other church, with a message more democratic and inclusive, and with a ministry which was part and parcel of the life of the frontier, came over the mountains with the great rush of emigration, and took over the spiritual command of the commonwealths which men were hewing from the wilderness—a command which it maintains to this day.[1]

Well into the twentieth century, Methodists held several propositions about themselves and their role in society. The propositions, still implicit in the above, are (1) Methodism was/is a child of providence. (2) Providence especially fitted Methodism and the Methodist connection for American society. (3) Methodist response to and stewardship of that providential calling had benefitted both church and nation, blessing the church with great numbers and the nation with troops of true believers in the American system. (4) The purposes and ultimately the health—spiritual and physical—of Methodism are bound up in this linked mission of nation and church.[2]

Thereby, Methodists conflated the kingdom of God with the nation, construed denominational purposes in terms of those of a Christian America, and in making the church subservient to Christian nationalism, intimately tied the former's health to the latter's. So the propositional or ideational evidence suggests.[3] Important and further implications follow, namely that the demise of Christian America, the event that Robert Handy called "the second disestablishment,"[4] shattered this mission that the church had taken as its own, that no comparable purpose of such energizing

21

dimensions has arisen to take its place, and that the present malaise of mainline denominations in general and Methodism in particular roots in this loss of purpose. This analysis locates mainline Protestantism's problem not in present agendas so much as in a faulty earlier purpose. The wedding of denomination to nation, however stimulating it proved to denominational growth, built a fundamental flaw into denominational foundations. When the promises of the First Amendment and the realities of pluralism exposed the fault line in Christian America, Methodists and perhaps also other mainline denominations suffered structural damage.

These propositions about denominational identity were widely shared. The Methodist pattern then is but an instance of a common story. So also their use in denominational history—the ideological use of history was not unique. The premium Methodists put on a historical fabrication of identity allows us to use them as a case study, an illustration of how in the quest for a Christian America, Methodists (and other Protestants) wrought fundamental changes in their purpose and perhaps in their character.

WHY HISTORY?

At a recent General Conference of The United Methodist Church, individuals and groups concerned to redirect the denomination and to return it to full health chose a curious vehicle for renewal. They recast the history of Methodism. They rewrote the "doctrinal history" in the *Discipline* so as to accent those aspects of Methodism that, if reemphasized, would rejuvenate the church.[5] The strategy was an obvious and well-tried maneuver for Methodists.

From the earliest *Disciplines* down to the most recent, Methodists have begun these formal, official self-presentations with a history of the movement. The first word that Methodists have wanted to say about themselves was an historical one. For the most part, these historical statements functioned to state and hence transmit the received Methodist identity. For long periods they would be carried over intact from one *Discipline* to another. But at points of significant change, as for instance in the 1939 and 1968 unions and in 1988, Methodists struggled to reshape the history to warrant the change.⁶

That orientation to historical self-understanding—a preoccupation derived from Wesley's practice and precept—reflected itself at a variety of points in the life of Methodism. Narrative self-presentations both stimulated and derived sustenance from the common Pietist passion for recounting individual and corporate religious experience. It "authorized" the production of endless histories of the movement, from competent surveys of the whole denomination to quite amateurish local and conference narratives. It expressed itself in myriad studies of Methodist "worthies," the bearers of the Methodist standard. It found expression in the papers and magazines, particularly the *Christian Advocates*, which reserved disproportionate space for the stories of Methodism. And it led them to require and feature history, particularly the history of the movement, in the preparation of Methodist ministers.⁷ History served to express and even to shape Methodist identity and to transmit denominational culture.

This chapter will explore shifts in Methodist identity and culture as they are reflected in Methodist histories and proceed then to reflect about history as bearer and transmitter of denominational identity. The historians treated (in chronological order) are Jesse Lee, Nathan Bangs, Abel Stevens, Matthew Simpson, James M. Buckley, the team of Halford E. Luccock and Paul Hutchinson, William Warren Sweet, and Frederick Norwood—each of whom, in some sense, spoke authoritatively for and about the movement.⁸

PROVIDENCE

In 1784, the newly organized Methodist Episcopal Church provided itself a constitution or quasi-constitution, adapting one elaborated by the British Methodists under John Wesley, a document known as *The Large Minutes*. The first American *Discipline*, that of 1785, followed the question and answer format of the British *Minutes* and its sequence of questions.⁹ The 1787 revision of the first *Discipline* put a new order to the questions and a historical frame on the constitution. The first asked, "What was the Rise of Methodism so called in Europe?" the second, "What was the Rise of Methodism, so called in America?" the third, "What may we reasonably believe to be God's design in raising up the Preachers called Methodists?" The answers briefly sketched the founding acts and founding impulses of the movement. The third answer deserves citation. It has been recited down to the present as a statement of Methodist purpose. It retained the substance of Wesley's answer but now nuanced to fit the new land. God's design was "to reform the Continent, and spread scriptural Holiness over these Lands. As a Proof hereof, we have seen in the Course of fifteen Years a great and glorious Work of God, from New York through the Jersies, Pennsylvania, Delaware, Maryland, Virginia, North and South Carolina, even to Georgia."[10]

These early Methodists had a vivid sense of America. Even as a small band of itinerants, they had traveled its roads, forded its waters, crossed its mountains, and penetrated its wilderness. This litany of states evoked their direct experience with the outpouring of God's Spirit upon the American landscape. The first proposition—that Methodism was providentially given and directed—expressed their very being. They found it axiomatic. Methodism was providential. The other propositions they would have found strange and discordant.

Jesse Lee shared the Christmas Conference's vision of Methodism as an impulse of providence. Indeed, we may fittingly view his *Short History of the Methodists*[11] as a fleshed-out version of this initial providential reading of the Methodist saga. Jesse Lee missed the 1784 constitutional gathering known as the Christmas Conference, missed it because he was some five hundred miles distant when he received the summoning word and nursed some grudges for being so belatedly informed.[12] He began travelling with Bishop Francis Asbury immediately thereafter, came to exercise considerable influence in the Methodist leadership, blazed the way for Methodism into New England, and served as chaplain to Congress. Lee missed election to the episcopacy by a narrow margin. And, of course, he could serve Methodism in only one place at a time. With due allowance for his frailty and finitude, however, we can say that otherwise Lee left his imprint on early Methodism. Sweet termed him "the most popular of all the early Methodist preachers."[13] He both made and wrote Methodist history, as would be the case for Methodist historians throughout the nineteenth century. His *Short History* was the first serious effort to sketch the contours of the movement. Lee's construction of the movement did not, however, please all. The General Conference actually rejected the volume; Asbury thought it inadequate on his own role.[14] Certainly part of the reason for controversy derived from the very personal vision that Lee provided.

Lee told the Methodist story as he saw it. He had seen enough of the whole that we get from him a remarkably well-rounded account. Subsequent historians have consistently drawn upon him for the documents that he reproduced, the events for which he provides the most complete eyewitness account, the very vividness of his portrayal. The revivals that he experienced and led; the conferences he attended and whose legislation he could then report firsthand; the penetration of "enemy" Puritan territory that he led; the general explosion of the movement over the new nation that his extensive travels documented; the advent of the camp meetings that he witnessed—these personal involvements in the development of Methodism give shape and vigor to his narrative. Doubtless, that very personal, idiosyncratic perspective offended his colleagues, who could not help but feel that Lee had implicitly claimed for his own what belonged to them all. And yet in another sense, this very personal vision did stand for them, in the way that the historical preface to the *Discipline* stood for them, for their conception of their history, history as immediate and perceivable instances of God at work. For that is how providence functioned for Lee. He offered no grand theory of providence at work. Nor did he explicitly claim the Methodist connectional system to be providential. Rather, he pointed concretely and specifically to the presence of God among the Methodists. For instance, of a 1788 Baltimore conference Lee reported:

> During the time of the conference, we were highly favoured of the Lord, and souls were awakened and converted. On Sunday, the 14th of September at 3 o'clock in the afternoon, Mr. Asbury preached in Mr. Otterbein's church; and the people were generally solemn and much affected; he then asked another preacher to pray and conclude: and whilst he was praying, an awful power was felt among the people. Some of them cried out aloud . . . and in a little time there was such a noise among them, that many of the Christian people were measurably frightened, and as there

was no opportunity for them to escape at the door, many of them went out at the windows, hastening to their homes. The noise had alarmed hundreds of people who were not at the meeting, and they came running to see what was the matter, till the house was crowded, and surrounded with a wondering multitude. In a short time some of the mourners lost the use of their limbs, and lay helpless on the floor, or in the arms of their friends. It was not long before some of them were converted. . . . This day of the Lord's power will never be forgotten by many who were present.[15]

Lee claimed Methodism to be providential by showing providence at work.

In similar fashion, Lee showed Methodism's attachment to the United States. He did not, most certainly did not, wrap the nation around the church. Indeed, with most early Methodists, Lee evidenced the pattern of affection-but-alienation that R. Laurence Moore shows to be so prototypically American—a kind of sectarian distancing of self and movement from nation and society at the same time that full loyalty is proclaimed and efforts are even made to convert and transform the society.[16] Lee did make unmistakable his own and American Methodism's patriotism. He criticized, for instance, the "head preachers . . . all from Europe," some of whom "were imprudent too freely against the proceedings of the Americans" during the Revolution.[17] And he presented the Methodists' own march to independence from Wesley and the British connection as an appropriate development.[18] But Lee did not providentially connect church and nation. He thought providence to be rather specifically focused on the work of salvation. Connections of general providence and the fate of nations therein did not interest him.

PROVIDENTIAL DESIGN

By 1792, according to Bangs, Methodism had brought "about one-twentieth part of the entire population" under its influence, some 198,000 attendees out of a population of four million. Such growth, "in the short space of thirty-six years," and despite the advantages enjoyed by other denominations, required explanation. Bangs found himself forced "to the conclusion that their prosperity must be attributed to the blessing of God upon their labors." He continued, "We therefore say again, that its forward course can be accounted for only by supposing the sanction of the most high God upon their labors."[19] At the end of the fourth volume, having brought the church down to 1840, Bangs rendered the same judgment—that the "success and influence of Methodism" had "one true original cause, namely, the divine agency."[20] Concern with Methodist numerical success led Bangs from the providential character of Methodism toward a second proposition—the providential connection of church and nation.

Like Lee, Bangs was an actor in that which he interpreted. He also made his mark on New England Methodism, particularly as Methodism's foremost spokesperson for Arminianism and against Calvinism. "Nathan Bangs: Apologist for American Methodism" one interpreter called him.[21] That he was and more. Bangs labored effectively not only to speak on Methodism's behalf to its "cultured critics" and the religious establishment but also to remake Methodism so that it might claim its place in the American religious establishment. Bangs played that reshaping role from his office as book agent, effectively the executive secretary and the teaching office of the church. What he wrought might be termed the revolution of the 1820s, the wholesale restructuring of Methodism—creating missionary, Sunday school, and tract societies; launching and editing a major weekly, *The Christian Advocate*, and a journal of theological opinion, *The Methodist Magazine*; establishing educational institutions; and founding the course of study, Methodism's four-year national reading course in preparation for ministry.[22] Bangs sought to make the church an effective force in national life.

When sketching the hand of providence in this Methodism on which he also had laid a hand, Bangs could not be content with simple and discrete providential instances, though he, like Lee, eagerly pronounced events both large and small to be of divine agency. No, Bangs saw that the divine agency extended also to Methodism as a system and its operation. And Bangs also recognized a providential connection between church and nation. To that end, he chose to begin the saga of American Methodism not with Wesley but with Columbus and proceeded to an examination of "the civil and religious state of the people at the time Methodism was introduced."[23] This was a self-consciously interpretive gesture on the part of a man with quite keen historical skills.[24] Bangs saw "benignant Providence" in the peopling of the land, the development of civil and religious liberties, the respect accorded Scripture and the Sabbath, the widespread profession of Christianity, the influence of revivals, the atmosphere of toleration—in short, the creation of a situation "highly favorable" to Methodist "evangelical labors."[25] Methodism's introduction into the land also showed providential design.[26]

At various points, his providential treatment of America was evocative of the Christian republicanism now recognized to be so significant in both national and mainstream Protestant life.[27] And yet Bangs did not really offer a providential reading of the nation as such; he did not provide a public theology. Bangs took interest in providence and Methodism, not providence and America. Or perhaps we should say he was interested in the public roles that providence exercised through Methodism. For instance, in measuring the impact of camp meetings and the revivals at the turn of the nineteenth century, Bangs spent some five pages on the "most happy and conservative influence upon our national character," "the conservative influence which vital, experimental, and practical Christianity exerts upon individual character, upon social and civil communities, and of course upon states and empires."[28] Though Methodism exercised a politically and socially constructive influence, Bangs insisted that it was purely religious in its intent and operation: "The influence therefore, which she has exerted upon the civil destinies of the republic, has been altogether of an indirect and collateral character, growing out of that moral and religious stamp with which she strives to mark and distinguish all her children."[29]

Bangs could be quite effusive about the political consequences of such indirection. For instance, he thought the national operation of Methodism functioned to cement the union together and to counter the politically divisive force of state governments.[30] But such notes were quite occasional. Bangs focused upon Methodism. It was the providential character of Methodism, not the providential character of the nation, that interested him. Incidentally, providence worked through Methodism and Methodists for the good of the nation. However, church, not state, remained providence's aim.

PROVIDENTIAL CONNECTION

Bangs had tentatively connected church and nation. Abel Stevens drew the providential connection of church and nation firmly. Firmness was characteristic of Stevens, who held a series of important editorships in the tumultuous middle decades of the nineteenth century: *Zion's Herald*, the New England Methodist paper, then *The National Magazine*, and finally *The Christian Advocate*. Through those immensely influential posts, he spoke a moderating, even conservative, word to the church, prizing its unity at the cost, some thought, of its witness.

Stevens entitled the first chapter in his *Compendious History* "Methodism—Its Special Adaptations to the New World."[31] The chapter and the volume begins with a striking but imaginary event of 1757.[32] That year, John Wesley, "inventor" of Methodism, and James Watt, inventor of the steam engine, found themselves at Glasgow University. Stevens imagined a chance meeting of these two in the university quadrangle, the inventors of the two machines for the conquest of the new world: "Watts and Wesley might well then have struck hands and bid each other godspeed at Glasgow in 1757: they were co-workers for the destinies of the new world."[33] Watts had produced the engine for the conquest of the new world physically, Wesley that for the conquest of the new world morally. With a series of assertions, Stevens exhibited Methodism's engine-like, conquering capacity as providentially given.

> Methodism, with its "lay ministry," and "itinerancy," could alone afford the ministrations of religion to the overflowing populations; it was to lay the moral foundations of many of the great states of the West....
>
> A religious system, energetic, migratory, "itinerant," extempore, like the population itself, must arise; or demoralization, if not barbarism, must overflow the continent....
>
> Methodism entered the great arena at the emergent moment.... It was to become at last the dominant popular faith of the country, with its standard planted in every city, town, and almost every village of the land....

Methodism thus seems to have been providentially designed more for the new world than for the old. The coincidence of its history with that of the United States does indeed seem providential.³⁴

Between and among these affirmations, Stevens sketched the contours of the Methodist system, a machine the elements of which seemed providentially suited to this American mission. Providence had indeed blessed America with Methodism and Methodism with America. Stevens saw in this new order that vision that Augustine had sought, "the city of God."³⁵

Though enunciating the third of the Methodist axioms, Stevens like his predecessors stopped short of a full-fledged public theology. Indeed, his affirmations about America touched land as much as state, the new world as much as the new republic. Watt and the steam engine, Wesley and the Methodist engine imaged a providential ordering of America as a whole—land, culture, peoples, society, economy. Providence extended its rule over America preeminently through Methodism.

A Conjoint Mission

Matthew Simpson focused Methodist attention more sharply on the American state and so articulated the fourth Methodist axiom. This was a fitting service for a man whose life was dedicated to politics, in church and in state.³⁶ College professor and president, like Bangs and Stevens an editor (*Western Christian Advocate*), delegate to General Conferences, then in 1852 a bishop, Simpson employed pen, platform, and power on behalf of antislavery and union. Confidant to Lincoln, Simpson used his access to Washington inner circles to gain appointments for Methodists and control over the Methodist Episcopal Church, South buildings in territory that fell to Union troops. When Lincoln fell, Simpson preached funeral sermons in Washington and at graveside.³⁷ Simpson's history, unlike that of Stevens, reflected Methodism's Civil War experience, an involvement that had wedded the Methodist Episcopal Church to the nation.³⁸

Simpson's *A Hundred Years of Methodism* appeared in observance of the American centennial. Appropriately, he began with a survey of national accomplishments, the contributions of America to the world. Then he flashed back to Wesley and British Methodism. It was American origins, however, not these "foreign" ones, that stamped American Methodism. "The rise of Methodism," he insisted, "was coeval with the Revolutionary spirit."[39] Both during the Revolution and thereafter Methodism suffered because of its British connection.

> It is somewhat singular that nearly all the troubles and secessions in Methodism have arisen from trying to introduce English ideas and plans into our American Church, or, in other words, from trying to condense our immense continent into the area of a little island. Every agitation has begun by extolling British usages and depreciating American.
>
> In every instance, however, the Church has adhered to American ideas, and has resolutely refused to change her policy at such dictation.[40]

Simpson's topic was an *American* Methodist church. It was this dynamic and rapidly growing church, the success story of American Methodism, that Simpson sought to explain. Like his predecessors, Simpson gloried in statistics, in growth.[41] He found "reasons of the remarkable increase of the Methodist Church" in three superior features of its life, "the superiority of its doctrines, the efficiency of its organization, . . . the piety, earnestness, and activity of its ministers and members."[42] Such claims had led his predecessors almost inevitably and immediately to invocation of providence. Simpson made much less of providence than they. When he did speak of it, the nation rather than the church came into focus. Of the war and emancipation, for instance, he said:

> We can now . . . see the guidance of an all-wise Providence, which overruled the counsels of men in the midst of all these commotions. It was the Divine will that slavery should be destroyed. With determined purpose, step by step, the South moved forward in the separation, first, of the Christian Churches, and then in the attempted division of the States, to that fearful war which resulted in the emancipation of the slaves. No instance in history more clearly shows how God has made "the wrath of men to praise him, and the remainder of wrath" he has restrained.[43]

Here was Mead's "nation with the soul of a church,"[44] or perhaps even a church whose soul was the nation. Simpson held all four Methodist propositions. However, the accent fell on the last, the providential linked mission of church and state. In the spirit of the centennial, Simpson spoke with confidence of this conjoint mission, mindful to be sure of the great cost with which it had been vindicated, but even so, especially so, with a providential, even millennial confidence.[45]

WHITHER PROVIDENCE?

James M. Buckley struck no such ebullient note. Rather he concluded his assessment and essayed twentieth-century prospects in *A History of the Methodists in the United States*[46] by pondering the question, "Has Methodism lost to a dangerous degree its original vital impulse?" and by invoking John Wesley's worry that "the people called Methodists" might become "a dead sect, having the form of religion without the power." Buckley obviously shared Wesley's worry: "The founders of Methodism had no enterprises that were not distinctly subordinate to the conversion of men and their spiritual training. Now its enterprises are many and complex, often pervaded by a distinctly secular element, which contends constantly with the spiritual."[47]

American Jeremiahs have typically prophesied doom to achieve revival and reform.[48] Buckley was no exception. He called for the renewal of the Methodist spirit and identified the requisite resources. And yet his rendering of Methodism's history, if carefully read, suggested grounds for pessimism. In Buckley's account, providence had seemingly loosed her grasp on church and on nation.

This judgment about Buckley and providence is extremely ironical, for in some ways Buckley was more self-conscious about providence than his predecessors. That concern he shared with the general editor of the important series in which his volume figured, the American Church History Series.[49] Philip Schaff designed the series to display the professional prowess of The American Society of Church History. For the Methodist volume he chose its preeminent spokesperson. Buckley played a major and a conservative role in its national affairs. He was delegate to General Conferences from 1872 to 1912. He edited the official and national paper of the denomination, *The Christian Advocate*, from 1880 to 1912. On several important matters, most notably women's role in the church, he stood steadfast and effectively against change. The past and history seemed, at times, to be his forte.

At two important places in his *History*, Buckley stopped to consider the relation of the human and the divine. He devoted chapter VIII to the work of the Spirit in early Methodists, specifically considering Benjamin Abbott, John Dickins, Caleb B. Pedicord, Thomas Ware, and Jesse Lee and the responses they elicited. Noting that Methodists construed the highly demonstrative behavior evident in conversions and revivals "to be direct results of the power of the Holy Spirit, and manifest proofs of His presence and approval of the work,"[50] Buckley inventoried other explanations—naturalistic and, particularly, psychological explanations—of the phenomena. He conceded that "various factors were involved in producing the effects of Methodist preaching and methods," but that among them "was the might of the Holy Spirit."[51] And the effects when carefully essayed and correlated with Scripture, Buckley affirmed, establish "the divine origin of the movement as conclusive as that furnished when holy men of old spake not of themselves, but as they were moved by the Holy Ghost."[52] So Buckley wrenched a providential meaning out of Methodism.

Buckley returned to the theme of providence at the end of his narrative, to worry again over Methodism's prospects. For the most part, however, Buckley remained uninterested in the providences underlying Methodist development and content to explain Methodism in naturalistic fashion. Quite a few of the stray exceptions—statements that God's hand can be found in Methodist affairs—occur in passages that he cited.[53] Buckley offered us, then, a curious irony. He insisted vehemently on the importance of providence but proved curiously unwilling or unable to point to its presence and activity. Providence had assumed doctrinal rather than historiographical force for him.

One could hardly assert that his reluctance to advance providential claims for Methodism typified the turn-of-the-century movement. Methodists generally continued the triumphalism so clearly evidenced in Scudder and Simpson.[54] Nor was he typical in his neglect of similar triumphal claims for the nation. Historians after him would entertain the four propositions and search for appropriate meaning thereof. Nevertheless, Buckley had taken Methodism around an important turn. He had effectively given up the affirmation that lent plausibility to the four propositions—that providence could be seen at work in Methodism.

This was a fitting posture to be taken in a volume that would stand cover-to-cover with histories of other American denominations. Buckley may well have felt constrained by the series. He certainly forewarned the reader that he could not, in good conscience, advance providential claims: "It is not within the province of the historian of his own communion, and in part of his own time, to pronounce judgment upon the motives of those professing 'like precious faith.'"[55] At most, he should aspire to present the developments so fairly that the reader would draw that conclusion.

The reader intent on drawing the four propositional conclusions would have received help from Buckley only on the first. He did present Methodism as "the lengthened shadow" of Wesley and construe Wesley as "The Man of Providence."[56] As we have seen, a limited providential meaning for Methodism can be detected. The other claims apparently did not interest him. He chose, in fact, an interesting place to begin the Methodist story, one wholly out of keeping with the other three propositions. He started with Henry VIII and the English Reformation. From such national and denominational humility interesting consequences flowed. They flowed gradually.

Humpty Dumpty

In spirit and assertions, Luccock and Hutchinson's *The Story of Methodism* resembled Simpson, not Buckley.[57] They chatted with the reader about Methodism; provided upbeat, celebrative and personal estimates of its power and significance; and claimed providential guidance for the movement with a frequency that recalls Lee or Bangs. Yet their very easiness with the providential claims is striking, perhaps worrisome. Do Buckley's critical premises haunt their breezy confidence? Do their assertions betray superficiality or conviction?[58]

Halford E. Luccock held pastorates, served as editorial secretary of the Board of Foreign Missions (1918–24), taught in several theological schools, including a long stint as professor of preaching at Yale (1928–53). A prolific writer, from 1924 until his death he contributed to *The Christian Century*. The *Century's* managing editor from 1924 to 1947 and its editor from 1947 to 1956 was Paul Hutchinson. Hutchinson shared Luccock's literary and missionary activities and concerns. He too was prolific. Their common journalistic bent is evident in this popular account of Methodism.[59]

Evident also is the premise they shared that the twentieth would be *The Christian Century*. They confidently traced the parallel development of nation and church. One early chapter, "A Tale of Two Villages," examined two English towns "which gave to the English-speaking world the most transforming spiritual forces of the seventeenth and eighteenth centuries."[60] Scrooby launched the Pilgrims; Epworth was home to Wesley. "From the first, in truth if not in actual chronicle, the Mayflower set sail to plant a new world. From the second, John Wesley went out to save an old one."[61]

Once they had Methodism firmly planted on these shores, they returned to the parallels of church and nation. In "Methodism in the New Republic," for instance, they implicitly compared Asbury and Washington and explicitly compared James O'Kelly and Patrick Henry.[62] They dwelt on Methodism's popular, even democratic, character and celebrated its pioneer and frontier spirit.[63] The genius of the movement, in fact, is its spirit of adventure, its willingness to experiment, its pragmatism. They did not invoke Frederick Jackson Turner explicitly but found their own term for the frontier spirit, Methodism's "irregularity."[64] The camp meeting typified Methodism's irregularity.[65] They found that spirit of adventure also in missions, to which they devoted considerable attention, making their volume in some respects a study of world Methodism. But again and again, they returned to Methodism and the nation. In the late nineteenth century, nation and church were paralleled on seven particulars—the application of polity, spirit, and organization to new conditions; elaboration of national organization; extensive building; the closing of the frontier; an increase in democracy, foreign affairs, and Negro education.[66] They also paralleled the international perspectives of nation and church in the period after the First World War.⁶⁷ And of course, they took great interest in the causes that riveted the church's attention on the nation—the Civil War, Reconstruction, temperance, the Social Gospel, and First World War.

Such challenges evoked the Methodist spirit of adventure, of irregularity. Luccock and Hutchinson end the volume on that positive note, hopeful that Methodism will in the future draw upon that experimental spirit and reach out to the world.⁶⁸ That note concluded a thoughtful discussion of problems—modern developments, post-World War I developments—that tested Methodism. They listed ecumenism, peace, technological-industrial matters, race. They also examined the great campaign that sought to address such challenges by transforming wartime religious mobilization into peacetime enterprise. This Centenary financial campaign Methodism initially pegged at one hundred million dollars. Luccock and Hutchinson entered their skepticism about the campaign, deftly but clearly. Their comments bear citation, for they point to the overreaching that Handy analyzes as constitutive of Protestantism's "second disestablishment."⁶⁹

They conceded that "the Centenary was not all permanent advance," that it made "too much use of war psychology," that its "promotional methods" made "the task of building the kingdom of God," seem "simply a task of perfecting a high-pressure organization . . . for the raising of certain definitely ascertainable sums of money," that it produced "an atmosphere of false excitement and achievement," and that gradually "this promotional fever evaporated." The Centenary, then, "left certain problems of adjustment which have perplexed many leaders, and many whom the church had commissioned for work in various difficult fields."⁷⁰

The hard-thinking that followed—Neo-orthodoxy it has been called—saw ironies where liberals had claimed providences, perceived an immoral nation where the Centenary had glimpsed the kingdom, recognized cultural enslavement in visions of a *Christian Century*. In Luccock and Hutchinson we find the now liberal Protestant establishment facing the implausibility of its premises. Methodism's four propositions come to rest on "irregularity," not providence, a sandy "human" foundation where Methodists had once found rock.

PROFESSIONAL, NOT PROVIDENTIAL, ESTIMATES

Luccock and Hutchinson wrote a historical idiom that Lee and Bangs would have understood. William Warren Sweet and Frederick Norwood simply did not.[71] The "second disestablishment" rendered the privileged, providential reading of American history impolitic and implausible. So for Methodists, the four propositions no longer guide historical analysis. Or, perhaps it would be more accurate to say, those dogmas have now recast themselves as historical generalizations.

Sweet found difficulty in claiming Methodism providential, but in the second chapter of *Methodism in American History* he treated "The Message of Wesley to His Time." That, once "providential," fit of movement and age could be diagnosed. "Methodism arose out of two great urges: the first was the religious experience of John Wesley; the second was the vast spiritual destitution of eighteenth-century England."[72] So the first proposition found objective form.

The second proposition, the relation of Methodism to American society, consumed Sweet. However, he found the relation to hinge not on providence but on Frederick Jackson Turner's frontier thesis.

> The greatest accomplishment of America has been the conquest of the continent.... The most significant single factor in the history of the United States has been the Western movement of population, and the churches which devised the best methods for following the population as it pushed westward were the ones destined to become the great American churches.[73]

A series of chapter titles charted that destiny: "Organizes for a Great Task," "Invades New England," "Crosses the Alleghenies," "The Circuit Rider Keeps Pace with the Westward March," "Shares in the Missionary Enterprise," "Begins her Educational Task." Conquest defines destiny. Methodism charted its destiny in the nineteenth century in conquest of the frontier, the conquest really of America, the missionary impulse to take the continent.

Stewardship of its missionary calling constituted the reason for Methodism's success, its rapid growth to become the largest Protestant denomination. Sweet rendered that third proposition also in objective or human rather than providential terms. Why did Methodism succeed? Sweet insisted that The Methodist Episcopal

Church "possessed, or developed, the best technique for following and ministering to a moving and restless population."[74] What were factors in that technique? Itinerancy, a centralized appointive power, circuits, short appointments, few repreached sermons, "zealous, energetic ministry," lay leadership, Arminian theology, a populist episcopacy, ample religious literature, and an "emphasis upon singing."[75]

Sweet's version of the fourth proposition followed readily. Sweet conceived of Methodism as the prototypical American church. He understood Methodism in terms of American society and American society in terms of Methodism.[76]

> As the title of this book implies, the history of American Methodism is here considered as a phase of American history, and it is assumed that it can best be understood in relation to the history of the American people.

So the church found itself caught in society's web, captive to American developments. Wealth was one.

> But such changes as were taking place in American Methodism were inevitable, for the church could not stand apart from the social, educational, and economic changes which were taking place in the nation. In the very nature of the case Methodists were bound to become economically prosperous....
>
> [And] the most serious problem faced by American Methodism as a whole at this time was its rapidly increasing wealth.[77]

In this and a variety of ways, Sweet transformed Methodist belief about itself into historical axioms. As such they could be tested by his graduate students at the University of Chicago. Sweet's intentions were laudable and widely shared by church historians. Church history would be a historical science, a species of history, a respectable university discipline. Sweet wanted American historians as colleagues. As president of the American Society of Church History and mentor to several generations of church historians, Sweet played a major role in secularizing and professionalizing the discipline. He gave such a reading to Methodist history.

Sweet taught at the University of Chicago from 1927 to 1946. For two years thereafter, from 1946 to 1948, he plied his craft at Garrett

Theological Seminary. Soon after his departure, in 1952 to be precise, Frederick Norwood assumed that Garrett position, which he held until his retirement. Norwood achieved what Sweet intended, the execution of a Methodist history fully respectful of "secular" historical canons. From its appearance, his *Story of American Methodism* enjoyed preeminence as the text of choice in the course required of United Methodist seminarians.[78] Had these theologians known about and gone searching for the Methodist propositions, they would have found them but in such a subtle and historiographically nuanced form as to be scarcely recognizable. Norwood dealt self-consciously and explicitly with these motifs that have been so important to Methodists. He did so in responsible interpretive fashion. A few citations provide some sense of his handling of Methodism's propositions:

> 1) Methodism began as a revival, and its history has been marked repeatedly by continuing revivals. From this point of view the denominational story is part of a constant theme in the history of Christianity in all times and places—continuing reformation. Inevitably, it seems, the church must go through such a process, as strong institutions languish and traditions ossify. The history of Methodism consistently demonstrates this theme. . . .
>
> 2) American Methodists, and to a lesser extent United Brethren and Evangelicals, were caught up in the heady surge of the westward movement. A couple of generations of historical scholars have attempted to disparage the hoary Turner thesis on the westward movement as the determinative factor in American History. But all they have been able to accomplish is to qualify it as one factor playing a part with others. For Methodism this surge west determined at least the size and influence of the growing institution, and to some extent its quality and spirit. . . .
>
> 3) [The Wesleyan or Methodist working theology] was so successfully peddled that it became a characteristic mark of American Christians of all kinds. The question remains to be discussed, whether this development was peculiarly Methodist or just plain American. Even Calvinism . . . was deeply affected. . . .
>
> Methodism became in many ways the most American of the churches. Not only in its inception but throughout its development it was most in tune with the American song. . . .

4) Does this mean that America was Methodized or that Methodism was Americanized? Probably some of both. . . . [Methodism's various developments] all point to a close and continuing love affair, for better or worse, between the Methodist Church and the United States. Who was the dominant partner?

The process of Americanizing and Methodizing brought on a tension which might be judged as the overriding theme of Methodist history in America.[79]

Here Methodism's four propositions found scholarly expression.

WHY METHODISM?

It would be uncharitable to lay at the feet of Sweet and Norwood a transformation that most church historians, including the present writer, presume and one that the whole denomination effected. The "second disestablishment," in fact, enveloped all mainline denominations. It would be more appropriate to see Sweet and Norwood as mirrors, as their predecessors were mirrors, reflecting the church's self-understanding back to church members. We should underscore, however, the importance of this historical reflection, this historical estimate of Methodist identity. As we noted above, Methodists have consistently turned to history when called upon to say who they were, to state purposes, to define themselves. History looms first in the *Discipline*. And these secular versions of the Methodist propositions now render United Methodism's understanding of itself and its belief. In the 1988 *Discipline's* "Historical Statement"[80] Methodism's propositions survive, as in Sweet and Norwood, only as historical axioms. Methodists continue to turn to their history for self-understanding. They find a narrative from which providence has departed. In this sense the making of church history into a historical rather than theological science has interesting consequences for the church. For it means that theological claims that once came readily to Methodist lips now simply are not heard.

"What may we reasonably believe to be God's design in raising up the Preachers called Methodists?" Many now do not find that Wesleyan purpose appropriately rendered by the four propositions and a vision of a Christian America. Certainly those propositions and vision no longer shape Methodist histories or the *Discipline*. That particular constellation is not, however, the only appropriate statement of the Wesleyan purpose. Early Methodists and their first historian, Jesse Lee, claimed providence but did not find it expressed in nationalism or a national ideology. It may be time for Methodists once again to recognize that they may be about reforming the continent and spreading scriptural holiness over these lands without domesticating that purpose into a vision of a Christian America.

PART 2
ITINERANT MINISTRY

CHAPTER 3

EVOLVING PATTERNS OF METHODIST MINISTRY

What a presumptuous title! What a presumptuous endeavor, to essay the history of Methodist ministry in one chapter. For the topic is, in one sense, fully canvassed. The history of Methodist ministry is, in truth, what all Methodist histories are about. The history of the church—of Methodism in this instance—has been written by minister-historians, with primary attention to ministers and with data and documents maintained by ministerial scribes. Ministerial perspective and concerns pervade Methodist history.[1] In addition to the denominational histories, which implicitly treat the history of ministry, there have been insightful analyses of Methodist ministry by William Cannon, Gerald Kennedy, Frederick Norwood, Dale Dunlap, Thomas Oden, Dennis Campbell, William Willimon, and others.[2] What more is there to be said?

Here I will not try to say better what has been well said (though historians never acknowledge the final word to have been spoken). Rather, I want to view the evolution of Methodist ministry from another angle. If previous treatments might be termed internal in the sense that they worked from within the denomination, employed categories that emerged out of Methodist self-consciousness, and pursued the changes in Methodist ministry in relation to polity, this exploration might be termed comparative or external. What I offer is a perspective on the evolution of Methodist ministry—really only the itinerant ordained ministry, the elders—from without. It is an outside view in two senses. First, I am endeavoring to relate the Methodist ministry to some overall patterns in the history of American ministry. And second, the overall ministerial patterns are related to leadership styles in American society as a whole. So there is a double externality to my assessment. Put succinctly, my approach is comparative and cultural—

comparative in that it attempts to see the Methodist patterns in relation to the evolution of ministry in Protestant denominations; cultural in that it invites comparisons of the Methodist and Protestant patterns with the evolution of leadership in American society. The virtue of this approach is that it permits us a fresh look at a very familiar story.

History of Ministry/Mythology of Ministry

We must begin in the history of ministry by confronting a myth, one that has dominated American ministerial self-understanding from at least the 1660s to the present.[3] The myth insinuates itself into formal, historical treatments of ministry. Declension, that's the myth. That the ministry in the old days, the ministry we knew in our youth, the ministry that we have heard about—was esteemed, was effective, possessed authority, transformed people and congregations, was undaunted by the challenges it faced, preached with vigor and conviction, overcame temptations and distractions presented by worldly, familial, financial considerations. It was a ministry—and note the male chauvinism—of real men. "Oh, if the church were to be again blessed with such a ministry!" That's the refrain that echoes through ministerial conversations, that shapes ministerial self-understanding, that structures histories of ministry. But that refrain has been sung by ministers ever since the second generation of New England pastors came on the scene. If ministerial decline approximated that perception, ministry would have long ago totally disappeared. Changed? Yes, changed it has. Changed dramatically. But declined? We shall see.

The Methodist variant of that myth was well named and exposed by Nathan Bangs 130 years ago. "It is contended by some, as an evidence of our declension," he observed, "that our circuits are shortened, and cut up into stations, and that thus the labour of the ministry is abridged, and, of course, its usefulness curtailed."[4] Such refrains became so common that the mythmakers earned the name "croakers."[5] Bangs thought not and saw the changes in his day in ministry and church and society as the earnest for the millennium. But the myth lives on, intimately tied up with the politics of appointments, the ongoing struggles between the power centers of the church, the relentless quest by every minister, church, superintendent, bishop, official, board to maximize autonomy and minimize external constraint. It is a myth that we must confront. We must move beyond a history of nostalgia, the mythology of declension, if we are to understand properly how ministry has changed. I hope my approach will help us battle this myth. Let me now turn our attention to the changing patterns in American ministry.

TYPES OF AMERICAN MINISTRY

Of necessity such a survey has to be highly selective and schematic. What follows is a brief version of a much fuller picture of ministry that I have attempted in other contexts. (1) Here I can only identify ministerial styles at certain points in American history, drawing on studies of ministry already noted. I shall isolate types or styles, realizing that reality was more complex. It is impossible in this chapter to follow the gradual transformations that produced these distinct ministerial styles. (2) I limit my presentation to the Puritan-Evangelical tradition, realizing that the richer texture of non-WASP styles is neglected. However, I would observe that the pattern discovered has something of a typological quality to it. Religious movements that followed the Puritans into the American wilderness have to a remarkable extent replicated the ministerial patterns identifiable in the New England experience. That attests either the enduring influence of Puritanism or the oft-made point that to an extent all American history is the history of immigration. I incline to the latter reading, namely that the history of all groups has an ethnic quality to it, that all movements have had to discover how to create and sustain a ministry in a new world. (3) I further sharpen the focus by examining the minister in society. That is, I will attempt to illustrate changes by looking at the *communal roles* played by ministers.

The first style of ministry made only a brief but important appearance in the 1630s.[6] It was that of the spiritual leaders of the exile—educated and ordained in England and well versed in the debates and doctrines that we label Puritan—who gathered the saints out of the mixed multitudes in New England. By testing one another's conversion experience, exiles created covenanted communities. The ministry labored from within these congregations to bring order into the emerging communities of New England. The minister shared the ordering role, with others, preeminently the magistrate whose equal the ministry very much was and around whom the civil covenant formed.

The second style of ministry—some now trained at Harvard—represented a stabilization and formalization of the highly visible, communal, local style of leadership. During the remainder of the seventeenth century and well into the eighteenth, the Puritan ministry became an office, sharply conceived in Calvinist dogma, highly esteemed within the town in which it was exercised through word, sacrament, and discipline within a town. As no town was complete without a church and no church without its minister, the ministry was, with the magistrate, the visible sign of local community. A town built around a church—a Christian utopian closed corporate community as one scholar has suggested[7]—this community expressed but also limited the minister's world.

During the Great Awakening, a revivalist ministry loosed itself from these local moorings, beginning to travel and to view an emerging American society as fitting into God's plans. With millennial visions that embraced the English settlements of the new world, the ministry joined hands across colonial lines in a community of affectionate unity, established in the transformative experience of conversion, and knit together by evangelical or pietist practices. The sign of the new community and of the new form of ministry was itinerancy, illustrated in George Whitefield, the Tennents, Jonathan Edwards, a translocal and highly disruptive leadership style—a leadership style, one must add, anticipatory of the political leadership that would bring the Revolution. Empowered by a new rhetoric of the Spirit, this ministry brought into being a new voluntary form of Christian community, community defined by religious experience (conversion) and profession of belief rather than geography. Itinerant revivalists worked across the Atlantic seaboard, effecting both a new unity and a new division in American society. Sometimes censorious—criticizing as "unconverted" clergy who ignored or opposed the awakening—the small party of revivalists put a higher premium on the renewed heart than the educated mind as credentials for preaching. As contrasted to the high office of the Puritan ministry, this was a popularly derived and spiritually communal style of leadership.[8]

During the Revolutionary period, the providential, covenantal, and millennial traditions of Puritanism and Evangelicalism were combined with the Republican ideology of English radicalism, applied to the nation and made available to the churches for statement of corporate purposes. After the Revolution in the succession of movements we call the Second Great Awakening, the ministry appropriated this new national corporate purpose in visions of Christian republicanism and programs of Democratic evangelicalism. To achieve these high purposes evangelical ministers assumed a national role—the building of a Christian civilization; exercised that role in new national communities called denominations and voluntary societies; and became thereby a cadre of national leaders. Not surprisingly, the ministerial style resembled the leadership style prevalent in early nineteenth century American society, that of the booster, the community builder, the propagandist for new opportunities. Like the local politician who would make a frontier land tract the new Philadelphia, like the merchant who envisioned his business the base of a new Wall Street, like the college president who foresaw a new Harvard in his handful of poor students and hastily erected buildings, the minister of that day was a booster for religious development with national pretensions. That peculiar style of revivalistic and missionary leadership so obvious in a Finney or a Cartwright was but the religious variant of the booster style.[9] Illustrative of the national community within which ministry was now set was a new pattern of ministerial mobility. Ministers held pastorates for brief periods and then moved on. This was true for Congregationalists as for connectionalists. Ministry deployed itself nationally. Ministers became agents for the creation of national community, a Christian America.

Before and after the Civil War, denominations internalized Christian culture, towns displaced frontier and ministry once again stabilized itself as a familiar and important feature of local community. Seminaries developed or grew to equip ministry for a broader range of pastoral tasks. And just as ministry was settling into civic and religious maturity in a small-town Christian America, this America was no longer. By century's end, Protestants awoke to discover massive immigration of non-Protestants; sprawling urban areas whose slums bred all manner of moral, economic, and political intemperance; labor strife; huge corporate structures lumbering across the economic frontiers and justifying their dominance with laissez-faire rhetoric framed for a simpler world; vast gulfs between rich and poor; and, of course, challenges to the Protestant worldview from Darwinism, history, sociology, socialism, and biblical criticism. Various new ministerial styles emerged in this complex new world. One numerically small but culturally significant new ministerial style characterized the prophetic, reformist, literary movement we call the Social Gospel. Not disposed to relinquish the vision of a Christianized America nor to labor for it in the older mode—through revivals—the Social Gospel ministry sought national leadership and national community by transforming both agenda and style. The Social Gospel ministry cautiously embraced the new intellectual trends, discovered its own social-ethical commitments in the prophetic writings of the Old Testament and the synoptic Jesus of the New and made itself the biblical herald of a liberalized Protestantism. Under the prophet's mantle lurked the leadership style of the Progressive Movement. Here as in previous styles of ministry, in both the national Protestant community to which it preached and in the reformist style it adopted, the Social Gospel partook of the communal and leadership styles of the day. Like Progressivism, the Social Gospel ministry's aspirations exceeded its attainments. In fact, the Social Gospel exposed and widened the divisions in Protestantism. The community of the Social Gospel, though indeed national, was but one wing of a divided Protestantism. The prophet's fate—to call all to a renewal of vision and capture only some.

In the twentieth century that social gospel style lived on, but so did older forms. And to them has been added a great variety of new forms of ministry, too many to adequately survey in this brief analysis. For purposes of comparison only, permit me to isolate the suburban style as one of a range of twentieth-century ministries whose sense of community and approach illustrates one twentieth-century trend. In suburbia, ministers became pastoral administrators.

Their roles were greatly constricted in terms of the external community but greatly expanded in terms of internal community. Serving long pastorates where Protestants lived and continuing long-established activity in local community, the ministers often lacked access to the work world in which much of their congregation participated. The religious community for which the minister was responsible was, in a sense, squeezed into the family. But at the same time as the external religious community was made peripheral to much of American life, the internal community within which the ministry now labored—the realm of the spirit, of spiritual and emotional problems, of family discord, of divorce—expanded greatly. Through the appropriation of psychology, ministry expanded pastoral counseling both directly and through sermons into the depths of the lives of the people. And through appropriation within congregations and denominations of corporate forms of organization, ministry transformed congregational and denominational life into complex institutions. Both psychological and organizational skills demanded sophisticated and well-trained leaders. Ministry, like much of American leadership, professionalized itself. Appropriate to this professional self-understanding and to the way in which professionalism divided up American life, ministry came to play a professionally dominant role in the smaller community.

EVOLUTION VERSUS DECLENSION

I noted at the outset that the myth of declension bedevils analysis of ministry. Some interpreters would treat change as decline. They would tell my tale as one of ever-increasing irrelevance of ministry as constriction of community and gradual professionalization, which moved ministry from the center of Puritan community as an office to the periphery of corporate, industrial America as profession. The analysis I have just given suggests another reading. The change in ministry is not a gradual slide from prominence into obscurity but rather of a ministry changing appropriately to suit the dominant form of community of the day and adopting a leadership style prominent in America of that day and pertinent to religious community as well.

Architect of order for exilic congregations, an office within the Puritan town, an itinerant and transcolonial style as Americans discovered one another, a national boosterism exercised through denominations and voluntary societies in the building of a Protestant culture, a small-town pastorate prominent in America as a network of villages, a prophetic and literary protest against a troubled and inhumane national community, and a pastoral administrator for a complex and professionalized America that has divided work and home—ministry has altered its style and expanded or concentrated its community to suit changes in American life.

The pattern is rather more a zigzag than a slide. And the future is very much open. We need not extrapolate from my analysis any pattern of irrelevance or secularization that diminishes the importance of ministry. Change it has; but decline, I think not.

THE METHODIST PATTERN

How might this investigation be applied to Methodist ministry? What might we gain from thinking about the evolution of itinerancy in comparative and cultural analysis? To what extent has the Methodist pattern resembled or diverged from one normed on Puritanism and Congregationalism? What might we gain from attacking the mythology that surrounds our ministerial self-understanding through a perspective from without? To answer these questions I have begun my investigation at a somewhat unconventional point. Rather than track legislation on the itinerancy, plowing through disciplines and general conferences, I have begun with ministerial manuals. Limiting myself to The Methodist Episcopal Church, I have analyzed selected how-to books, those formal and published efforts by members of the guild to counsel apprentices. My assumption is that such works both reflect and shape ministerial self-understanding. The assumption is warranted because the books used carried one of several kinds of imprimatur. (1) They were included in the course of study (note that for the MEC the course was the standard mode of theological education until the turn of this century, required even for seminary graduates);[10] (2) they were issued by the Methodist Publishing House of the day; (3) they were written by a Methodist leader.

THE DECLINE OF THE ITINERANCY?

If one is dead set upon documenting the decline of the itinerancy, the dismounting of the circuit rider, and the congregationalizing of the connectional system, one can certainly read the manuals to sustain that prejudice. Certainly Methodist itinerancy has changed. Six-month appointments lengthened to a year, to two years, to four, and now to longer, open-ended assignments. Health concerns have changed as well. Adam Clarke's *Letter to a Methodist Preacher*, which went through several American and a number of English editions, bespeaks the travails of itinerancy.

> From the nature of your work, you must be unavoidably exposed to all kinds of weather—damp houses, bad beds, innutritious food, and a terrible catalogue of *et cetera*. The bad effects of these you may in some measure endeavour to counteract, or to suspend for a time; but you cannot ultimately prevent them from hurrying you into eternity. Whatever deference I may feel myself inclined to pay to the assertion of a great man, vis., that a *minister of the gospel is immortal till his work is done*; yet I am satisfied that he who preaches the gospel as he ought, will, unavoidably, sooner or later, become a *martyr* to his work.
>
> Never sleep in a dampt bed; this is certain death, especially to a delicate constitution.
>
> Do not keep the same shirt on during the day in which you have slept the preceding night; the matter of insensible perspiration is expelled from the body because it is noxious, and cannot be reabsorbed without doing the constitution great injury; and reabsorbed it must be, if you continue to wear the same linen during the day, in which you slept all night.
>
> Never dry your wet clothes while you have them on; this is very injurious. If you have no change of raiment, (and it often happens that a Methodist preacher has but one coat,) walk in the open air till they are dry, or go to bed that they may be dried at the fire.[11]

Clark then gave extended counsel on regularity, for which I will refer you to the original.

Matthew Simpson's *Lectures of Preaching*, given as the Beecher lectures at Yale and doubtless shaped for that audience but carried on the 1880 and 1884 courses of study, attends to health concerns of a different order—those of a stationed pastor. (Do his musings suggest a medical rationale for the waning of the Methodist spirit?):

> The principles of ventilation are generally but poorly understood by sextons. They usually confound warm air with pure air, and keep the rooms closed to have them warm. The interest of many a service is destroyed by this means. People wonder what is the matter with their preacher and with themselves. They have no life, no enthusiasm. They cannot have any when their lungs are loaded with impure exhalations, and the brain is oppressed with imperfectly oxygenated blood. I believe that the health of many a minister suffers severely, and his life is not infrequently shortened, in consequence of the poor ventilation of crowded houses.[12]

By the twentieth century, the health concerns were not only localized but internalized. The *Ministerial Ethics and Etiquette* of Nolan Harmon and the Abingdon publications of Seward Hiltner, *Preface to Pastoral Theology*, and by John Spann, *The Ministry*,[13] suited a ministry whose significant itineration was to the hospital and home of the physically or emotionally diseased.

The health concerns in the manuals illustrate—what might be as readily documented with other aspects of ministry—that the meaning of itinerancy has changed dramatically. But is change necessarily decline? The manuals can be read to confirm the decline of the itinerancy, if the three- or six-month appointments of Asbury and the double form of itinerancy—itinerancy from circuit to circuit and itinerancy within the circuit—is taken as normative. But do we not gain a fresh perspective on the changes in itinerancy if we view the changes as occasioned by the changing character of community in America, the shifts in ministerial style adopted by other denominations, and the Methodist participation in both community and leadership transformation?

Exilic Ministry: Ambassadors of Spiritual Community

Let us look briefly at the evolving understanding of Methodist ministry. Methodists generally and early Methodist historians in particular deemed their itinerant connectionalism providentially given for spreading scriptural holiness and reforming the nation. Well they might. For early American Methodism rather effectively combined the first and third styles of American ministry—the exilic leadership, which quested after order and discipline, with the revivalistic itinerancy, which sought spiritual community. This unity of styles gave Methodist ministry a rather unique power. It was able both to preserve and order the faith of those who by heritage or outlook were predisposed to Methodism and to capture persons and communities spiritually and morally at sea in this new society. Methodists knew their business.

The earliest American Methodist ministerial manual was the *Discipline*. Like Wesley's *Large Minutes*, which it superseded and on which it initially depended very heavily, the *Discipline* outlined Wesley's pragmatically and providentially derived counsel for men exiled from home to preach on the itinerant plan. The first, the 1785 *Discipline*, even employed Wesley's term *helper* for minister and faithfully reproduced with but minor alterations, "The Rules of a Helper."[14] Hence the first style of American Methodism ministry was a Wesleyan and British invention. That may have been superficially obscured by the rearrangement and Methodizing of the *Discipline* that began with the 1787 edition. But the Rules of a Helper recast as "the Directions given to a Preacher" still read:

1. Be diligent. Never be unemployed. Never be triflingly employed. Never trifle away Time; neither spend any more Time at any Place than is strictly necessary....

11. You have nothing to do but to save Souls. Therefore spend and be spent in this Work. And go always not only to those that want, but to those that want you most....

12. Act in all Things, not according to your own Will, but as a Son in the Gospel. As such it is your Part to employ your Time in the Manner which we direct: Partly in reading, Meditation and Prayer. Above all, if you labour with us in our Lord's Vineyard, it is needful you should do that Part of the Work which we advise, at those Times and Places which we judge most for His Glory.[15]

The American communities evoked by such Wesleyan ministry were also intense and single-minded, very much like those initially called into being by Puritan divines, though nurtured by an itinerating rather than a settled ministry.

One of the early Methodist manuals, containing both Adam Clarke's *A Letter to a Preacher* and Thomas Coke's *Four Discourses on the Duties of a Ministry of the Gospel*,[16] counsels and illustrates the sharply focused character of early itinerancy. Clark directed, "Your call is not to instruct men in the doctrines and duties of Christianity merely; but to convert them from sin to holiness. A doctrine can be of little value that does not lead to practical effect; and the duties of Christianity will be preached in vain to all who have not the principle of obedience."[17]

Echoing the language and instructions of Wesley's "Rules of a Helper," Clarke and Coke desired self-educated, experiential Christians who shunned politics and poetry, felt the truth they preached and preached it alone. Traveling ambassadors of spiritual community they must be:

> Never disappoint a place.
>
> Be punctual. . . .
>
> Never leave any place you visit without reading a portion of Scripture and praying with the family.
>
> Should you be invited to any place where you are not permitted to pray with the family, never go thither again; and give them your reason. An ambassador of God should be transacting the business of his Master withersoever he goes; and where he is not permitted to do it, there God has not sent him.[18]

Coke drew out the implications for ministerial style:

> The ambassador of a king speaks only in the name of his employer: he knows no other man while he acts from the authority, and is concerned with the interests of the kingdom he represents: he lays aside the private character, and appears always in his public capacity.[19]

As ambassadors, Methodist ministers exercised authority in this world but belonged not to it. No court or palace for them, they presented their revivalistic credentials on the circuit, in quarterly meetings and especially in camp meeting. Itinerants were truly exiles, ambassadors of the spiritual realm. Hence as Coke insisted, "The spirit of our ministry is a spirit of separation from the world."[20] Exilic ministry it was, reinforced by the separation from friends and family occasioned by constant travel and sharply focused upon exercising a revivalistic ambassadorship. And Clarke's directions to the people echo that sense of a narrow ambassadorial mandate: "Receive the preacher as the ambassador of God, sent particularly to *you* with a message of salvation. Listen attentively to every part of the sermon—there is a portion for *you* somewhere in it; hear *all*, and you are sure to discern what belongs to yourself."[21]

He continued with language that suggested the liabilities and limitations of community dependent upon only periodic ministerial sustenance of poorly trained but earnest and dedicated young men.

> Do you think that this or the other preacher cannot instruct *you*. He may be, comparatively speaking, a *weak* preacher: but the meanest servant of God's sending will at all times be directed to bring something to the wisest and holiest Christians which they have not fully known or enjoyed before. You do not depend upon the man's abilities; if he be a preacher of God's making, he is God's mouth; and by him the Holy Ghost, the Spirit of unerring counsel, of infinite wisdom, and eternal love, will speak to you.[22]

Coke summed it up well:

> I am very conscious, brethren, that our itinerant plan is to be preferred to any other *in this* as in a thousand respects. *We* are seldom tempted to be in the world. *We* must love it exceedingly if we find many occasions to be in it. Our time is spent between the mount, the multitude, and our own people. We almost continually reside in families which look for, and which love and honour, the seriousness and gravity of their preacher.[23]

The Booster

The exilic-revivalist style of ministry—alienated from the world, dependent upon families for sustenance and community, meagerly equipped for pastoral work and narrowly focused in its concerns—transformed itself quickly, almost immediately, into national boosterism through the Methodist connection. I have not yet uncovered an early nineteenth-century manual that reflects that transition. By the 1830s publications clearly indicate that Methodism was very much at home in American society. Nathan Bangs' *An Original Church of Christ: Or A Spiritual Vindication of the Orders and Powers of the Ministry of the Methodist Episcopal Church*, a defense of Methodist against its detractors, attested that sense of legitimacy in the community of Christian America. Bangs insisted:

> The method of propagating these doctrines and enforcing these rules, by an itinerant ministry, with all those auxiliaries afforded us by class leaders, stewards, exhorters, and local preachers, is admirably adapted to give a diffusive spread to the gospel of God our Savior, and to build up the people in holy living.

At the same time he noted that Methodist ministry had changed:

> In the extension of the work, it has been found expedient so to modify some of those external features of the system as to meet the exigencies of the times, and take advantage of the improvements of the age, and to reach the greatest possible portion of mankind with the benign influences of religion.[24]

In a later work, *The Present State, Prospects, and Responsibilities of the Methodist Episcopal Church*, he spoke even more directly of the change in ministry concomitant with the change in community.

> Under the joint superintendency of Bishops Asbury and M'Kendree, I was appointed, in 1813, to the Rhinebeck District, which then comprehended what are now Poughkeepsie, Rhinebeck, New-Haven, and Hartford districts, in all of which there was but one single station, and that so feeble as scarcely to show signs of life. After going around the district once or twice, I said to the preachers, "You might as well go home and go to sleep, as to preach in the manner you do, so far as building up Methodism is concerned. You may indeed be instrumental in the awakening and conversion of sinners; but while you preach once in two weeks in a place on week-days and Sabbaths, and are absent from your appointments all the rest of your time, though

sinners may be awakened, yet, during your absence, other denominations, who have stated ministrations every Sabbath, and whose ministers are constantly among the people, will gather the principal part of them into their churches, and thus you lose all your labour, so far as the Methodist Episcopal Church is concerned." "What shall we do?" It was asked. I answered, "We must go to work and build meeting-houses, and have a preacher stationed in every city and considerable village in the country, in order to establish Methodism."[25]

Bangs was more than just pragmatic here. He saw in such changes, as had Wesley, that both problems and success had disclosed a more appropriate style of ministry.

> The fact is, a competent preacher stationed in one place, if as diligent as he ought and may be, will soon familiarize himself with his people; can visit the sick, the delinquents, and incite them forward in the discharge of duty; bury the dead, perform the marriage ceremony, meet the classes, attend prayer-meetings, and perform all other pastoral duties, and then have time enough for study.[26]

Revivals and membership growth, Bangs believed, attested the providential character of the change, but he nonetheless played an important role in changing the Methodist ministerial style to suit new and more stable forms of American community. "The present system, therefore, of a more contracted sphere of labour, is the natural result of the improved state of society, of the greater populousness and compactness of the villages and settlements."[27]

The changing character of Methodist and American community and of Methodist ministry that Bangs perceived, was the grounds on which advocates of theological education in the 1850s pled their case. Randolph S. Foster in *A Treatise on the Need of the M. E. Church With Respect to Her Ministry* insisted that "Methodism is not now, either positively or relatively, what it was in its inception, or early manifestations; other Church organizations are not what they were; society is not what it was."[28] He noted how piety, thrift, industry, prudence had wrought a change in the Methodist people, leading them to respect for education and culture; how other churches had caught "the reformation spirit," "provoked by our example, and emulous of our zeal," producing "A new race of ministers," and how society had also "undergone and is yet undergoing, a great change—a rapid and glorious transformation," epitomized in progress and the diffusion of information. In these altered circumstances, Foster saw a mandate for an educated and well-trained ministry: "Hence . . . an emergency is upon us. We must adapt ourselves to the change or our mission is accomplished, and other hands now ready will enter into our labors, and gather our ripe and ample harvest; or it will remain ungarnered to rot in the unreaped field."[29]

Not all sized up the situation as Foster did. Persons like Alfred Brunson in *The Gospel Ministry: Its Characteristics and Qualifications* knew theological education to be the ruin of Methodist ministry. Speaking of graduates of such institutions, he affirmed:

> But of this class of preachers, experience proves, that one fourth have so ruined their healths in their *modern* cloisters, as to be *unable* to endure the fatigues and privations of the itinerancy; another fourth are so in debt that they much teach school or enter into some other more lucrative business than the itinerancy to raise means to pay for their education, and by the time this is done they will have contracted tastes, habits of living, etc., and that can never be met in the itinerancy unless very specially favored, and therefore never enter that field; another fourth, if they enter this field, do it with such exalted views of their superior advantages and qualifications, that they must be favored with the best, easiest, and best paying appointments; and, of course, but one fourth are ready and willing to take share in "the rough and tumble work" of the itinerancy.[30]

The debate on theological education, an important one, had long-term implications for Methodism. At stake, among other things, were the very nature of Methodist community and the style of Methodist ministry. It is instructive to note that both sides saw that the issue was whether the ministry evolved culturally as the Methodist people climbed the socioeconomic ladder or targeted itself at the common people. Their choices differed. And the choices are well illustrated by the secular leadership with whom Foster and Brunson compared the minister. Foster thought of the doctor and the lawyer. Brunson ranged more broadly—"The farmer, mechanic, doctor, lawyer, sailor, or soldier."[31] Both assumed that ministry through Methodism was to be instrumental in the building of a Christian America. Methodist ministers were to be boosters of a Christian nation either by shaping culture or by conquering its people *or* both.

The differences on ministry and mission produced more than debate and founding of theological seminaries. Some who shared Brunson's angle and felt that Methodism must sustain its commitment to the poor followed B. T. Roberts in a prophetic revolt that led, on the eve of the Civil War, to the formation of the Free Methodist Church.[32] Free Methodists were not the first nor would they be the last to hold up earlier styles of camp meeting and revivalistic ministry as essential for reaching the unchurched in American society. Others shared Bangs's conviction that the already-churched-but-prone-to-wandering-or-backsliding needed their primary attention.

Pastor in Small Town America

After the Civil War, Methodism enjoyed through its leadership a national prominence but with other denominations, I would argue, came to exercise its primary influence in American society through ministry to the stable communities that dotted the land. Matthew Simpson's *Lectures on Preaching*, speaking out of Methodism to a wider audience, described and prescribed a ministerial role appropriate for American town community. Comparing the minister with other servants of the local community—the doctor, lawyer, and politician—Simpson posited that the minister must be both preacher and pastor:

> Preaching is the chief work, but not the only work, of a Christian minister. He organizes Churches, leads the public devotions of the people, administers the ordinances, and superintends important movements both within and without his own congregation. Yet all these works bear a distinct relation to his office as a preacher; they either issue from it, or are auxiliary to it.[33]

Simpson portrayed the minister as the center of two communities, the congregation and the society. He envisioned the minister as exercising the pastoral office in its fullness—visiting, praying, preaching, superintending the Sunday school and selecting its books and teachers, organizing the church, evangelizing and enlisting new members, managing buildings and property, dealing with church officers, supporting the benevolent and missionary enterprises of the larger church, controlling the access to his people by evangelists. He also urged labor in the society as a whole. Though the minister should be wary of purely political involvements, he should use his influence on the organizations and associations in society to shape their directions and bind them to the church, he should mount the platform, and he should participate actively in the benevolent movements. Here was a ministry very much at home in the stable communities of a Christianized culture. Reflecting that at-homeness, Simpson provided the minister counsel on how to carry on pulpit exchanges in a cooperative fashion and how to find work for every member of the congregation. Already looming over that well-ordered community were the intrusive strains of the Gilded Age. Simpson alluded to the growth and complexity of corporations and organization, welcomed the findings of science and insisted on the power of the pulpit in American society.

The Prophetic Preacher

A generation later, Protestants were no longer so sanguine. Not in the vanguard of the Social Gospel, Methodists took it into the system and contributed mightily to it. The ministerial manuals of the early twentieth century—and by then they proliferated—vary in the degree to which they explicitly counseled Social Gospel activity but more generally reflected this new style of ministry and the complexities of twentieth-century religious community. William A. Quayle's *The Pastor-Preacher* published in 1910, which remained on the Course of Study for five quadrennia from 1912 to 1932, framed the ministry so as to fit it for Social Gospel battles even while he urged entry into civic concerns only cautiously. He could think of no "manlier business than preaching." For Quayle, "Preaching is a robust business. It is in nothing ladylike. . . . The preacher is not a man of cartilage: he is a man of bone and sinew. He feels the riot of mighty deeds. Life is epic to him." The Social Gospel imagery defined the role:

> We shall not fill up the ranks of the ministry by talking smooth talk of ease of emulment. THAT IS NOT HOW THE MATTER IS. The battle beats fiercely. It is against principality and powers,

against spiritual wickedness in high places; it is tireless as the dreadful fight before Port Arthur. The easy brother should not undertake this job. I call it "job" because that is what it is. Put preaching where it belongs, not with the so-called learned professions, but with the eternal working professions, the serious sweaty toils of men, where the corn is planted and the wheat is reaped and the trenches are dug and the sewers laid—the everlasting labors of mankind.[34]

Quayle wanted activities; he said at one point, "The football men are the men wanted here.... I would have every candidate for the ministry play football. It would teach him impact and to see with quick eye the need, and with spirit and body agility to cope with the need. The great, bleak, angry line of Sin, what shall a preacher do with that? And the only logical reply as well as the only Scriptural reply is, 'Rush against it.' "[35] Interestingly, Quayle was equally eloquent on the importance of cultivation of intellectual strengths and has some timeless counsel to offer on how the minister should read. Broadly, sums it up. One excerpt gives us a hint of his insight:

> If a congregation can discover by a preacher's Sunday utterances where the preacher's week-day reading has been, then it is that preacher in sore need of amplifying. A preacher's entire life of reading (in so far as a book may) should minister to each Sunday's utterance, and not some book on which he browsed during the week.[36]

Quayle urged ministers to combine this wide knowledge with a comparable knowledge of human nature acquired through visiting and to focus sharply through the Book of God on "life from God's standpoint."[37]

In his *The Theology of a Preacher*, which appeared in 1912, Lynn Harold Hough reflected the Social Gospel's desire to make theology relevant to life. He insisted that "the first important thing about a preacher is that he should be alive... rich in vital qualities, ... quickly responsive to all the currents that play through human experience,... vividly, deeply, and vigorously alive." A "deep experience of human things and a deep experience of divine things"[38] would make preaching and theology alive and would create Hough's ideal, the preacher-theologian.

Methodism's more thorough appropriation of the Social Gospel ministry is to be seen in the fact that it mandated a current edition of Washington Gladden's manual, *The Christian Pastor and The Working Church*[39] on the 1924 course of study. Further, one of the premier Methodist social gospelers, Francis John McConnell, produced his own manual, *The Preacher and the People* in 1922.[40] The church carried on the 1928, 1932, and 1936 courses yet another work that reflected the Social Gospel, James A. Beebe's *The Pastoral Office*. Beebe called Gladden's manual "the most impressive description of the work of the Protestant minister in more than a quarter of a century," and sought a similar aim in his own effort. One statement will have to suffice as illustration of his concern: "The church must become social toward its several parts and be filled with the spirit of cooperation toward all other community institutions. It must learn to think of itself, not as an end, but as a means (and not the only means) of Christianizing society."[41]

This progressive trend culminated perhaps in the manuals of G. Bromley Oxnam, particularly, *Preaching in a Revolutionary Age* and his edited volume, *Preaching and the Social Crisis*.[42]

The Pastoral Administrator: Professionalization of Ministry

The transition to the final style of preaching and community, that of pastoral administrator, was prefigured in Beebe's manual Beebe had placed most of the work of ministry under "administration"—"The Administration of Worship," "The Administration of Evangelism," "The Administration of Religious Education," "The Administration of Service," and "The Administration of Finance"—and he prescribed means to structure the church and establish committees "to supervise the great essential tasks of the church."[43]

Methodists appropriated the other half of the intellectual-practical resource for a ministry of pastoral administration, that from the psychological revolution, somewhat more gradually, at least insofar as it was attested by Methodist manuals for clergy. By the 1940s, however, Methodists evidenced such appreciation in the rubrics descriptive of the minister's work in a volume edited by J. Richard Spann and entitled simply *The Ministry*. Spann and company treated the minister as preacher, priest, comforter, counselor, religious educator, leader of people and program, and director of public relations. Experts in each of these fields gave the ministers their professional advice. A fuller integration of the administrative and psychological roles into a professional ministerial style is found in the Abingdon publications by the Princeton pastoral theologian, Seward Hiltner, especially in his *Preface to Pastoral Theology*. Hiltner gathered the operations of ministry under the rubrics of shepherding, communicating, and organizing. In his brief for pastoral theology from those perspectives, Hiltner made the pastoral administrator style triumphant.

I need not dwell on this style. Seward's work and that of his many colleagues and students is familiar to most of us. The style was well described by H. Richard Niebuhr in *The Purpose of the Church and Its Ministry* with the rubric, "pastoral director."[44] I would bid you to turn to that work for further illustration.

CONCLUSION

Myths exercise great power over the human mind. United Methodists function with a myth mediated by pictures like this

and by its more stylized and iconic version on publications from The United Methodist Publishing House.

In so imaging our itinerant ministry in its circuit rider version, we imprint a peculiarly Methodist myth of declension in our individual and collective consciousness. The icon can have enervating consequences. By no stretch of the imagination can we equate the long, relatively stable, parishlike appointments of today with the onerous travels of our ancestors. The familiar—no, almost constant—imaging of itinerancy invites us into a rather easy and negative judgment of present-day ministry. Such images, I believe, govern standard readings of Methodist ministry at one level or another. Charting the changes in and timetables of the itinerant system, we tend to impulsively do so with this iconic image and Methodist categories derived therefrom that reinforce (implicitly) a mythology that treats the initial Wesleyan horseback pattern as normative and deviation as declension.

Here I have sought to break the power of that mythology. Instead, I invite us to view the changes that Methodist ministry underwent as part and parcel of significant alterations in the style of leadership—religious and secular—in American society. To be sure, one can construe the convergence of Methodist with societal (and overall Protestant) patterns as compromise or capitulation to society or culture. Those who read changes in that fashion, I believe, fail to recognize the significant role that Methodists played in the creation of those patterns. That point is covered elsewhere in this volume. Here I would only insist that the convergence of Methodist and societal patterns can be read as incarnation as well as compromise. My own inclination is to value positively the successive stages in Methodist ministry and to see them as highly relevant to the religious needs and social realities of those whom the church sought to save and serve.

It seems fitting to conclude with a statement from H. Richard Niebuhr, who concerned himself both with the nature of ministry and the relations of religion to culture. One statement helps us assess what I have attempted here. Niebuhr observed:

> Whenever in Christian history there has been a definite, intelligible conception of the ministry four things at least were known about the office: what its chief work was and what the chief purpose of all its functions; what constituted a call to the ministry; what was the source of the minister's authority; and whom the minister served.[45]

It is on the first and last that I have dealt, endeavoring to share several definite, intelligible conceptions of ministry in Methodist history. It is easy when we look back to permit nostalgia to breed inferiority, to recognize the accomplishments of past ministry in such a way as to minimize those of the present, to so mythologize the ministerial heritage as to place us much beneath those who have trod before. When Gibson Winter wrote of *The Suburban Captivity of the Churches*[46] and when we speak out of our rich Social Gospel heritage of the great ethical challenges of our day, we rather belittle the suburban ministry that so many of us now exercise. I certainly would not want to prescribe suburban pastoral administration as the only and future style of Methodist ministry. Neither would I want to demean it. Rather I would insist, as this chapter has sought to show, that ministerial style evolves appropriately with the changes in community—religious and societal—into forms fit for the day. Our future is every bit as glorious as our past. To think otherwise is to malign the Holy Spirit.

CHAPTER 4

DISTRICT SUPERINTENDENCY: A RECONSIDERATION

The district superintendency, this chapter suggests, deserves better. It ought to be the chief missional, evangelistic, and strategic office of The United Methodist Church. We ought to have a vision for, a theology of, and *Discipline* protocols for the office that summons superintendents to such dimensions of leadership. And we as a United Methodist community ought to invest the district superintendency with the affirmation and support that their exercise of *episkopé*[1] warrants and as Scripture and our tradition demand:

> Now as an elder myself and a witness of the sufferings of Christ, as well as one who shares in the glory to be revealed, I exhort the elders among you to tend the flock of God that is in your charge, exercising the oversight, not under compulsion but willingly, as God would have you do it—not for sordid gain but eagerly. Do not lord it over those in your charge, but be examples to the flock. And when the chief shepherd appears, you will win the crown of glory that never fades away. (1 Peter 5:1-4)

Charles Wesley, "A Prayer for Labourers"

1 Jesu, thy wand'ring sheep behold!
    See, Lord, with yearning bowels see
Poor souls, that cannot find the fold,
    Till sought, and gather'd in by thee.

2 Lost are they now, and scatter'd wide,
    In pain, and weariness, and want,
With no kind shepherd near to guide
    The sick, and spiritless, and faint.

3 Thou, only thou the kind, and good,
      And sheep-redeeming Shepherd art,
Collect thy flock, and give them food,
      And pastors after thine own heart.

4 Give the pure word of general grace,
      And great shall be the preachers' crowd,
Preachers, who all the sinful race
      Point to the all-atoning blood.

5 Open their mouth, and utterance give,
      Give them a trumpet-voice to call
A world, who all may turn and live
      Thro' faith in him that died for all.

6 In every messenger reveal
      The grace they preach divinely free,
That each may by thy Spirit tell
      "He died for all, who died for me."

7 A double portion from above,
      Of that all-quick'ning Spirit impart,
Shed forth thine universal love
      In every faithful pastor's heart.

8 Thy only glory let them seek,
      O let their hearts with love o'erflow,
Let them believe, and therefore speak,
      And spread thy mercy's praise below.[2]

THE MIDDLE JUDICATORY LEADER AND THE CONGREGATION

In an Alban Institute study of the middle judicatory, Gil Rendle asserts that such offices, as for instance district superintendents, are and should be about service to congregations:

> Middle judicatory offices and staff are increasingly shifting away from the assumption that the work and ministry of the denomi-

nation's middle or national offices makes the decisive difference to people and that local congregations therefore will align with them, and shifting to a widespread recognition that it is the local congregation that makes the difference. The role of the middle judicatory office is now seen to be the first line of defense and the closest point of support for the important work and ministry of the local church.[3]

This reorientation of judicatory or denominational services toward the congregation the Alban study both describes and prescribes.

The 2004 United Methodist *Discipline* makes the same congregational prescription and claim, albeit in stages. It defines the "purpose of superintending" as "to equip the church in its disciple-making ministry."(¶401) And, as we all well know, the *Discipline* states "The Mission" of the church narrowly: "The mission of the Church is to make disciples of Jesus Christ. Local churches provide the most significant arena through which disciple-making occurs" (¶120).

In many ways, this congregational focus should come as no surprise. A congregational understanding of the church has been the norm in American religion since the Puritans established their New England "Way" and the Anglicans empowered their vestries in the South. From colonial days, the congregational norm has bedeviled connectional churches (Roman Catholic, Presbyterian, Episcopal, Methodist) that have sought to exercise their connectional authority. In various ways, the society challenged the legitimacy of power and authority lodged above the local level. In particular, courts initially tended to function out of a Puritan (we would call it "Baptist") conception of the church as a locally gathered church, "owning" its property and "calling" its ministry. Eventually judicial procedures recognized our "trust clause," and the connectional and missional understanding of church therein embodied, ones we had held since Wesley. The cultural lure of congregationalism, however, comes back in ever-new forms to tempt and beguile connectional churches, Methodism included. The most recent specters have presented themselves in the church growth, parachurch and megachurch impulses, each of which encourages local control and local initiative. Intrinsic factors have also pressed toward more local or congregational patterns, including pressures for increased consultation, the constraints of second-career and two-career ministerial families, encouragements toward longer pastorates, and the difficulties of accommodating ethnic and other special need situations. This trend, whatever its appropriateness in other traditions and its celebration by religious think tanks, has decidedly undercut district strategies and the role of the district superintendent (DS) as regional strategist.

CONGREGATIONALIZING UNITED METHODISM

The role of the DS as the chief missional and evangelistic strategist seems to be now a faint memory, difficult even to imagine. Methodism has gradually bought into the congregational paradigm, apotheosizing parish ministry and the "local church" and making our connection and connectional apparatus subservient to the congregation.[4] The most dramatic expression of this can be found in the 2004 *Discipline*. It now makes "The Local Church" the first word said about the church as organization or institution. That long section, almost sixty pages, follows immediately after our constitutional, theological, and ethical professions and thereby essentially forefronts a congregational understanding of the church, notwithstanding what is claimed elsewhere about the connectional offices and agencies and about the conference as the basic body of the church.

The *Discipline* has not always so privileged parish ministry and the local church. Historically, American Methodists—like their Wesleyan counterparts globally—functioned with a very different missional, connectional conception and ordering of the church and, of course, an understanding of ministry as itinerant, missionary, and "sent." The church was more than what the Articles of Religion described ("a congregation of faithful men in which the pure Word of God is preached, and the Sacraments duly administered according to Christ's ordinance.") Indeed, it would have been envisioned as a series of ever-larger "conversations" or "conferencings" about how to be a holy people and to spread scriptural holiness across this land. The most local of those conversations was not called *conference* but instead *class*. But it, like the quarterly conference and annual conference and general conference, was a community within which the word was read and preached, discipline exercised, and on occasion (but rarely) the sacraments celebrated.

Most typically, the quarterly conference (ancestor to charge conferences) featured the sacraments, multiple preaching services, love feasts, and other services as needed. There, in the event over which the presiding elder (district superintendent) presided, Methodism was most fully church. There in quarterly conference would gather the various officers of Methodism from class leaders to presiding elders (and often bishops). Often huge crowds came as well, to be fed with two days of spiritual nourishment. These basic church meetings became great evangelistic affairs. And like other levels of the conference structure of Methodism, the quarterly conference sent forth persons to appointments, that is, into mission.[5]

Such a "conferencing" ecclesiology looked outward rather than inward. It gathered to disperse. It had incidental relation to buildings. It oriented itself regionally to where people lived and worked. There it appointed its meetings and services, using the most public space available, including particularly the homes of the faithful and its own meetinghouses where existing. It behaved missionally, strategically, evangelistically.

The shift from such connectional and itinerant to more congregational and parish notions of church and ministry happened gradually. The forces making for the adjustment were various but certainly the increase in the number, proportion, and importance of station churches proved critical. I have catalogued those changes elsewhere.[6] Here I would simply note that the succession of Methodist *Disciplines* chronicles the change, gradually pulling together instructions and expectations about ministry in relation to local church and parish ministry, reflecting ways in which the church's mission came to center on congregations and buildings. The 1928 (MEC) *Discipline* indexed "The Local Church" but spread treatments of it over various rubrics. The 1930 (MECS) *Discipline* included a subsection entitled "The Local Church" but lodged it under Christian education. The first *Discipline* of The Methodist Church, that of 1940, devoted a section to "The Local Church" and positioned it last under Part IV, "The Conferences." So placed, it belonged still to the conference order of Methodist reality. By 1944 and from 1944 to 1960, "The Local Church" became Part II of the (MC) *Discipline*, following immediately after "The Constitution" and preceding Part III, "The Ministry" and Part IV, "The Conferences." Within "The Local Church" were embraced treatments of the quarterly conference and the church conference, as well as the official board. "The Local Church" entirely subsumed the once regional quarterly conference. Within that section as well was placed "Church Membership," once a major rubric in its own right.

By 1976, Wesley's ministry within United Methodism—once itinerating and connectional, continental and worldwide—had been embraced by or collapsed into the local church. Ministry was characterized as local and the (UMC) *Discipline* recognized non-local ministry under a new rubric—"Appointments Beyond the Local Church." Increasingly, Methodists thought not in connectional but in local and parish terms. They spoke of ministry as parish ministry. And they reflected thereby the overall therapeutic and professional changes through which American ministry was passing. Boards of ordained ministry treated parish ministry as the only ministry and rejected or grudgingly accepted persons who aspired to teaching or one of the chaplaincies. As one wit put it, United Methodists had inverted Mr. Wesley's adage ("The world is my parish") to affirm "My world is the parish" or "My world is my parish." By 1990 when the bishops produced a "Vision for the Church," they rendered it in congregational terms: *Vital Congregations, Faithful Disciples.*[7]

Let's consider whether this development has been good for our church. And let's do so with particular attention to the office that has been perhaps most affected—*debased* would be my term for it—by this congregationalizing trend. For one of the greatest anomalies in the present ordering of ministry is where the *Discipline* locates the district superintendency. The superintendency—in many ways the most connectional, itinerant, typical of our offices—lies outside the norm, as an extension ministry or, to use the earlier formulation, as an appointment beyond the local church. How bizarre!

THE SUPERINTENDENCY: TEN HYPOTHESES

The following ten hypotheses constitute an outline for this enquiry. I suggest that

- district superintendents have a much grander, more important purpose than "servicing" local suppliers (that is, congregations);
- United Methodists have swung too far in a congregational, parish direction;
- the superintendency, like the presiding eldership before it, has responsibility for the mission of the church, for envisioning and defining, not just responding to and serving, the mission of the church;
- the office's character as "itinerant," virtually ignored, strangely ignored, in the *Discipline*, should be reclaimed and given its programmatic, conceptual, and theological due;
- the superintendency has sacramental dimensions, a "presiding-at-table" role, better indicated in the former title, "presiding elder," that should also be reasserted;
- the district superintendency might, perhaps should, be understood in relation to superintending roles within other traditions, as for instance, the suffragan episcopacy in Anglicanism;
- also in need of recovery is its function as the chief evangelistic or missional office of the church;
- the office desperately needs theological attention and conceptual overhaul;
- another full-fledged study of the district superintendency is long overdue, undertaken of course in relation to the episcopacy but also in relation to ministerial orders and offices generally, providing a theological and biblical grounding for the entire leadership system;
- such a study, perhaps again undertaken in a reassessment of general superintendency generally, should consider whether persons should be installed through consecration or in some similar sacral act, within annual conferences, and in connection with commissioning and ordination.

The discussion that follows reflects on these assertions, mostly in passing, on a few at more length.

Background

I should note, as an indication of the perspective governing this discussion, the interests and involvement that motivate and shape my own concerns on district superintendency:

- Most immediately, as writer for the Task Force to Study the Episcopacy created by the 2004 General Conference;
- As author with Thomas Frank of the 2004 book prepared for that year's General Conference, *Episcopacy in the Methodist Tradition: Perspectives and Proposals*;
- Through ongoing involvement in the United Methodist-Episcopal (UMC-ECUSA) national dialogue and long interest in ecumenism;
- From undertaking earlier a history of that domain within which the presiding elder and district superintendent labor, namely conference: *The Methodist Conference in America*;
- As principal investigator in the Duke study on "United Methodism and American Culture" and contributing studies on connectionalism and conference;
- From longtime interest in denominational structures, particularly those above the congregational level;
- As participant in the Hartford Seminary project "Organizing Religious Work," as part of the United Methodist team, the results of which were published as *Church, Identity, and Change*;[8]
- Through lifetime as a PK (preacher's kid), faculty member at three UMC theological schools, and elder in the North Carolina and North Georgia conferences of the UMC.

Having invested heavily in studying the organizational fabric of Methodism, particularly at the middle judicatory level, I should concede that the district superintendency is perhaps the central feature of Methodism about which I know least.

An Ignored Office?

The superintendency, I would suggest, has not been well studied. It is not that Methodists do not talk about the superintendency.

Indeed, I suspect that district superintendents constitute one of the most chatted about aspects of and offices in our system. (Perhaps we could test that out by bugging randomly selected pastor's offices or planting hidden mikes in the hallways and toilets at annual conference.) But genuine, careful studies of the superintendency seem to be few and infrequent. Perhaps this chapter will elicit from readers notations about a sizable literature about which I am ignorant.

If I am correct that we lack recent good, basic, full-length analyses of the office, why is this the case? Is the superintendency too familiar, too obvious to be worth studying? I found that to be the case with the annual conference. It was such an obvious, day-to-day, familiar constant in Methodist life that it did not seem to need analysis. My *Methodist Conference in America* became the first real effort to examine the conference and to trace its evolution. Is that familiarity why such a paucity on the district superintendency?

The relevant paragraphs in the 2004 UMC *Discipline* promise much about the office but establish foundations not developed fully. What we have now in the *Discipline* derives from the 1972–1976 Quadrennial Commission for the Study of the Offices of Bishop and District Superintendent. The report, recommendations, and legislation of this commission, "Leadership and Servanthood: Episcopacy and District Superintendency in The United Methodist Church," came through with modest changes into the *Discipline*.[9]

The report, which underlies the current disciplinary understanding, duties, and responsibilities, had behind it some quite important work on the two offices, namely Gerald Moede's *The Office of Bishop in Methodism: Its History and Development* and Murray H. Leiffer's two studies, *The District Superintendent in the United Methodist Church* and *What District Superintendents Say*.[10] Much of the work of that commission also informed the overall study of ministry by Egon W. Gerdes, *Informed Ministry: Theological Reflections on the Practice of Ministry in Methodism*.[11]

Since the commission did its work, two significant studies of the presiding eldership have appeared, but both confine their attention to the decades after 1784.[12] Beyond that we have some Doctor of Ministry studies and a few specialized analyses from research institutes—Hartford Seminary, the Ormand Center, the Alban Institute, The Center for Parish Development. However, given the centrality of this office to American Methodism, essentially from the beginning, the office of presiding elder or DS has been remarkably understudied.

THE DISCIPLINE'S PROMISE

The *Discipline* does reflect important aspects of the 1972–1976 Commission's report. In particular, the *Discipline* locates the discussion of the district superintendency within the chapter on "The Superintendency" generally. It understands the two offices of bishop and superintendent together, rather than burying discussion of the latter within the section outlining the duties of traveling preachers. Prior Methodist *Disciplines* had connected DS (or presiding elder) to the episcopacy operationally but had, over time, separated the treatments and so buried the relation. UMC *Disciplines* since 1976 have made it possible to think theologically about the superintendency as *episkopé*, that is, in relation to the overall superintending that the church requires. The Commission had identified and provided legislation paralleling dimensions or features of episcopacy and district superintendency—some of which come through clearly in the *Discipline*, some of which do not. For instance, the report and *Discipline* insist that both offices should be understood as having personal, collegial, and corporate dimensions.

THE MISSING EMPHASIS ON THE DS AS THE CHIEF MISSIONAL STRATEGIST FOR THE DISTRICT

Here we need to discuss what this legislation treated lightly, namely, the missional possibilities in the office and to remark on how little encouragement the UMC *Discipline* (since 1976) gives to DSs to conceive of their office in strategic and missional terms. The discussion of responsibilities starts off in a permissive, if not promising fashion: "The district superintendent shall oversee the total ministry of the clergy and of the churches in the communities of the district in their missions of witness and service in the world" (¶419). Note, however, that the *Discipline does not say*: "The district superintendent shall oversee the total ministry . . . of the district in *ITS* missions of witness and service in the world." Instead, it locates the church's mission in the parish clergy and local churches, not with the DS and on a regional level. It extends to the DS merely an instrumental or helping function.

A long list of responsibilities follows. The DS is called on for spiritual and pastoral support of clergy and churches—certainly important. And the *Discipline*, within the itemization of duties, returns to missional instructions in rubrics (g) and (h) of ¶419. There too, however, the emphasis falls on being helpful to the mission that belongs in and derives from the congregation. The *Discipline* permits the DS "by enabling" and "by working in cooperation with" to participate in the mission of the district. The notion of the DS as the chief missional strategist for the district, its churches and its clergy, is *missing,* or at least *underdeveloped.*

One can hardly argue that the post-1976 UMC *Discipline*'s protocols about the office of DS, and the limitation on the strategic or missional dimension of this office, were imposed on district superintendents. Murray Leiffer carried out a serious study of the superintendency over a quarter century ago.[13] As noted earlier, his study informed the 1972–1976 quadrennial study that yielded our present Disciplinary protocols. Leiffer's survey of a nationwide cohort of 475 district superintendents in 1970 indicated that they viewed their pastoral role—as pastor to pastors—at the top of their responsibilities. They ranked "Training pastors as 'enablers'" and "Friend, counselor to minister and wives" as the two top responsibilities. The DSs put those two decidedly above "Serving on Cabinet," "Work with 'problem' churches," "Conducting Charge Conferences," and thirteen other duties. Leiffer observed a critical discrepancy between where the DSs placed their priorities and how they actually spent their time. The heaviest demands on time came from charge conferences, office work, and serving on cabinet. Counseling pastoral families and training pastors as enablers came in fourth and ninth, respectively. I would note that the strategic, missional, or evangelistic priority—put as a question to the DSs as "Studying the territory of the district for purposes of long-range, district-wise planning"—ranked down the list in both importance and as a claim on the DS's time. It was seventh in importance and twelfth in expenditure of time and energy.[14]

THE MISSIONAL MANDATE

So far the discussion has covered the first two points on my bulleted list. My third point—that the superintendency, like the presiding eldership before it, has responsibility for the mission of the church, for envisioning and defining, not just responding to and serving, the mission of the church—can be summarized with a further series of bullets:

- congregations and clergy SHOULD NOT define and confine the church's and a district's mission;
- they SHOULD find their appropriate place within the district mission;
- like the parishes of Mr. Wesley's England, the local churches do have a critical role in disciple making;
- however, the mission of the church then and the mission of the church now should not be bottled up in buildings;
- our church desperately needs the regional strategizing that the district superintendency can uniquely and only provide; and
- the role is not a new one but an old one for the office.

The presiding elder's missional role was spelled out most clearly in the early MEC *Disciplines*, with their terse stating of regional duties:

Of the Presiding Elders, and of their Duty

Quest. 1. By whom are the presiding elders to be chosen?

Answ. By the bishop.

Quest. 2. What are the duties of a presiding elder?

Answ. 1. To travel through his appointed district.

2. In the absence of a bishop, to take charge of all the elders, deacons, travelling and local preachers, and exhorters in his district.

3. To change, receive, or suspend preachers in his district during the intervals of the conferences, and in the absence of the bishop.

4. In the absence of a bishop, to preside in the conference.

5. To be present, as far as practicable, at all the quarterly meetings: and to call together at each quarterly meeting all the travelling and local preachers, exhorters, stewards, and leaders of the circuit, to hear complaints, and to receive appeals.

6. To oversee the spiritual and temporal business of the societies in his district.

7. To take care that every part of our discipline be enforced in his district.

8. To attend the bishop when present in his district; and to give him when absent all necessary information, by letters of the state of his district.[15]

When Bishops Francis Asbury and Thomas Coke glossed this section of the 1798 MEC *Discipline*, they concluded by crediting the presiding elders, to a significant extent, with the missionary or evangelistic successes of the young movement.

> In the year 1784, when the presiding eldership did *in fact*, though not in *name*, commence, there were about 14000 in society on this continent; and now the numbers amount to upwards of 56000: so that the society is, at present, four times as large as it was twelve or thirteen years ago. We do not believe that the office now under consideration was the *principal cause* of this great revival, but the Spirit and grace of God, and the consequent zeal of the preachers in general. Yet we have no doubt, but the full organization of our body, and giving to the whole a complete and effective executive government, of which the presiding eldership makes a very capital branch, has, under God, been a grand means of preserving the peace and union of our connection and the purity of our ministry, and, therefore, *in its consequences*, has been a *chief instrument*, under the grace of God, of this great revival.[16]

One gets some sense of the rough and tumble missional and strategic character of the office, particularly as it led the evangelistic expansion of the church into frontier areas, in the autobiographical, tall tales of Peter Cartwright, notably his *Autobiography of Peter Cartwright, the Backwoods Preacher* (1856) and *Fifty Years as a*

Presiding Elder (1871).[17] The most thorough study of the exercise of the office up through Cartwright's period, by Fred Price, makes the case for its strategic nature. His theme is that the presiding eldership was missional in character, the key to Methodism's explosive growth, the missional operational agency of the church, the chief evangelistic office.[18] The presiding elder's role now might seem more akin to what one finds in Baptist or in megachurch circles—where congregations outplant a new congregation, function with house or apartment congregations, encourage bivocational ministries, train for new church planting, and itinerate—all patterns "stolen" from Methodists. In times past, it was the duty of the presiding elder to oversee just such aggressive evangelism. The presiding elder (PE) or DS envisioned how circuits should be laid out to encompass his (and it was "his") region, where new circuits should be started or existing ones divided, when preachers needed to change, how best to use exhorters and local preachers; in short, how the human resources at his command ought to be deployed to meet the human needs of the district. Bishops, with multiple conferences to oversee, depended on the presiding elders, individually and collectively, to be the strategists. The presiding elder, like the bishop, gained the wisdom for the superintending role by traveling through the district—preaching and presiding.

REAL ITINERANCY

District superintendents, the 2004 UMC *Discipline* asserts, are "an extension of the general superintendency" (¶417). The *Discipline* understands the episcopal and superintending offices as "an integral part of the system of an itinerant ministry" (¶401), but it says amazingly little about the itinerant character of the superintendency and its participation in the "itinerant general superintendency," which our Restrictive Rules protect constitutionally as the defining feature of the offices. Since 1808, the MEC and successor denominations have stipulated in the Restrictive Rules that

> the general conference shall have full powers to make rules and regulations for our church, under the following limitations and restrictions, viz. . . . 3. They shall not change or alter any part of

rule of our government, so as to do away Episcopacy or destroy the plan of our itinerant general superintendency.[19]

We have not been as articulate about the district superintendency as we should have been. Lacking a full-fledged recent study of the office, the treatment in the Appendix to this chapter from Thomas Coke and Francis Asbury's 1798 annotated edition of the MEC *Discipline* is one of the best, albeit very short, treatments available. That statement may also come closest to being a forthrightly theological assessment. We *need* a more thoroughgoing study that includes a theology of the office.

If and when there should be such a study, should it not begin with the superintendency's incarnation of the central Wesleyan commitment to, indeed belief in, itinerancy? Are not district superintendents the most itinerant of our ministers—and, in fact, more itinerant than the bishops? To be sure, bishops travel more extensively across the globe, to more general agency meetings and to their semi-annual confabs in vacation locales. But where is the itinerant activity in getting on a plane and into a cab for a meeting? Compare that to constant driving at high speeds along the dusty back roads of a district or between the district and conference offices. Now, there's itinerancy! Itinerancy is an odometer thing. Asbury taught us this. He counted up the miles at the end of the year. DSs do as well, I suspect—for "Uncle Sam" if not for their own purposes. And I suspect that DSs do not get "frequent flyer" points for the miles logged.

I would remind us that this reality in the lives of the DS is in keeping with our tradition, for the first duty from the original legislation on the presiding elder was *to travel*: "*Quest.* 2. What are the duties of a presiding elder? *Answ.* 1. To travel through his appointed district."

Perhaps we lack an adequate theology of the superintendency—for Bishop as for DS—because we have not done as well in theologizing itinerancy as we might have done.[20] At any rate, United Methodism would profit by elaborating a genuine theology of "itinerant superintendency" within which both a general superintendency (that of the bishops) and a district and conference superintendency (that of the DS) might be understood.[21]

A SACRAMENTAL OFFICE?

In his study that emphasized the missional character of the presiding elder, Fred Price also delineated and discussed the primary roles of the office. The first item on his list was "Provider of the Sacraments." The others bear mention at this point as well:

Apologist	Propagandist
"Visioner"	Connector
Celebrator/Revivalist	Preserver
Innovator	Trainer
Nurturer	Advisor
Disciplinarian.[22]	

The PE provided sacraments as he presided over quarterly conferences (predecessor to charge or church conferences). In some, he might not be the only elder present. Indeed, it was common for the quarterly conference or quarterly meeting to gather PEs and preachers from other districts—and bishops, if in the vicinity—and to draw huge crowds. In other circuits, he might well have been the only person fully ordained. His quarterly appearance accustomed Methodists to quarterly observance of Eucharist. An annual sacramental appearance of the DS at the charge or church conference might not suffice to reclaim this historic role but would be a worthy new habit (unless, of course, it encouraged congregations or congregants to commune only once a year).

One can discern the sacramental quality of the early presiding eldership by taking note of the activities associated with the PE's primary task, that of presiding at quarterly conferences (quarterly meetings). Very early these became two-day affairs, frequently but not always on the weekend. Saturday would feature some preaching but also care for all the business prescribed by the *Discipline*. Sunday would be a glorious liturgical festival, often beginning with a love feast and featuring multiple sermons, the Lord's Supper, and memorial services and baptisms as needed. They drew huge crowds, particularly in warm weather, and frequently were combined with camp meetings when that institution emerged.

William Colbert, who traveled extensively in the middle Atlantic states from 1790 to 1838, left us a typescript journal that extends to ten volumes and describes one quarterly meeting after another.²³ For instance, one held on March 13-14, 1802 at Bowen's Meetinghouse, on the Somerset and Annamessex Circuit, involved himself and four other preachers: Thomas Ware, P.E., Edward Larkins and Daniel Ryan (both on that circuit with Colbert), and the probationary preacher, Henry Boehm (the son of Martin and a later traveling companion of Asbury).²⁴ Colbert reported:

> Saturday At night we had a glorious Love-feast among the blacks.
>
> Sunday 14 Brothers Ware, Larkins and Ryan preached to as many as the house would hold, and Bro. Boehm and myself took the Black people in the woods. I preached . . . Brother Boehm gave an exhortation: and indeed we had a great time, many tears were shed and many joyful shouts were heard. We left them shouting the praise of God, and went to the Meetinghouse. . . . We then administered the sacrament and held a Love feast, and a glorious time we had. It is not according custom to hold Love-feast after preaching but I believe it would be best on many accounts. Lodged at Sister Esther Purnells.²⁵

Such accounts, highly typical, deserve more analysis than we can devote here, as for instance on the biracial but segregated character of early Methodism. We should note, however, both the sacramental and evangelistic quality of these presiding elder events.

The same can be discerned a couple of months later, when Colbert was appointed presiding elder to the Albany District. The district then featured ten circuits. Colbert started off conducting a quarterly meeting every weekend, beginning June 5 and extending to September 3 and 4, when he began a second round of quarterly meetings.²⁶ The pattern of presiding weekly at a quarterly meeting can be tracked in his daily accounts into December when there is a break in the manuscript and typescript journals. Why the weekly sacramental-evangelistic-disciplinary event? Simple math. As a PE with ten circuits, each of which had a quarterly meeting *quarterly*, Colbert would need to conduct at least forty in the course of the year. Moreover, since he left his Albany District a month before the Baltimore conference, in order to make the long trek, and needed to allow a month after conference to wend his way back, he had to do a quarterly meeting every week just to cover the ten circuits on his district. In fact, on his way to and from conference he took a busman's holiday and attended other PE's quarterly meetings. PEs appointed closer to the meeting site of their conference would have fewer weeks in transit but would have paralleled Colbert's exciting but grueling pattern of virtual weekly quarterly meetings. The aspect of these occasions on which Colbert reported was their eucharistic evangelistic character, a reporting pattern highly typical.

For instance for a quarterly meeting on the Herkermer Circuit on Sunday, July 4, he noted:

> A glorious morning. Many of the friend[s] spoke with life and power in the Love-feast. The Lord displayed his power. One man who had been under conviction was so wrought upon, that he lost the use of his limbs, and was brought to experience the goodness of God, (I trust) in the conversion of his soul. After the Love-feast we took the congregation into the woods. To me it was pleasingly romantic, to Behold the people seated on the old logs, and in their wagons, Beneath the lovely shades of the stately Maple and Beach Trees listening to the joyful sound of salvation. I stood in the Waggon, and preached to them from Acts 16 ch 30, 31 Brothers Wilkerson Hoyer and Willy exhorted. The Lord was present, but more power fully at the administration of the sacrament. Numbers were brought on their knees, crying for mercy and one was brought to rejoyce in the God of her salvation ... [A woman wept, then went motionless, rose up testifying, to be knocked over by another who though opposed to shouting herself went stiff and fell on the first].[27]

Or similarly for August 28-29 on the Otsego Circuit:

> Sunday ... I had to stand in a waggon on a Dunghill and preach to the people ... Toward the close of administering the ordinances the Lord display'd his power, and several were brought to cry for mercy. The times of administering the Lords supper, and the Love feast I have found, in this Country times of great power. We have had a number of open communion Baptists in our Love-feast, they profess to be a happy people, and I do not doubt their having religion among them, but at the same time, I fear there is so much of Calvinism among them that we may by their mixing

so much with us find it attended with disagreeable consequences. For my own part, I like the pure old unmixt Methodism better than any thing I have yet made myself acquainted with.[28]

Colbert does not always tell us whether or not he was the celebrant, though he probably often was. Either way, as PE he lived a constant, or at least weekly, diet of sacramentlike love feasts and Lord's Suppers, a weekly diet of quarterly conferences.

So to speak of the district superintendency as a sacramental office is to accent what had been one of its constitutive dimensions. In addition to what reclaiming a sacramental role for the office might do for our conception of it theologically, the reenvisioning might also work wonders for the image and self-image of the DS. Congregations and clergy who have thought of charge conferences as a play in which "The Tax Man Cometh" and of the DS as primarily a fiscal and personnel officer might grasp other dimensions of the office and of our connection, as charge conferences regained their once sacramental character and the DS's presiding there took on more than an organizational character.

SUPERINTENDING

Reasserting the sacramental aspect of the office might make it more feasible in our understanding of the ordering or superintending roles to lay claim to understandings of *episkopé* from other traditions. In particular, the Anglican or Episcopal suffragan episcopacy might be one to study; though the Anglican office may represent more of "an extension of the general superintendency" (2004 *Discipline*, ¶417) than Methodists could stomach. Suffragans are full, real bishops, elected to the office, and ordained and consecrated, with the full panoply of sacramental authority of the episcopal order.

Methodists have been so resolute—in the face of repeated challenges—in keeping the presiding eldership and district superintendency under episcopal appointment that we have tended to erode its episcopal dimension, its presiding character, its superintending function, its call to exercise *episkopé*. The original legislation, to which we have already called attention, accented the "suffragan" character of the office clearly. In the schema below, the answers omitted (for brevity) outlined "episcopal" duties that the PE would exercise on his own, in his district. The answers retained empower the PE to exercise *episkopé* "in the absence of a bishop."

> *Quest.* 2. What are the duties of a presiding elder? . . .
>
> *Answ.* 2. **In the absence of a bishop**, to take charge of all the elders, deacons, travelling and local preachers, and exhorters in his district.
>
> 3. To change, receive, or suspend preachers in his district during the intervals of the conferences, and **in the absence of the bishop**.
>
> 4. **In the absence of a bishop, to preside in the conference.** . . .
>
> 8. **To attend the bishop** when present in his district; and to give him when absent all necessary information, by letters of the state of his district. (bold added)

As contrasted with this original, one might argue that the 2004 UMC *Discipline* has augmented greatly the "episcopal" duties that the DS would exercise on her or his own in the district. Less clear, one might further argue, is the DS's authority and stature to exercise *episkopé* "in the absence of a bishop."

Is it time, therefore, to imagine procedures of installation in this office, modeled in some fashion after those for bishops. Why do we not consecrate persons for this service? We consecrate and have consecrated for various roles, short- and long-term. Surely DSs could be brought into the office during annual conference, amongst those with whom they will serve, in a fashion that appropriately acknowledges their being set aside to exercise *episkopé*. No small part of the problem with the DS is our undeveloped or at least underdeveloped appreciation for and theology of the office.

A THEOLOGY OF THE OFFICE?

A theology of district superintendency might, perhaps should, parallel that of the bishops. If so, we might play with the former as *itinerant presiding superintendents.* Such a theologizing with an eye to the definition of superintendency protected by the Restrictive Rules—not itinerant general superintendents but perhaps itinerant presiding superintendents—draws together three of my bullets, those three just discussed:

- The office's character as "itinerant," virtually ignored, strangely ignored, in the *Discipline* should be reclaimed and given its programmatic, conceptual and theological due (WORD).
- The superintendency has sacramental dimensions, a "presiding-at-table" role, better indicated in the former title, "presiding elder," that should also be reasserted (SACRAMENT).
- The district superintendency might, perhaps should, be understood in relation to superintending roles within other traditions, as for instance, the suffragan episcopacy in Anglicanism (ORDER).

These three rubrics—itinerant, presiding, superintendent—would permit us to parallel roles of the district superintendency with Word, Sacrament, and Order, three defining marks of the church in classic Reformation and Methodist theology.[29] These rubrics invite as well our invoking the traditional offices of Christ: prophet, priest, and king. Both the ecclesial and the Christological terms, when applied to the office, would permit an extraordinarily rich resource for understanding its theological promise. The terms, as theologically developed, in turn would allow us to claim or reclaim the "episcopal" duties to be exercised in the district *and* the call to exercise *episkopé* "in the absence of a bishop."

A theology so developed would ground and be grounded in the work of the office, either as currently exercised or as potentially developed. Currently exercised are the DS's Word, preaching, itinerant, prophetic work; as also the royal, Order, superintending work. Perhaps less clear today, less utilized, less emphasized is the second, the priestly, the Sacramental role, the presidency, including presiding at the table.[30] It can and should be reclaimed, so as to offer a full-orbed understanding of the office.

SERVANT LEADERSHIP?

Recently General Conference, as it sought to reclaim the office of permanent deacon and the diaconal shape of the whole ministry of the church, added to the calling to ordained ministry and the definition of the church an additional defining mark—service: "Ordination is fulfilled in leadership of the people of God through ministries of Service, Word, Sacrament, and Order."[31]

If the church sustains this fourfold development, it may well need and want to reflect on the relation of these four marks to the traditional anointings of Christ—prophet, priest, and king. I suggest this not because there is any difficulty understanding Christ's ministry as one of service but because simply adding "servant" to the other three of Christ's anointings may produce some distortion in our understanding of the three.

This is of particular concern in relation to Christ's royal office, the ordering office. In exercising his kingship on earth, Jesus rejected Satan's offer of earthly power, identified with the Suffering Servant, embraced the marginalized, gained a crown of thorns, and assumed a lordship spiritual in character. The "royal" anointing—when rightly developed, as for instance out of the passage from 1 Peter cited at the beginning of this chapter—points to such service, the suffering service of Christ. Merely adding "service" might invite a misunderstanding of the royal and ordering office, creating a tendency to construe it even further toward earthly power.

Moreover, if we add "servant" to the anointings of Christ, why stop there? Would we not need to include also "teacher," "healer," and any number of Christ's other offices?

Whatever our reservations about the addition of the fourth rubric, United Methodists will likely sustain and develop the fourfold ministerial-ecclesial schema. In this case, a theology of district superintendency, as well as that of general superintendency, needs to follow suit. The first point I would make is that "servant" should be used carefully in understanding and reconceptualizing the district superintendency. The DS should be about service, but about more than "servicing" local suppliers. The DS should serve in the fashion outlined by 1 Peter. DSs should serve as Charles Wesley envisioned, as gatherers of the lost sheep, as chief evangelists, as missionary tacticians, as strategists for the district.

In our effort to attend to Service, Word, Sacrament, and Order in relation to the office of episcopacy, Tom Frank and I paralleled those four with the three traditional Methodist rubrics—itinerant, general, superintendent—and drew attention to another word in the pertinent Restrictive Rule, namely "plan." With respect to the DS, the fourth term ought, I would suggest, to call attention to the strategic, evangelistic, and missional potential of the office. I do not have a word to propose but would encourage those who live and study this office to bring forth the appropriate fourth rubric.

If Methodism should choose not to invest in the Christological and theological work of developing the fourth ecclesial, ministerial term, then the evangelistic, missional, and strategizing functions of the district superintendency can be appropriately embraced, respectively in the existing three: Word (itinerant, evangelistic), Sacrament (presiding, missional), Order (superintending, strategizing).

Whatever we do in reconceptualizing, clearly we should heed the precept of Paul Dietterich and Donald Arthur, *The District Superintendent, Key to District Revitalization*.[32] We need to recover the DS's function as the chief evangelistic or missional office of the church. That might be as simple as bringing some coordination to the outreach that we already have. I long to be able, for instance, to go into a city and to find in the yellow pages or the newspaper religion sections or the church advertisements a sense that United Methodism has an organized, coordinated presence in that locale. I will be excited to find an ad—like some I have seen from Lutherans—that lists the churches of the city or district, their location, and the time of their Sunday service. I will be thrilled by evidence in the papers or yellow pages of a district strategy of evangelization and mission. And one can imagine many other far less simple and far more effective ways of mobilizing a district and its clergy and lay resources to care for the human needs of the area. We have middle judicatory servant leaders. Do we permit them to lead?

Concluding Exhortations

We need to redo the *Disciplinary* conception and the tasks of this critical office. I conclude with that affirmation and by pointing back to and recalling all ten, but particularly the last three, of my ten bullets:

- The office desperately needs theological attention and conceptual overhaul.
- Another full-fledged study of the district superintendency is long-overdue, undertaken of course in relation to the episcopacy but also in relation to ministerial orders and offices generally, providing a theological and biblical grounding for the entire leadership system.
- Such a study, perhaps again undertaken in a reassessment of general superintendency generally, should consider whether persons should be installed through consecration or in some similar sacral act, within annual conferences, and in connection with commissioning and ordination.

CHAPTER 5

THE TEACHING OFFICE

The *Minutes* of the first annual conference:

The following queries were proposed to every preacher:

Ought not the authority of Mr. Wesley and that conference, to extend to the preachers and people in America, as well as in Great Britain and Ireland?

Ans. Yes.

Ought not the doctrine and discipline of the Methodists, as contained in the minutes, to be the sole rule of our conduct, who labour in the connexion with Mr. Wesley, in America?

Ans. Yes.[1]

The 1808 MEC *Discipline*:

The General Conference shall have full power to make rules and regulations for our Church, under the following limitations and restrictions, viz.:

The General Conference shall not revoke, alter, or change our Articles of Religion, nor establish any new standards or rules of doctrine contrary to our present existing and established standards of doctrine.[2]

The current (2004) UMC *Discipline*:

The General Conference shall have full legislative power over all matters distinctively connectional, and in the exercise of this power shall have authority as follows: . . . To enact such other legislation as may be necessary, subject to the limitations and restrictions of the Constitution of the Church.

Restrictive Rules.

Article I.—The General Conference shall not revoke, alter, or change our Articles of Religion or establish any new standards or rules of doctrine contrary to our present existing and established standards of doctrine.

Article II.—The General Conference shall not revoke, alter, or change our Confession of Faith.[3]

Speaking for the Church.—No person, no paper, no organization, has the authority to speak officially for The United Methodist Church, this right having been reserved exclusively to the General Conference under the Constitution.[4]

Bishop Nolan Harmon:

The General Conference . . . is the supreme governing and law-making body of United Methodism.[5]

Theologian Thomas Langford:

General Conference holds the teaching office in United Methodism. It is the final authority and officially speaks for the Church.[6]

This chapter reflects on the teaching office in the history of Episcopal Methodism.[7] Such an exploration might seem, as the preceding quotations should suggest, a rather unpromising venture. What history is there to tell? After all, on this point as perhaps on virtually none other, Methodism has spoken with great precision and finality. Conference, and particularly General Conference, is supreme. On whatever the issue of the day, to General Conference (since 1792) has Methodism looked for a definitive statement of its position. Since 1792, General Conference has occupied the teaching office. What history is there to write? Would it not suffice to say that this precept has no history but has been quadrennially reproclaimed?

This chapter gives to General Conference's actual exercise of the teaching office less attention than it deserves. Its purpose is to explore other agencies of Methodist teaching. All during its existence, General Conference has found ways to speak to and for the church. Obviously, it did so forcefully by its quadrennial revision of the *Discipline*; by legislation; by authorizing catechisms, hymnbooks, liturgies, and the like; by the various offices and agencies it established (which we will examine); by its stipulation of and initial control over the course of study; and by direct efforts to speak to the Methodist people through pastoral letters.[8])

RESTRICTIVE RULES BUT . . .

Subject to the limitations of the 1808 Restrictive Rules, General Conference does occupy, as closely perhaps as an agent in any Protestant church can occupy, what Catholicism has understood as the *magisterium*, the teaching office, the supreme doctrinal authority of the church.[9] To employ that rubric is, to be sure, to exaggerate the authority that any human vessel can occupy and, perhaps to inappropriately qualify the Protestant belief in the sovereignty of the Word and the priesthood of believers. So one can speak only metaphorically of a Methodist teaching office. Yet insofar as Methodists can be said to have a teaching office, is that not clearly General Conference? Is not that where such teaching authority as does exist is lodged?

Well, perhaps. For a variety of reasons that will become clearer as we proceed, General Conference's actual exercise of the teaching office has been less clear, unambiguous, uncontested, than the theory would suggest. General Conferences, after all, come into being, sit for a short period, revise the *Discipline*, legislate, perhaps issue a pastoral address, and then disappear for four years. If for no other reason, that four-year interim—the quadrennium that has such magical value in Methodist calendars—leaves, and has left, time and space for others to exercise the teaching office

- through transmission,
- in interim capacity,
- by execution,
- through interpretation,
- in application,
- even in preparation for General Conference itself.

Over the years, various agents of/claimants to General Conference's teaching function have, to some degree at least, encroached upon, perhaps even threatened, General Conference's authority. And beyond the infringements of General Conference's teaching office that, at least in theory or appearance, respect its authority lie other efforts to connive at authority that can only be seen as, in some sense, an effort to displace General Conference and to exercise the teaching office in Methodism.

In addition, from the very start teaching belonged in a special way also to the episcopal office, indeed to the ministerial office generally. And the episcopal claim to teaching authority has from time to time been reentered, perhaps no more vigorously than at present. Here too the *Discipline* notwithstanding, the actual exercise of the teaching role may be somewhat different than envisioned.

Our concern, then, is with the actual exercise of the office, the intellectual leadership of the movement, General Conference's delegation of its authority, the effectual tutelage of the people called Methodist. This will not be a review of the constitutionality of General Conference's authority. Rather, we focus on how, in Methodism, a teaching office was actually exercised.[10] Who or what addressed the church, the whole church? Who or what posed the questions for the church's consideration? Who or what called to mind the bearing of Scripture or tradition on the issue? Who or what elicited conversation and debate and brought various constituencies into dialogue? Who or what worked toward consensus, compromise, resolution? And who then educated the church on the question as resolved? Who really taught the church?

To appreciate the present exercise of the teaching office, we need to review its history.

THE TEACHING OFFICE IN EARLY METHODISM

Methodism might be permitted some unclarity about the nature of the teaching office. After all, deeply imbedded in its memory lies the realization that the teaching office once took rather different and specific form. In early Methodism the teaching office rested firmly, unequivocally, definitely on Mr. Wesley. He constituted the intellectual and theological center of the movement. Very self-consciously and deliberately, he dedicated himself and the movement to instruction. Wesley embodied that teaching role. Doubtless much that passes for Wesleyan teaching originated elsewhere, as we seem to learn with every new publication by Richard Heitzenrater.[11] And yet, it comes to us through Mr. Wesley's pen. And that is what constitutes the teaching office.

In thinking about this role, we naturally revert to those deposits of Wesley's teaching, *The Large Minutes*, *Explanatory Notes Upon the New Testament*, *Standard Sermons*, and for Americans, Wesley's modified version of the Anglican Articles of Religion, all of which came to us from Wesley's hand. The controversy over the present standards reinforces that focus.[12] These deposits of Wesley's teaching are, of course, very important, absolutely decisive. Yet we should not lose sight of the underlying factor that makes them decisive—namely, that Wesley consistently taught, that he did very little that did not have some teaching purpose, that virtually the entire Wesleyan system evidences his teaching role, and that he exercised his teaching office in so much of what he did. His correspondence, tracts, republications, sermons, controversial and apologetical pieces, magazine, schools, classes and societies, rules, republished libraries, encouragement to families and societies to create libraries, Sunday schools, conference sessions, training and supervision of his assistants and helpers—indeed the entire system—consitute a remarkable drive to educate his people in the faith, to identify the heart of the Christian gospel, to teach the faith.

Even where that authority and function was in some sense formally shared, as in conference, we know all too well that Mr. Wesley exercised the teaching role. Thomas Neely put it succinctly:

> But let it not be supposed that the Conferences which Mr. Wesley called had any governing power. The members discussed, but Mr. Wesley decided. They debated, but he determined. Mr. Wesley was the government; and, though he invited the preachers to confer with him, he did not propose to abandon any of his original power. They had a voice by his permission, but he reserved the right to direct.[13]

As Neely suggests, Wesley's voice possessed a political (governing, polity) as well as an instructional (teaching) force, and eventually British as well as American Methodists had to decide how voice in both senses would be cared for and whether they would be cared for in the same office. At any rate, American Methodists know and have known of Mr. Wesley's authority, and though they might not formulate his exercise of authority as embodying the teaching office, it was just that.[14] Indeed, when we array the great variety of his instructional resources and efforts, we can see that he exercised the teaching office regularly, intensely, extensively.

EARLY AMERICAN METHODISM

Would American Methodism also have the voice highly concentrated in the person of Wesley's assistant, later superintendent, or exercised by conference? And would the instructional and political voice—the teaching and polity functions—coincide? The Christmas Conference of 1784 addressed but did not entirely resolve these questions. To be sure, Asbury's maneuver for a conference to receive and act on Mr. Wesley's acts and documents, the actual role that the Christmas Conference played in establishing a superintendency and episcopal government, and its exercise of authority over Wesley's *Large Minutes* in altering and adopting them as a *Discipline*, laid the groundwork for conference's supremacy. And behind those symbolic acts lay a decade of American governance and legislation through conference, a pattern that at Fluvanna had brought Methodism very close to presbyterial style of conference authority. During that period, however, the movement experienced also firm, autocratic guidance at the hand of Mr. Wesley's appointed assistants. In 1784, American Methodism stood poised between two principles of authority, one fairly broadly shared, the other highly focused and personalized. Which would it be—a sovereign conference or a personified center?

Ambiguity prevailed. The Christmas Conference received directives and documents from Wesley, the designations of Thomas Coke and Francis Asbury as superintendents, and provisions for the life and work of an independent church. But it also acted to confirm those by elections and adoptions. What had more force—the fact that Wesley made provision for the church and specified its leadership or the fact that conference acted in acceptance and approval? Where was the supreme power to be located, in superintendency or in conference? And more to the point of our enquiry, where was the intellectual leadership of the movement to be lodged? At virtually every turn, the Christmas Conference left that ambiguous.

THE EPISCOPAL TEACHING OFFICE

There is no question but that Coke prepared and conducted himself to exercise the intellectual leadership of American Methodism—studying on shipboard the texts that bore on church order, carefully crafting sermons that would lay the groundwork for a Methodist "episcopal" self-understanding, conducting a planning session for the Christmas Conference, speaking eloquently on the conference floor, advocating the establishment of an academic institution, preaching throughout the connection, championing antislavery—in so many ways providing ideas for the new American church.[15] But how was that received? Would conference and American Methodism consent to Coke embodying the teaching office?

Had that question been distinguishable from the issue of Coke's authority as a whole—had the teaching office been distinguishable from the appoitive and administrative powers of the superintendency and had Coke's authority been distinguishable from that of Wesley—American Methodists might have answered differently than they did.

They actually attempted such a resolution for Mr. Wesley's authority. In the *Discipline,* the Christmas Conference pledged the new church to Methodist unity: "During the Life of the Rev. Mr. Wesley, we acknowledge ourselves his Sons in the Gospel, ready in Matters belonging to Church-Government, to obey his Commands."[16] This pledge, like the acquiescence in Coke's leadership, proved more than the Americans could actually concede. By 1787 when Wesley, by letter, summoned the Americans into conference and selected two new superintendents, Richard Whatcoat for the United States and Freeborn Garrettson for Nova Scotia, conference found that stipulation of Wesley's authority and his actual exercise of it unacceptable and stripped the preceding acknowledgment from the *Discipline*. Conference did not assent to Wesley's nominations. It also acted to curtail Coke's authority drastically. The *Minutes* asked "Quest. 1. *Who are the Superintendents of our church for the United States?* Ans. Thomas Coke, (when present in the States) and Francis Asbury."[17]

A direct line runs from this action, through the experiment with and repudiation of the Council, to the 1808 constitutional provision for General Conference plenary authority. American Methodists resisted governing authority when it preempted a legitimate place for conference's participation and assent. The constitutional resolution seems clear. The year 1808 indeed settled that. But how would the church care for its intellectual leadership, for doctrinal authority? And could and would conference distinguish between the teaching and governing authority in some way?

Indeed, it could and would. It did so particularly with respect to Wesley. Even as it resisted Mr. Wesley's governing hand, American Methodism honored his intellectual leadership. Throughout this period, Americans respected both the formal provisions for Wesley's teaching, *The Large Minutes* (*Discipline*), *Explanatory Notes upon the New Testament*, *Standard Sermons*, and *The Articles of Religion* and the entirety of the Wesleyan teaching as mediated in Wesley's writings and their own preaching. In a quite real sense, Wesley continued to exercise the teaching office in American Methodism both while he lived and long thereafter.

Nor did the bishops (superintendents) give up on the teaching role. Coke found himself chastised, notably on the matter of antislavery preaching, but continued to press for the intellectual development of the movement, especially for schools. In their frequent reference to him as "the Doctor" or "Doctor Coke," American Methodists at once deferred to Coke and gave bemused and somewhat judgmental opinions of Coke's efforts and effectiveness. Such appellations suggest both some actual authority and the American church's wariness of and resistance to it.

ASBURY IN A TEACHING ROLE?

Asbury was another matter. Unlike Coke, Asbury was really ill equipped for the task. He struggled to lead the movement intellectually and succeeded. Yes, succeeded. His teaching authority may come as a surprise, for we generally evaluate his work in other terms. Yet intellectual leadership constituted, in my judgment, an important aspect of his role. The dimension of it in which he probably most succeeded is lost to us—namely through his sermons and prayers, his statements in conference, his conversations, and especially his talks with horseback companions. Asbury taught, as early Methodism taught, in a seminar of the road. He exercised the teaching office preeminently in oral fashion. Unfortunately, the dimensions of this can only be inferred from notations of texts in his *Journal*,[18] from the concerns that prompt his letters, from the chance comment that his companions note at the end of the day. There we see that Asbury exercised the teaching office orally; we have access to very little of its character.

Asbury had his hand in ventures that remain on record. The most important, though perhaps not immediately obvious, teaching instrument was his *Journal*. The earliest parts appeared in serial form in the short-lived American *Arminian Magazine* in 1789 and 1790. They were published in separate form again in 1802.[19] Then in 1810, he gave attention to the preparation of yet another edition.[20] Something of what he expected from this publication can be inferred from his frequent entries while editing, as for instance in 1798: "I have well considered my journal: it is inelegant; yet it conveys much information of the state of religion and country. It is well suited to common readers; the wise need it not. I have a desire that my journals should be published, at least after my death, if not before."[21]

A second type of publication for which Asbury should receive some credit is the *Arminian Magazine* (Philadelphia, 1789–90), in which his journal initially appeared. He had a hand as well in the second effort that American Methodists made at a journal, *The Methodist Magazine*, which similarly lasted but two years (1797–98). More important than the few Asbury letters contained therein was the effort itself, to create an intellectual medium for the movement. In this, as in so much of his leadership, Asbury modeled himself after Wesley. He wanted the American movement to have a literary medium and a literature.

And so, third, Asbury took an active interest in other publishing possibilities, including, for instance, an American version of

Wesley's works.[22] Asbury's broader concern for publication is especially evident in his letters to John Dickins and Ezekiel Cooper, the book agents. Asbury played a vital part in Methodism's early publishing, particularly in suggesting items that ought to be printed. He bears, at least, partial responsibility for the publications that early Methodism generated for itself.[23]

Fourth, Asbury produced some of the literature himself. In these efforts, we can see something of what he took to be the special needs of the American Methodists. One concern was for an American hymnody and so he put out his own version of a *Hymn Book*.[24] Asbury resorted to print also to deal with the threats to the unity of the movement. He had worked for some time on a volume that would heal Methodism's wounds. It eventually appeared in time to address the James O'Kelly schism. He entitled it graphically *The Causes, Evils, and Cures of Heart and Church Divisions, Extracted from the Works of Mr. Jeremiah Burroughs and Mr. Richard Baxter*.[25]

Perhaps the most self-evident exercise of the teaching office came in 1798. In that year, Asbury (with Coke) issued an annotated version of the *Discipline*,[26] an endeavor to instruct the Methodist faithful through and about Methodist belief and practice. In many respects the immediate precedent to the "Doctrinal Standards" in the 1972 and 1988 UMC *Discipline*, this MEC *Discipline* had been prompted, like Asbury's volume on schism, by division, in this case the O'Kelly movement. The explanations, rendered in smaller type, frequently exceeded the section explained. For instance, the half page of Disciplinary statement on the episcopacy received seven and a half pages of commentary. Where appropriate, the commentary adduced scriptural warrant, appeal to tradition, the example of Wesley. This experiment was not to be repeated. The General Conference of 1800 did not like the idea or the result as much as had that of 1796.

One more illustration of Asbury's publishing: he endeavored at various points and through several media to provide Methodism with a self-portrait, a way of understanding itself. He called these efforts "history." One that actually appeared began with his directives to the presiding elders to give him reports of their districts and the religious state and events therein.

> Once in a year all the presiding elders ought to write to the Episcopacy, to collect into a focus the work of God, for the press,

and I wish the preachers of [today] would write a brief of their conviction, conversion and call to preach and where they had laboured. I will select all the most spiritual parts of letters to print and to keep a history of what God is doing in the South. . . .

Would the presiding elders write to me one letter only of the state of the work, I should rejoice and the city preachers also of the cities. We could give great personal information to the conference and individuals of the work of God.[27]

The resulting volume, copies of which are now quite rare, Asbury entitled *Extracts of Letters Containing Some Account of the Work of God Since the Year 1800*.[28]

Finally, Asbury addressed himself to Methodism in his valedictory statements.[29] In such formal last statements as well as in the immediacy of his journals, Asbury sought to shape the mind of Methodism. Thereby he gave intellectual leadership to the Methodist movement. His may have been a crudely exercised teaching authority, but he gave it his best, and he claimed the connection's attention. Moreover he did so, obviously, during the very period in which General Conference came to define itself as the formal teaching authority of Methodism. General Conferences came and went every four years. Asbury moved daily so as to traverse the length and breadth of Methodism. And his practical efforts set the terms for later successful exercise of the teaching office.

THE EPISCOPACY, A FOOTNOTE

Intellectually more gifted persons would follow Asbury to the office and yet, not until our own day, has the episcopacy successfully reclaimed the teaching authority vested in Asbury. As we shall see, an important reason for this was that Methodism discovered some other ways to structure the teaching office. But it was also the case that never thereafter were the superintendency and the teaching function concentrated and personified as they had been in Wesley and Asbury. Later bishops actually had better vehicles with which to exercise the teaching office. McKendree, for instance, initiated the episcopal address to General Conference, which would, down to our own day, set denominational agendas and constitute an important dimension of Methodism's teaching office.

Beginning with John Emory, some would be elected to the office because of their intellectual gifts. And they used them. In a real sense they endeavored, individually, to sustain a teaching function. The bishops produced apologetics, histories, biographies, constitutional interpretations, theology, guides to the *Discipline*.[30] And yet, despite all that production, the office shifted to other shoulders after Asbury's death. In part, the shift had to do with the many other burdens the bishops bore; in part with their very plurality—the several bishops in place of the one Asbury; in part, with their increasingly regional deployment and orientation; in part, with their absence from one another. For a variety of reasons, the bishops and particularly the collectivity of the episcopacy became less effective at teaching than a succession of persons who ostensibly worked under them.

The Book Agents, Stewards, and Editors

From the very start, the bishops selected as book agents persons dedicated and committed to the life of the mind. Gradually these appointees discovered the intellectual potential of the position and assumed genuine leadership of the movement. In time, Wesley's mantle would fall on their shoulders. The agent or steward gradually became his successor as teacher-through-publication. John Dickins, Ezekiel Cooper, John Wilson, Daniel Hitt, and Joshua Soule each played an important role in building a small-scale distribution and reprint business into a national media empire, the Methodist Book Concern.[31]

Under Soule, in particular, the Concern took the step that actualized the teaching potential of the office. Soule began (or relaunched) *The Methodist Magazine*, the first of a number of serials through which he and his successors would turn from being publishers into being editors. Thereby, they achieved a voice. Thereby, they became the voice of Methodism. The editors possessed what the episcopacy lacked, namely, a medium through which to be heard on a regular and consistent basis across the entire connection at the same time. In the great age of the serial, the editors became the great spokespersons to and for the church.

Soule's successor, Nathan Bangs, who assumed the position in 1820, discovered the potential of that voice. Assuming editorship of *The Methodist Magazine*, Bangs transformed it from a Methodist *Reader's Digest*, a mere vehicle for republication of British items, into a genuinely American medium. In the process his teaching, his ideas, his opinions gave shape to American Methodism. This enlarged role doubtless had much to do with the controversy into which *The Methodist Magazine* was soon pressed.

The reform movement of the 1820s had established its own medium, the *Wesleyan Repository*, later titled *Mutual Rights*.[32] The denomination needed a channel of official response. So the impulses that divided the church—the cries for democracy that eventuated in the Methodist Protestant Church, the controversies with the Episcopalians and Congregationalists, and eventually the slavery and sectional crisis—created a teaching office. Controversy made the editor and his vehicle, *The Methodist Magazine* and later *The Christian Advocate*, an essential and powerful force in the church. The editors became figures to be reckoned with. Certainly Bangs was such a figure. His power had something to do with the circumstances. It had as much to do with his recognition of the potential in the office.

Bangs was an initiator, a go-getter, an entrepreneur, what that age knew as a "booster." Sustaining the active book publishing role of the Book Concern, he launched in 1823 the *Youth's Instructor and Guardian*, an instructional magazine for children. In the years thereafter he moved into tracts, Sunday school literature, and Bibles. In 1826 he consolidated several regional papers into what would become a national voice to the laity, the *Christian Advocate*. And when he yielded the office of book agent to John Emory, he continued as editor of the *Advocate*.

The potential in the medium soon generated regional *Advocates*, including important papers like *Zion's Herald*, *The Western Christian Advocate*, and the *Nashville Advocate*. The agents launched other ventures—Sunday school *Advocates*, *The Ladies Repository*, missions magazines—to tap the differentiated Methodist reading public. The church witnessed a virtual explosion of popular media and sustained, at the same time, the serious scholarly endeavor, *The Methodist Review* or *Methodist Quarterly Review*. And when the church split, literary media typically played a role in the division and found themselves the voice of the new entities. German Methodism also had its important papers and magazines.[33]

The editors were no more a united voice than were the bishops, but they were a readily accessible voice. By virtue of their election to the office, they constituted something of an official voice. And so in the decades leading up to and following the Civil War, and despite their plurality, the editors effectively spoke to and for the church. Beginning with Bangs, they saw themselves as the church's defenders. They wrote the apologetics and the histories that delineated the church's position. At the helm of *Advocate* or *Methodist Review* sat those whom we today regard as the Methodist theologians of the mid-nineteenth century—Nathan Bangs, John McClintock, Daniel D. Whedon, and Daniel Curry of the (MEC) *Methodist Review*; Bangs, Thomas E. Bond, George Peck, Abel Stevens, Curry, and James M. Buckley of the *Advocate*; Thomas O. Summers, Albert T. Bledsoe, J. W. Hinton, and J. J. Tigert of the (MECS) *Methodist Quarterly Review*;[34] H. N. McTyeire and Summers of the Nashville *Advocate*; and William Nast of *Der Christliche Apologete*.[35] The church(es) obviously put persons in the editorial positions from whom it expected leadership. Those persons rendered that service. It should come as no surprise that the church moved such individuals from this position to the episcopacy and into theological education.

Across the connection others who aspired to or exercised leadership also found the press vital. Reformers, critics, other voices sought the media. So through the *Guide to Christian Perfection*, later *Guide to Holiness*, the first great Methodist woman theologian, Phoebe Palmer, found a national audience.[36] At a later period, one of the great theologians of Black Methodism, Henry McNeal Turner of the AME Church, would exercise his intellectual leadership through a journal, the *Southern Recorder*.

NATIONAL PLATFORMS

The denominational press helped foster a national reading audience, one increasingly open to the larger world that magazines and papers mediated. In the mid-nineteenth century and continuing into the latter part of the century, various other agencies bid for

Methodist attention. In so doing, each carried some portion of Methodism's teaching office. Each had a platform.

One that would continue to gain power over the century was the network of reform movements and voluntary societies, each typically dedicated to a special cause, that with its own literature, paper, agents, and national structure, knitted Methodists together. The mission societies, both those (male) bearing the denominational name alone and those qualified by "female" or "women's," proved remarkably adept at this. For much of the rest of the century, they focused the church's attention, efforts, and resources on evangelization and expansion, at home and abroad. Women as well as men rose to prominence as teachers—mentoring through example, writing, editing, speaking, organizing. Reform efforts also, notably abolition organizations and particularly the temperance crusade, mobilized support through instructional campaigns. So persons like Frances Willard became tutors to the church and indeed the nation. Eventually, as we note below, such voluntary organizations stabilized as the internal structure of the denomination and then transformed their teaching into board and agency roles.

The Sunday school constituted a second platform, a related network with rather obvious responsibilities for the transmission of the faith. Its orientation toward youth may lead us to dismiss it as an aspect of Methodism's teaching office. And initially, it did little more than publish literature for the Sunday schools. Even in that it made Methodism a national school. Over time, the church discovered the potential of the Sunday school as a medium for the whole church and as a creator, not just a transmitter, of doctrine. Key in this development was John Heyl Vincent, who assumed the leadership of the Methodist Sunday School Union in 1866. Over the rest of the century, in a variety of initiatives, he transformed the Sunday school into the shaper of Methodist lay life. Through teachers' institutes, loose-leaf lessons, the *Sunday-School Journal*, the international lesson plan, particularly the Chautauqua Sunday-School Teachers Assembly, and itinerating and correspondence versions of Chautauqua, Vincent, transformed Methodism into a gigantic classroom. By the end of the century this system claimed the intellectual leadership of the church as its teachers and writers. Through this complex system, the Sunday school quite literally both taught and shaped the church. This was a social construction of reality—the church organized around an evangelical and missionary educational enterprise run essentially on correspondence principles.

Ministers were also shaped by a third platform, a great correspondence school, employing the principles of the Sunday school. It was called the Course of Study. Initially administered by the bishops through the annual conferences, General Conference made it in 1844 a uniform four-year program of study.[37] As the only way into the ministry, the course quite literally shaped the mind of the Methodist ministry. Unlike the teaching agents already discussed, the course did not really formulate doctrine or generate literature. Yet by the selection process, by the identification of a normative Methodist posture—John Wesley, John Fletcher, Richard Watson, John Miley, Henry Sheldon, Albert Knudson—Methodism itself underwent change.[38] In that limited sense, the course did define doctrine.

THE SEMINARIES

In the twentieth century, and through more theologically constructive efforts, three agencies would vie for the teaching office. They were the seminaries that succeeded to the course of study's role; the boards and agencies into which the publishing, missions, and educational efforts of the prior century institutionalized their offices; and the College of Bishops, which after two unifications and particularly that of 1968 found a voice with which to teach the church.

The seminaries and also the colleges with which the church dotted the land garnered Methodism's intellectual elite from the start. There is a difference, however, in placing the intelligentsia in schools and in actually recognizing the schools as the intellectual center and official voice of the church. The former came easily; the latter shaping role emerged gradually as the seminaries maneuvered to monopolize ministerial education, as seminary teachers published the volumes that the church read, as the church came to look to the seminaries for doctrine, as seminary deans and faculty assumed church leadership.[39] In the latter part of the nineteenth century, the church located its theologians at Boston, Drew, and Garrett in the North and Vanderbilt in the South. John Miley at

Drew, Miner Raymond at Garrett, Borden Parker Bowne at Boston, Thomas O. Summers and John J. Tigert at Vanderbilt wrote the systematic and philosophical statements that defined Methodist theology. They were the first of several generations of seminary theologians who had or gained a national platform. To the seminary, then, rather than to the editors, the church turned for authoritative statement of the faith. And in their hands the church increasingly put its ministerial candidates. Seminary rather than Course of Study gradually became the normal pathway to ordination.

That latter function obviously continues to this day and remains normative.[40] The seminary's premier place as the teaching authority has been otherwise eclipsed. That may seem a surprising statement given the role that Albert Outler played in the 1968–1972 UMC *Discipline* and that Thomas Langford played in that of 1988. Their prominence, however, had more to do with their individual effectiveness as political actors at General Conference than in the deference that the church paid to the seminaries. Sometime around the 1939 unification and the period of neoorthodoxy, the seminaries lost their place as the teaching office.

The reasons for this are many and complex and really beyond what we can attempt here. There is an incredible irony here, for seminaries claimed national public attention even as ecclesiastical constituencies lost interest. It was during this period that American seminaries gained national prominence as intellectual centers, spoke on matters of national social policy, took their ethical and theological posture with great seriousness, became research facilities, and began to turn out PhDs in numbers. The seminaries continued to perform a teaching office. But it ceased to be effective as the church's teaching office. Seminaries increasingly lost sight of their prior audience; they lost sight of the fact that their teaching office was for the church. So though the faculties continued to write and the church to read, authorship and readership diverged. Faculty increasingly wrote for one another and with such specialization and technicality that laity and even ministers had difficulty in following. Theology differentiated itself into technical academic disciplines and professional societies. The seminary turned away from the church; the church turned a deaf ear to the seminary. So Bishop Paul N. Garber could denounce the school of which he had been dean as "un-Methodist."[41]

Within The Methodist Church and later within United Methodism, the number and competition of the seminaries doubtless played a role as well. No one seminary claimed quite the dominant position that Boston had enjoyed initially in the North and Vanderbilt in the South. The multiplication of seminaries muffled and divided the seminary's voice in Methodism. Recently even the Ministerial Educational Fund may be a contributory factor, necessitating as it does an essentially financial and promotional relationship between the schools and the church. At any rate, in the middle decades of the twentieth century the church increasingly attended to other theological voices.

THE ORGANIZATIONAL REVOLUTION

Some may find difficulty in taking seriously the teaching authority of its next holders, the national boards. Of late, the boards and agencies have become somewhat the whipping boy for the church. Strident voices suggest that the church does not need bureaucracy and should not have ever built it. So a frequent refrain. Many view the managerial or organizational revolution that occurred across American society around the turn of the century as a misfortune and tragedy for the church.[42] This mood, apparently widespread across the church, makes life difficult and budgets slim for the boards. And the reaction does not confine itself to the national level. Conference agencies and conference budgets also take their hits. A powerful current of localism, of congregationalism, is sweeping the connection.[43] So it may be difficult to make credible the role that they played in earlier decades as teachers of the church.

In the early twentieth century, however, both laity and clergy saw in business organization a creative way in which the church could structure itself for its life and work. In the effort to make the church effective in its mission, these reformers sought to make the church work. They adapted techniques being used in the national corporate world—scientific management, professional leadership, coordinating structures, business procedures of finance and promotion, a sophisticated nation-to-conference-to-congregation communication system, modern media. The actors in this drama were not small-minded robber barons but the great heroes and leaders of Methodism's witness—the missionary and ecumenical leaders like John R. Mott, the social reformers like Francis J. McConnell and Frank Mason North, the deaconess leaders like Lucy Rider Meyer and Belle Harris Bennett. It was on behalf of the great causes—the Social Gospel, ecumenism, temperance, pacifism, labor rights, race relations, education, missions—that the boards and agencies emerged.[44] By the 1920s, if not before, they had become the effective leadership of the church and played increasingly a teaching role.

Bureaucracies are not typically known as tutors. What gave a teaching dimension to these enterprises? In part, their purposive character. They emerged as vehicles for embodying a message and conveying it to the church. They bore and expressed some compelling cause—missions, temperance, education. Also, essential to their effectiveness was the church's willingness to structure itself top to bottom along the lines established on the national level. The principle is now so well established, so much a part of operating assumptions, that we scarcely even think about it. We assume that at every level—national, jurisdictional, conference, congregational—the denomination must have a uniform structure—finance and administration, council of ministries, church and society, discipleship, missions, higher education, archives and history, Christian unity, religion and race, education. However, such linked organizational structure emerged gradually over the nineteenth century. So structured, of course, the boards and agencies had a channel into every local church. Each strove to use that channel to educate the Methodist faithful on its cause or purpose.

The teaching office that resulted differed from but drew upon that exercised through earlier instruments. Obviously, it lacked the cohesion possible when the office centered on Asbury. Yet the agencies sought the leadership that he had once exercised over national Methodist policy. The boards depended heavily on publication but had a far more programmatic and less editorial and opinion-shaping character than the nineteenth-century editors. They made good use of many of the instrumentalities developed by the several platforms of the mid-nineteenth-century but gave them a polished and professional form. *Motive*, for instance, far excelled any publication that the church had aimed at the youth market. The boards did not typically compete with the seminaries by issuing systematic theology, but in their own way they shaped an ecumenical, social, expansive theological posture for the church. Though not self-consciously systematic, this theology had a remarkable inner coherence.[45] And the boards mediated it to the churches—weekly, diffusely, energetically, on a massive scale, through innumerable publications, and so set agenda for the church. So, in lumbering fashion, they defined its belief, conveyed it to the faithful, and formed the church.

That teaching system communicated effectively for much of this century. It no longer does. The church lacks a general circulation magazine; its effort to produce an electronic substitute, *Catch the Spirit*, seems doomed; the national *Advocate* has, in a sense, gone into independent (but friendly) hands; the many churchwide media serve markets, sectors, professions, or interests.[46] Though the national machinery continues to run at high speed, it almost seems out of gear. The wheels at the local level do not want to mesh, keep the pace, or even follow the direction set on national levels. The system does not work. The reasons for this are not entirely clear. Part of the blame lies outside the church. The 60s and post-60s revolt against Washington effectively discredited national organizations, including ecclesial ones. Bureaucracy cannot be trusted, we were told. Some of that distrust derives from the social crises associated with race, war, and poverty. The boards and agencies took high profile leadership in what have proved to be intractable problems. They have suffered in the confusion over directions. So also mainline denominations, their programs, and their communications have been eclipsed by more hot media. Television, both commercial and religious, orients Americans to a personal reality, not a structural one.

The changes, strains, and conflicts in American society have found their way into the churches. But the churches, really all the so-called mainstream denominations, have their own peculiar set of problems. Despite a number of efforts over the past fifteen years to kick the church back into gear, the faithful do not seem to be responding. They really cannot. The organizational grammar, the infrastructure for action, is in collapse. This is particularly obvious in the youth and college networks from which the church once recruited its leadership and built its agencies. That constituency now belongs to the parachurch outfits. Beyond that, the purposes that had once generated enthusiasm and constituency for boards and agencies have themselves faltered. Missions is the most obvious illustration and the key casualty. The evangelization of the world in this generation no longer energizes the church. The most successful teaching organizations within the church actually function to criticize the church and its practices. The Commission of the Status and Role of Women (COSROW), Religion and Race, Good News, the several ethnic caucuses—"struggle groups" as one analyst terms them[47]—seem more effectual as teachers than the program agencies. At least, information now flows more effectively along these other channels. However, if they serve to unite and communicate with those who share a perspective, they also function to alienate those who do not and to divide the church. The struggle groups are effective in teaching, but not the whole church, only a part. Recognizing the leadership gap, the episcopacy has sought to reclaim a national teaching function.

A Teaching Episcopacy

The bishops have reclaimed national leadership. Their initiative has been a long time in developing. Ambiguous incentives derived from the 1939 union. In some ways the polity that emerged in 1939 actually accelerated the momentum toward a diocesan episcopacy. Considerable blame could be allocated to the jurisdictional structure. By electing and deploying bishops on that regional basis, the church effectively imaged the bishops as sectional leaders. The bishops' efforts to reduce the number of conferences they serve and to lengthen their tenure have also given them a diocesan cast.

On the other hand, the 1939 union provided a structural foundation for episcopal leadership. The southern church brought into union the principle of an effective College of Bishops. Its successor, the Council of Bishops, gave the episcopacy a structural cohesion, a vehicle through which to act collectively on behalf of the whole church. The Council did not immediately reclaim national leadership. It has taken some time for the Council to overcome two centuries of centrifugal, parochial, and regional inertias. One hurdle, perhaps a fairly high one, was the essential social character of their unity. The bishops made themselves into a great family; they had come to use their gatherings for social and peer-support functions. They became a family of regional superintendents. In reclaiming the teaching office, the bishops have had to develop the will to work together, the patterns of work that would give them a united voice, the discipline to labor as a magisterium.

Stimuli to concerted action were various. The 1968 union was one. The faltering of other leadership, particularly that of the boards and agencies, was perhaps another. The U.S. National Conference of Catholic Bishops modeled what might be achieved. The Methodist bishops enjoyed success with various initiatives, including pastoral letters. Internal structures, particularly a Committee on Episcopal Initiatives for Ministry and Mission, focused the Council's growing resolve to act collectively. And finally, the sense of crisis in the church over faltering programs and declining membership doubtless also had a role.

And so, they reclaimed something of the mantle of Wesley and Asbury. They did so dramatically with *In Defense of Creation: The Nuclear Crisis and a Just Peace*.[48] The entire process—from the hearings and gathering of opinion in its preparation, to first release, to formal presentation, to the mandated reading in its pastoral letter form, to the study of the larger statement in the congregations—represents an incredibly important experiment in episcopal exercise of the teaching office. Whatever one thinks of the actual posture, the document and the claim made on the church with it, brought the bishops into a new relationship with the faithful. Here, really for the first time in almost 200 years, the bishops in united fashion gave theological leadership to the church. Something of the same process of sustained study, research, consulting, reflection, and writing yielded the 1990 statement *Vital Congregations, Faithful Disciples: Vision for the Church*.[49] Thereafter followed other initiatives replicating the engagement procedures for teaching the church—on urban ministries, children and poverty, and the children of Africa. Increasingly the bishops have used their gathering to bring in scholars and resource persons, to produce and work over their own position papers, and to use various opportunities collectively and individually to exercise theological leadership for the church.[50] So the bishops bid to reclaim Asbury's and Wesley's mantle and exercise the teaching office. They now have the resolve, the leadership, and the internal structures[51] to act with something of the unity that the episcopacy could when it was, in effect, one person.

GENERAL CONFERENCE AND THE TEACHING OFFICE

Ironically, just as the Council of Bishops rediscovered the magisterium and mechanisms for staking its claim thereon, General Conference found ways to make good on its own constitutional authority.

Here too the critical date seems to be 1968. The merger of that year prompted self-consciousness about authority, belief, and witness. One aspect of that was attention to constitutional questions, including the issue as to what are the doctrinal standards.[52] This chapter takes less interest in the resolution of the ensuing debate than in the fact the question was raised and the debate happened. Here it is important to underscore the exercise of General Conference's authority. Perhaps symbolic was *The Book of Resolutions* with which, beginning in 1968, General Conference spoke to the church. Yet those documents, valuable as they are, have had, at best, quite modest impact and represent a one-stroke statement.

Far more important was the creation of the Study Commission on Doctrine and Standards and its product, the statement for the 1972 UMC *Discipline*. In and through that document, General Conference spoke to the church in a particularly powerful way. It was not the most controversial statement that the church has made in recent years. At one level, it represented little more than what General Conference has always done, namely, recast the *Discipline*. However, it differed markedly from prior General Conference's recension efforts in its importing the theological statement into the *Discipline* (an exercise of the teaching office, as we note below). Further, it set precedents for other study commissions, which have sustained that teaching role, including particularly the sequel "Committee on Our Theological Task," authorized by the 1984 General Conference, which prepared the draft that, as revised, went into the 1988 *Discipline*.[53] The statement on "Social Principles" and the process that brought it into being could also be cited, as also the baptism study and the long series of study commissions on ministry.[54]

The study commission functions effectively, then, to carry out important discovery and teaching responsibilities. Of special note were the two that produced the 1972 and 1988 doctrinal statements. Several points about them and their products in particular deserve remark.

The 1972 and 1988 statements have been read, particularly by the church's leadership, and read as authoritative. The status of the 1972 and 1988 statements, as annotations on our doctrinal standards, gave/give them a peculiar privilege. Like the marginalia of the Scofield Bible or perhaps the more recent Serendipity Bible, the statement actually upstaged the standards. The statements bear comparison with Asbury and Coke's annotation of the 1798 *Discipline*. And it is worth recalling that the church never let Asbury and Coke repeat that effort; the annotations had preempted the standards.

The two doctrinal statements present themselves and their claims in a remarkably confident tone. On key matters, like pluralism, the quadrilateral, what constitute doctrinal standards, and the distinction between doctrine and theology, the statements seemed to be speaking *ex cathedra*.

The authority of such points, and indeed the statements as a whole, gained wide currency, even adherence. My own sense of that is quite vivid. In twenty years of reading theology of ministry papers by graduating seminarians and recently in reading theology statements for the Board of Ordained Ministry, I recall few that missed the opportunity to expand upon these distinctive formulations as, for instance, the quadrilateral, often indeed favoring those, because of their prominence, clarity, and confident tone, over the doctrine they interpreted.

Obviously, across the church those renderings of our theological posture, particularly that of 1972, produced controversy and opposition, as well as adherence. And so, petitions to the 1984 General Conference called for the second study commission.[55] This is really the key point, that the 1972 statement elicited a conversation between General Conference and the Methodist people, a conversation on doctrinal matters.

The process that followed, with three major study commissions, gave General Conference a mechanism with which to think with the church, ongoing committees with lines out to the church, bodies set up to listen and gather insight. The process was followed again in anticipation of the 1992 General Conference and with similar effect, though with highly controversial matters—like sexuality—speaking with and listening to the church can become highly politicized. Perhaps teaching in a huge church must have a political edge to it. At any rate, the entire procedure of gathering in opinion, reporting out tentative drafts for comments, conducting hearings and consultations, eliciting media coverage, establishing great groups or other listening structures, receiving various declarations and technical opinions, and finally referring to General Conference can engage and has engaged the church in theological dialogue.[56] General Conference sustains that theological activity in its own legislative committee and plenary action.[57]

The 1988 statement actually goes a considerable way toward describing and thereby sanctioning the very process by which it was produced, the dialogue between General Conference and those it represented. This seems the intent, tenor, and thrust of the entire section, "Our Theological Task" (¶69). We are invited into theological reflection understood as critical and constructive, individual and communal, contextual and incarnational, practical.

That ongoing reflective and renewing activity is grounded in the crucial theological distinction, central to the statement, namely, that between doctrine and theology. Doctrine as the received witness to, in, and of the faith takes and requires expression in the life of the community. That expression—the "testing, renewal, elaboration, and application of our doctrinal perspectives"[58]—is a shared theological obligation. Hence, General Conference does that in such ongoing, structured relation to the United Methodist faithful.

Given such an understanding, General Conference fittingly acted as had the bishops with their pastoral letter. It mandated study of the 1988 statement, the new annotations. They, like the 1972 statement, come to us as a teaching document. Finally, General Conference established its committee as a permanent body. In these ways, General Conference found a way of exercising its teaching office, *in the interim*.

CONCLUSIONS

With both the 1972 and 1988 statements, the process by which they came into being and the manner in which they are presented to the church, General Conference discovered an ongoing process by which to sustain its constitutionally given teaching functions. The study commissions have proved essential. Though hardly a new venture, nor more obviously linked to General Conference than any other aspect of our connection, they nevertheless have behaved in a more attentive and responsive way to both the United Methodist people and General Conference itself. Whether over time they will evolve into something with a separate life and operate—as did Asbury, the editors, the platforms of the nineteenth century, the seminaries, the boards and agencies, or the Council of Bishops—as teaching authorities in their own right, we surely cannot know. However, at present they represent an interesting Methodist experiment.

The question ahead of us, I suppose, is whether Methodism can and will really attend to two teaching authorities—the Council of Bishops and General Conference through its study committees.[59] We clearly do need national leadership and, in particular, a teaching or intellectual leadership. The cry for that reverberates throughout the denomination. The church stands at one of those points of structural ferment and possibility. Who or what will emerge in leadership? How will the church configure itself so as to respond to that leadership? Key to our movement ahead will be effective national leadership, the exercise of the teaching office.

CHAPTER 6

ITINERANT GENERAL SUPERINTENDENCY

"Nothing," affirmed bishops Thomas Coke and Francis Asbury, "nothing has been introduced into Methodism by the present episcopal form of government, which was not before fully exercised by Mr. Wesley." They continued:

> He presided in the conferences; fixed the appointments of the preachers for their several circuits; changed, received, or suspended preachers, wherever he judged that necessity required it; travelled through the European connection at large; superintended the spiritual and temporal business; and consecrated two bishops, Thomas Coke and Alexander Mather, one before the present episcopal plan took place in America, and the other afterwards, besides ordaining elders and deacons.[1]

An "itinerant general superintendency" our first bishops thought absolutely key to the Methodist system.

> *Our grand plan*, in all its parts, leads to an *itinerant* ministry. Our bishops are *travelling* bishops. All the different orders which compose our conferences are employed in the *travelling line*; and our local preachers are, *in some degree*, travelling preachers. Everything is kept moving as far as possible; and we will be bold to say, that, next to the grace of God, there is nothing *like this* for keeping the whole body alive from the centre to the circumference, and for the continual extension of that circumference on every hand.[2]

Methodism has made this Cokesbury (Coke + Asbury) understanding its doctrine. Since the General Conference of 1808, of the Restrictive Rules, which function as a constitution, one has affirmed:

> The general conference shall have full powers to make rules and regulations for our church, under the following limitations and restrictions, viz.
>
> ... 3. They shall not change or alter any part or rule of our government, so as to do away Episcopacy or destroy the plan of our itinerant general superintendency.[3]

In the current UMC *Discipline* the quaint formulation of 1808 has been modernized to read:

> ¶19. Article III.—The General Conference shall not change or alter any part or rule of our government so as to do away with episcopacy or destroy the plan of our itinerant general superintendency.

However, when *The Book of Discipline of The United Methodist Church 2004* gets around to elaborating the episcopal office, it speaks not a whisper of itineration. In delineating the duties of bishops, it underscores their "general" and "superintendent" roles. "Bishops are elders in full connection," it affirms, "who are elected from the elders and set apart for a ministry of general oversight and supervision (¶401)." It continues with terms and language drawn from the business world, from American culture, from ecumenical conversations that Coke and Asbury would not have understood:

> As followers of Jesus Christ called to servant leadership, bishops are authorized to guard the faith, order, liturgy, doctrine, and discipline of the Church; to seek and be a sign of the unity of the faith; to exercise the discipline of the whole Church; to supervise and support the Church's life, work, and mission throughout the world; and to lead all persons entrusted to their oversight in worship, in the celebration of the sacraments, and in their mission of witness and service in the world. Bishops carry a primary responsibility to support and encourage the ministry of all Christians. They share with other bishops in the supervision of the whole Church, encouraging and supporting all baptized people in the exercising of their gifts and ministries, praying for them, and proclaiming and interpreting to them the gospel of Christ. Bishops are to be prophetic voices and courageous leaders in the cause of justice for all people. Bishops are also authorized to appoint ordained clergy to their responsibilities, consecrate, ordain, and commission persons in ministry to the Church and world (¶404.1).

What follows is my attempt to understand contemporary formulations, to recover the full richness of the Wesleyan charism, to be self-conscious about the witness of Scripture, to draw on ecumenical insights, and to encourage United Methodism to develop a full-orbed theology of the episcopal office. Why the presumption to offer the church such counsel? Several invitations to do just that! Most recently, I was invited to serve as writer for the Task Force to Study the Episcopacy created by the 2004 General Conference for which much of the following was drafted.[4] After 2004 I was invited to address the Connectional Table as it began its work. In anticipation of the 2004 General Conference and from The United Methodist Publishing House, I was invited to prepare a volume that would help delegates understand episcopacy and provide background for proposals coming from the Council of Bishops (COB) And still earlier came the invitation to address the COB on matters connectional.

Such invitations can make one heady. However, counsel is only counsel. Thomas Frank and I discovered that when, in the organizational motions of the 2004 General Conference, the volume just mentioned, our *Episcopacy in the Methodist Tradition*, was cited and our names invoked. A motion for bishops to chair legislative committees, one of our several proposals to strengthen the episcopal office, went down to glorious defeat. That seemed to put our efforts to nought. However, in creating a Task Force to Study the Episcopacy, General Conference provided a wide-open agenda. Both Tom and I, along with James Kirby and others who have studied or lived with the episcopal office, spoke to the Task Force. At its invitation, I became its writer, Tom serving in comparable fashion for the parallel Ministry Commission. And so the counsel continues. I begin with some assumptions that guide my thinking, which I shared with the Task Force, and which I would presume to suggest ought to guide others as they reflect about episcopacy.

ASSUMPTIONS

In thinking about episcopacy in the Methodist heritage and especially upon United Methodist episcopacy, I have worked with the following assumptions:

(1) Given the above Disciplinary tasks and duties, a first priority is to discern what ought to be the role of the bishop in fulfilling and providing oversight for the mission of The United Methodist Church in the twenty-first century. Guiding efforts to think about episcopacy, therefore, are the mission of the Church, the well-being of the people called Methodists, and the effectiveness of our witness to the world.

(2) Inherent in, indeed central to oversight and supervision—to the *episkopé* to which bishops are called and consecrated—is their stewardship of the Church's resources in aiding it to fulfill its mission. As the Church's chief stewards the bishops and the episcopal office should model and exemplify that good order to which they summon all the faithful. Such stewardship encompasses all the Church's talents—spiritual, human, environmental, material, financial, cultural—and entails effective deployment of all these limited resources.

(3) Until recently, the UMC has been spared some of the financial impact of mainstream Protestantism's decline and the challenges of stewardship under such constraints because our members have given beyond the level that might have been projected. Now projections of income and of ballooning expense factors (rising medical costs, longer life spans, earlier retirements) oblige many annual conferences to reduce Conference staff, the number of DSs, and support of programs; connectional agencies experience similar constrictions; and the Episcopal Fund cannot be excepted from the financial impact of our decline. Itinerant general and district superintendency can and should be reshaped to lead and model stewardship in a time of diminishing resources.

(4) No matter how much we wish to enhance episcopacy or how monumental the changes we propose, we do not start afresh to conceive and define the office but instead work out from itinerant general superintendency as lived in our heritage, from Scripture's witness about leadership, from the wisdom about office and order derived from tradition and mirrored for us in other communions, from best practices and our best thinking in relation to these givens, and from discernment of what the Gospel beckons us toward.

(5) Itinerant general superintendency is so central and integral to the United Methodist connectional system that any change to episcopacy affects everything else—including particularly our ministry

as a whole, the conference structures (both those within Jurisdictions and those organized as Central Conferences), our congregations, the agencies and the work they all undertake—and even minor changes to the episcopacy can produce large alterations in the connection.

(6) In keeping with traditions inherited from John Wesley, refined through the centuries by Methodists, Evangelicals, and United Brethren, and codified in the *Discipline*, we affirm the distinctive leadership roles in all roles and offices, lay, licensed, consecrated, commissioned, and ordained ministry and in particular the ministry of the whole people of God and the distinctive roles of the laity.

(7) Our purpose, therefore, ought to be to think in terms of and to enhance the connection and to strengthen the whole people of God, laity in their various roles, and ministry at all levels and in all dimensions—spiritual, teaching, serving, evangelizing, caring.

(8) In particular, acceptable renewal of the episcopacy ought therefore to strengthen, to make more effective and faithful, and to help the Church's leadership generally to fulfill the mission of the Church.

(9) Insofar as possible, proposals for change ought to reflect our Wesleyan theology and practice of ministry.

(10) As we probe the nature and purpose of itinerant general superintendency, we ought to think of the worldwide nature of the church, most specifically of United Methodism but also of the autonomous/affiliated churches, of our larger communion as represented in the World Methodist Council, of the episcopal churches with which we are engaged bilaterally and multilaterally, and of the councils of churches within which our leaders function. Alterations in our understanding and practice of episcopacy ought to move the UMC toward the unity of the body of Christ for which Jesus prayed.

TOWARD A THEOLOGY OF EPISCOPACY: REFLECTING THEOLOGICALLY AND MISSIONALLY

A faithful statement of the Wesleyan understanding of itinerant general superintendency must begin with consideration of

Scripture and *episkopé*, draw freshly and imaginatively on the Wesleyan charism, take special note of episcopacy as lived out in the Methodist[5] experience (with particular attention to the United States), and reflect the fullness of the ecumenical witness. That is to say, a Wesleyan understanding must be quadrilaterally undertaken. Beginning with Scripture, it reasons with Wesleyan terms and practices, acknowledges how under the guidance of the Holy Spirit we have lived into that Scriptural-Wesleyan paradigm and tests our notions against the ecumenical traditions. Our norms, then, are

> Scripture: Texts on leadership generally and episcopacy particularly
> Reason: Terms and practices expressive of the Wesleyan charism
> Experience: Episcopacy as lived (with particular attention to North America)
> Tradition: Including particularly that mediated by the ecumenical witness

Scripture and Episcopacy

Ministry—lay and ordained; licensed, appointed, commissioned, consecrated; diaconal, presbyterial, episcopal—norms itself on that of Christ (¶¶301, 403).[6] So the Apostle Paul exhorts (Philippians 2:5-7): "Let the same mind be in you that was in Christ Jesus, who, though he was in the form of God, / did not regard equality with God / as something to be exploited, / but emptied himself, / taking the form of a slave, / being born in human likeness." All ministry must emulate that of Christ and insofar as humanly possible look to Christ's servant ministry. Bishops as "followers of Jesus Christ," are "called to servant leadership" (¶404.1). In that servant style, bishops exercise for the church and the world the three offices of Christ's ministry, those of prophet, priest, and king.

On the *royal* office in servant style, Christ himself provided directive and example, as John informs us:

> Then he poured water into a basin and began to wash the disciples' feet and to wipe them with the towel that was tied around him. He came to Simon Peter, who said to him, "Lord, are you going to wash my feet?" Jesus answered, "You do not know now what I am doing, but later you will understand." Peter said to him, "You will never wash my feet." Jesus answered, "Unless I wash you, you have no share with me." Simon Peter said to him, "Lord, not my feet only but also my hands and my head!" . . . After he had washed their feet, had put on his robe, and had returned to the table, he said to them, "Do you know what I have done to you? You call me Teacher and Lord—and you are right, for that is what I am. So if I, your Lord and Teacher, have washed your feet, you also ought to wash one another's feet." (John 13:5-9, 12-14)

The royal office certainly involves oversight, guidance, ordering, leadership, discipline, and superintendence, but it is "lordly" not according to societal patterns but to that of the one who washed his disciples' feet. Understood and exercised in such fashion, the "kingly" office inverts what history remembers about the conduct of kings. Bishops lead in diaconal fashion, that of basin and towel. They indeed "exercise the discipline of the whole Church" and "supervise and support the Church's life, work, and mission throughout the world" (¶404.1). They guard, supervise, support, encourage, oversee. They appoint, consecrate, ordain, commission, and order (in various ways) the church's ministry. They do so after the style of Christ and, as we will note below, through Christian conferencing.

The *priestly* office in servant style might appeal, as well, to the John passage. The retrospective from Hebrews also reminds us that it was as suffering servant that Christ exercised intercessory priestly submissions on our behalf.

> In the days of his flesh, Jesus offered up prayers and supplications, with loud cries and tears, to the one who was able to save him from death, and he was heard because of his reverent submission. Although he was a Son, he learned obedience through what he suffered; and having been made perfect, he became the source of eternal salvation for all who obey him, having been designated by God a high priest according to the order of Melchizedek. (Hebrews 5:7-10)

As priestly followers of the Suffering Servant, bishops guard, model, teach, and celebrate the church's liturgy. Bishops "lead all persons entrusted to their oversight in worship, in the celebration of the sacraments, and in their mission of witness and service in the world." They minister to all those who minister (lay, licensed, commissioned, and ordained), praying for, encouraging, supporting, and enabling them. And of course, they lay hands on to bless, "consecrate, ordain, and commission persons in ministry to the Church and world" (¶404.1).

The *prophetic* office in servant style might well look to the beginning of Christ's ministry.

> When he came to Nazareth, where he had been brought up, he went to the synagogue on the sabbath day, as was his custom. He stood up to read, and the scroll of the prophet Isaiah was given to him. He unrolled the scroll and found the place where it was written:
>
> > The Spirit of the Lord is upon me,
> > because he has anointed me
> > to bring good news to the poor.
> > He has sent me to proclaim release to the captives
> > and recovery of sight to the blind,
> > to let the oppressed go free,
> > to proclaim the year of the Lord's favor.
>
> And he rolled up the scroll, gave it back to the attendant, and sat down. The eyes of all in the synagogue were fixed on him. Then he began to say to them, "Today this scripture has been fulfilled in your hearing." (Luke 4:16-21)

Bishops are servants of the Word. They lead the church in the proclamation of the kingdom, spreading the good news, especially the good news to the poor, the outcast, the marginalized, the exploited. "Bishops are to be prophetic voices and courageous leaders in the cause of justice for all people" (¶404.1). They promise redemption. They call to discipleship. They witness to the radical demands of Christian living. Under the mandate to preach the gospel, they exercise the church's teaching office. Bishops are authorized, indeed charged, "to guard the faith, order, liturgy, doctrine, and discipline of the Church"(¶404.1). As such, United Methodist bishops labor on behalf of the whole church, sharing with all those who exercise *episkopé*, responsibility for interpreting and transmitting the gospel of Christ, seeking "to be a sign of the unity of the faith," and "are to be prophetic voices and courageous leaders in the cause of justice for all people" (¶404.1). They also have an ecumenical episcopal prophetic teaching office, which I will elaborate below.

Scripture has much to say about leadership, indeed witnesses throughout in both Testaments to ways in which God calls and directs God's servants in the exercise of *episkopé*. And in several places, the early church gave counsel about the episcopal office, as for instance from Timothy and Titus:

> The saying is sure: whoever aspires to the office of bishop desires a noble task. Now a bishop must be above reproach, married only once, temperate, sensible, respectable, hospitable, an apt teacher, not a drunkard, not violent but gentle, not quarrelsome, and not a lover of money. He must manage his own household well, keeping his children submissive and respectful in every way—for if someone does not know how to manage his own household, how can he take care of God's church? He must not be a recent convert, or he may be puffed up with conceit and fall into the condemnation of the devil. Moreover, he must be well thought of by outsiders, so that he may not fall into disgrace and the snare of the devil. (1 Timothy 3:1-7)

> For a bishop, as God's steward, must be blameless; he must not be arrogant or quick-tempered or addicted to wine or violent or greedy for gain; but he must be hospitable, a lover of goodness, prudent, upright, devout, and self-controlled. He must have a firm grasp of the word that is trustworthy in accordance with the teaching, so that he may be able both to preach with sound doctrine and to refute those who contradict it. (Titus 1:7-9)

In interpreting such biblical passages, with their culturally limited conceptions of appropriate leadership, Methodists have, of course, been drawn by the Spirit's guidance, by the wider Scriptural witness, and by other elements of the quadrilateral to broaden our sense of who should occupy the episcopal office. It is also the case that Methodists have their own take on Scripture and a Wesleyan reading of leadership, indeed, one that sees "itinerant general superintendency" as *the* faithful expression of the apostolic pattern. To that we now turn briefly.

The Wesleyan Charism

In the chapters on "Episcopacy and Methodism" and "Itinerant General Superintendency: Asbury's Precept and Practice" of *Episcopacy in the Methodist Tradition*, Thomas Frank and I attend at some length to the very distinctive leadership style(s) and norm(s) exemplified by John Wesley and Francis Asbury.[7] The chapters appeal to the consensus in early American Methodism that its practice of superintendency faithfully followed that of John Wesley, adjusting and adapting it as necessary to the North American context. And they indicate that Asbury, Thomas Coke, and their successors in the episcopal office understood itinerancy in general, and itinerant general superintendency in particular, to be not just Wesleyan but a recovery of the New Testament pattern of leadership, that of Christ and the apostles. Coke and Asbury spell this out in their annotations on the 1798 MEC *Discipline*, insisting their episcopacy was "the primitive and *apostolic plan*." Methodism, the first bishops argued, reached back past the centuries of settled, diocesan episcopacies to effect a distinctive recovery of apostolic leadership—ministry as missional, evangelistic, sent, appointed/appointive—"a royal priesthood that has apostolic roots" (¶403).

As apostolic, Methodism's conception and practice of episcopacy was pneumatological, an understanding spelled out in some detail in *Episcopacy in the Methodist Tradition* and therefore not reiterated here. When truly pneumatological, when truly faithful, Methodism has been Spirit-led in its exercise of *episkopé* and its understanding and exercise of superintendency, making it accordingly dynamic in character, subject to renewal and to critique. A full discussion of its pneumatological character would require much attention to the long, dynamic process of Methodism's growing in the Spirit, a rehearsal of the history of the church's understanding and practice of superintendency. This would be a theological reading

- of the adoption of the "Restrictive Rules,"
- of episcopacy as contested in virtually every Methodist squabble and deeply implicated in and affected by the fight over slavery,

- of bishops as bearers of Methodism's evangelical doctrines and witnesses to social holiness,
- of the witness brought into our several unions out of the MEC, MECS, Methodist Protestant, and EUB experience,
- of dimensions of the office lost with the creation of the Judicial Council and gained with the establishment of the Council of Bishops,
- of the discoveries that the global dimension of the COB has yielded,
- of the effect of leadership transformations in American society (our next topic).

Such a quick overview should suggest what Frank and I indicate, as do James Kirby, Gerald Moede, and others, namely that the Methodist/Wesleyan pattern does not remain static.[8] American Methodist episcopacy has evolved as has our connection as a whole. Bishops have done much to effect change as they are both agents and creatures of connection.

Certainly another Wesleyan emphasis, though not absolutely unique, is our understanding of bishops as a special ministry, not a special order, elected from the elders and consecrated, not ordained, to their ministry of general oversight and supervision (¶403, ¶404). Given that commitment, we might question the warrant for separating the treatment of superintendency from the overall discussion of "The Ministry of the Ordained," a change made with the 1976 *Discipline*. Prior *Disciplines* considered the episcopacy as a chapter within the larger section on ministry, a placement rather more in keeping with our doctrine. Alternatively and positively, one can make a strong case from the current *Discipline*'s organization for revising our theology to construe episcopacy as in fact a separate order. While that would revise two centuries of Methodist self-understanding, it would accord with the way clergy and some laity reverence bishops, with the manner in which bishops treat one another, with the relocation of their membership on election to the Council of Bishops, and with the office's life character. If General Conference does not wish to elect either option—of relocating treatment of superintendency back within "The Ministry of the Ordained" or of considering episcopacy as a third order—it might consider doing a little of both, namely, treating episcopacy alongside deacons and elders and discussing the exercise of superintending (for both district and general superintendents) as a separate chapter.

Episcopacy as Lived (with Particular Attention to North America)[9]

In reflecting on episcopacy experientially, we might take note of the long-term effect of (1) American (U.S.) democratic protocols, (2) certain functional or best-practice dictates, (3) the power of contemporary leadership patterns, and (4) ways that the UMC and its predecessor churches (EA, UBC, MEC, MPC, MECS) have interacted with these societal influences.

1. American Democratic Protocols

At least from the moment of Asbury's decision to accept the office only if elected, Methodist superintendency has felt the pressure of civil political practice. For some around Asbury and his successors, including some of the bishops' closest coworkers, mere election did not begin to care for the monarchical power inherent in the Wesleyan pattern. So began two centuries of efforts to widen participation in governance, decision making, appointments. Virtually every schism turned, in one way or another, on episcopal power and authority or perceived abuse thereof. And virtually every development in the church has had its effect on the episcopal office, sometimes by design, other times by accident—presiding elders (district superintendents), the Council of Bishops, General Conference, delegation, Restrictive Rules, boards and agencies, *Christian Advocates*, cabinets, contests over race and slavery, lengthening of term limits, colleges and seminaries, admission of laity, women in ministry, unification, Judicial Council, jurisdictional elections, consultation, accountability, the increasingly global makeup of the denomination.[10] The litany could go on and on, listing new or altered features of our connection that in one way or another brought American democratic precepts or practices into juxtaposition with episcopacy. From these "experiences" the UMC has come to expect bishops to exercise *episkopé*—to superintend, to lead, to appoint, to govern, to equip, to teach, to guard the faith, to evangelize—in some accord with the wisdom, practices, and procedures of American democracy.

2. Functional or Best-practice Dictates

Bishops and Methodist episcopacy have experienced and been affected by a second set of societal/cultural best-practice norms. These sometimes touch the authority or power of the office but more typically affect its exercise. Here too the list might be long. Included would be educational practices and patterns that shape how bishops exercise the teaching office. So also expectations about good business practice, about accountability and transparency, about administrative effectiveness, and about financial management and fiscal integrity. The episcopal office also is shaped by and shapes itself by the practitioners whom it employs and who extend its work. Here one might list various new roles and offices on local, regional, and national levels, including communication specialists, program coordinators, chancellors, executive assistants, directors of ministerial services, directors of connectional ministries, information technocrats, directors of new church development. Adopting best practices and enhancing its leadership with specialists, United Methodist episcopacy textures itself, adds competences, and develops nuances that await full articulation.

3. Contemporary Leadership Patterns

A third experience, closely related to the prior two, is with ideals or models of leadership. More so than other experiential norms, this one is time sensitive, one ideal giving way to another. Sometimes those derive from societal styles, sometimes from politics, sometimes from the corporate or business arena, sometimes from other religious communities. The appropriation of servant leadership and its introduction into the *Discipline* as it became a powerful, indeed, the "in" form of corporate practice, illustrates how experience contributes to our conception of episcopacy. The UMC could, as we suggest above, find ample New Testament warrant for servant leadership and servanthood and, of course, it is central to our understanding of the diaconate. However, the underdeveloped biblical and theological warrant would lead one to suspect that the notion has been imported from corporate America.

Leadership as exercised in other religious communities can also influence Methodist practice. One form of leadership that is highly visible—namely the media-savvy, contemporary-culture–sensitive, charismatic preacher/worship leader; a leadership style dominant in religious broadcasting and modeled by self-anointed "bishops"—is unlikely to gain Disciplinary status any more than did its nineteenth-century counterpart, the camp meeting preacher. But as the latter did affect episcopal practice, so a few United Methodist bishops will, we suspect, draw some inspiration from that media model. United Methodism would more likely borrow (and arguably already has borrowed) ideals or models from other episcopal churches, Anglican and Roman Catholic especially. Their patterns add precedent and warrant to what has been a gradual shift away from "itinerant general superintendency" and toward a diocesan mode—with administration, budgetary roles, pastoral oversight, and problem-solving focused locally.

Leadership styles do change and the current forms in society, politics, business, communications, and religious communities offer United Methodism ways of being effective, being incarnational, for the day. So we should expect episcopal leadership to change—some patterns (as for instance that of the CEO that normalized executive ministry) giving way to new ones for a new day. With that assumption, the Task Force to Study the Episcopacy recommended the removal of the now dated leadership terms of *Mode, Pace,* and *Skill,* introduced in the 1976 *Discipline* as ¶502, and continued until 2004 (as ¶402).

4. The UMC (EA, UBC, MEC, MPC, MECS) Experience

The prior three experiential resources for shaping the understanding and practice of superintendency derive from the church's and bishops' engagement with the world and with leadership beyond the church. Methodism learns also from itself. Indeed, sometimes Methodism teaches the world about effective leadership. Methodist connectionalism and its successful expansion by planting relatively uniform order, liturgy, practice, and governance across the nation (and eventually the world) taught the business community a trick or two. Methodist itinerancy and stump-preaching shaped nineteenth-century political practice. Methodist national communication systems—the *Christian Advocates*, Sunday school materials, missionary magazines—outpaced its secular counterparts and doubtless influenced business practices.

So, if superintendency in some respects has been confined or crowded (as the first two experiential norms might suggest), it has expanded on, developed, experimented with, shaped leadership, its own and that of Methodist ministry generally. Methodist bishops have from the beginning modeled leadership. Asbury did so self-consciously and deliberately, from the moment he landed in North America, conscious of setting a Wesleyan example, especially with regard to itinerancy. Later bishops may not have been quite so self-conscious in their exemplification of leadership. However, their actual practice, more so than precept, modeled ministry—on itinerancy, daily and weekly rhythms, work, reading, spirituality, speech, writing, self-expectations, residency, sabbaticals, discernment, and holy conferencing—each of which deserves a dissertation. One illustration of the bishops leading by example will have to suffice. The trend in UMC ministry toward longer pastorates tracks the shift of bishops from multiple conference itinerating superintendency into a diocesan mode and into two and more quadrennial terms.

American Methodist bishops have been the church's chief strategists—exercising missionary, evangelistic, envisioning, initiative-taking roles. Focused preeminently in the person and authority of Asbury, these strategic responsibilities over time have been divided, diffused, differentiated, and delegated. The *Discipline* nevertheless specifies the charge (¶401):

> The purpose of superintending is to equip the Church in its disciple-making ministry.... It is also their task to facilitate the initiation of structures and strategies for the equipping of Christian people for service in the Church and in the world in the name of Jesus Christ and to help extend the service in mission.

Bishops have shared that strategic role and the superintending office with a distinctive Methodist office, that of the presiding elder (PE), now district superintendent (DS), to whom superintendency or *episkopé* is extended (¶401). The PE or DS historically functioned as chief strategist within his district, a vital delegated role when bishops presided over multiple conferences and not necessarily the same ones year-to-year. A contested office—one of the denomination's bitterest fights and longest enduring schism came over whether the presiding elders should be elected or appointed—the district superintendency needs more theological treatment.[11] The *Discipline* is long on responsibilities (¶¶419, 421, 422, 423, 424) and short on the qualities for the office (¶420). Nor has Methodist literature been very helpful. Insiders will have to provide our theology, exegeting practice in the manner of Asbury and Coke, of our corporate, collegial superintendency.

Another Methodist distinction, related to the DS, has been the practice of corporate and, more recently, collegial superintendency, represented preeminently in the institution of the cabinet. The bishop-in-cabinet as well as the office of DS, deserves more adequate description and theological commentary. Again, such treatment will have to come from an insider, since the work of the cabinet and much of the activity of the DS are conducted in camera or governed by expectations of confidentiality.

The Church has been more explicit on the corporate and collegial dimension of the Council of Bishops (COB) and certainly the bishops themselves are. Their practices of covenanting and covenant groups, discernment decision making, holy conferencing and restructuring for mission have set the terms for similar practices at conference and local church levels. These episcopal patterns and their diffusion represent but the present expression of episcopal modeling of "conference," of the church's corporate nature, and of collegial leadership. That practice of modeling and diffusion can be traced from Wesley and from Asbury onward. Among the recent ways in which the bishops have established patterns for the church as a whole has been in its living into the diversity and global nature of the church. Although it may not yet be fully evident to those outside the COB, and not yet adequately theologized, the election to the episcopacy and presence in the Council of African Americans, Asian Americans, Hispanic Americans, women, and the Central Conferences is reshaping United Methodism's understanding and practice of episcopacy and of leadership generally.

As the bishops model leadership for the denomination, so also the episcopacy responds to the development of other offices and institutions. In addition to those already mentioned within conferences, cabinets, and extended cabinets, the general agencies, the colleges, universities, hospitals, camps and homes, the Judicial Council, and, more recently, the caucuses have affected the episcopacy in important if sometimes subtle ways. Power-sharing with other leaders reshapes what bishops do and redefines the office. In the past, for instance, the teaching office that belongs by Christian tradition to the bishop came to be exercised de facto by the *Christian Advocate* editors and then passed along to educators and to the program agencies.[12] More recently, the Council through its theological initiatives and individual bishops in conferences has labored to recover the teaching office. The episcopacy, then, defines and is defined in its interaction with the array of United Methodist leadership.

The office is shaped as well by the elections that produce it, by the processes for nomination, and by the politicking around episcopacy. Those dynamics need as well to be reflected in our theology of the office.

THE ECUMENICAL WITNESS

In its search for unity, the ecumenical movement, to which United Methodism is constitutionally committed and to which Methodism has contributed materially and consistently, has turned to the witness of the early church and of Scripture. The harvest of this wisdom out of the tradition on ministry, on much of which we have already touched, can be found in the 1982 Faith and Order publication, *Baptism, Eucharist and Ministry*.[13] BEM's consensus on episcopacy is a study in conciseness:

> Bishops preach the Word, preside at the sacraments, and administer discipline in such a way as to be representative pastoral ministers of oversight, continuity and unity in the Church. They have pastoral oversight of the area to which they are called. They serve the apostolicity and unity of the Church's teaching, worship and sacramental life. They have responsibility for leadership in the Church's mission. They relate the Christian community in their area to the wider Church, and the universal Church to their

community. They, in communion with the presbyters and deacons and the whole community, are responsible for the orderly transfer of ministerial authority in the Church. (M29)

BEM posits the threefold pattern of ministry (bishop, elder, deacon) as based in Scripture, as sustained in the traditions of the churches, and as ecumenical norm. It treats episcopacy as preeminently sacramental, pastoral, teaching—presidency and proclamation exercised so "as to be representative pastoral ministers of oversight, continuity and unity in the Church." (M29) Bishops are to be exemplars and witnesses to the "apostolicity and unity of the Church's teaching, worship and sacramental life" (M27). Their leadership, as that of all in ministry, should be personal, collegial, and communal (M26). Bishops should be representative—a term that we used in prior *Disciplines* but now slight—pointing to dependence on Christ but also representing the community to God, and leading the community in its representation of Christ to the world. Many of the other themes in *BEM* have been touched upon already as they have become staples in Christian thinking about leadership. Not heretofore treated are the notions of the historic episcopate that *BEM* treats under the rubric of the "Apostolic Tradition," offering reinterpretations that also inform the UMC's conversations with the Episcopal Church (ECUSA).[14] Such bilaterals, the important multilateral Pan-Methodist Commission,[15] as well as the larger ecumenical conversations,[16] indeed help Methodism claim the larger, longer traditions that see bishops as servants of the whole church, as exercisers of the teaching office, as signs of and laborers for the church's unity. So now Lutherans and United Methodists can affirm:

> Bishops are given authority to preach, teach, and uphold the apostolic faith of the church: to lead all persons entrusted to their oversight in worship and in the celebration of the sacraments; to supervise and support the church's life, work and mission throughout the world; and to consecrate, commission, ordain, or authorize the ordination of persons for the ministries to which they are called.[17]

United Methodism configures the office and bishops exercise their authority so as to further the church's ecumenical commitments and apostolic faith.

The Church lodges a special ecumenical and doctrinal charge with the bishops collectively. By Constitution, (¶2, Article IV and ¶6, Article VI), Doctrinal Standards (¶101), Theological Task (¶104), and various Disciplinary precepts committed to the unity of the church, United Methodism asks the COB to guide the church's ecumenical endeavor. Specifically, it "expects the Council of Bishops to speak to the Church and from the Church to the world and to give leadership in the quest for Christian unity and interreligious relationships" (¶427.2). And the *Discipline* further specifies that "in formal relations with other churches and/or ecclesial bodies, the Council of Bishops shall be the primary liaison for The United Methodist Church" (¶2401.1). In its exercise of these ecumenical responsibilities, the Council is guided by one of its own, who serves as the denomination's chief ecumenical officer and this liaison (currently William Oden) and the COB are aided by the General Commission on Christian Unity and Interreligious Concerns (¶1903.20, 22, 23, 25; ¶1904; ¶1905.4; ¶2401.2). Under the liaison's leadership, United Methodism and other UM bishops participate in our several ecumenical conversations. This "holy conferencing" radiates beyond the participants to "tradition" the Council, the bishops as individual leaders, and the denomination. The UM office of bishop thereby claims the rich heritage of wisdom and practice of *episkopé*.

CONCLUSION

Our norms for thinking about episcopacy, then, are of course the diverse biblical counsels and models (*Scripture*), the Wesleyan charism (*Reason*), episcopacy or superintendency as lived, with particular attention to North America (*Experience*), and the ecumenical witness (*Tradition*). The quadrilateral provides a working guide for leadership that orients United Methodism to its mission and offers us Faithfulness + Hope + Love. Our charge as a denomination, we think, is for us to be in our rethinking episcopacy as in all else:

- Faithful to Scripture, the Wesleyan norms, the Constitution

DOCTRINE IN EXPERIENCE

- Instructed by our experience with itinerant general superintendency
- Cognizant of best practices of leadership, teaching, ministry
- Drawn by our vision of the kingdom of God and our hope for the unity of Christ's church
- Committed to and oriented by the church's apostolic witness

CHAPTER 7

MINISTERIAL FORMATION

The title "Ministerial Education" should conjure up the complaint of Edward Farley and others that theological education has collapsed into the clerical paradigm.[1] "Ministerial Education" indicates that this chapter considers a subset of Methodist theological education, namely those processes, relations, and institutions that prepared persons for Methodist itinerancy. It takes that focus without conceding to Farley that Methodist theological education collapses into the clerical paradigm. Indeed, it suggests that another paradigm—the seminary paradigm—bedevils analysis and that the clerical "collapse" may have to do with how scholars have isolated and portrayed Methodist education, not how it actually behaved. For Methodists, it will be argued, ministerial education belonged to the larger pattern of education in the faith, of sanctification, of the way of holiness, and theological or seminary education constituted only one of several modalities of ministerial preparation.[2]

My argument, simply put, is that there were indeed *several* ways in which early Methodism prepared persons for ministry. I distinguish four:

- The first is termed *fraternal* to capture the largely oral apprenticeship model that trained and educated by yoking a junior itinerant to an older, by modeling, by interaction "on the road," by practicing under supervision, by conference enquiries that assessed growth and maturity.
- The second might well be called *Wesleyan* or *connectional* to suggest how preparation through a course of study respected John Wesley's precept and example, brought somewhat more serious reading into the apprenticeship, and made conferences the agent of ministerial training.
- The third should properly be termed *collegiate* in recognition of the importance played by the church colleges and

baccalaureate studies—education of ministers side by side with those who would remain laity—in preparing generations of persons for ministry.
- The fourth, *seminary*, denotes not all the institutions in the early nineteenth century that bore that label but only those postbaccalaureate endeavors that modeled themselves after Andover, Princeton, and Yale and that segregated professional studies under a theological professorate.

The progress of Methodism through these four phases is a well-told tale, often related as a triumphal pilgrimage, a pilgrim's progress. In the earliest period, from 1784 to 1820, the church failed in several valiant efforts to establish a central educational institution and had to make do with informal educational procedures. Then, from 1820 until about midcentury, annual conferences proceeded on their own in a two-pronged fashion, formulating a course of study for all candidates for ministry and establishing academies and colleges to assure that their leadership would be trained under Methodist auspices. The pilgrimage culminated, so it is suggested, around midcentury with the establishment of distinct theological schools in 1839–1840 at Newbury, Vermont, the predecessor to Boston, in 1854 of the Garrett Biblical Institute and in 1866 of Drew Theological Seminary.[3] Toward the seminary, then, the pilgrim, the Methodist "Christian," progresses.

This retelling draws whatever distinction it possesses not in new data on one or more phases, or new insight into the dynamics of their unfolding, but rather in the simple claim that the tale should not be related as pilgrim's progress at all. The four ways of doing ministerial education—fraternal, Wesleyan (connectional or conference), collegiate, and seminary—are each legitimate, indeed important, in their own right. They may have appeared in succession. However, each needs to be examined and respected for the distinctive dimension it contributed and contributes to ministerial preparation. To interpret the first three as only phases toward fulfillment in seminary, or even as preparatory stages in individual ministerial development, is to miss the very different ways in which each construes and undertakes the educational process. It is also to lose sight of the fact that the first three models or patterns continued to function, indeed, continue to this day (a point to which we return briefly in the chapter's conclusion.). The linear, progressive schema obscures the ways the four have worked readily together and construes their competition as a simple division between friend and foe of education.

FRATERNAL

> They were like a band of brothers, having one purpose and end in view—the glory of God and the salvation of immortal souls.[4]

"Fraternal" well describes early Methodist ministry. Bound in covenant to travel, to submit to the appointive power, to accept a common wage (when it could be raised), to suffer together, to preach the Word, this fraternal order educated and trained in the same way that it worked—together on the road. William Burke, who began itinerating in the late 1780s, reported:

> In the fall, at the beginning of October, brother Lowe insisted that I should accompany him round New Hope circuit. Accordingly, I arranged my business so as to make the tour of six weeks. We went on together, preaching time about, till he was taken sick and returned home, and left me to complete the round.[5]

By inviting the neophyte or prospective minister to travel along, Methodism did its theological education and preparation for ministry on the road. The individual was "on trial," learning while doing, but also under supervision and frequently traveling with an experienced itinerant, a mentor, a sage, capable of giving instruction. The pattern was well established by the first decade of the nineteenth century, linking a young with a more experienced minister.[6] Charles Elliot described it as an apostolic plan:

> When the young or inexperienced are actually employed in preaching, under the watchcare and instruction of experienced Ministers, such as the Apostles under Christ, and Mark, Timothy, and Titus under the Apostles, we have as exact a specimen of apostolic and primitive training for the ministry as can be furnished.[7]

In the traces, but in relation to other itinerants, ministers learned. The learning went on while in appointment, in riding to camp meetings and conferences, in the conferences themselves, in hearing one another preach, in counseling sessions thereafter, in coaching in spirituality—in short, in and through the operation of the Methodist connection.

The fraternal, apprenticeship style of instruction for ministry belonged to a larger pattern of Methodist teaching. Guidance, direction, counsel, discipline—the business of class and quarterly meetings—made the Methodist system a great school for growth in the Christian faith and the life of Methodism itself an educational process toward sanctification.[8] And the teaching medium was Christian experience, the experienced leading the neophyte and experience being shared and experiences being related. The relational character of such learning they conveyed with familial language; they called one another brother, sister, mother, father. Much of that sharing of experience was direct and oral. But experience could also be conveyed in print, so realized these American sons and daughters of Wesley. Robert Roberts reported that his early tutelage in the faith involved exposure to the writings of John Fletcher and John Wesley, as well as the Bible, an instruction that preceded his formal schooling:

> I had counsel, advice and prayers of the preachers, which I consider among the happiest circumstances of my early life as they took much pains with me. I began to read Fletcher's *Appeal*, Fletcher's *Checks*, and felt myself firmly established in the doctrines of the Methodists, and all that I desired to make me a Methodist was an evidence of my acceptance with God through the merits of the Redeemer.[9]

Training for ministry simply continued this process and included the reading specified as normative, Wesley's *Sermons*, his *Notes upon the New Testament*, the *Discipline* (which replaced Wesley's *Large Minutes* for the American church), and the hymnbook. Also important were the publications of the Methodist Book Concern, in effect, the ongoing version of Wesley's *Christian Library*. Of this library, the ministers were both the students and the librarians and tutors; the dissemination of books and tracts was a central part of their business.

Illustrative of the process was the saga of James Quinn. He went as a youth of thirteen to an Asbury-led conference in Uniontown, Pennsylvania, in 1787. Several years later he was converted under two itinerants. He then apprenticed himself to and lived with several local preachers. He rode on his first appointment with Joseph Shane. A later assignment put him in the vicinity of several itinerants, including Enoch George, later bishop, then temporarily located, from whom he continued to learn. He says of them:

> These had all been successful and popular traveling preachers, and were considered men of first-rate talents; and, although none of them were classically educated, yet were they men of sound, well-improved mind. . . . At the feet of these excellent men I took many useful lessons in theology; for I was more than willing to learn, and they were apt to teach.[10]

Looking back from a later day to that period before his ordination in 1803, Quinn described himself as "at that time a student of the fourth year in the Methodist theological seminary, which had its establishment in all the United States, and a few branches in the western wilds."[11] He later spoke with pride of his having "had the honor of being some kind of president in BRUSH COLLEGE for eight years, during which period I had something to do with the theological training of such men as Finley, Strange, Bigelow, Bascom, etc."[12] Quinn's editor/biographer defended this "brush or road seminary" against midcentury detractors who favored formal theological education by comparing early Methodists to the Romans and "Washington and his brave fellows" who learned the art of war "on the toilsome march, the tented field, or battleground." "And where and how did the Methodist preachers learn to preach? By preaching." He continued and made explicit the implicit contrast of "road" training to that gained at college or seminary:

> I once knew a college graduate, an A.B., thrown quite into confusion on being asked by the examining committee, "What was the object proposed by Fletcher in writing the Appeal? and what method of argument did the author pursue?" But the graduate of the Brush College could tell you very promptly almost every thing about Fletcher and Wesley. The Bible, however, was their stronghold. They were at home here, and you seldom heard from them a lame or inappropriate quotation.[13]

The apparent effectiveness of such instruction led some early Methodists to disparage formal schooling altogether. So, at least, reported S. R. Beggs of Indiana Methodism around 1820. After serving as assistant class leader and receiving a license to preach, he proposed taking a couple of years of schooling. The Rev. James Armstrong dissuaded him. "He held that I could better receive my education and graduate in the 'Brush College', as most of our preachers had done."[14] In similar terms, Joseph Trimble spoke retrospectively of his apprenticeship in the Ohio area, circa 1830:

> There were no Theological schools at that day, for the training of the young men of the church for the work of the ministry in the Methodist Church. Indeed, some of the fathers desired them not, believing that the circuit system, with a senior and junior preacher, proffered the best possible advantages for theological study and for training the young men of the Conference to be useful ministers of the Lord Jesus. This was my school.[15]

COURSE OF STUDY

The perfection of theological study in the school of apprenticeship that Joseph Trimble experienced did not obtain universally. The New England Conference heard to that effect from its president pro tempore, George Pickering: "The President addressed the Conference concerning the necessity of Preachers being diligent in their Studies and Labors."[16]

The 1816 General Conference discovered a number of grave problems affecting Methodist ministry, among them "the admission of improper persons into the itinerancy." The committee charged to examine the problems and propose remedies affirmed:

> Although a collegiate education is not, by your committee, deemed essential to a gospel ministry, yet it appears absolutely necessary for every minister of the gospel to study to show himself approved unto God, a workman that needeth not to be ashamed. Every one, therefore, who would be useful as a minister in the Church, should, to a sincere piety and laudable zeal for the salvation of souls, add an ardent desire for useful knowledge—he should strive by every lawful means to imbue his mind with every science which is intimately connected with the doc-

trine of salvation by Jesus Christ, and which will enable him to understand and illustrate the sacred Scriptures.[17]

General Conference assigned to the bishops "or a committee which they may appoint in each annual conference" the duty of pointing out "a course of reading and study proper to be pursued by candidates for the ministry."[18] It fell then to annual conferences to take responsibility for theological content in ministerial preparation and to monitor the two-year reading course.[19] Conferences (with the bishops) became the educational system, setting the curriculum, enriching the apprenticeship to include explicit attention to the reading program, monitoring individuals' progress each year at the annual gathering, and certifying completion and theological adequacy.

The year after the General Conference mandate, the Baltimore Conference acted to implement the mandate. It spelled out doctrines on which the candidate must be familiar; prescribed knowledge of Scripture, geography and history; and set forth the following program:

> The art of conveying ideas with ease, propriety and clearness is of great importance. The Candidate should understand the Articles of Religion, and the doctrines and discipline of the Church, to which he is to subscribe, and by which he is to be governed
>
> 1st. On Divinity, a constant use of the Holy Scriptures. Wesley's Sermons – Notes – answer to Taylor – Saints Rest – Law's Serious Call – Benson's Sermons – Coke's Commentaries – Fletcher's Checks – Appeal – Portrait of Saint Paul – Wood's Dictionary – Newton on the Prophecies – and Wesley's Philosophy.
>
> 2nd. Rollins' Ancient History, Josephus's Antiquities, with Wesley's Ecclesiastical History.
>
> 3rd. The Rudiments of the English language, Alexander's, Murray's, or Webster's Grammar.
>
> 4th. Morse's Universal and Paine's Geography.[20]

Thus came a specifically communal and theological journey into the four-year period of being on trial; thus also conferences joined the senior itinerant in traveling with the candidate into maturity in ministry. Conference examinations gave the program its rigor. Such examinations developed naturally out of the annual review of the characters of the ministers, an exacting process that had from the very first consumed much of the time of annual conferences.[21] To the review of character now was added scrutiny of the individual's formal, but individualized, program of reading. On this reading program, annual conferences examined candidates. As early as 1819, the New England Conference was appointing a committee to give special assistance in that examination.[22]

Something of the operation of the course of study can be discerned in the experience of The Reverend Jacob Lanius,[23] born in Virginia, moved as a child to Missouri, licensed to preach in 1831, and accepted on trial by Missouri Annual Conference. Midway in that four-year process, specifically in mid-1883, Lanius began to note his reading, the first item being Volney's *Ruins*.[24] Over the next two years his reading drew frequent comments:

> Tues. 14th [Jan. 1834] I spent the morning in reading "Watson's Institutes and the Christian Advocate and onward About noon I rode to Bro. Marrs where I spent the night in my usual employment of reading and conversation.[25]

> [Nov. 25, 1834] This evening I learned from Mosheim's Ecclesiasticale History that Infant Baptism was first derived by a branch of the Manichian Paulician Sect in the Eleventh Century.[26]

> [Mar. 31, 1835] After dinner I took Dr. Mosheim's History of the Church and went to the grove and spent the remainder of the evening in reading, meditation, and prayer. We often find it necessary in this new and frontier country thus to retire because the people have but one room in the general and a fortune of children who surround us crying and hollering to such an extent as to render it impossible to read and understand and very often we are interrupted by a question or a statement from a good brother or sister which the rules of ministerial and Christian etiquet require us to attend to.[27]

> [May 2, 1835] [P]assed the night with the family and Bro. Estes our class leader at this place in conversation on various subjects, reading the Masonic constitution which I had in my saddle bags, singing, prayer, sleep, etc.[28]

[Sept. 1836] [S]addle bags washed down stream.... My loss was about seven dollars worth of valuable books that I had bought in St. Louis.[29]

The reading program apparently succeeded. Lanius was ordained elder in September 1835.

Over the years the church made various improvements to the course.[30] One was lengthening it to encompass the whole trial years—that is, making it a four-year program. Another change, doubtless motivated by somewhat varied success with the course from conference to conference, was greater standardization across the connection. That this was already happening, probably through the coordinating efforts by the bishops, can be seen in 1840 in the newly established North Carolina Conference. In organizing itself, it adopted a series of resolutions commending the New York Conference course of study and examination procedures and calling for the bishop to implement that program.[31]

At its organization, the Methodist Protestant Church had adopted a single, Disciplinary course (in 1830). The same decision came in 1844, the year of the division, for the Methodist Episcopal Church, so thereafter both the MEC and MECS had a single, national course. About the same time the German Methodists, the United Brethren, and the Evangelical Association also created courses of study; subsequently the MEC established them for the various language conferences that emerged in the nineteenth century.[32] Only at a later period, however, did the administration become centralized nationally. For the nineteenth century, this was a conference course.

Until the twentieth century the course was the way into ministry, normative for candidates who took a college degree, normative for candidates who received a seminary education. Seminary graduates alone gained exemption from the course, beginning in 1900 for the MEC, in 1908 for the MPC, and in 1914 for the MECS. When the three churches united in 1939, "more than half of all ministers who joined Annual Conferences on trial had no professional training in theological schools."[33] Seminary was made the normative route into ministry finally in 1956.

For much of its history, then, Methodism equipped for ministry through conference and through a course of study administered by conference and in a process in which judgments of satisfactory completion, preparation for ministry, and theological adequacy were made by the collegium of ministers.

COLLEGIATE

Methodism undertook the founding of colleges out of various motives, including concern for education per se, aspirations for respectability, worries about denominational (Presbyterian especially) domination of educational institutions, and fear of losing its own elite. The 1834 Indiana Conference passed a resolution memorializing the Legislature concerning Presbyterian control of the State College at Bloomington:

> We look in its charter and read that the places of president, professors and tutors are open, soliciting capacity to occupy them without regard to religious professions or doctrines. We then turn our eyes on the faculty from the organization of the institution up to this hour, and we see one common hue, one common religion characterize every member, as if capacity and fitness were confined to one church and one set of religious opinions.[34]

Concurring, Stephen Olin, an early president of Wesleyan University, appealed for support in an 1844 speech by conjuring up the specter of Methodism's losing its elite by forcing them no alternative but to attend other denominational schools. "No Christian denomination can safely trust to others for the training of its sons. . . . History has too clearly demonstrated that, without colleges of our own, few of our sons are likely to be educated, and that only a small portion of that few are likely to be retained in our communion."[35]

He estimated that three-quarters of those who have attended other denominational schools had been lost. "Many of them have gone to other denominations, many more have gone to the world. All were the legitimate children of the Church. They were her hope, and they should have become the crown of her rejoicing."[36] The danger he thought more likely was the loss of religious influence altogether. "It must not be forgotten that the years spent in college are those in which most conversions take place, and if the youth does not submit to obey the religious influences that surround him then, the danger is imminent that he will never become a Christian."[37]

In worrying about denominational interests, Methodists did not waiver in their commitment to the unity of piety and learning nor to their desire to participate in the Christianization of American society. Also motivating the church were genuine concerns about preparation of persons for ministry and recognition that the system of apprenticeship had its faults.[38]

Enunciating such concerns, the General Conference of 1820 added another motive, namely, its own mandate, by resolving "that it be, and is hereby, recommended to all the annual conferences to establish, as soon as practicable, literary institutions, under their own control." In setting forth the case, a working committee sounded the denominational alarm:

> The committee appointed to take into consideration the propriety of recommending to the annual conferences the establishment of seminaries of learning . . . regretted that the cause had not sooner claimed the attention of the General Conference . . . considering the rapid improvement of society in almost every science, and the extension of our Church.[39]

It went on to affirm:

> Almost all seminaries of learning in our country, of much celebrity, are under the control of Calvinistic or of Hopkinsian principles, or otherwise are managed by men denying the fundamental doctrines of the gospel. If any of our people, therefore, wish to give their sons or daughters a finished education, they are under the necessity of resigning them to the management of those institutions which are more or less hostile to our views of the grand doctrines of Christianity. . . .
>
> Another capital defect in most seminaries of learning, your committee presume to think, is, that experimental and practical godliness is considered only of secondary importance; whereas, in the opinion of your committee, this ought to form the most prominent feature in every literary institution. Religion and learning should mutually assist each other, and thus connect the happiness of both worlds together.[40]

General Conference's worries animated the Virginia Conference in the 1820s. John Early, chair of the examining committee noted marked deficiencies among candidates for the ministry in history, grammar, geography, and philosophy.[41] Out of that concern and with the prompting of General Conference to annual conferences, Virginia created a committee in 1825 to establish a "seminary of learning." The committee of twelve included John Early, as well as seven laypersons. In its "Address to the Members and Friends of the Methodist Episcopal Church," the body set forth several aims, among them:

> Another great and noble object is contemplated in the establishment of this College or Seminary, and that is to afford young men, who give evidence of their being called by the Lord Jesus Christ to preach the Gospel, and that they possess the gifts and graces of the Holy Spirit, an opportunity to obtain important qualifications for the Ministry.[42]

John Early, the visionary who foresaw such purposes in the future Randolph-Macon, found himself well-positioned to bring them to fruition. He served the school as president of the board of trustees from 1832 to 1868.

In fact, the colleges did not typically set up a distinctive ministerial track, structure their curricula for ministerial preparation, or feature biblical and theological studies.[43] Nevertheless, absent alternative theological programs, the colleges did serve that purpose and many of the future clergy did further their preparation at the Randolph-Macons (even as they prepared themselves through the course of study).

The place of ministerial training in the founding and operation of Randolph-Macon and similar colleges needs to be underscored in counterpoint to more recent interpretations that have minimized both their denominational and ministerial character. These interpretations have themselves corrected, indeed overcorrected, even earlier readings that made the church colleges narrowly denominational and failed to recognize the wider views and significant local support with which they came into being.[44]

When established, Randolph-Macon understood its purposes to be communal and cosmopolitan, not narrowly sectarian (Methodist), a necessary stance in a Virginia still Jeffersonian, wary of religious establishments, and unwilling to charter institutions not deemed as serving the public trust. Randolph-Macon would, then, like other early colleges, define its mission broadly, as in service to church and country,[45] structure its board to represent the community (as well as Methodism), open its doors to persons of all denominations, orient its training to the needs of the citizenry (not just persons who would eventually turn to ministry), and seek strong community support. James Scanlon observes, "No denominational test was made for admittance or continuance (references to openness are seen as early as 1833), and not only was the student body diverse, but the Methodists were in the minority."[46] However, Scanlon minimizes the Methodist imprint on the school and its service to the Methodist community, noting statistics for 1856, which put the Methodist presence in the school at 31 percent and the preministerial at only 9 percent.[47] But he also describes the role of the Methodist president, the Methodist majority of the trustees, the efforts made to hire a Methodist faculty, the support given the school by the Virginia, South Carolina, and Georgia Methodist Conferences, the special consideration given to the sons of ministers, the recurrent revivals at the school, and the significant eventual output of ministers.[48]

Scanlon's portrayal and his own statistics suggest a different conclusion—that the college was a very Methodist institution. In a counting of the occupations of the 210 early graduates by the Society of the Alumni there were

48 teachers (13 of these professors)

43 clergy (12 also taught or served as school president)

39 lawyers (8 legislators)

31 farmers

29 physicians.[49]

So Methodism educated its leadership; so it trained persons who did go into ministry alongside persons preparing for other professions; so it tutored its leadership in the evangelical liberal arts.[50]

Key to making the institution really Methodist and useful in preparation of the Church's leadership was the president, typically a distinguished member of the clergy.⁵¹ Stephen Olin played such roles at two of Methodism's important early institutions. He assumed the presidency of Randolph-Macon in 1833, after having taught at the University of Georgia. Olin taught mental and moral science, belles-lettres, and political philosophy; preached occasionally; delivered formal addresses; built a faculty; raised money; cultivated conference support.⁵² He led in a very clerical fashion, using the gifts and strengths of the ministerial office and relation, and building a national reputation for the school and himself.

After a period of ill health and European travel for curative purposes, Olin was elected to the presidency of Wesleyan University and continued the educational vision and legacy of the first president, Wilbur Fisk. In an 1845 statement on Wesleyan's behalf, Olin spoke of its graduates "as a class, such men as the Methodist Church most wants as instruments in the various departments of her work for fulfilling her great commission."⁵³ The statement would hold up. In its first half-century (1831–81), close to half its graduates entered the ministry, 90 percent into Methodist ministry. During this period, the percentage of Methodists among students, faculty, and trustees climbed, the student percentage from 50 percent in 1831 to over 80 percent in 1881, the faculty from 65 to 100 percent, the trustees from 65 percent to 90 percent.⁵⁴ Wesleyan became Methodism's first national educational institution. There much of its leadership received the kind of classical education that would equip them to make Methodism itself a full player in national life.

Elsewhere the pattern was similar. A good vantage from which to view it is through Matthew Simpson's *Cyclopaedia of Methodism*, a boosterish volume, as its subtitle indicated: *Embracing Sketches of Its Rise, Progress and Present Condition, With Biographical Notices and Numerous Illustrations*.⁵⁵ Entries for the several Methodist colleges repeatedly cite their service in preparing persons for ministry. Of Augusta College, Bishop Simpson noted: "In its halls were educated many young men who became prominent both in the ministry and in the various professions of life." Of Wofford, "A goodly proportion of its graduates may be found in the ministry." Simpson reported that by 1877 Ohio Wesleyan had graduated 683 "of whom nearly 200 have become ministers, 10 are missionaries in other lands."⁵⁶ Comparable statements about collegiate preparation of ministers occur for Madison College, Allegheny, Emory, McKendree, and of course, Wesleyan.[57]

Methodists took these ventures in collegiate education very seriously. And for good reason. When the 1834 Indiana Conference noted that the Presbyterians controlled the State College at Bloomington, their explicit concern was that their youth were "abandoning and renouncing the institution because the religion of their fathers (is but tolerated) and not domiciled," leading them to request that the faculty contain "a due proportion from other religious denominations."[58] They also took various measures at that conference for secondary education, its staffing, and financing. By the next year they had given up on transforming the state university and proposed the creation of Indiana Asbury University.[59]

The North Carolina Annual Conference came into being amid Methodism's collegiate frenzy and its early sessions illustrate how central education and colleges became to denominational purposes. The conference met for its initial session on January 31, 1838. Various organizational activities went on. Commanding the preponderant attention, if the Minutes are a reliable guide, was education. The conference "recommended the publication of Wesley's Christian Library." It took action to recommend Leasburg Academy "to the patronage of our people," appointed a committee of trustees "to cooperate with the existing board in the supervision of the School," made arrangements for nominating persons for five scholarships and "resolved 4th that the Bishop be requested [to] appoint Bro. Lorenzo Lea to the Leasburg Academy: which on motion was adopted." The next day it took action extending similar "patronage" to the Clemmonsville Academy, appointing "5 individuals to be elected as trustees by the present board," and charging the Salisbury presiding elder with the "duty of having the property of said academy properly secured to the trustees appointed from this Conference." In additional action it instructed "the committee on the Leasburg and Clemmonsville Academies . . . to report suitable persons to be elected as trustees of those academies."[60] The next report concerned a "female Collegiate Institute"—appointed trustees, created a committee to pursue incorporation, authorized the acquisition of land (211 acres), addressed issues concerning staffing and operation and requested that the bishop "appoint from this body an agent for the

Greensboro Female Collegiate Institute." The next morning the conference heard a report by the agent of the flagship southern college, Randolph-Macon, set aside a time of prayer for this cause and requested an agent for it as well.[61] In the following years, the academies and colleges commanded similar extensive attention, the conference created a standing committee on academies, made provision for collections, and began to insist on reports.[62]

These efforts for education and successes with colleges came in the face of some indifference on the part of the Methodist faithful and open opposition on the part of some of its leadership.[63] Many of the colleges failed. But others survived and to their number would eventually be added universities. That topic brings us to the fourth style or phase of Methodist education for ministry.

SEMINARY

"I will not allow this opportunity to pass," wrote Stephen Olin, future president of Wesleyan, to Nathan Bangs, then president of Wesleyan, "without expressing my most deliberate conviction that the establishment of theological schools is indispensable to our future progress."[64] That statement, made in 1839 to accompany a centenary donation, occurred in a long letter in which Olin summed up what Methodism had achieved in a hundred years and what it still needed to accomplish. Its future greatness, thought Olin, required greater support for education and specifically for theological education. This was a sentiment Olin had expressed at least ten years earlier.[65] Others were coming to the same conclusion, including key leaders like Randolph S. Foster, John Durbin, and John Dempster, as well as reformers like La Roy Sunderland.[66] So Methodism, albeit belatedly, created institutions specifically for the preparation of persons for ministry. These initiatives came, Glenn Miller has suggested, without the great debate and the intense opposition that have been alleged.[67]

The first, organized in 1839–40 at Newbury, Vermont, lasted only a few years but brought to its faculty the person who would symbolize Methodist theological education, John Dempster.[68] Appointed to teach theology, Dempster also did fund-raising and promotion for the institution and figured in its transformation into

The Methodist General Biblical Institute and its removal to Concord, New Hampshire, where it reopened with three faculty (among them Dempster) and seven students. The school did not prosper and was again moved, as part of the Centenary financial campaign of 1866, to become part of what would be Boston University. The same campaign launched another theological enterprise at Drew University in Madison, New Jersey. Dempster meanwhile had become instrumental in founding the second theological institution, Garrett Biblical Institute, which opened in 1854. Northwestern developed as an adjacent institution.[69]

In annexing seminary to university, these three set what would be an important Methodist pattern, a kind of institutionalization of Methodism's hymnic pair: "knowledge and vital piety."[70] Such a balance clearly informed the theological schools themselves. They would be institutions set in a university context but very clearly oriented to church and ministry. Revivals and study, prayer meetings and ministerial service went hand in hand. And students came to school already active in ministry, under appointment and under supervision in the fraternal apprenticeship; continued ministerial service during their program; and left with their diploma only to be subjected to the common regimen and hurdle of Methodist ministry, qualification under the standards of the course of study. (In 1883, the three seminaries of the MEC boasted a combined student population of 432. By contrast, the total number of preachers in the course of study was 2,550.)[71]

CONCLUSION

Seminary, like college, remained an option, an enhancement, an enrichment to ministry and ministerial preparation. Seminary complemented the course of study, some apprenticeship, and preparatory college work. So because it shared its work with other agencies (or later incorporated such agency into its own life), Methodist theological education acquired a distinctive character. David H. Kelsey recognizes that character in making the Methodist pattern one of three distinctive styles of theological education. Kelsey does so by distinguishing the kinds of communities theological schools endeavor to be: the first, a Catholic pattern, aiming to be congregation or church, a doxological community; the second, a Reformed model, adjoining training to church through apprenticeship to adept ministers, in more self-consciously academic community; the third, peculiarly Methodist, and elaborated under circuit and course of study conditions, having the loosest, adjunctive or extension, relation to church and congregation (but a close relation to connection) and reaching for missional community. So, for Methodists, he affirms "what constitutes the school community is its basic focus on equipping its students with professional ministerial skills and competencies."[72]

It had such a character, we would add, because it belonged within a fourfold pattern of Methodist ministerial education. Methodists, we conclude, did not succumb to Farley's clerical paradigm. More to the point they did not, at least in the nineteenth century, succumb to the seminary paradigm. Instead, the fourfold pattern oriented ministerial candidates and ministerial education toward the larger universe of education (collegiate); toward the collegium of ministers, the church's theological community (the conference course of study); toward the Methodist people and the populace generally whom Methodists sought to reach, a people who would also be invited into a discipleship of apprenticeship (fraternal); and toward serious engagement with scripture and with God in three persons, Father, Son, and Holy Spirit (seminary). So Methodists embraced, however imperfectly, what Glenn Miller has termed the four covenants of theological education—

> covenant with the educational world (collegiate);
>
> covenant with the theological community (conference course of study);
>
> covenant with the socio-cultural milieu (fraternal apprenticeship);
>
> covenant with God and Christ (seminary).[73]

PART 3
CONFERENCE AND CONNECTION

CHAPTER 8

METHODIST CONNECTIONALISM

Commentators on the American scene sometimes speak of churches as "connectional." With that term they differentiate denominations with strong corporate, centralized, or hierarchical authority systems from those with systems that are self-consciously or operationally congregational, independent, or free church.[1] Although the word lacks precision, it handily marks off episcopal and presbyterian from congregational polities. So the Roman Catholic, Lutheran, Episcopal, and Presbyterian churches are connectional, while Baptist, Congregational (UCC), Christian, and Mennonite churches are not.

Connectional communions, if Protestant, by and large derive from the Magisterial Reformation and often have enjoyed privileged status as state or established churches. By contrast, many, though not all, of the nonconnectional churches have roots in or affinities with the Radical Reformation and a free-church ecclesiology.[2] The latter fit comfortably within American social and legal patterns, where voluntarism, separation of church and state, localism, and individualism hold sway. The former have had episodic clashes with the courts or with popular opinion that presume that churches are local bodies "owned" by trustees. To a public, and even a membership, that "knows" religion to be voluntary, connectional churches have had to explain themselves. This burden has been borne most heavily by the Roman Catholics but virtually all connectional churches can recall some moment of conflict around connectionalism.[3] It is, perhaps, this angularity of connectionalism with respect to American values and practice that puts it forth as a term for distinction.

United Methodism and many other American Methodist communions would certainly place themselves among the connectional churches. Our connectionalism, most Methodists would know, does not derive, in the first instance, from the Magisterial

Reformation or privileged status as a state church. While United Methodism and other episcopal Methodisms do owe much to Anglicanism, it was the Wesleys—John and Charles, preeminently John—who defined our connectionalism.[4] And the term has a very special meaning for Methodists. Wesley's connectionalism was decidedly enriched by elements of Anglican ecclesiology and practice and by American organizational experience. For some, it is these later accretions that most define connectionalism—accretions like apportionments and corporate bureaucratic boards and agencies that spend the apportionments. And when Methodists reshape the church through mergers, these later accretions tend to preoccupy the architects of the new order, as Robert Sledge shows.[5]

Apportionments certainly vividly convey certain notions of connection and connectionalism. They image the claim, for every charge or church, that centralized authority, program, board, and agency make: the claim that comes as an "obligatory" budgetary asking. To the typical United Methodist, connectionalism means taxation, begrudged even for the pension and salary portions that she understands. Connectionalism has always had its fiscal dimension. Indeed, one might argue that connectionalism had its foundation in the collection of 1742 that inaugurated the class system and that being in connection with Mr. Wesley thereafter had its price. Certainly, early American Methodism depended entirely on the collections brought to quarterly conference, the quarterage equally shared among itinerants, presiding elders and bishops. Nor is this the first generation of Methodists who have chafed over collections that supported far-off ministries.

However, though impossible and unthinkable without its fiscal dimension, connectionalism has always meant more than sharing a financial burden and indeed has been bearable as a financial burden because it was embraced and indeed celebrated for its multiple values. To recall those multiple values helps us understand why we speak of ourselves as a connectional church and why we must, simply must, think of more than apportionments when we think *connection*.

The remainder of this chapter explores those multiple values. First, I look at the theological principles that undergird or are latent in Methodist connectionalism. Then, I explore Methodism as a changing covenant, noting the different forms or styles of connectionalism that have emerged over the history of American Methodism.

CONNECTIONALISM: A PRACTICAL DIVINITY

At its best, Methodist connectionalism has been more than a form of corporatism, more than a polity, more than a classificatory term. Connectionalism has been a Wesleyan precept, an ecclesial vision, a missional principle, a covenantal commitment, an ethic of equity and proportionality, a tactical stratagem, an elastic and evolving standard, a theology in praxis. Only if these richer meanings are grasped can one appreciate why we give them fiscal expression.

First, connectionalism is a Wesleyan precept, a first-order affirmation, an identifying statement, a recognition of Wesley's authority and that of those who have succeeded to his apostolic superintendency. To be Methodist has meant locating ourselves within a system that evolved around and through John and Charles Wesley. To be Methodist has meant singing our hymns, accepting our doctrines, reading our literature, knowing our story, recognizing the Methodist way as a full and adequate expression of the gospel witness, and accepting our place within a set of gracious relations. The latter—the acceptance of our acceptance into class, society, conference—gave connection its form by tying those fleeing the wrath to come into bond with one another and with Mr. Wesley. Americans first named themselves Methodist by precept, "Preachers in connexion with the Rev. Mr. Wesley."[6] Connectionalism makes a statement, a statement about authority, a statement about identity.

Second, connectionalism appeals to an ecclesial vision. Indeed, connectionalism represents a distinctive Methodist manner of being the church, a multifaceted, not simply political, mode of spirituality, unity, mission, governance, and fraternity that Methodists lived and operated better than they interpreted. Methodists came closest to articulating this vision in what they said, and more important, what they did, with conference. The same might be affirmed of the United Brethren and Evangelical Association.

In "The Large Minutes" Wesley recognized "Christian conference" as one of five "instituted" means of grace. That designation and the character of the other four—prayer, searching the Scriptures, the Lord's Supper, and fasting—suggest how very central to the Christian life and the Methodist movement Wesley placed *conference*. The reference here was not specifically to the annual or to the quarterly Methodist meetings or conferences but rather to the mode of engagement, discipline, purpose, and structure that they shared with all serious Christian encounter and that characterized all the Methodist structures. Conference was the way Wesley sought to conduct his affairs with his people.

The connection of preachers became a family headed and governed by John Wesley; it was a monasticlike order held together by affection, by common rules, by a shared mission, and by watchfulness of each member over one another; it functioned as a brotherhood of religious aspiration and song; it served as a quasi-professional society which concerned itself with the reception, training, credentialing, monitoring, and deployment of Wesley's lay preachers; it became a community of preachers whose commitment to the cause and to one another competed with all other relationships; it was a body whose resources provided for the wants and needs of its members. When one of its members died, it constituted the agency of memorial and memory. It served as the spiritual center of Methodism; it was multivalent.

This gracious vision, this notion of structure as grace, characterized all dimensions of connection, not just conference. The several structurings of the Wesleyan spirit had emerged in stages and in relation to entities named as the occasion suggested—societies, bands, classes, stewards, trustees, circuits, connection, conference, quarterly meeting. These were the spatial *and* temporal outworking of a set of religious impulses, never fully integrated into theory, but nevertheless characteristic of a peculiar Wesleyan style of organization, unity, mission, reform, spirituality. Constituting the Wesleyan economy, these features and practices expressed Wesleyan spiritual and religious emphases, the accent on the priesthood of all believers and the insistence on the mutual interdependence of all parts of the body of Christ. They cohered because Methodism cohered, because they belonged together in the religious experience and administrative style of John Wesley, because they possessed a center in him, because Wesley envisioned Methodism as an integrated connection.

Third, connectionalism actualizes a missional principle, a principle expressed perhaps best by itinerancy and general superintendency. Itinerancy has meant that the connection has first claim and it makes its claim on behalf of its purpose—namely, "to reform the Continent, and spread scriptural Holiness over these Lands."[7] Connectionalism and itinerancy constitute the church as missionary by nature. Ministers are sent, and they are sent where most needed. A certain amount of consultation always went on—even before the *Discipline* so required—but such conversation served to guide the appointing authority to the wisest decisions for the whole. So ministers are ordained in conference because the call is not to some locale but to mission, to the connection, to the world. The missional principle inherent in itinerancy belongs, however, to the whole people. We all are sent, commissioned, missionaries.

It is, perhaps, because connection is missional that we have had such difficulty in making it function as a formal ecclesiology. When we think ecclesiologically, we revert rather automatically to the language of the Articles of Religion—"a congregation of faithful men in which the pure Word of God is preached, and the Sacraments duly administered according to Christ's ordinance."[8] We do not mine our connectional pattern, practice, and heritage for their ecclesiological implications because we have other resources and because, if we do reflect about connection in other than polity terms, we do so soteriologically. Connection belongs for us to doctrines of salvation, the Christian life, mission—not to Christology or ecclesiology. If Methodists were to structure their theology systematically around the creed, discussion of connection might well come up, not when talking about Christ and his Body or in expounding upon the holy catholic church or the communion of saints, but rather when discussing forgiveness, resurrection and life everlasting. Connection might well be treated under soteriology.[9] It makes a statement about how we will effect the salvation of souls and the redemption of the world. It speaks about our mission.

Fourth, connectionalism expresses a covenant to carry through on the missional commitment. That covenant has often been spoken of in relation to those "in full connection," whose membership in conference put them in covenant relationship with one another, with all the people whom they committed to serve, and, of course, preeminently with God. But Methodism initially treated all members in the same fashion, holding them to their disciplinary obligations, expecting them to care for their neighbors, pressing on them the counsels of perfection, issuing tickets to those in good standing for love feast, and excluding those whose walk diverged from the Methodist way. Such a larger covenantal bond, in principle, continues to this day. It is one of the resources for our renewal.

Fifth, connectionalism, as a covenant, necessitated an ethic of equity and proportionality. That always took fiscal form. Those who had much paid more to support the shared ministry than those who had little. That sharing according to means is especially obvious in the early collections of American Methodism and is accessible today in the records of early conferences. For instance, in the early nineteenth century the Baltimore circuits constituted something like twelve percent of the Baltimore Conference but delivered more than twice that percentage in its collections. But equity and proportionality applied across the board, not just fiscally. In appointments, bishops and cabinets sent itinerants (who were paid equally) where the connection needed them. Today, when the reverse potential holds sway—the gifted are sent, not to where the need is greatest but to where the reward is greatest—it is worth recalling that salary differentials initially emerged so that persons with families and individuals sent to higher-cost urban areas would not suffer. Mark Wethington and Charles Zech show that financial policies and the ethic of connectionalism can go in quite different ways. Wethington urges United Methodism to bring its expenditures in line with its true mission.[10] Zech explores financial dissent from mission not understood or appreciated on a congregational level.[11]

Sixth, connectionalism was a tactical stratagem. It worked. Methodism—with its principles of itinerancy and connectionalism—elaborated a national, frontier-oriented ministry-delivery system.[12] With our orientation to the whole, to continent and world, we early adopted new mechanisms that took or brought the gospel to those who needed it. We pioneered, literally in forest and plain, but also with camp meetings, Sunday schools, newspapers, women's organizations, church extension, Freedmen's Aid, missionary organization, and eventually corporate structures. The stages in this pioneering are outlined below. Suffice it to say here that the boards and agencies and apportionments that now seem to some a burden, ironically, emerged initially and were enthusiastically embraced for their ability to carry the Methodist message. They connected gospel with need.

Seventh, as just implied, connectionalism has been an elastic and evolving principle and pattern. It has permitted, indeed needed, innovation, creativity, fresh starts, some break from the denominational norm. By such new ventures, connectionalism found new expressions of itself. John Vincent, for instance, experimented with Sunday schools in Chicago, his innovations earning him leadership of that enterprise for the denomination. He then guided us and much of evangelical Protestantism into the international lesson, training institutes for teachers, standard curricula—a new educational connectionalism. As his example indicates, innovation led to new commonalities and sharing, to new norms, to consolidations that served the whole. An indication of the value put on his efforts by the Connection was his election to the episcopacy.

This novelty-to-connectional-norm is strikingly exemplified in Methodist institution building. First with colleges, then with seminaries and universities, next with hospitals, then with homes, orphanages, camps, and retirement facilities, Methodist laity and clergy ventured daringly in new enterprise, confident that the institution would serve the connection and hopeful that the Methodist people shared the vision. Often the people did, as for instance did the visionaries and boosters who founded Methodist colleges, universities, and educational ministries. The story of risk-taking makes the narratives of our nationally renowned Methodist universities and hospitals truly inspiring, a claim made for Duke as for many of our schools. But the larger picture also includes false-starts, missteps, and failures. And today, some of United Methodism's greatest institutions seem less than attentive to their heritage and the constituency they were created to serve. Nevertheless, they have stood, if they do not always stand today, as icons of connectionalism.

Eighth, then, connectionalism rests on just such institutional outworkings of the faith. Connectionalism constitutes a Wesleyan theological style, a practical theology, an experimental divinity. As with other aspects of our praxis, connectionalism's theological dimension has not been sufficiently developed systematically and formally. Still, connectionalism has served to express, give shape to, choreograph, structure our notions of who we are, what we affirm, and what we are called upon to do. Connectionalism displays our theological system, a programmatic and operational statement of the Wesleyan theology of praxis. We live our theology. Connectionalism expresses it.

CONNECTIONALISM: A CHANGING COVENANT

In living their theology, Methodists gave connectionalism different form in different periods. They held themselves together, undertook their mission, defined their identity, communicated with one another and structured governance in styles appropriate for the day. Each style had its own grammar and rules touching form, substance, procedure, and structure. Seven different styles seem distinct enough to warrant mention and brief characterization. They are Wesleyan (episcopal), popular, voluntary, corporate, federal, professional, and postcorporate. I have arrayed them here in roughly chronological order, though the first two emerged at virtually the same time, the federal has been in the process of development over the whole of our history, and several others have also evolved over long periods of time. Further, they all live on. One style does not disappear after its period of dominance but instead remains to find altered place in the successive style. These seven styles, then, represent continuing options for Methodist self-understanding, definition of mission, and connectional shaping. They function as historical generalizations, as a typology, as models.

ORAL/AURAL CONNECTION

How, over the course of its history, did American Methodism connect itself? Of what did its connectionalism consist? How did it structure and display its theology?[13] In its first decades, American Methodism depended upon the connectional, missional, and disciplinary provisions that Wesley had made, provisions enriched and decorated after 1784 with the episcopal features taken over from Anglicanism.[14] Conferences, itinerating general superintendents, a national itinerant ministry, and classes for the Methodist peoples gave voice to Methodism's Arminian and gracious word. Connection had a preeminently *oral* character (a style every bit as characterizing of the United Brethren and Evangelical movements as of the Methodist Episcopal). Preaching mediated a Wesleyan reading of Scripture, hymns instilled our doctrines, class meetings translated promise into practice, love feasts expressed the joy that young and old, rich and poor, white and black, English and German had *heard* and *experienced*. Methodist connectionalism *voiced* itself and measured its effectiveness by the quality, intensity, and volume of its utterance. Did one preach with "liberty"? elicit tears? demand or produce shouts and cries? Virtually any journal or diary of this period attests and assesses this voiced connectionalism. For instance, Jesse Lee noted for late 1783 and for 1784:

> [Dec.] Saturday 31st, I preached at Mr. Spain's with great liberty to a good congregation, and the Spirit of the Lord came upon us, and we were bathed in tears—I wept—and so loud were the people's cries, that I could scarcely be heard, though I spoke very loud. I met the class—most of the members expressed a great desire for holiness of heart and life, and said they were determined to seek for perfect love.
>
> Sunday 1st of February, I preached at Coleman's with life and liberty, to a weeping congregation. When I met the class, we were highly favoured of the Lord, with a comfortable sense of his love shed abroad in our hearts; the brethren wept, and praise God together...
>
> Saturday 14th.—We held our quarterly meeting for Amerlia Circuit, at old father Patrick's—we had a good meeting for the first day. One Sunday morning we had a happy love feast; at which time I wept much, and prayed earnestly that the Lord would take every evil temper and every wrong desire out of my heart, and fill my soul with perfect love. I felt the pain of parting with my friends in that circuit.[15]

Preaching, singing, testifying—early Methodists voiced their love for one another and so quite literally heard themselves together. And in connecting themselves to one another and to their mission, they heeded the variety of rubrics and practices and offices that Wesley had given them. Connectionalism had a specifically Wesleyan grammar and vocabulary. And the rules were those taken over from Wesley and adjusted to the American scene and episcopal governance in what Americans called a *Discipline*. In its thirty pages or so,[16] Methodists found guidance for spreading scriptural holiness. So Methodism connected itself through an itinerant general superintendent (and specifically Asbury), annual and general conferences, and a nationally itinerant traveling ministry, (itinerants and presiding elders whom Asbury appointed across conference lines and on a national basis, reinforcing his own itinerant general superintendency with an itinerant general ministry). The ministry, the episcopacy, and the conferences constituted a particularly important and underappreciated connective voice. Methodism hung together in hearing a common Arminian gospel.

CONNECTED BY EVENT

A second form or style of connectionalism—dynamic, revivalistic large gatherings—also derives from the earliest phases of Methodism and is so intertwined with the first as to be infrequently distinguished. William Everett and Thomas Frank described it as popular public assembly.[17] This designation contextualizes early Methodist gatherings—crowds taken outside for preaching, the quarterly meeting and love feast, the camp meeting, the assemblages around conference—in the long tradition of Christian (and secular) popular gatherings. I prefer a more regional understanding, namely, as the religious counterpart to the event-based community of the upper south and lower middle states.[18] Like elections, musters, dances, horse races, Methodist community was event, defined less by space or place than time, something that occurred. Connectionalism *occurred—by appointment*. It was *event*.

Its event character was well captured by the admonition, "Don't disappointment an appointment!" Of the events constitutive of and connectional for Methodism, that most important and expressive was the quarterly meeting. In it the ecclesial dimensions of conference, outlined above, came most fully alive. One key to the quarterly conference's connective role came from an early change in design and length. *In 1780* the American conference recommended that quarterly meetings be a two-day affair and a weekend event, whenever possible.[19] From that point, the quarterly meeting quite literally brought the connection together, as this account indicates:

> I went next morning to brother Hobb's. Next day, was our quarterly-meeting, and a great many people came out; here I met brother Whatcoat and brother Morrell; one of them preached, and the other exhorted. Next day, brother Whatcoat opened the lovefeast; and after the bread and water were handed round, divers young converts spoke very feelingly of the goodness of God, and his dealings with their souls: we had a precious time. There was a large congregation, and one of our brethren preached, and the other gave an exhortation: we had a solemn, and I trust, a profitable time to many souls.[20]

The next account, for 1818, is particularly interesting because it comes from a British Methodist and describes the American quarterly meeting as something novel. The observer describes the whole event and captures a common feature of the quarterly meeting, namely, its gathering preachers, as well as people, from far and wide, connecting Methodists within and beyond the circuit.

> I had an opportunity of attending a quarterly meeting on Redding circuit; and as it was the first I ever attended, I will describe it as faithfully as I can. . . . The place where the quarterly meeting was held, was Weston. The Presiding elder was Ebenezer Washburn. The preacher in charge was James M. Smith, brother of Eben, and his colleague was Theodosius Clark. Beside these the other preachers present were Hawley Sandford, Samuel Bushnell, Cyrus Silliman, and Oliver Sykes. The exercises began at eleven o'clock on Saturday. The presiding elder preached the sermon, and the preacher in charge exhorted. After this a call was made to know how many persons wanted places of entertainment; that point being ascertained, another call was made to know who would entertain them. On this point there was no backwardness on the part of the people. One said, I can take *four*, another *six*, another *eight*, &c. The preacher then made the distribution accordingly. The members of the quarterly conference tarried for business, which was soon disposed of, as there were no

complaints, no appeals, no licenses to be renewed, no applications for recommendation for deacon's or elder's orders, or for admission into the traveling connection, no reports to be acted upon, and not a great deal of money to be divided among the preachers. The presiding elder had lost his horse, and a handsome sum was made up by the members of the conference toward purchasing another.

In the evening there was a general prayer-meeting at the Church. I did not enjoy it much. There was, according to my judgment at that time, too much noise by far. To some, probably, it was a good meeting, but my ears had not become accustomed to such lively singing and loud praying. The next morning the love-feast commenced at nine o'clock, and closed at half-past ten. After the love-feast the sacrament of the Lord's supper was administered. One probationer was publicly admitted into full membership; one who had been expelled was read out; and the bans of marriage published for one happy pair. The presiding elder preached again on Sabbath, and brother Sykes administered a startling exhortation, during the delivery of which some cried and screamed aloud. . . . I had never witnessed anything like such manifestations of feeling, either in London or elsewhere, and was therefore unprepared to judge whether the excitement proceeded from the depths of penitential distress, or from an ecstasy of joy. The sermons both days were sound, orthodox, and powerful; but the exhortations seemed to be based upon a principle which I had not, as yet, considered to be the correct one—namely, that the greatest noise does the greatest good.[21]

The event-based character of Methodist connectionalism displayed itself most extravagantly in the institution that housed warm-weather quarterly meetings, namely, the camp meeting. Camp meetings, as events, oriented the Methodist connection toward its mission, namely, redeeming individuals and society. This engagement with the world and the worldly gave them their storied character. Order seemed always perilous. But then conquests over the worldly, the melting of the stony heart, the conversion of the recalcitrant spouse seemed the more momentous. Camp meetings and even quarterly meetings as popular assembly gradually waned as Methodism put down roots in place, traded preaching houses for proper churches, stationed pastors, circumscribed community by space, and slowly transformed the camp meetings themselves into spas and the quarterly conference into a congregational business meeting. The holiness protests of the Civil War era endeavored to return Methodism, not just to perfection, but also to event-based community. So they created a new connection, a national organization devoted to camp meetings, the National Camp Meeting Association for the Promotion of Holiness. Recollections confirm the holiness assessment, making clear how important the institutions of quarterly and camp meetings had been and that they no longer retained that importance.

> The old quarterly meeting conferences and love-feasts! what was more characteristic of practical Methodism than they? The horses and carriages, and groups of men, women, and children plodding the highways on foot, for twenty miles or more, as on a holy pilgrimage; the assemblage of preachers, traveling and local, from all the neighboring appointments; the two days of preaching and exhorting, praying and praising; the powerful convictions, and more powerful conversions; and especially the Sunday morning love-feast, with its stirring testimonies and kindling songs; its tears and shoutings—how precious their reminiscences! Alas, for the changes which are coming over us![22]

What would connect Methodism—connect Methodists to one another, voice their common affirmations and give expression to their mission—as event (camp meetings) and orality (the shout) waned? Itineration increasingly occurred within conferences. Multiple bishops lacked the cohesive and connective power that had been Asbury's and the bishops soon began itinerating by region. General conferences, as we will note below, became, especially after the 1808 provisions for constitutional status and delegation, the important legislative connection.[23] But general conferences met only every four years. Who or what would connect, day-to-day, week-to-week, as had Asbury and his lieutenants? How would Methodism hear a common Word?

CONNECTION BY PRESS AND VOLUNTARY SOCIETY

The *printed page* gradually assumed the connecting, mediating, grace-delivering, missional role previously carried by the spoken word and *voluntary association* much of what had been provided through the large popular event. Under the leadership of Joshua Soule, book agent/editor (1816–1820), and particularly his successor, Nathan Bangs, the Book Concern became the most innovative and connecting force in Methodist life (a role clearly increasing in importance during the preceding decade). The publishing enterprise developed in a number of directions but none more important than the establishment of media for regular communication. *The Methodist Magazine* (1818) and the *Christian Advocate* (1826) provided the church with a clear voice, one that could convey across the connection complicated and complex ideas in coherent fashion, one that could get through with a uniform message despite itinerants' varying efforts in and enthusiasm for the published wares. The magazine for clergy, and more importantly the weekly paper for the whole church, focused the entire church's efforts for nurture and outreach. (The United Brethren published the *Zion's Advocate* from 1829 to 1831 and followed with the paper that lasted till union in 1946, *The Religious Telescope*, a biweekly and an English-language venture from the start. The Evangelical Association launched its journal, *Der Christliche Botschafter*, in 1836. Initially a monthly, it lasted till the union as a German paper but gradually was upstaged by the English paper, *Evangelical Messenger*, begun in 1848.) Connection came through paper, tract, hymnbook, discipline, and Bible. Every itinerant peddled for the Book Concern. Regional *Advocates*, their editors also elected by General Conference, came eventually to nuance Methodism's written word for our many audiences. Through them, Methodism transmitted its "word" to its many publics. Through them Methodists heard one another across the entire connection.

Also keeping Methodists, United Brethren, and Evangelicals on the *same page* were the new *voluntary* societies that focused the common faith toward concerted witness. The Missionary Society of the MEC was formed in 1819–1820 and the Sunday School Union in 1827 (counterpart organizations for the EA and UBC formed in 1838 and 1841 [missions] and roughly 1820 and 1835 [Sunday schools]). These two programmatic associations came to have great connective power across the Methodist peoples, drawing them into local and conference associations and drawing these associations into action on behalf of the cause. They prospered (as did voluntary movements across American Protestantism) because the church threw its shoulder behind this reorganization and because the new media from the Book Agency reinforced the organizational efforts. Popular literature, particularly for Sunday schools, made the program of the church available to every Methodist community.

Nathan Bangs saw the importance of these new institutions within the larger Methodist connectional system. After commenting on classes, stewards, exhorters, local preachers, itinerants, conferences, and bishops, he noted:

> In addition to this regular work, in which we behold a beautiful gradation of office and order, from the lowest to the highest, there is the book establishment, which has grown up with the growth of the church, and from which are issued a great variety of books on all branches of theological knowledge, suited to ministers of the gospel, including such as are suited to youth and children, as well as those for Sabbath schools, and a great number of tracts for gratuitous distribution by tract societies, Bibles and Testaments of various sizes, a quarterly review, and weekly religious papers. This establishment is conducted by a suitable number of agents and editors, who are elected by the General Conference, to which body they are responsible for their official conduct, and, in the interval of the General, the New York Annual Conference exercises a supervision of this estimable and highly useful establishment.
>
> In the last place, we may mention the Missionary Society of the Methodist Episcopal Church, which was organized in 1819, and has since spread itself, by means of auxiliary and branch societies, all over the United States and Territories, and, by means of its missionaries, has extended its operations among the aboriginal tribes of our wildernesses, among the descendants of Africa in the south, the new and poorer white settlements of our country, and also has sent its living heralds to Africa, to South America, and to the Oregon Territory. May its boundaries continually enlarge![24]

Both Sunday School and Missions channeled Methodist lay imagination and energies into the building of great networks of loosely-related societies, male and female, zealously committed to evangelization of youth and the "heathen." Methodists still connected with oral testimony and the written word but increasingly channeled their witness through societies with a missional or programmatic purpose. They did so by joining, and joining with others. The program of the church ran with *voluntary* societies.

PROGRAMMED AND CORPORATE CONNECTION

By the 1870s, such societies—then including, for the MEC, the Missionary Society, the Church Extension Society, the Board of Education, the Sunday-School Union, and the Tract Society, as well as the more loosely related Freemen's Aid Society and Book Concern, not to mention temperance organizations, preachers' aid societies, and various others—had become too successful, General Conferences thought, to be allowed to run themselves, to compete with one another, to remain self-governing. And so in 1872 and 1874, the MEC and MECS took action to make the boards elective and thereby accountable to General Conference, thus turning voluntary societies into national, corporate denominational boards. The magnitude of the change A. J. Kynett explained in relation to his own agency four years later, noting that previously:

> Although organized by order of the General Conference, the corporate body was, by the terms of its Constitution and Charter, a "Society" composed of such members and friends of the Church as might contribute to its funds the sum of one dollar per annum, or twenty dollars at one time. These had the legal right to elect its managers; but only such as could be present at the annual meetings in Philadelphia could share in the exercise of this right. It was, therefore, clearly beyond the reach of the Church government, and equally beyond the reach of all contributors to its funds, except only a portion of those who resided in the city of Philadelphia.[25]

The change effected in 1872 was structural and legal as indicated in the enabling report:

> The special Committee "appointed to consider and report concerning the relations of our various benevolent societies to the authorities of the Church, and whether any action is necessary, and if so what, to place them under the full control of the General Conference," has considered the subject stated.[26]

With respect to the Missionary Society incorporated by the New York Legislature, it noted, "To place this corporation under the control of the General Conference, it will be proper to procure an act of the Legislature to amend the charter so as to provide that the Board of Managers shall be elected by the General Conference."[27]

Connectionalism had, at last, a denominational-structural expression, *a corporate structure*. Agencies proved remarkable connectional delivery systems, serving missional, identity-providing, communicative, and governance functions. These roles, their operation on a national level, and their corporate structure imprinted itself as well downward through the denominations to conference and local levels. Local Methodists, conference committees, and national boards embraced corporate structure for what it facilitated—effective programs. And programs expressed Methodist ideals and ideas in missions, education, witness, and reform.

Until 1939 or so, the boards and agencies were surrounded with other bodies, also active on a national level, that bound the connection together and worked programmatically. These included, of course, the college or board of bishops and general conferences but also other national organizations (women's, youth, reform, temperance, and so forth), national papers, clergy magazines, the seminaries (particularly Boston for the North and Vanderbilt in the South), and the publishing houses.

FEDERAL-STYLE CONNECTION

Ironically, the union of 1939 (MEC, MECS, MPC), in the endeavor to create a more national church, tore much of the connectional fabric—dropping power and authority into jurisdictional conferences, including particularly the power to elect; making bishops regional, not general, superintendents;[28] bloating general conference by intention and regionalizing seminaries and other teaching agencies by accident; consolidating boards into even more significant bureaucracies and empowering those boards to select their professional staff. The net effect of these changes was to leave the agencies as *the* connecting power nationally *and* to undo the accountability that 1872 had achieved. In the union of 1939, rather than that of 1968, lie many of the concerns that trouble agency critics today.

The actions of 1939 also consolidated within Methodist *governance* patterns and practices that had long characterized American politics, in particular,

- —separation of powers and distinct legislative, executive and judicial agencies;
- —provision for judicial review;
- —delimitation of national authority and reservation of powers and prerogatives to regional bodies (jurisdiction and conference);
- —construal of Methodist conference structures at all levels as representative bodies and therefore to be inclusive of laity as well as clergy in accord with principles of equity and proportionality.

Concern to make Methodist polity behave according to American precept had begun when the first conferences convened. It had been made operative by Asbury's call for a general conference and elective episcopacy. It had found expression in the 1808 constitution and provision for delegated representation. It had animated the reform efforts of African Methodists, Republicans, Methodist Protestants, Wesleyans, Free Methodists, and Nazarenes. It had encouraged women and Blacks in their quest for representation, ordination, episcopal orders. Yet, while Methodists accommodated themselves to American political practice over the course of their history, only in 1939 did they accord American civil theory full disciplinary status. The reunion of 1939 made *federalism*, political rights, representation, separation of powers into Methodist principle. The linchpin in this federalism is the jurisdictional conference, an accommodation to Methodist racism and (Southern) regionalism.

PROFESSIONAL CONNECTIONS

Decisions in 1939 probably disguised, though by no means discouraged, another long-term trend in Methodist connectionalism, namely, its reliance upon professions, professionalism, and professional association. What 1939 disguised with the new jurisdictional structures and its ratification of full laity representation was the way in which conference structures, particularly annual conferences, had evolved into professional organizations.[29] Conferences increasingly functioned for clergy the way the state bar did for lawyers. They set standards, reviewed credentials, admitted to practice, guarded prerogative, pressed for compensation, contracted for health-care, maintained pensions, oversaw professional ethics. Conference professionalism, ironically, continued and grew even as conferences became representative and laity were included. Professional interests and concerns lodged themselves in boards or committees, particularly the Board of Ordained Ministry, executive sessions, and various clergy-only affairs.

Professionalism was by no means limited to conference. Indeed, many sectors of Methodist leadership gradually developed professional patterns. Sarah Sloan Kreutziger shows how, for instance, urban missions, settlement houses, urban volunteers, and deaconesses were affected by professionalism and how these prophetic actions yielded the new profession of social work.[30] Similarly, Robert C. Monk notes that campus chaplaincy gradually took on a professional aspect.[31] The same might even more readily be demonstrated for other forms of chaplaincy, military and hospital especially. Each role or vocational niche in the church seemed to acquire a professional aspect; persons in that calling gathered together in regional and national meetings; once organized, they sought denominational recognition or relation to some board or agency. New offices and old created new professional or quasi-professional associations, new networks that connected the church to offer or receive the special expertise and counsel. So various church professionals—Christian educators, lay workers, evangelists, missionaries, information officers, large-church pastors, musicians, fiscal officers, church and society persons, and, after 1968, council directors—gathered from across the country in annual professional or professional-like meetings. And what they sought was comparable to what other professional groupings sought when assembled—how to become more effective in the particular service to which they had been called, how to be better leaders, how to offer the church the guidance or counsel which they alone could give. The connection was well-served by such professionalism. *And* the church was connected through these professional networks, connected by the service they offered for the whole, connected in their very existence as the religious counterparts to the webs that held American society together, professional association.

The servant-character of Methodist guidance gives to Methodist professionalism, indeed to religious professionalism generally, an ambiguous, even self-contradictory, character. Professionals exert influence and lead out of expertise, specialized skills, privileged knowledge. The church at one moment honors and requires such human elitism and in the next moment reminds itself of the priesthood of all believers, the sinfulness of all, and the gifted nature of truly gracious leadership. Charisma and dependence upon God, not professionalism alone, it knows, characterize the true servants of God. Ambiguity, even conflict, over professional expertise lies under some of the strains in connectional affairs, beginning in the late nineteenth century and continuing throughout the twentieth century. Bradley Longfield has exposed some of the ambiguity over professionalism by exploring the tensions over Methodist higher education.[32] So does Monk, describing how campus ministry dealt with the growing professionalism of campus ministry, the eager advocacy and interventionism of student leadership, and the uncertainty by the church at large over both. The 1960s and 1970s brought campus ministry and its politicized connections; indeed, it brought Methodist connectionalism as a whole into crisis.

POSTCORPORATE CONNECTIONALISM

The three dominant styles of twentieth-century connectionalism—corporate, federal, and professional—are under siege. The attacks on agencies, centralized governance of any sort, and elitism are not Methodist-specific but are paralleled in other denominations, in large-scale business enterprise, and in government at all levels. Americans have apparently tired of working in, under, and through corporate, bureaucratic structures, tired of having the shots called at national or even conference headquarters, tired of kowtowing to experts. They protest in various ways—tax-payer revolts, rebellions against headquarters, voting the rascals out, dropping out.

Organizations respond by downsizing, outsourcing, applying the most current measures of influence and communication, and adopting total quality management, *Good to Great* counsel, or whatever touted by the organizational guru of the day—regulation, grant making, franchising, consulting, credentialing—tactics that do work, at least in the short run. Virtually every one of these tactics has found its way into denominational repertoire. So United Methodists find themselves offered various franchise opportunities by boards and agencies, Disciple Bible Study being the most dramatic instance. The few successful ventures in franchising, grant making, consulting do not "redeem" the boards and agencies but instead seem to dissociate themselves from agency programs and so undercut rather than bolster goodwill toward the connectional structures.[33] And other tactics in organizational vogue—particularly those more controlling, intrusive, accountability-prepossessed and regulatory—do not meet with such favor. Indeed, they both foster and function with an enervating suspicion. Their efforts to make the system work and to command the funds necessary for effective functioning are met with hostility and suspicion. And, boards, committees, commissions, task forces function in an atmosphere where accountability is the first order of business, where every slate is immediately assessed for its representativeness, where suspicion reigns that money is not being equitably or properly expended, where leadership is experienced only as power. Balkanization reigns in church, as in American politics.

Disquiet over United Methodist agencies, then, belongs within the larger cultural traumas and the desperate quest for new modalities of community, cooperation, labor, and governance. In finding such new modalities of connection, Methodists can and should lead. It is a Methodist specialty. And Methodists are leading. All around are experiments in connection—in the caucuses, in media ministries, in new and old efforts at discipleship, in listening groups, in Council of Bishops' initiatives, in Disciple Bible studies, or Emmaus Walks. Such experiments have not solidified into a new paradigm of connection. Instead, what haunts connectional gatherings and efforts to put up new connectional fabric are calls for *accountability* and hermeneutics of suspicion. Any new ventures now face the immediate challenge as to whether all constituencies have been properly represented. Reformers find it difficult to move through and beyond the politics of accountability to discerning, much less addressing, the missional ends which connection should serve. To term these quests for connection a new style, overstates, then, their functionality and acceptance. Our category "postcorporate connectionalism" indicates a point of departure rather than an arrival.

Conclusion

Methodism behaves in certain ways like other connectional churches. Shared, for instance, are the crises, uncertainties, and inner turmoil outlined immediately above as "postcorporate connectionalism." Methodism, however, has, at least in its better historical moments, understood its connectionalism as something different than just a polity classification, something more than just a strong corporate, centralized, or hierarchical authority system, something complex and variegated.

The second part of this chapter explored those multiple values, identifying theological principles that undergird or are latent in Methodist connectionalism. Connectionalism has been, I suggested, a Wesleyan precept, an ecclesial vision, a missional principle, a covenantal commitment, an ethic of equity and proportionality, a tactical stratagem, an elastic and evolving standard, a theology in praxis.

In the last section, I treated Methodism as a changing covenant, noting the different forms or styles of connectionalism that have emerged over the history of American Methodism. Seven forms of connectionalism, I argue, each with its distinctive organizational style, have emerged and, for their day and for the Methodism of their day, have been judged as appropriate measures in enunciating and achieving corporate purposes:

Wesleyan (episcopal)	oral/aural
popular	event
voluntary	printed page
corporate	program
professional	guidance
federal	governance
postcorporate	accountability

In its own way, each style sought to define corporate praxis (a piety and ecclesiology), to provide mechanisms for collective hearing (our doctrine), to delineate an organizational language (an ecclesial vision), to orient Methodists toward goals (a mission), and to call forth effort (covenant and ethic). Some of these served better and more faithfully as theology in practice, as practical divinity, than others. And none, at this point, seems quite adequate, including particularly the style we have awkwardly labeled *postcorporate*.

As we think and act ourselves toward a new vision for United Methodism, understanding the rich potential in our connectionalism might help us get our bearings.

CHAPTER 9

METHODIST CREATION OF THE DENOMINATION

The great iron wheel in the system is itinerancy, and truly it grinds some of us most tremendously; the brazen wheel, attached and kept in motion by the former, is the local ministry; the silver wheel, the class leaders; the golden wheel, the doctrine and discipline of the church, in full and successful operation. Now, sir, it is evident that the entire movement depends upon keeping the great iron wheel of itinerancy constantly and rapidly rolling round. But, to be more specific, and to make an application of this figure to American Methodism. Let us carefully note the admirable and astounding movements of this wonderful machine. You will perceive there are "wheels within wheels." First, there is the great outer wheel of episcopacy, which accomplishes its entire revolution once in four years. To this there are attached twenty-eight smaller wheels, styled annual conferences, moving around once a year; to these are attached one hundred wheels, designated presiding elders, moving twelve hundred other wheels, termed quarterly conferences, every three months; to these are attached four thousand wheels, styled traveling preachers, moving round once a month, and communicating motion to thirty thousand wheels, called class leaders, moving round once a week, and who, in turn, being attached to between seven and eight hundred thousand wheels, called members, give a sufficient impulse to whirl them round everyday. O, sir, what a machine is this! This is the machine of Archimedes only dreamed; this is the machine destined, under God, to move the world, to turn it upside down.[1]

The genius of the Methodist organization has often been remarked. George Cookman in the above passage employed the vision of Ezekiel as a figure to suggest the heavenly design of its operation. Abel Stevens, seeing the danger of barbarism in the spread of population beyond the reaches of religious influence, conceived of Methodism as a "religious system, energetic, migratory, 'itinerant,' extempore, like the population itself" necessary for and "providentially designed" for the United States.[2] This theme expanded and secularized received scholarly affirmation by William Warren Sweet in his works on Methodism and American religion. Methodist organization has been celebrated; it has also had its detractors—prophetic voices from within, some of whom exited in the name of republicanism or antislavery, and critics from without. One such critic, the Baptist J. R. Graves, organized his reflections under Cookman's image of *The Great Iron Wheel*. Its machinelike characteristics impressed Graves as "a crushing military *despotism*," "the very system of the Jesuits of Rome," "Antichrist," "spiritual tyranny," "clerical despotism," a threat to free institutions.[3]

It is not the purpose of this chapter to review or resolve the debates over the character, efficiency, methods, leadership, and impact of Methodist organization that have raged from the earliest days of British Methodism. Rather, the purpose of this chapter is to pursue a point implicit in the fact and substance of the discussion about Methodist polity. The thesis expressed in the title is that the distinctive form of the church that we know as the American denomination and designate as "denominationalism" is deeply indebted to Methodism. The principle of organization in Methodism has become the principle of denominationalism. And Methodism was the religious movement that first fully, effectively, and nationally exemplified that principle. Methodism, to borrow (with alteration) H. Richard Niebuhr's phrase, was a significant social source of denominationalism. This thesis will have to be qualified in a number of important respects, Methodism's borrowings acknowledged, the role of other denominations and religious movements admitted, and the place of denominationalism in larger societal and intellectual transformations noted. The qualifications should serve to suggest the complexity of the history of denominationalism and to raise questions about the ethical and sociological reductionism that has allowed to stand as explanation of denominationalism. The thesis when appropriately qualified should suggest that the form (as well as the idea) of denominationalism is rooted in vital religiosity. Denominationalism as a form of the church is not simply the result of the several divisive compromises of the Christian gospel.[4]

DENOMINATIONALISM AS A PROBLEM

A contemporary of the maturity of American denominationalism, Robert Baird, celebrated its basic principle. The voluntary principle, he suggested, evoked Americans' "energy, self-reliance, and enterprise in the cause of religion."[5] More than adequate to the challenge posed by disestablishment and an expanding population, it betrayed the real genius of free enterprise, the American (Anglo-Saxon) peoples and American religion and bespoke the will (hence voluntarism) of Americans to make religious freedom work for the kingdom of God. That it produced separate denominations was not disturbing because the denominations, at least the evangelical denominations, were unified in a common mission.

Baird's treatment epitomizes a basic strength, but perhaps also a weakness, in analyses of denominationalism. Baird looked through the denominations and denominationalism to more fundamental realities—evangelicalism, mission, voluntarism, religious freedom. Many of the most penetrating discussions of American religious institutions have shared this trait; they have looked through or around denominationalism to what appeared most basic. Hence the best treatments of religious structures are to be found in works on evangelicalism, missions, voluntarism, religious freedom, toleration, religious pluralism, separation of church and state, religion and the nation. There are, of course, no want of studies of particular denominations and ample numbers of works treating the denominations together. But Americans have been strangely reluctant to look directly at what is celebrated frequently in passing, the denominational form of the church. This reluctance must be attributable, at least in part, to a Christian conscience uneasy about divisions in the body of Christ. This uneasiness, expressed most eloquently in H. Richard Niebuhr's *The Social Sources of Denominationalism*, has occasioned the search for unitive realities and unwillingness to speak about what is experienced on a day-to-day basis. Denominationalism has been left to the sociologists, whose ideal types (suggestive as they are) do not exhaust what historians and members of denominations ought to know about the phenomenon.

Denominationalism as a Form of the Church

The denomination and denominationalism, dynamic religious structures and processes, have altered considerably in the several centuries during which the term *denomination* was being employed to designate religious movements. For that reason it is important to specify that denominationalism will be used for the pattern of interinstitutional and intrainstitutional structures, processes and relations that existed among mainstream American Protestants in the nineteenth century. That delimitation, while arbitrary, provides the term with specific social meaning and is necessary for discussion of the origins and character of denominationalism.

It must be acknowledged at the outset that to unravel the thread of denominationalism is to separate it from the fabric into which it was woven and thereby to remove it from that to which it belongs and that gives it shape, purpose, and significance. To affirm this is to acknowledge the value of the treatments of denominationalism under the rubrics mentioned above. Denominationalism is a form of the church possible in a society characterized by toleration or at least the spirit of tolerance, laws and customs supportive of religious liberty and *de facto* (if not legal) disestablishment. Denominationalism, then, has to be understood in relation to the sagas of religious liberty, the democratic state, and bourgeois society. Quite clearly, Baptists, Quakers, and other Dissenting groups in their advocacy of and embodiment of religious freedom were social sources of denominationalism.[6] So too the struggles in this direction within other religious groups in several colonies were part of the social origins of denominationalism. The development and appropriation of the voluntary form of the church proved an essential ingredient, perhaps a precondition of denominationalism.

Histories conceived under the several rubrics related to freedom, therefore, describe important dimensions of the beginnings of denominationalism. They point to denominationalism's place within the larger story of Western voluntarism, societal differentiation, organizational specialization, and secularization. The denomination belongs within the array of associations—the free and often competitive institutions (essential to bourgeois, democratic society)—upon which Alexis de Tocqueville, William Ellery Channing, Ralph Waldo Emerson, and others commented. Association seemed the principle of democracy and of American society. Association in political life and association in civil (and religious) life were mutually reinforcing.[7]

Denominationalism, then, is to be seen as a form of the church adjusted to the realities of American society. It clearly is an adjustment to the realities of religious pluralism and voluntarism that characterized American society. The most important descriptions of denominationalism have been sketched against this background. Among the most perceptive remains Sidney Mead's depiction. It is worth quoting at some length:

> The denomination is the organizational form which the free churches have accepted and assumed. It evolved in the United States during the complex and peculiar period between the Revolution and the Civil War.
>
> The denomination, unlike the traditional forms of the church, is not primarily confessional, and it is certainly not territorial. Rather it is purposive..... A church as church has no legal existence in the United States.... Neither is the denomination a sect in a traditional sense and certainly not in the most common sense of a dissenting body in relationship to an established church. It is, rather, a voluntary association of like-hearted and like-minded individuals, who are united on the basis of common beliefs for the purpose of accomplishing tangible and defined objectives. One of the primary objectives is the propagation of its point of view.[8]

Mead elaborated the meaning of this purposive form of the church by noting a number of traits characteristic of denominations. They are (1) sectarian, primitivistic, and antihistorical; (2) voluntaristic, self-promotional, and activistic; (3) missionary; (4) revivalistic and therefore oversimplifying, Arminian, pragmatic, emotional, egalitarian, and anti-intellectual; (5) antirational (anti-Enlightenment); and (6) competitive.[9]

Second to its purposiveness is another feature of denominationalism to which Winthrop Hudson as well as Mead drew attention.

Denominationalism is predicated upon an understanding of the church as pluralistic yet united and in a sense ecumenical. "Denominationalism," Hudson suggested, "is the opposite of sectarianism."

> The word "denomination" implies that the group referred to is but one member of a larger group, called or denominated by a particular name. The basic contention of the denominational theory of the church is that the true church is not to be identified in any exclusive sense with any particular ecclesiastical institution. The outward forms of worship and organization are at best but differing attempts to give visible expression to the life of the church in the life of the world. No denomination claims to represent the whole church of Christ. No denomination claims that all other churches are false churches. No denomination claims that all members of society should incorporate within its own membership. No denomination claims that the whole of society and the state should submit to its ecclesiastical regulations. Yet all denominations recognize their responsibility for the whole of society and they expect to cooperate in freedom and mutual respect with other denominations in discharging that responsibility.[10]

Never adequately articulated but implicit in the self-understanding of denominations was the recognition that there was a unity of the church that transcended the observable disunity. The disunity, an inevitable result of human diversity, did not undermine unity on essentials, on fundamentals. It did not mean that individual denominations were schisms (as Niebuhr's analysis would suggest). It did mean that unity was not to be achieved through coercion. And, most important, it meant that the true church and its unity were not to be fully manifested in human institutions.[11] Denominationalism was a witness to the true church by its pointing beyond the divisions in human structuring of the church to the shared unity.

The denomination in the view of Mead and Hudson is a purposive structure and conception of the church implicitly unitive or ecumenical in character. A third feature of denominationalism related its purposive character to this wider vision. The denomination was instrumental to the Protestant endeavor to Christianize society—to Christianize the new Republic and eventually also the world. The several Protestant (and specifically evangelical

Protestant) denominations collaborated in working to build a Christian commonwealth in preparation for the coming of Christ's kingdom. In some instances this common task motivated and expressed itself in cooperative endeavor. The various voluntary societies—Bible tract, Sunday school, reform societies—were the most obvious reflections of the common end. As frequently, the common end was sought through competition, competition among the denominations and competition of denominations with the voluntary societies. The competitiveness has sometimes obscured the common end. But commentators on American religion from Robert Baird to H. Richard Niebuhr, James Maclear, Elwyn Smith, Martin Marty, Robert Handy, George Marsden, Mark Noll, and others have described the common efforts to erect a Christian (Evangelical Protestant) society.[12]

As Baird recognized in dividing American religion into Evangelical and non-Evangelical denominations, and as more recent commentators have recognized in analyzing the building of a Christian empire (society, establishment, kingdom), this unitive end of the denominations permitted and elicited degrees of participation. Religious, ethnic, racial, and regional factors affected the level of participation. Roman Catholics, Jews, and Unitarians were by definition and hostility excluded. Lutheran and certain Reformed bodies allowed ethnic and theological factors to regulate the degree of their participation. Episcopalians, Presbyterians, Methodists, and Baptists struggled over the implications of participation for tradition, theology, and polity. Black denominations, while animated by the passions of the Christianization of society, were by racial exigencies and racial prejudice excluded from full participation. Mormons, millenarian groups, and utopians defined their Christian societies over against the dominant society. Slavery and sectionalism finally wrought divisions within denominations and in the nation as a whole in the labor for a Christian empire. But when the spectrum of participation in the cause of building a Christian America is recognized, the fact remains that the dominant or normative conception of the denomination was this instrumental one. The denominations (Evangelical) singly and collectively were means, that is, instruments, for the Christianization of society and the building of the kingdom of God.

H. Richard Niebuhr in *The Kingdom of God in America* recognized the dynamism, unity, and force in American religion. In emendation of his stance in *The Social Sources of Denominationalism* he analyzed the ideal of the kingdom of God on earth, showing it to have been a central preoccupation of American religious movements. But he continued to view the denominations as the halting places, the forms for preserving, the institutionalizations of these dynamic processes. Denominationalism marked the end of the dynamic movements in the church. It was the end in the sense that in attempting to conserve and preserve, leaders created institutions which killed the spirit of the movements. It was an end in the sense that the denomination became an end in itself, thus displacing with a static structure the dynamic ideal of the kingdom of God.[13]

Niebuhr's conception is at variance with the view just set forth of the denominations as purposive voluntary associations, possessed of a vision of their place in a wider Christian unity and instrumental to the Kingdom of God and to the Christianization of society. Niebuhr was probably right in viewing the denominations as eventually becoming ends in themselves. The question is whether they were intrinsically the death of Christian vitality; or more to the point, perhaps, whether they are by definition static, conservative, lifeless. Much depends upon the attitude held toward institutions and upon at what point in the life of the several movements they are to be defined as denominations (only in their mature late nineteenth- or early twentieth-century form or in their more dynamic phases). And this is related to the inevitability of the sect-to-denomination process that Niebuhr posited.[14]

These broad theoretical and historical questions cannot be addressed directly here. What can be investigated is the appropriateness of the view here set forth to the development of one denomination, The Methodist Episcopal Church (a major contributing stream to successor denominations, The Methodist Church and The United Methodist Church). What can also be shown is how the vitality of institutional development within Methodism served as a model for the denomination-building process in other religious movements. Implicitly, then, Niebuhr is answered by showing Methodism in its dynamic phases to have been a social source of denominationalism.

METHODISM AS A SOCIAL SOURCE OF DENOMINATIONALISM

The Evangelical denomination in early nineteenth-century America was, as we have suggested, a purposive voluntary association, possessed of a vision of its place in a wider Christian unity and structured as an instrument for bringing in the kingdom of God and Christianizing society. The denomination was then a missionary structure and by intention national in its aspirations. Where were its origins, its fabricators, its early manifestations? They were, as the second section above indicated, imbedded in the American and European experience, in the thrust of various religious movements, in the fact of pluralism, and in the conditions of religious freedom and disestablishment. To single out one religious movement as a social source of denominationalism is only to suggest a prevalence within it of influences from other religious movements and of trends affecting various facets of American and European society. To argue that Methodism was a social source of denominationalism is only to suggest that Methodism was representative, an early embodiment, an available model.

Methodism's role as exemplar of the purposive, ecumenical, and instrumental church structure derived from the genius of John Wesley; from the ambiguous status of early Methodism; from the new meaning conferred on Methodist structures and activities by its transference to the American environment where its Anglican context and ecclesiology were largely lost; and from its very successes. These factors and certain strategic and ethnic ones were to make it, rather than Moravianism, a similar embodiment of the denominational principles and also a forceful mediator of Pietism's practical (purposive), ecumenical, and reforming (instrumental) impulses, the effective transmitter of denominational form of the church.

What was Methodism's genius? It was largely the genius of Wesley.[15] By upbringing, education, inclination, and theology John Wesley was, as Frank Baker has argued, a High Church Anglican, an early bigot for the Church of England, whose later comprehensiveness represented an appropriation of that other spirit of the Anglican Church.[16] Wesley's experientially and theologically derived eclecticism, his maturation as a folk theologian,[17] or catholic theologian[18] did not dissolve Wesley's dedication to the church or his resolve to maintain the evolving Methodist connection within it. By principle and prejudice averse to falling in with the Dissenters, Wesley through the force of his own indomitable will and a richly textured Evangelical-Anglicanism kept his connection in a formally and legally anomalous position. Methodism was not a new church; nor was it to be during Wesley's lifetime one of the denominations within Nonconformity. Poised between theologically and legally constituted systems of ecclesiastical authority, the Methodist structures could, like the Pietist structures that preceded them, be governed by their purposes. Methodism was purposive, a leaven within the Anglican Church, a movement to spread scriptural holiness across the land. "The chief design of His providence in sending us out is, undoubtedly, to quicken our brethren."[19] "We look upon the Methodists," Wesley affirmed, "not as any particular party . . . but as living witnesses, in and to every party, of that Christianity which we preach."[20]

Affirming Methodists to be distinguished only in their commitment to "the common principles of Christianity" (not by opinions, emphasized phrases or parts of religion, or "actions, customs or usages, of an indifferent nature"),[21] Wesley asserted:

> By these marks, by these fruits of a living faith, do we labour to distinguish ourselves from the unbelieving world, from all those whose minds or lives are not according to the Gospel of Christ. But from real Christians, of whatsoever denomination they be, we earnestly desire not to be distinguished at all, not from any who sincerely follow after what my Father which is in heaven, the same is my brother, and sister, and mother. And I beseech you, brethren, by the mercies of God, that we be in no wise divided among ourselves. Is thy heart right, as my heart is with thine? I ask no farther questions. If it be, give me thy hand.[22]

Methodism was a purposive religious society, a people, dedicated to the spread of scriptural holiness as a way of life and it was, at least by its own intentions, unitive in character. Its structures and disciplines were instrumental to these ends. Wesley was candid on this point.

> What is the end of all ecclesiastical order? Is it not to bring souls from the power of Satan to God, and to build them up in His fear

and love? Order, then, is so far valuable as it answers these ends; and if it answers them not, it is nothing worth.[23]

Wesley's understanding of the development of Methodism betrays this instrumental or pragmatic view of order. Methodists, he insisted,

> had not the least expectation, at first, of any thing like what has since followed . . . no previous design or plan at all; but every thing arose just as the occasion offered. They saw or felt some impending or pressing evil, or some good end necessary to be pursued. And many times they fell unawares on the very thing which secured the good, or removed the evil. At other times, they consulted on the most probable means, following only common sense and Scripture: Though they generally found, in looking back, something in Christian antiquity likewise, very nearly parallel thereto.[24]

Also reflective of Wesley's instrumental view of order or structure was his willingness to borrow what seemed to work—classes, bands, love feasts, covenant services, watch nights. The efforts to save souls produced a remarkable freedom over the structuring of the religious life.

Expediency, "inspired practical improvisation," common sense, pragmatism, eclectic borrowing, the ability to recognize the general applicability of a successful local experiment, the willingness to be tutored or corrected by experience and the Holy Spirit Wesley made the Methodist way.[25] His experimental approach to structure, appropriate to the experiential mood of the eighteenth century, evidenced itself throughout the development and records of Methodism. Wesley structured Methodism instrumentally to its evangelical and unitive purposes. The bands, classes, and societies; itinerancy, circuits and conferences; rules, directions, minutes, sermons, *Notes upon the New Testament*; the preachers and leaders—the social network that comprised the Methodist connexion—was, as Wesley declared in the "Large Minutes," "to reform the nation and to spread scriptural holiness over the land."[26]

The Wesleys, John and especially Charles, sought to keep the British Methodist movement within the Church of England and to prevent it from separating into a distinct denomination or church.

Yet in its national aspirations and missionary style, in that its structures were instrumental to its unitive purposes, Methodism embodied what was to become the denominational principle. Of course, British Methodism's denominationalism was in the very real sense suspended. Wesley's churchmanship kept the connexion from perceiving itself and being perceived as a new form of the church, the denomination. However, as my former colleague Richard Heitzenrater has shown, despite Wesley's rhetorical commitment to remaining within the Church of England, his many initiatives in providing missional infrastructure to the movement oriented Methodism toward separation and independence.[27]

By Wesley's death, when the connexion was in the process of becoming independent, the organizational and missional principles constitutive of the denomination would be appropriated by the Dissenting denominations in England and by other Protestant denominations in America. The common early nineteenth-century commitment to evangelization and appropriation of missionary structures have obscured the development of denominationalism and Methodism's contribution thereunto. It appears that Methodism's denominationalism consisted in its break with the Church of England and reconstitution as an independent body. The survival after the founder's death, accompanied by the agonies over authority, ordination, licensing, and sacraments make this reading plausible and in one sense accurate. However, British Methodism could not be fully a denomination until the structural principles it embodied were allowed to become fully determinative of the connexion. This could happen when British Methodists gave up on efforts to remain part of the Church of England. But the break alone, and legal standing under appropriate English laws, would have made Methodism a denomination in name only. Wesley had already given it its denominational style and substance, the inner missional structuring that would characterize nineteenth-century denominationalism.

By the same token the Dissenting denominations may appear to have been denominations for the duration of the eighteenth century. They bore that name and standing under the Toleration Acts. Were they not denominations? By the criteria established here—purposive, unitive, instrumental, national, missionary organization—they were, in fact, not. Until midcentury the primary institutions in Dissent were Dissenting (rather than missionally denominational) and the Presbyterians, Congregationalists, and General and Particular Baptists were names, denominations, given to ministers and congregations loosely bound by history, belief, and practice. The primary self-identification was that of Dissenter.[28] Internal structuring of Congregationalism gathered momentum in response to the growth of rational and heterodox currents in Dissent in the 1730s. It was not until evangelicalism impacted itself upon both Congregationalists and Particular and General Baptists in the final third of the century, that they developed structures or recast structures—ministerial associations and academies initially—for purposes of self-propagation and mission. Their maturity as denominations was as evangelical denominations, purposive in character, whose unitive and missionary intentions manifested themselves in the work of the founders of the modern missionary movement, William Carey and company. Whether Baptists, Congregationalists, and Anglicans borrowed missionary, purposive denominational form from Methodism is difficult to show. What can be said is that the evangelicalism that through the agency of Wesley informed the organization of Methodism came by the end of the eighteenth century to inform Baptists and Congregationalists as well. The Presbyterian interest languished until revivified by Scottish missions in the South. The Unitarians who emerged out of Presbyterian, Congregationalist, Baptist, and Anglican ranks began the process of organization in the 1790s. In their own way—hardly evangelical—they developed structures for growth and elaborated a theology in its own terms unitive that together provided them the denominationalism necessary for the stabilization of their cause.[29]

Methodism's contribution to denominationalism proved ironical. Wesley's efforts prevented it from falling in with the Dissenters and becoming a Dissenting denomination. Yet the principles in the Methodist movement—what, among other factors, assured its growth and what fellow Methodist but Calvinist George Whitefield and company lacked—were to become the essentials in Dissenting denominationalism. While critical of the Methodists for the bulk of the century, the Dissenters came eventually to emulate them. A movement that at all costs avoided becoming a denomination was, despite its best efforts, to be the quintessential one, not in the details of its polity or ecclesiology but in the principles that, in fact, underlay them. Methodism, which has probably not received its proper recognition as a preliminary phase of the missionary movement, has also lacked credit for its contribution to denominationalism. Priority has been given to those who possessed the name—denomination—rather than to the movement within which the denominational principles were elaborated.

DENOMINATIONALISM AND AMERICAN METHODISM

The Methodist contribution to American denominationalism is not totally unacknowledged. Martin Marty in *Righteous Empire* comes close to crediting Methodists with the most basic change "in the administrative side of Christian church life in fourteen hundred years."[30] William Warren Sweet argued that Methodists were the first to organize nationally.[31] The overall importance and influence of Methodism has driven some to speak of the nineteenth century as the "Methodist Age" or to credit Methodists along with other popular denominations in the democratization of American Christianity.[32] The "stirrings" toward denominationalism within the Wesleyan movement noticed by Marty, the example of Methodist organization nationally cited by Sweet, and the Methodist mediation of revivalistic, Arminian, practical, emotional, lay Christianity analyzed by Hudson suggests a large but diffuse Methodist contribution to denominationalism (of which the stirrings, organization, and religiosity are expressions) that Methodism witnessed to most effectively in America. Methodists embodied the principle that the church or denomination (church order, church structure, polity, the church as a visible reality) must be purposive, instrumental, missionary, and though in aspiration national yet cognizant of sharing that aspiration with other denominations. The principle implied that the church order did not emanate from God, nor by divine constitution, nor by Scriptural dictate. It was a human creation. Of course, humanity created order in response to the guidance of the Holy Spirit, but nevertheless by an ordering of the church achieved in the present and designed to suit its activity. This denominational principle required *de facto* surrender of claims to be *the one, true* church—to be the church continuous with the early church or to be the only church exemplificative of the New Testament. Methodism by the accidents of its creation and implantation in America witnessed to this principle.

Methodism witnessed to this principle less ambiguously, indeed, much clearer in America than it had in England, where it functioned as *ecclesiola in ecclesia*; sought to reform, not leave, the Church of England; and did not in Wesley's lifetime surrender the claims to be part of "the church." In America, especially after Independence, ongoing disestablishments, the agony of the transfer of Wesley's authority, and the establishment of an independent Methodist Episcopal Church, the movement became clearly what one critic quoting Coke called a "new plan." Indeed, the critics perhaps best saw Methodism's strange role. From the Episcopalian John Kewley in the early nineteenth century to the Landmark Baptist J. R. Graves in the latter part of the century, opponents denounced Methodism as "merely a human device."[33] Graves put it crassly:

> Were you asked if the economy of the Christian Church is of divine origin and appointment, you, in common with every other Christian, would answer, most emphatically, YES.... Why, sir, in what light would a Protestant Christian be regarded in our day, who held and taught that the Christian Church was merely a human institution—a man-invented society or organization, like the institutions of Odd Fellowship or Masonry, and like them, subject to all the modifications of man's ever fluctuating and capricious fancy! Would not Christendom unite in a holy crusade against the sentiment? ...
>
> Now, Methodism, considered as a church or society, is purely and clearly of *human origin* and device, and of a *very recent date*—indeed, it cannot boast of as illustrious a founder as Masonry, nor of as high antiquity, by some thousands of years. Solomon is claimed (I do not pretend to say it,) as the inventor of Masonry, and the cause of its organization, the building of the Temple; while John Wesley, *when an unconverted* man, is the boasted founder of Methodism, and the cause of *its* being organized into a Church was the *Revolutionary war*!![34]

Methodists could and would defend their episcopacy, church order, and theology, invoking providence and the Spirit. Not being the only imitators of the primitive church, experiencing their growth before American eyes, and making their pragmatic changes in Wesley's structures, Methodists were not in a good position to claim to be the unchanged church of the New Testament. They did, in the main, remain loyal to Wesley. But Wesley himself had charged them to chart their own purposive course: "They are now at full liberty simply to follow the Scriptures and the Primitive Church. And we judge it best that they should stand fast in that liberty where with God has so strangely made them free."[35] That freedom American Methodists had exercised and continued to exercise. From what Frederick Norwood calls its "lay beginnings,"[36] through the labors of Wesley's missionaries; through the early phases of organization by Rankin, Asbury, and others; through the gradual elaboration of conference structures; through the trials of the Revolution; through Wesley's ordinations, abridged Articles of Religion, revised *Sunday Service*, and appointment of Coke and Asbury as joint superintendents, "Methodists stumbled their way from society to church."[37]

With John Wesley's blessing and provision of basic documents, The Methodist Episcopal Church in a Christmas Conference of 1784 constituted itself a distinct denomination. And considerable formation lay ahead. The process of building denominational infrastructure had just begun. The definition of episcopacy, refinement of the conference system, development of a delegated general conference, nurturing of the traveling ministry and class system, establishment through the *Discipline* of definite shape to the denomination, creation of a Methodist Book Concern and periodicals, and the testing of the denomination in early internal and external controversies made of Methodism a church order by intention national and governed by its purpose. However, in certain respects 1784 changed little, as the small American Methodist movement already had shaped itself and defined its ethos in Wesley's energetic, missionary, evangelistic, purposive style and had already accustomed itself in the Wesley mode to working alongside other religious communions. Colonial Methodism had already become a missionary order. Independence in 1784 made that ecclesial principle into a denomination.

To be sure, there were limits to Methodism's purposive or functional character. These were clearly indicated in the circle-the-wagons response to the republican revolt led by James O'Kelly and his brief for ministerial rights, the defensiveness evidenced on a variety of polity issues, the retreat from antislavery, the authoritarianism of Asbury, and the conservatism so pronounced in the six restrictive rules of 1808. But to note some inertias and inabilities to respond freely to new opportunities and challenges is only to say that the Methodists were not fully conscious of the significance of their own novelty nor capable of living fully into its promise. The Methodist witness to the new purposive, missionary form of denominationalism attracted adherence and emulation. In particular the United Brethren under Phillip William Otterbein, and the Evangelical Association under Jacob Albright, adopted and adapted Methodist structures and procedures for Reformed and Lutheran German constituencies and translated Pietist ideals, including that of being *ecclesiola in ecclesia*, for the American environment. In time other denominations would join these three in making their structures instrumental to the spreading of scriptural holiness over the land.

Though Presbyterians, Congregationalists, Baptists, and Christians reached that stage following different paths and by adapting and altering their own traditions, nevertheless in so doing they were replicating the Methodist pattern. As denominationalism reached maturity in the early decades of the nineteenth century, it did so as the joint testimony of distinct peoples and traditions that the Christianization of American society was to be their individual and common endeavor. That mission, as Robert Handy has so carefully shown in *A Christian America*, was the purpose of the denominations. Denominations were, and denominationalism was, purposive. To be sure, there were social sources for each and all. But transcending the theological and ecclesiastical differences and the social, class, and racial distinctions was a common endeavor. The denominations were instruments of the kingdom of God. Denominations were not, then, as Niebuhr argued, the end of the kingdom. They were, under the conditions of disestablishment and religious freedom, its beginning. They were not, in their earliest phases, ends but means. That they later became ends in themselves—as Niebuhr quite rightly asserts they did—was a sign that denominations as well as the quest for the kingdom has lost the original vision.

CHAPTER 10

CONNECTING THROUGH EDUCATION

Four propositions frame the task of this chapter:

- American Methodism has been, and United Methodism continues to be, a connectional church.[1]
- At the heart of the connection, of that Methodist connectionalism, lies education.
- The expression of connectionalism and the way Methodism has related to education and specifically to higher education have differed over time.
- We seem to be at a point now of rethinking the connection and redefining education's place therein.

Implicitly in these propositions I make several contentions. The first is that Methodist higher education has always been connectional. This point runs counter to common assumptions about church and education and to the point of view of the otherwise excellent study by Beth Adams Bowser of the century-old Methodist accrediting body, the University Senate. She says:

> The Senate's work was designed originally to bring a sense of "connectionalism" to the institutions of learning that considered themselves, or wanted to be considered, under the auspices of The Methodist Episcopal Church. This had been missing in the planning and administration of these institutions since 1820, when Annual Conferences received the authority to act autonomously in establishing schools. The resulting chaos was unacceptable to the Methodist Episcopal Church, especially if it was to have a *system* of "quality" schools that could compete with the best schools in any given region.[2]

To the contrary, I will argue, connectionalism has been a defining attribute of Methodist higher education, as also of Methodism.

A second point, implicit in the propositions, follows and constitutes the purpose of this chapter. It is that connectionalism has not always been bureaucratic and national in character and that a lively and substantive and mutually enriching connection between United Methodism and its colleges can survive and perhaps be enhanced by radical changes in the existing largely national corporate, bureaucratic structures and systems of accountability.

A third implicit point will be evident as I proceed, namely, that one can envision at least four stages in the connection of education to the church. The first might be termed *episcopal*; the second, *conference* or *regional*; the third, *agency* or *bureaucratic*; and the fourth, *professional*. An apparently fifth and emerging stage has yet to reveal its character sufficiently to be labeled. Each stage turned a different facet of the church toward higher education, engaging colleges in slightly different ways, connecting Methodist educational systems to the church through different adhesive principles. How ought a fifth and emerging stage to look? Where will it engage the higher education? How will college and church be joined? That question remains open.

THE INHERITED PATTERN

Methodism's connectionalism and the centrality of education to the connection derive from John Wesley. When we think of Wesley, both his own classical education and formation at Oxford and his endeavor to supply education to his people at Kingswood come immediately to mind. Those important marks of Wesley's commitment to education, however, constitute but a small part of lifelong, systemic, well-institutionalized, indeed pervasive educational endeavor. The entire Wesleyan system evidenced his teaching or the educational role. Indeed, Wesley's educational endeavor and the religious reform that we know as Methodism were coextensive.

Here I would stress the noninstitutional but pervasive, intensive, and personal educational roles that Wesley played. Wesley was the teacher for Methodism. Wesley consistently taught. At some level one can find a teaching purpose in most of what Wesley undertook. Virtually the entire Wesleyan system evidences his teaching role. And he seemed to exercise his teaching office with any with whom he came into contact who proved in any way open and responsive. Certainly he taught his preachers, in conference and out. And he held them accountable to educate themselves, using the resources that he provided. He gave similar incentives to the people, directly and through correspondence. And the systems he created clearly served educational purposes. His correspondence, tracts, republications, sermons, controversial and apologetical pieces, magazine, schools, classes and societies, rules, republished libraries, encouragement to families and societies to create libraries, Sunday schools, conference sessions, training and supervision of his assistants and helpers—indeed, the entire structure of Methodism—betray a remarkable drive to educate his people in the faith, to identify the heart of the Christian gospel, to teach the faith.

Through much of this, Wesley wrote what one might term *curricula*. He did so formally and self-consciously in creating deposits of his teaching. "The Large Minutes," *Explanatory Notes on the New Testament*, *Standard Sermons*, and for Americans, Wesley's modified version of the Anglican *Articles of Religion*, all of which came to us from his hand, Wesley identified as touchstones of faith and practice.[3] In making such provisions and in giving guidance to his people, Wesley exercised what theologians call the teaching office. That mantle, in the Christian tradition, has been worn by the bishops and in Roman Catholicism by the chief of the bishops, the pope.

A scriptural *episcopos* Wesley could term himself and so he has been acknowledged by Methodists. When sometimes affirmed, Wesley's exercise of the scriptural episcopal office points to his governing and appointive authority. I pursue that remarkable connectional power in other chapters. Here I would stress that Wesley, by what he did and what he created, made Methodism into a giant classroom. And the activities and structures and processes by which he taught were also what connected Methodists to him and to one another. The educational was connectional; the connectional was educational. At the heart of both was Mr. Wesley.[4]

EDUCATION AND THE AMERICAN EPISCOPACY

There is no question but that the first two American bishops, Thomas Coke and Francis Asbury, aspired to play a comparable educational and connective role for the American Methodists. Here too when we think of American Methodism and education, what comes to mind is the ill-fated and several-times started Cokesbury College, modeled after Kingswood.[5] Or we think of the horseback reading to which the circuit riders were challenged. But as in the case of Wesley and British Methodism, the American pattern involved substantial informal educational processes that deserve mention.

Coke clearly envisioned himself as inheriting, embodying, and exercising Wesley's role, Wesley's teaching authority for the infant American Methodist movement. He prepared and conducted himself to exercise the intellectual leadership of American Methodism—studying on shipboard the texts that bore on church order, carefully crafting sermons that would lay the groundwork for a Methodist "episcopal" self-understanding, conducting a planning session for the Christmas Conference, speaking eloquently on the conference floor, advocating the establishment of an academic institution, preaching throughout the connection, championing antislavery—in so many ways providing ideas for the new American church.[6]

Neither Asbury nor the American preachers could suffer Coke's presumption and style. Does that mean that Wesley's model of episcopal teaching disappeared? Not exactly. Asbury, whom we do not think of as much of an intellect or as an educator, proved more successful in exercising Wesley's educational roles.[7] Some of the roles are obvious. Asbury encouraged Methodists, particularly in Virginia, North Carolina, South Carolina, and Georgia, in their efforts to found boarding schools, none of which flourished for long.

Less obvious were the ways Asbury, like Wesley, found other conduits for education. He oversaw the publishing efforts of the movement, issuing directives and counsel to the book agents, first John Dickins and then Ezekiel Cooper. They and he, by making the itinerating preachers agents into colporteurs and salesmen for the publishing enterprise, turned all of the circuit system into a giant distribution network.

Among other education projects earning his sponsorship were a magazine (which appeared as the *Arminian Magazine* in 1789 and 1790, and as *The Methodist Magazine* in 1797 and 1798, not a stunning success obviously), an American version of Wesley's works,[8] a variety of republications of British items, and a few American originals.[9] For the rather considerable list of titles produced by the little American Methodist press under Asbury's general editorship, see the Appendix to this chapter. Beyond the many republications, Asbury attempted to be an author in his own right. Among the items he issued were his own journal, initially serialized, and then published as an independent book; his own version of a Hymn Book;[10] a compilation intended to address the James O'Kelly schism, entitled graphically *The Causes, Evils, and Cures of Heart and Church Divisions, Extracted from the Works of Mr. Jeremiah Burroughs and Mr. Richard Baxter*;[11] and Asbury's effort at a history of the movement, *Extracts of Letters Containing Some Account of the Work of God Since the Year 1800*.[12]

Perhaps the most self-evident educational effort on Asbury's part clearly involved Coke as well. It came in 1798, an annotated version of the *Discipline*,[13] an endeavor to instruct the Methodist faithful through and about Methodist belief and practice.

Finally, Asbury played his most important educational roles orally. The aspect of this that is most accessible is his effort to direct the movement through several valedictory statements.[14] More important but more elusive than that were his daily interventions—throughout his ministry—in the lives of all those with whom he traveled, resided, and spoke. The educational roles in which he probably most succeeded are lost to us—namely, through his sermons and prayers, his statements in conference, his conversations, and especially his talks with horseback companions. Asbury taught, as early Methodism taught, in a seminar of the road. He exercised the teaching office preeminently in oral fashion. Unfortunately, the dimensions of this can only be inferred from notations of texts[15] in his journal, from the concerns that prompt his letters, from the chance comment that his companions minute at the end of the day. Thereby he gave intellectual leadership to the Methodist movement.

These "educational," teaching efforts, we should stress, held Methodism together, connected it, made it genuinely a connectional church. Asbury moved, spoke, and "taught" daily so as to traverse the length and breadth of Methodism. He gave reality to the formal notion to which we still subscribe, namely, that our bishops function as itinerant general superintendents. His connective and educative functions interplayed, indeed, were the same. Methodism held itself together by an itinerating bishop and to a lesser extent a ministry also itinerating nationally. Itinerating teacher-preachers offered what education Methodism could claim. As education went, it was not very high; it was not very formal; but it was extensive and connective.

THE COLLEGE ERA

Asbury's—and Coke's—dream of schools for Methodism materialized after both had died, Coke in 1814, Asbury in 1816. The General Conferences of 1820 and 1824 charged annual conferences with the establishment of schools, literary institutions, and colleges. The imperative led to the creation of some ninety secondary-level institutions. Gradually, conferences, often collaboratively, also launched collegiate institutions, beginning with Augusta College in Kentucky (1822), followed by Randolph-Macon in Virginia (1830) and Wesleyan University in Connecticut (1831). The first women's college, Wesleyan in Georgia, was approved and chartered in 1836; the second, Greensboro College, soon thereafter.[16] By the Civil War Methodism had established or was affiliated with some two hundred such collegiate institutions. Many—being poorly funded, staffed, supported, and attended—did not long survive. By one estimate Methodism succeeded in establishing thirty-four "permanent" colleges before 1861.[17]

Bowser comments on this pattern and this stage negatively—as one of disarray, inconsistent standards, poor planning, misuse and inadequacy of resources, isolation, unnecessary competition.[18] From her vantage, indeed that of late nineteenth-century Methodist leaders, conferences did not seem to be very obvious resources for managing educational enterprises or holding them in relation to the church. In truth, for the earlier period, conferences were what connected Methodism, what held the church together, what did its work. Conferences managed Methodism's enterprises from the death of Asbury through the Civil War. The bishops were then many and not working together very successfully.[19] The agencies (the Missionary Society) and Advocates functioned to channel resources and to communicate across the church. But the necessary work of whatever nature—missions, fund-raising, evangelism, education—had to be delegated to the conferences. Methodism functioned then with a highly decentralized system but it functioned quite successfully, thank you. The church connected itself through a network of regularly meeting conferences—quarterly, annual, general—with annual conferences playing the key administrative roles.

Among the first successful projects of this conference-style connectionalism were colleges. Augusta, for instance, derived from the initiatives in 1821 of the Ohio and Kentucky conferences. Leadership came from both conferences, Ohio contributing the first president, Martin Ruter, who came to the office from the helm of *Western Christian Advocate* and also John P. Durbin as a faculty member. The latter would go on to edit *The Christian Advocate* and from there to assume the presidency of Dickinson College. The latter college, taken over by the Methodists, enjoyed the sponsorship of Methodism's two strongest conferences, Baltimore and Philadelphia.

If Asbury epitomizes the first "episcopal" phase of Methodist education and connectionalism, Durbin does the second "college" phase.[20] Born in 1800 of Methodist parents in Bourbon County, Kentucky, Durbin was apprenticed as a cabinetmaker at fourteen. At eighteen he experienced conversion and about the same time a call to preach. Accepted into membership one week and licensed to preach the next, he was immediately sent to the Limestone Circuit. In 1820 when the Western Conference was divided, he went with Ohio. During appointments in the 1820s he began his education, responding to the tutelage of several senior itinerants, including Martin Ruter, whom he would join later at Augusta.

The idea of the circuit rider reading on circuit, Wesley-like, may be mostly myth. Durbin gave reality to the myth. He started with the requisites—Wesley's and Fletcher's *Works* and Clarke's *Commentary*—moving on to grammar, Latin and Greek. Eventually he enrolled formally as a college student. He attended Miami University while appointed in that vicinity and Cincinnati College while there, graduating finally M.A. Soon thereafter Durbin was made professor of ancient languages at Augusta. He held that position for a few years, relinquishing it for health reasons, only to continue as agent for the college, in effect the itinerating admissions and development officer.

Durbin served briefly as chaplain of the United States Senate and also briefly as editor of *The Christian Advocate* (New York). In 1834, he became Principal (President) of Dickinson College, a post he held until 1845.[21] He transferred to the Philadelphia Conference in 1836 and eight times earned the conference's token of highest respect, election to represent it at General Conference. Five of those times he led the delegation, the highest accolade that conferences then—or now—accord their own.[22] Philadelphia turned to him at every point. The 1845 Conference appointed or elected him to preach the Conference Sermon (for 1846). He also served as examiner in the Committees for Examination of the second-year exam on the "Bible as to ordinance or Sacraments."[23] Durbin also headed the Visiting Committee to Dickinson College in 1846 (the agency through which the church exercised its oversight of institutions).[24] In 1849, the bishop concurred in the Conference's high estimation of J. P. Durbin and made him Presiding Elder of North Philadelphia.[25] A year later, in 1850, Durbin succeeded Charles Pitman as secretary of the Missionary Society.[26] He would make that office perhaps the most visible and important leadership position in the church.

Durbin's prominence during his presidency at Dickinson and his overall career well symbolize the nature of the college-church relationship and also what served to connect Methodism at this juncture. If Asbury-the-bishop incarnated Methodist connectionalism in the early years, Durbin-the-president incarnated connectionalism for the pre–Civil War decades.[27] The Durbins quite literally knit the church together on education's behalf. From the 1830s to the Civil War, colleges constituted the Church's primary benevolence, the focus of its efforts at social and cultural uplift, its training ground for ministry, its center for enquiry and theologizing, the agency through which the Church exercised the teaching office.

Into the colleges the Church poured its (limited) financial resources. On their behalf the emerging lay elites began to take leadership roles. There the church equipped its ministry—with Wesleyan, Dickinson, Randolph-Macon, and others serving, in effect, as the seminaries of their day.[28] Through the colleges the church would carry on its larger mission of reforming the nation, joining with other denominations in common endeavor to instill Protestant commitment, republican ideals, and civic virtue in the nation's rising leaders.

The Protestant effort to build a Christian America produced much collaboration but even more competition. The churches competed for and with the hearts and minds of the rising leaders of the next generation. Until the Methodist Church could found enough of its own institutions, the potential new leaders in Methodism had resorted to colleges belonging to other denominations, some of them "straying" into other ecclesial folds. Methodist colleges would definitely, so insisted founders and benefactors, hold for the church its youth whom they thought had heretofore been lured into other denominations by attendance at their institutions. So insisted Stephen Olin, president of Wesleyan, in 1844 sounding a then common refrain: "No Christian denomination can safely trust to others for the training of its sons. . . . History has too clearly demonstrated that, without colleges of our own, few of our sons are likely to be educated, and that only a small portion of that few are likely to be retained in our communion."[29]

He estimated that three-quarters of the Methodists who had attended others' colleges had been "lost": "Many of them have gone to other denominations, many more have gone to the world. All were the legitimate children of the Church. They were her hope, and they should have become the crown of her rejoicing."[30]

The biographer of Wilbur Fisk, founding president of Wesleyan, sized the matter up similarly:

> The Methodists had become the most numerous body of Christians in the United States, and had greatly increased both in wealth and intelligence. As they became able to educate their children, they found the importance of having institutions of learning under their own control. Prior to this they had been satisfied to send their children to colleges under the influence of other denominations, and, as a natural consequence, many became alienated from the views of their parents. Besides, most of the colleges in the country were under the direction of some

one denomination, and this secured to those churches who had most influence in this line, a control over public sentiment that was hardly compatible with the equal rights of the several churches.... Moreover, while we had no such institutions among ourselves, the importance of education was not likely to be so generally felt as it ought to be.[31]

The colleges indeed educated the church's youth for service. Of Randolph-Macon's early graduates, 210 in all, the large bulk entered the professions:

48 teachers (13 of these professors in one of the church's colleges)

43 clergy (12 also taught or served as president of school)

39 lawyers (8 legislators)

31 farmers

29 physicians.[32]

Of Wesleyan's first forty years of graduates (919), a third entered the Methodist ministry. According to Duvall, Wesleyan produced three-quarters of the ministers who had college degrees.[33]

How Methodist were these institutions? Recent scholarship has divided on that point. Charles Sellers pronounced Dickinson after the Methodist takeover as "sectarian."[34] By contrast, James Edward Scanlon accented the more public, civic, and local nature of Randolph-Macon's early years, as did David Potts for Wesleyan.[35] Agreeing, Glenn Miller observes, "These schools were more secular than the present-day observer might suppose from their presidents' rhetoric." What Miller found—really across American higher education—was a pattern of schools under denominational governance but operated clearly in communal and "public" interest; chartered by colony or state but eschewing religious tests and opening their doors to individuals from various denominations; providing for religious and moral character formation through a regular pattern of worship; and offering a classical, liberal arts educational diet capped by moral philosophy. Miller terms the denominational college "a curious hybrid," a public, incorporated institution yet under the control of trustees accountable in some fashion to a denomination.[36]

These divergent estimates derive, to some extent, from looking at different aspects of collegiate life but, perhaps more importantly, from differing estimates by interpreters as to what then constituted a denomination and how denomination related to college. Those who minimize the Methodist character of the pre–Civil War college expect to find denominational control from some central agency or judicatory. For Methodists such centralization did not exist. The denomination was but a collection of conferences and the conferences themselves had little in the way of permanent machinery, no conference headquarters, no bishop's office. Conferences convened once a year. The bishops rotated among them. The presiding elders kept on the move as well. The secretary, himself a "traveling preacher," represented the conference's ongoing consciousness and its memory. Agents for the colleges and various causes kept on the move, as did the corresponding (executive) secretaries for the several denominational societies (missionary, Sunday school, tract). The editors of the *Advocates* represented perhaps the most stable offices in prewar Methodism.

Furthermore, a school might relate to more than one conference. Each would appoint members to a visiting committee. Indeed, by the 1870s Wesleyan claimed thirteen patron conferences.[37] Even such oversight functioned also as patronage or support, encouraged as much from the college as from the conference side.

What Methodist influence on colleges was to be had came from within rather than from without the institution and derived from the informal influences, rhythms, lifestyle, and ethos that a Methodist president, faculty, and board gave the place. Visiting committees from the conferences—Baltimore and Philadelphia in the case of Dickinson—could observe and report on a day's or week's activities. Touring agents would render the same report across the conferences. But since these were the connections, the Methodist character could be measured by nothing else.

The proof really came in the pudding. In substance, style, purpose, agenda, and ethos the colleges radiated Methodism. Not surprisingly, these schools in fact produced the church's leaders. Noteworthy, as we've already remarked, were the numbers entering the ministry, probably including some of the persons identified as teachers. And, as the colleges produced the leadership cohorts in their graduates, they also contributed the bishops and agency heads from their faculty and presidents. Indeed, for the middle decades of the century the stepping-stone to the episcopacy was a college presidency.

For good reason then Wesleyan would be termed in the 1870s and 1880s "the mother of our denominational institutions," "the crown and glory of our Church," or as the Methodist press in New York and Boston put it, the "mother of us all."[38] And yet by the time such accolades became common, the nature of Methodist connectionalism and of the relation of college to church was changing.

A NATIONAL CHURCH

Northern churches emerged from the Civil War and from their involvement in the war effort having learned what mobilization on a national scale could do for denominational enterprise—for adequate funding, for coordination, for quality control, for uniformity, for efficiency, for fair distribution of time and resources. Methodists especially recognized that activities or projects previously undertaken or overseen by conferences could be rendered more accountable and supported better on a national level. So in 1872 (1874 in the MECS, still later for the MPC, UBC, and EA),[39] the MEC General Conference responded to "The Report of the Special Committee on the Relation of Benevolent Institutions to the Church" by directing the Bishops "to take such measures as they may deem proper to secure by law such form of organization of the various benevolent corporations of the Methodist Episcopal Church as will place all under the full control of the General Conference."[40] By this action the church turned the once voluntary societies of common endeavor into formal, national denominational agencies, accountable to General Conference through elected boards and corresponding secretaries. Two of the Boards, founded within the prior four years, symbolized the will of the church to achieve such national policy in higher education. One was the Freedmen's Aid and Southern Education Society that would coordinate northern Methodist educational ventures for African Americans.[41] The other was the Board of Education that had initially been established in 1868 on the plan extended to all agencies in 1872.

The problem of accountability had been identified earlier in the decade. In 1860, General Conference had taken up the question of whether it, rather than annual conferences, should have control and supervision over collegiate education and conceded themselves "unable to fix upon any plan for the organization of a permanent Board of Education which they deem practicable." They affirmed:

> What of ecclesiastical control has been exercised has been by the Annual Conferences.... without any established law or uniform plan, and with but little concert between the Conferences or the different institutions....
>
> The committee are confident that the Annual Conferences would not consent to a transfer of the control of the literary institutions under their care to the General Conference, or a board created by its appointment; nor are they sure, could this be done, that the educational movement of the Church would not be robbed of much of its vitality and freedom of action in adapting itself to the peculiar wants of the different sections of the country by attempting to direct it by a uniform and rigid system.[42]

By the late 1860s Methodists recognized that vitality and freedom were being purchased at too high a price. Methodism had simply become too big, too complex, too institutionalized, too wealthy to run itself by conferences that met only periodically. And its enterprises deserved the care, resources, and oversight that could only be appropriately garnered and distributed nationally. What was needed was something that did not come and go annually like a conference or quadrennially like a general conference but functioned week-to-week, day-to-day, hour-to-hour. What was needed were boards and agencies, boards and agencies genuinely accountable to the church. Hence the revolution of 1872.

Aspiration for national and, what we would now term, bureaucratic control came not only from General Conference and the national level. Those committed to the cause at hand, in this instance education, clearly saw the need for greater efficiency by the denomination. For instance, arguing for a better educational system, George R. Crooks, editor of the New York paper *The Methodist*, called during the 1860s for some transregional association of Methodist colleges: "Methodist institutions . . . holding the Methodist name . . . culturing Methodist piety and . . . chiefly of Methodist patronage."[43] Like sentiment recurred through the Methodist press.

Moreover, as David Potts has shown with respect to Wesleyan, friends of the college sought through a variety of stratagems to put that institution into ever-wider Methodist systems of support and influence.[44] Indeed, one can plausibly argue that it was the colleges and their friends who engineered the establishment of national, denominational, corporate boards charged with both oversight and support. The process was a gradual one. We can see, for instance, the same John Durbin who taught at Augusta and led Dickinson, experimenting as head of the Missionary Society with greater system and national coordination. And the search continued, as far as education was concerned, until the creation of the University Senate in 1892. The work of that body reinforced and completed the several tendencies toward centralized denominationalism.

The University Senate has come into prominence in the late twentieth and early twenty-first centuries as United Methodists jockey over theological education, the Ministerial Education Fund, and where and how seminarians should be educated. Its purposes have been larger than theological education. Indeed, United Methodists generally may be surprised to learn that it was we—rather than the now prominent regional accrediting organizations or those of other professions—who established the first accrediting organization. The Senate served, in relation to the Board of Education, to establish academic standards, to apply them to individual institutions, to determine which schools qualified according to those standards and as "Methodist," to identify those Methodist institutions, to visit and investigate, to give counsel and guidance, to play a role in distribution of resources.[45]

The Senate decided what counted as quality education. It also determined what counted as "Methodist." Denominational identity now possessed a national connectional touchstone. We take this today so much for granted—that the national church would determine who a Methodist is and who can use the name—that we fail to recognize its novelty in the late nineteenth century. But new it was. And Scanlon and Potts and others who see the colleges becoming more Methodist in the closing decade of the century can be rightly forgiven for failing to recognize the earlier conference-based connectionalism and identity. The year 1892 indeed marked something of a watershed. The northern church created the Senate, also mandated a national fund for the support of students, looked forward to a national educational system, and to that end authorized the establishment in the nation's capitol of a central graduate-level university "to be called The American University, which should be the crown of our educational system."[46]

Comparable national efforts for education went into African American communities channeled through what was founded in 1866 as the Freedmen's Aid and Southern Education Society. Coordinating its efforts with those of the Board of Education and the Woman's Home Missionary Society, it boasted by 1892—when observing twenty-five years of operation—"A Federated System of Schools," a "thoroughly unified system of schools," "so graded and located, and related in courses of study, as to form a federation of institutions, including professional, classical, academic, and industrial schools."[47] This "federated" system ran under national management, under a Board of Managers elected by General Conference, which in the interim of General Conferences reported to a General Committee. Its corresponding secretary took "personal direction" and responsibility for "the buying of lands, the erection of buildings, the employment of teachers, and the superintendence of institutions of learning of various grades."[48] The general committee took responsibility for determining "what institutions shall receive aid for the ensuing year; the total amount to be expended as far as practical; the amount each school shall receive . . . what amount shall be apportioned to each Annual Conference to be raised." It was also "to counsel and direct the board in the general administration of its affairs."[49]

In its twenty-five years, the Society had expended close to three million dollars, a million of that in the prior quadrennium (1887–1891), $1,010,980.25 to be exact. Real estate, the Society valued at $1,808,800. In the prior fiscal year, the Society had disbursed monies to the following collegiate or higher-level institutions: Bennett College, Central Tennessee College, Claflin University, Clark University, Gammon Theological Seminary, George R. Smith College, Little Rock University, Morgan College, New Orleans

University, Philander Smith College, Rust University, Samuel Huston College, U. S. Grant University, and Wiley University.[50]

The Society claimed for that year 447 teachers and 9,310 mostly precollegiate students, and 172 students in college. It boasted 326 persons preparing for the ministry and over the prior quadrennium "twelve hundred and fifty conversions . . . among the students."[51]

In its report, the Freedmen's Aid and Southern Education Society assured General Conference of the following results:

1. The property is absolutely safe to the Church.
2. Schools of similar grade have substantially the same courses of study.
3. Local responsibility and cooperation are being developed as rapidly as the financial ability of the people will justify.
4. College degrees, in course or honorary, are only conferred by institutions of collegiate grade, and then, as a rule, only in consultation with the authorities of the Society.
5. No new schools will be founded in the South, among our people, either white or colored, without the consent and cooperation of the central office.
6. No teachers can be employed not in thorough accord with the doctrines and usages of the Church.
7. The English Bible is introduced as a text-book in all grades of every school, whether theological, collegiate, or academic.
8. To a very great extent the same text-books are used in all schools of the same grade, making it possible to contract for them at the lowest rates, as well as to insure the use of the best books.[52]

Here, then, was the national system as the church wanted it; written post–Civil War, on a blank slate as it were; without the distraction of pre-existing institutions and their support systems; with nothing to stand in the way of national control, standardization, efficiency, purpose; a system that produced both teachers and conversions, both new citizens for the South and new ministers for the denomination.

National efforts, of course, never sufficed, either for the Freedmen's Aid Society or for the Board of Education and University Senate. More local and regional support for institutions continued in the new era.[53] But from the 1890s through the first half of the twentieth century a national connectionalism predominated and set the terms for what was implemented more locally. The University Senate, the Board of Education (now General Board of Higher Education and Ministry), the General Board of Global Ministries, and organizations like the National Association of United Methodist Schools, Colleges, and Universities (NASCUMC) effectively served the Methodist interest in higher education.[54]

A PROFESSIONAL STAGE?

The role of the national church in education continues so visibly to the present—through such organizations and institutions—that we might readily conclude with Bowser and others that the new age began and ended with the establishment of the University Senate. However, the terms for Methodist connection and connectionalism shifted subtly in the twentieth century. They did so generally. They did so in relation to higher education. Both generally as a denomination and specifically in higher education Methodism appropriated patterns and practices of association, communication, credentialing, specialization, and connection that can be termed *professional*. Over the course of the century professionalism increasingly became the new mode of connection.[55]

Professionalization generated new organizations, as we shall note below, but it also transformed existing structures in interesting and strange ways, in ways not frequently acknowledged. Most important, Methodist conference structures, annual conferences specifically, came increasingly to behave like professional organizations, like the American Medical Association or the American Bar Association. They did so during a period when the lay presence in annual conferences gradually increased and conferences took on qualities of representative democracy. Lay equalization, formalized in the union of 1939, which brought Methodist Protestant and the two Methodist Episcopal churches together, furthered the full participation of laity in all aspects of denominational governance. Subsequent struggles toward inclusion and empowerment of women and of Methodism's several ethnic minorities have made the twentieth-century denominational story to be one of democratization. And indeed it was. However, the story was also one of professionalization. Both stories, both trends interplayed in complex fashion. Both could be accommodated because conferences divided their life, reserving for certain committees and the executive sessions what was truly professional and exercising the more governmental roles elsewhere. In the former, conferences dealt with those concerns that defined professional life generally—setting standards; determining who would be admitted; raising the minimum salary;[56] improving quality by heightening educational requirements and controlling admissions; guaranteeing insurance coverage;[57] establishing and interpreting pension programs;[58] exercising ethical oversight; protecting professional ministerial privilege. So conferences behaved like professional societies.

Professionalism also affected virtually every other aspect of American life, higher education included. It did so in relation to other long-term trends—the nationalization of culture, the prominence of new media (radio and then television) and of advertising in setting cultural standards, the subsuming of economic life under huge national and international corporations, the growth of the military as employer and purchaser, gradual shifts in gender roles and race relations, secularization, the increasing diversity, individualism, and pluralism of society, the growing prominence of technology and science, and the general commodification of life.

Colleges and universities participated in and contributed to these trends. Especially affecting colleges, including the better church-related colleges were

- the growing fiscal and regulatory roles of the Federal government,
- the dominance in higher education generally of the research university and its values,
- the consequent displacement of the liberal arts ideal as an integrative principle,
- the fragmentation of faculty and curriculum into disciplinary specializations,
- the pressure to accommodate the careering orientation of students (and parents),
- the emergence of religious studies as a field of study freed from its earlier Protestant commitments, methodologies and concerns,
- the increased pluralism of American society.

In consequence, religion found its place pushed to the margins in religious studies, student groups, chaplaincies, and the Christian college.

These larger societal trends affecting higher education and the plight of the church college have been so overwhelming, have so dominated the consciousness of those in church and college leadership, and have so shaped our interpretive framework that we have tended to neglect the more insidious way in which professionalism subtly refashioned the relation of college to church. We can be forgiven the oversight. After all, what has been most dramatic has been what was and is imaged as the war between religion and science, a war that cost the church its most prized institutions, north and south, east and west—Wesleyan and Vanderbilt, as first casualties, University of Southern California and Northwestern as later losses. And that war continues, rather more as a cold than a hot war, as Douglas Sloan and my former colleague George Marsden have so eloquently shown.[59] Now not attacks on religion and the loss of institutions but the pervasive domination of an Enlightenment epistemology—naturalism, Kantian dualism, rationalism, materialism—reduces the whole life of the spirit (aesthetic, ethical, religious) to what can be observed and counted, and eviscerates the spiritual innards from academic life. We have yet to find, argues Sloan, a qualitative mode of knowledge that would give faith a foundation, within the university, on which to build.

It should come as no surprise then that interpreters have focused on religion in higher education and the church-related college as questions, as problems, as challenges. What remains of church relationship, they ask? In denominational identity? In religious ethos? In curricular coherence? In faith community? In leadership sensitive to the church? In the shaping of persons for church professions? The substantive questions and the pursuit of the several components thereof—pursued so resolutely by Merrimon Cuninggim in *Uneasy Partners: The College and the Church*, remain terribly important.[60]

The substantive side of those questions and subquestions must be addressed. Also of interest, though, is the way in which the several subquestions have resolved themselves into professional endeavor and the matter of church relationship transforms itself into a variety of professional prerogatives.

Denominational identity belongs to those who work interstitially—denominational executives, presidents, board members. Religious ethos and community have been delegated to the chaplain. To curricular coherence department chairs and deans give passing attention, though many do not see much beyond the interests of their own discipline. Departments of Religion oversee specifically religious curricular matters and, in some places, worry over whether persons go on to seminary. Few of the faculty can be counted on to belong to sponsoring denomination and fewer still to have ordination. Each of the ingredients or dimensions of church relationship then has resolved itself into a professional prerogative. Each takes professional form. Each belongs to a professional cohort.

Before we distress too much over that point, we need to acknowledge that professionalism defines the whole of American society and The United Methodist Church. Professional networks constitute the communities through which the church and much of our society now do work. The church quite literally ties itself together, connects itself, through these networks. Typically each will have some official sheltering—under a denominational board, commission, caucus, or affiliated group; with its own contact person, coordinator or staff person at the national level; some mechanisms and procedures for recognition or accreditation; a newsletter and perhaps now a website or blog; jurisdictional and conference affiliates; a regular, perhaps annual, gathering; ongoing programs and promotional efforts dedicated to furthering that profession's interest; in short, a group identity.[61]

Conference directors, communicators, business administrators, youth ministers, church growth experts or evangelists, chaplains, librarians, Christian educators, editors, continuing educators, spiritual directors, church musicians, financial officers, legal counselors, camping ministers, and special ministries of all sorts have their professional gatherings. Other affinity groups, not typically thought of as "professional," nevertheless function in a similar, quasi-professional fashion. To some extent, professional status may be disguised by a particular occupation's accountability to, connection with, or official relation to an agency. For instance, a number of groups might be seen as enjoying professional status, credential or recognition in relation to the General Board of Higher Education and Ministry—Christian educators, chaplains and campus ministers, deacons (and earlier diaconal ministers), field educators, teachers of religion and divinity, presidents of United Methodist colleges, and seminary heads.

The church connects itself, binds itself together, undertakes its tasks through these professional and quasi-professional networks. Like so many twisted wires, the church hangs together by what also divides it. For even as these professional groups connect, they also, like the caucuses and various "struggle" groups, divide and disconnect.[62]

And higher education experiences such disconnect as much as other sectors of American life. Campus-based individuals and groups that ought to be in conversation are not, nor do they connect with persons within the denomination with whom they really share concerns. Religion departments increasingly differentiate themselves from campus ministries and chaplains. The left hand knows not the business of the right. Campus life, like denominational life, like American life generally, divides as well as unites along these strange professional lines.

Important in relation to the concern of this chapter is the further and perhaps obvious point that professional groupings and professionalism no longer bridge between church to higher education, no longer connect Methodism with its institutions. Neither religious studies nor chaplaincies typically coordinate their activities with the youth workers or local pastors of neighbor United Methodist churches. Theoretically, faculty members who are ordained and college chaplains could or should connect with the denomination through their "appointment" as extension ministries and their relation in that capacity to an annual conference. However, as I explore elsewhere in discussion of extension ministries generally,[63] inclusion exists only on paper, chaplains and other extension ministries remain marginalized and are popularly regarded as having left the ministry (that is, the profession). Chaplains sustain ties with the church and resource themselves through the General Board of Higher Education and Ministry, but that connection does not translate into meaningful engagement at other levels. And United Methodist faculty, whether ordained or lay, lack even that connectivity.

The professionalism, then, that honeycombs both church and college internally effects a yawning division between church and college. For none of the professional groupings effectively bring together church and academe. A kind of professional no-man's or no-person's-land divides church and college cohorts. I know this firsthand from having served on at least four committees of three of our general agencies, committees that intentionally tried to put together academics and church leaders. We also structured our Duke-based Lilly Endowment-supported project on United Methodism and American Culture to include both academics and clergy. In each case overcoming the divide between church and academe constituted the major work of the body. Little else could be accomplished until the groups negotiated the tensions and mistrust and misunderstanding and different rules and distinct languages. And while within those specific but isolated initiatives we found some rapprochement by the time our meetings concluded, we never succeeded in translating that mutuality into meaningful and programmatic connection between the church and higher education or into a new mode of connectionalism more generally. We returned home to our professional interests and niches.

So professionalism both connects and divides. Professionalism connects but in Balkan-like, in caucuslike, in tribal fashion. Professionalism produces a new tribalism—tribes competing within church, tribes competing within academe, tribal groupings that pit college against church. The actual caucuses—highly visible in their public celebration of identity through gender, ethnicity, program, or ideology—figure prominently in denunciations of the divisions and acrimony in American and denominational life. As apparent symbols of the divisive and obstructionist and self-interested element in common life, they take the heat for structural lines that run much deeper and broader. Professional identities, professional credentials, professional associations now connect in church, higher education, and society. Professionalism divides as it unites, in college as in church. Professionalism, perhaps earlier resourcing the connection, now divides higher education from the church.

A FURTHER STAGE?

So then what will connect denominations in the decades and century ahead? And what will connect church to higher education?

Will it again be the bishops? or conferences? or national boards? or professions? Or will it be yet something new that educators and clergy or boards and institutions create? Will it be a mode of connectionalism that overcomes the incredible challenges that knowledge has posed for faith in the twentieth century? And finally, whose responsibility is it or whose initiative ought it be to propose and initiate the new connectionalism and establish the relation between college and church? Might it be in the future as in the past that higher education leadership join with counterparts in the church to forge the new connection and the new relationship?

CHAPTER 11

METHODIST CULTURE WARS

Conventional wisdom today holds

- that denominational loyalty, at least among mainline denominations,[1] has weakened, decidedly;
- that the once-prominent "establishment" denominations[2] as institutions are fading;
- that individuals, congregations, and regional judicatories are staging "Boston Tea Parties" protesting decisions, priorities, inefficiencies, waste, monetary claims and the onerous, oppressive burden of the bureaucratic board and agency structure that seems to be the cohesive principle in denominations today;
- that caucuses and struggle groups have balkanized denominations, turning conventions, assemblies, and conferences into contentious and demoralizing rather than unifying and galvanizing experiences;
- that many of these struggle groups and caucuses align themselves into two broad coalitions, liberal and conservative;
- that these coalitions transcend denominational, indeed religious, boundaries;
- and that liberal and conservative[3] or liberal and evangelical[4] identities threaten now to divide, perhaps even destroy, denominations.[5]

The range of such problems, including especially the divisions within denominations, spell, some would suggest, the end to denominationalism.[6] At the very least they portend, as a United Methodist bishop and a seminary president both prophesied in the aftermath of the 2004 General Conference, the clean division of such mainline denominations into new conservative and liberal entities and the end to United Methodism as we know it.

DENOMINATIONALISM AS DIVISION?

This chapter endeavors to show that denominational divisions do not constitute a new threat at all. Division has haunted denominations and denominationalism rather continuously throughout American history. Indeed, were theology rather than history and sociology to be the thrust of this essay, one might affirm with H. Richard Niebuhr that division is the essence of denominationalism:

> For the denominations, churches, sects, are sociological groups whose principle of differentiation is to be sought in their conformity to the order of social classes and castes. . . . They are emblems, therefore, of the victory of the world over the church, of the secularization of Christianity, of the church's sanction of that divisiveness which the church's gospel condemns.[7]

Even on historical grounds, one might view division to be a characteristic of denominations. Divisions or near divisions constitute the story of virtually any denomination or denominational family, a fact readily discernible in the annual *Yearbook of American and Canadian Churches*[8] or any other effort at the full mapping of American religion. And the larger pattern of denominations or denominationalism evidences periods of intense fracturing and fragmenting—periods when existing bodies experience internal strain, when some denominations do split and when new denominations emerge, often with commentary on the prior denominational order as constitutive of their purpose and self-understanding.

The "great awakenings" of the eighteenth and early nineteenth centuries represent such periods of fracturing and fragmenting. So also do the slavery and sectional crisis of the middle nineteenth century and the late nineteenth; as well as the early twentieth-century time of centralizing, professionalizing, corporate restructuring, and cultural realignment. The latter period, with its great Pentecostal effervescence, has sometimes been portrayed as one of cultural crisis, as though the new denominations sprang *ex nihilo*. Recent scholarship suggests that Pentecostalism has stronger ties to Methodist and other existing traditions than has sometimes been supposed and that those as well as the Holiness and Fundamentalist movements ought to be seen as developments from, if not divisions out of, earlier denominational stock. At any rate, the Holiness, Pentecostal, and Fundamentalist eras represent times, if not a time, of serious denominational sifting and shifting. And so too does this period from the 1970s to the present. Division within the denominational house may be, to borrow an image from Robert Handy but employ it differently, the religious counterpart to economic depression.[9]

Certainly all denominational divisions do not occur in these periods of fracturing and fragmenting. Some movements, as this chapter will indicate with respect to the Methodists, have shown a genius for dividing every decade. And yet we should not lose sight of these larger patterns in the history of denominational division. Individual denominational divisions have coincided sufficiently with these larger processes of restructuring for one to suspect that denominationalism, in effect, renews and reconstitutes itself (that is, reshapes the denominational form) through divisions and severe tension.[10] The Presbyterians perhaps best represent in their saga the larger pattern of tension, division, and reunion. They took their rise amidst the Puritan crisis within and without the Church of England, divided new side and old in the First Awakening, suffered significant losses from the Cumberlands and to the Christian (Disciple) movements in the Second Awakening, split New School and Old over issues that would ultimately divide the nation, and narrowly escaped a major division during the fundamentalist controversy. Current turmoil within Presbyterianism, paralleled across mainstream Protestantism, suggests that once again individual denominations and the larger pattern of denominationalism is in a period of transformation.

CONSTITUTIVE DIVISION: THE METHODIST STORY

Division is not only part of the fabric of denominationalism, it is also woven into the life of individual denominations. Such a history of division is well illustrated, perhaps fittingly illustrated, by the Methodists. Methodism began, of course, as a reform movement within the Church of England, pledged in deference to, if not always agreement with, the Wesleys—John and particularly Charles—who insisted that Methodism did not and would not separate from the Church. To that pledge British Methodism remained committed through and beyond John's life. And yet, as Richard Heitzenrater has demonstrated, even under Wesley, Methodism increasingly structured and conducted itself in ways that pointed toward separation.[11]

The inertial pressures toward separation from the Church of England that the Wesleys resisted were, if anything, more intense in the colonies. Methodists immigrating from Ireland or England and persons here who developed Methodist or Methodist-like sympathies found it more difficult to structure Methodist life within an Anglican parish, for that system was not everywhere established and even where established not always well led or maintained. The parish system deteriorated dramatically during the Revolution when Anglicans—clergy and laity—fled to Canada or to Britain (as did preachers whom Wesley had sent over, Francis Asbury excepted).

The first division occurred during this period, even before Methodism officially separated from the Church of England in 1784. The movement split badly. In 1779, during wartime hostilities, the regularly called conference, meeting in Fluvanna County, Virginia, proceeded to establish American Methodism as a church through autonomous acts and presbyterial ordinations. They asked,

> Q. 14. What are our reasons for taking up the administration of the ordinances [sacraments] among us?
>
> A. Because the Episcopal Establishment is now dissolved and therefore in almost all our circuits the members are without the ordinances, we believe it to be our duty.
>
> Q. 19. What forms of ordination shall be observed, to authorize any preacher to administer?
>
> A. By that of a Presbytery.
>
> Q. 20. How shall the Presbytery be appointed?
>
> A. By a majority of the preachers.
>
> Q. 22. What power is vested in the Presbytery by this choice?

A. 1st. To administer the ordinances themselves. 2d. To authorize any other preacher or preachers approved of by them, by the form of laying on of hands and of prayer.[12]

This declaration of independence had been anticipated and countered by an "irregular" conference held the prior month in Delaware to accommodate Francis Asbury, then in hiding, and clearly convened to contravene the anticipated separation.[13] This conference, almost exactly the same size as the later "regular" body, queried:

Q. 10. Shall we guard against a separation from the church, directly or indirectly?

A. By all Means.[14]

And the following year, this Chesapeake group queried:

Q. 12. Shall we continue in close connexion with the church, and press our people to a closer communion with her?

A. Yes.

Q. 20. Does this whole conference disapprove the step our brethren have taken in Virginia?

Ans. Yes.

Q. 21. Do we look upon them no longer as Methodists in connexion with Mr. Wesley and us till they come back?

A. Agreed.[15]

This latter group, which insisted on awaiting John Wesley's provision for ecclesial order, eventually won out and the schism was healed.

CONTINUOUS DIVISIONS?

I have dwelt at more length on this particular separation than I can on subsequent ones to make two points: (1) that American

Methodism was already dividing internally before it officially "divided" itself from the Anglicans and established itself as a distinct denomination, and (2) that the formal separation in 1784 actually involved a threefold disengagement—(a) from the Church of England; (b) from the North American Anglicans among whom the Methodists had labored, who were then also being reconstituted as an independent church and among whom were kindred spirits, chief of them, perhaps, Devereux Jarrett, who were deeply offended by the Methodist departure; and (c) eventually from Mr. Wesley and British Wesleyanism. The latter also was to be an occasion for offence, for in their first *Discipline*, the Americans pledged:

> During the Life of the Rev. Mr. Wesley, we acknowledge ourselves his Sons in the Gospel, ready in Matters belonging to Church-Government, to obey his Commands. And we do engage after his Death, to do every Thing that we judge consistent with the Cause of Religion in *America* and the political Interests of these States, to preserve and promote our Union with the Methodists in *Europe*.[16]

American Methodists found this pledge and the unity it prescribed impossible to honor when Wesley sought to exercise church government. In 1787 Wesley ordered the convening of a general conference and the election of specific persons as bishops. The Americans resisted these commands and stripped the above pledge from the *Discipline*. So American Methodism began in a complex division, though one it has consistently celebrated rather than bemoaned.

To 1787 is often traced yet another division, namely, the beginnings of the African Methodist Episcopal Church, traditionally associated with Richard Allen's walkout from St. George's church. Full separation took a number of other provocations. In 1816 several African American churches formed in similar reaction to Methodism's racial policies covenanted to establish the denomination. From these small beginnings and those of the African Union Church and the African Methodist Episcopal Zion Church, much of Methodism's significant black membership was drained off.[17]

These losses were gradual and the actual break between black and white Methodists more gradual and more gradually recognized on both sides than we have sometimes been led to believe.

These were divisions caused by white racism and unfortunately rather ignored because of racism. By contrast another division, largely among whites, registered itself immediately and traumatically. It came in 1792, when Methodists from the Virginia-North Carolina area followed James O'Kelly, an erratic but prominent leader, in demanding "democratic" rights for preachers, protesting monarchical behavior by the bishops, especially Asbury, and witnessing against slavery. The break came over a proposal made to the General Conference of that year that would have given preachers a right of appeal over their appointment, a popular initiative that seemed destined to pass.[18] When the legislation failed, O'Kelly's supporters, later called *Republican Methodists*, walked out.

Their departure, from the vantage point of the late twentieth century, looks like a minor one, primarily because the *Republicans* proved stronger in protest than they did in subsequent organization and evangelizing. Their *schism* was not minimized in the 1790s. Then it seemed a major "culture war," a battle over the soul of the movement, a question as to whether Methodism would be a Wesleyan or an American cause, a denomination shaped primarily by the culture, practices, beliefs, style, and ethos of the inherited Wesleyanism or of the republicanism of the new nation. The latter had tremendous appeal and seemed to capture essential elements of what both the New Testament and Pietism envisioned for the Christian life. Republican Christianity, as O'Kelly articulated it, offered a vision of equality, fraternity, justice, human rights. And it made sense to persons, particularly the preachers, who experienced any arbitrariness on the part of the appointive authorities, the bishops. A new church for a new nation, a democratic church for a democratic nation, so urged O'Kelly. Was the choice, as he presented it, between Wesleyanism and Americanism? To move beyond that dilemma and contain the schism took a decade of concerted effort on the part of Asbury and his supporters.

In appreciating the significance of this division and several of the subsequent Methodist schisms, we might well keep in mind the close divisions in the presidential contests within the Southern Baptist Convention in those years when moderates still mounted resistance to its conservative drift. A number of those votes were extremely close, suggesting a SBC that was deeply divided. Such proportions do not register, however, in the much smaller numbers of churches and clergy now formally affiliated with the moderate southern Baptist organizations. The depth and extent of a fault line and the size of the parties divided thereby do not then always correspond with, nor are they accurately measured by, the size of a party that departs. This was clearly the case for the Republican Methodists and would prove to be the case in the subsequent nineteenth-century divisions. Similar, major "cultural" and social issues surfaced—in virtually every decade of the nineteenth century—to split Methodism again and again.

DIVISIONS: MINOR AND MAJOR

To be sure, not all the cleavages within the Methodist family can be traced to a decisive moment and a legislative contest or produced such serious trauma. The separate organization of the German movements, the United Brethren and Evangelical Association, reflect their distinct origins in the broader evangelical movement and the specific leaven of Reformed, Mennonite, and Lutheran pietism. Still, the first conference of the former in 1789 and its formal organization in 1800, and the first conference of the latter in 1803 and its formal organization in 1807, represented failures (on both sides) to carry through on the looser comity they had enjoyed with the Methodists. Unification was revisited in the next decade and repeatedly thereafter until the two movements, united in 1946, joined with The Methodist Church in 1968. Early Methodism experimented with intercultural, bilingual community but found differences along language lines difficult to bridge.

Three protests of the early nineteenth century had regional or local effect. William Hammett, ordained by Wesley, settled eventually in Charleston. He built a strong following, resisted the authority of Asbury and Coke, and led a schism of Primitive Methodists (there and in North Carolina) that began around 1792 and largely dissipated after his death in 1803. At the northern reaches of the movement, a group of "Reformed Methodists," led by Pliny Brett, who had itinerated from 1805 to 1812, sought church government and local authority more akin to that appreciated in New England. They protested episcopacy, emphasized the attainability of entire sanctification, and repudiated war and slavery.

Formally organized in 1814 at a convention in Vermont, they drew several thousand adherents across New England, New York, and Canada. By the Civil War, most of the Reformed movement had affiliated with the Methodist Protestants.

In the second decade of the century, the African Methodist Episcopal (1816) and the African Union (1813) churches organized, as we noted. Their centers were located and remained in Philadelphia and Wilmington, respectively. The organization of the African Methodist Episcopal Zion Church in 1820 was closely related with a separation among white Methodists also in New York led by Samuel Stillwell, a trustee at the flagship John Street Church, and his nephew, William Stillwell, a preacher then in charge of two of the African American congregations. At issue in both divisions was ownership of church property and control over ministry. The Stillwellites grew to some 2,000 members in the New York, New Jersey, and Connecticut areas, continuing until the younger Stillwell's death in 1851. Another separate Methodist body, also with the name *Primitive Methodists*, developed around the figure of Lorenzo Dow, the export of American-style camp meeting revivalism to Britain after 1805, and import-of-the-export as a distinct denomination, beginning in 1829. The Primitives developed strength in Pennsylvania and, especially, in Canada.[19]

The democratic themes associated with these several movements came in to focus in the reform efforts of the 1820s—to permit election of the episcopal lieutenants or surrogates known as presiding elders, to allow some conference role and representation to the two-thirds of the Methodist ministry functioning as local rather than itinerant preachers, and to permit laity a say in the governing annual and general conferences. Here, as with the Republican Methodists, a set of legislative proposals gave focus to concerns, practices, and styles that went far deeper and presented the church again with the question as to how its internal life would draw on the best aspects of democratic society. Here too the reformers initially carried the day. They passed (decisively, 61 to 25) legislation at the 1820 General Conference providing for election of presiding elders, a proposal surfaced early in Methodist history and repeatedly urged up to the present, but vehemently resisted by the bishops, by William McKendree in his opening episcopal address to that conference and by bishop-elect Joshua Soule, the architect of Methodist constitutional order. Soule pronounced the change unconstitutional and insisted that he could not "superintend under the rules this day made." Soule's resignation prompted the conference to suspend the new legislation.

A decade of intense, bitter, recriminating politics followed. New media emerged to carry the campaign to the populace. Popular conventions met to broaden the reform agenda. Bishops and conferences suppressed dissent and excommunicated dissenters. The reform movement found support from some of the strongest of Methodist leaders and its following at the heart of the Methodist movement, namely, in the upper South and in the middle states. In 1830 a new denomination, the Methodist Protestant Church, came into being to consolidate the reforms. And here too the rather modest size of the new denomination scarcely registers the deep division and cultural war through which Methodism had passed.

SLAVERY, REGION, RACE

Each division produced not only losses—of persons, of richness and diversity, of leadership, of principle—but also countermeasures that sometimes paralleled, sometimes negated the points of the reformers. Losses and reactive countermeasures certainly attended the divisions of the 1840s and 1850s, the exiting of abolitionists to form the Wesleyan Methodist Church in 1842, the split of the Methodist Episcopals north and south in 1844, and the emergence of the Free Methodists in the late 1850s (formally organizing in 1860). In each of these divisions, high principle on one side produced compensating efforts on the other. The MEC, particularly in New England and the "burned-over district," became more receptive to abolition in the face of competition from the Wesleyans. The MECS intensified its mission to the slaves in the wake of the division of 1844. And New York Methodists contended with the witness of reformers who criticized elite control of the annual conference, the use of pew rents, slippage in the church's teaching on sanctification, and irresolution on slavery. "Freedom" emblemed their several-pronged attack on Methodism's bourgeoisification and compromise with society's practices and their call for a return to primitive Methodism.[20]

The division of 1844 produced differing ecclesiologies and notions of the relation of church to the civil order, north and south, and both churches have, at times, read the division as though it primarily concerned notions of the power of general conference, the authority of bishops, the limits of social witness. Underneath these theological and polity concerns, of course, lurked slavery and the differing sectional attitudes thereunto. Sectional division of the churches produced intense moral warfare, principled posturing, undergirded by fears and hopes about slavery. The several church splits anticipated and aggravated, if they did not "cause," the growing division of the nation.[21] The 1844 division, creating a Methodist Episcopal Church and a Methodist Episcopal Church, South, left scars that continue to this day and fault lines that now vibrate over abortion and homosexuality rather than slavery. If these current issues constitute banners in a larger and deeper culture war, so might we also portray the contest between slave and free civilizations of the 1840s and 1850s.

The 1860s saw massive population shifts among Black Methodists and one major new African American denomination, the Colored Methodist Episcopal Church. The latter, formalized in 1870, represented the culmination of MECS efforts to minister to slaves and then freed persons under strict racist guidelines and can be read as either extrusion of or exodus by African Americans.[22] One stimulus to MECS cooperation in the establishment of the CME was the success enjoyed by the MEC (the northern church) with the ex-slaves and the even greater and politically more radical advances of the AME and AMEZ.[23] All these population shifts, and not just the emergence of the CME, ought to be seen as important divisions. Also of a divisive quality was the decision by the MEC in 1864 to authorize the creation of separate Black annual conferences, a segregating gesture "perfected" in the North before it was spread across the South. This *de jure* separation of black and white proved as complete as and longer-lived than the division of the MEC and MECS.

LANGUAGE, GENDER, CLASS

Some internal divisions look benign in hindsight but raised then, as they raise today, questions about the character and unity of the church. I refer to the establishment of distinct language conferences, an issue that has resurfaced recently as highly controversial when requested by Korean Americans. The year 1864 saw the authorization of German annual conferences by the MEC. German mission conferences had been established in 1844, as also had a mission conference for Native Americans. Swedish, Norwegian, Danish, Spanish, Japanese, and Chinese conferences would emerge later.

Episcopal Methodism granted laity rights in General Conference only gradually (in 1866 and 1872 in the MECS and MEC respectively) and had even greater difficulty with overtures to include women as lay leadeers or to ordain them. But Methodism did sanction women-run voluntary societies that functioned like conferences, notably the Woman's Christian Temperance Union (1874), interdenominational but always heavily Methodist; the Woman's Foreign Missionary Society (1869); the corresponding entities for the MECS (1878) and MPC (1879); and the Ladies' and Pastors' Union (1872). There was no threat of division along gender lines but the internal structural differentiation deserves notice.

Class differences were not so easily contained. From the 1860s on, the holiness cause increasingly took on aspects of class war. Church leaders who initially embraced their fervent piety increasingly reacted to sustained holiness criticisms and freelance itineration with a heavy, disciplining hand. Schisms proved inevitable. The Free Methodists had, we noted, already exited in 1860. The National Camp Meeting for the Promotion of Holiness of 1867 led to the formation of a National Camp Meeting Association. Holiness camp meetings and itinerating holiness preachers called Methodism to return to its primitive practices. They recalled a prewar and pre-1844 Methodism of entrepreneurial circuit riders, of outdoor quarterly meetings conjoined with camp meetings, of shouting preachers and demonstrative religiosity, of discipline through class meetings, and of side-street preaching houses. Many felt ill at ease in the grand, uptown gothic cathedrals, lavishly appointed and funded with pew rents; unnourished by worship centered in the Sunday service rather than the camp; ill equipped to function in the increasingly nationalized and centralized program of the church and in the corporate board and agency structure authorized in 1872;

unsatisfied by a view of the Christian life as nurtured by home and in Sunday school and provisioned through John Vincent's uniform lesson plan, teacher institutes, and Chautauquas. The holiness camp meetings represented one side in a culture war that pitted the anxious bench and class meeting against the Sunday service and the Sunday school. The prophetic spirit became, in places and at times, a come-outer spirit. And so in the 1880s and 1890s, regional and state holiness associations and conventions gradually transformed themselves into new denominations, the Church of God (Anderson), Church of God (Holiness), the Holiness Church, and the Church of the Nazarene. The later separate organizations make it hard to recall and envision the broader war within Methodism in which they had campaigned. The same, with important qualifications, might be said of the Pentecostal movements.

CODA

The twentieth century, of course, represents something of a different story. Its agenda was reunion, the ending of denominational divisions, ecumenism, Christian unity. Methodism experienced several major reunions—the MEC, MECS, and MPC uniting in 1939 to form The Methodist Church; the EA and UB uniting in 1946 to form the Evangelical United Brethren Church; the two new bodies uniting in 1968 to form The United Methodist Church. And the reunions have not yet ended. Recent general conferences have authorized proceeding with COCU/CUIC; with rapprochement with the AMEs, the AMEZs, and the CMEs; with bilaterals with Lutherans and Episcopalians; and with other ecumenical explorations.

Yet unifications, as well, have proved immensely divisive in ways that need to be recalled if one wishes to understand internal and transdenominational coalitions today. For instance, the prospect of unification of the MEC and the MECS caused near division in the South (the MECS), with race as the major concern. And when unification came, it did so with an accommodation to the South that built a radical division into the very fabric of the denomination—namely the segregation of African Americans nationally into a Central Jurisdiction. And the ending of that scandal coincided with the birth within Methodism of the caucuses and special interest groups.

Division and culture wars have been a rather constant feature of Methodist denominational life and, if not an every-decade affair for others, at least very common. Conventional wisdom has a short memory.

CHAPTER 12

ARE THE LOCAL CHURCH AND THE DENOMINATIONAL BUREAUCRACY "TWINS"?

Proposals for reform of United Methodism surface frequently. Often they would free the local church from the perceived burden of remote, inflexible, centralized, hierarchical rule by boards and agencies; from the obligation to render up apportionments to this Caesar; from the yoke of mandated denominational structure; from perceived centralized control. Such concerns have resulted in greater flexibility for local churches and, to a lesser extent, annual conferences to adapt structure and organization to reflect size, context, resources, and mission. Bishops attempt to relieve meetings and especially annual conferences of the burden of business and to make them occasions of Christian conferencing. They and leaders at all levels push decision making away from motions, debates, and divisions of the house toward discernment. And in an important symbolic attack on centralization, the 2004 General Conference abolished one symbol of denominational authority, the General Council of Ministries, replacing it instead with a Connectional Table.[1]

This essay responds by suggesting that such reforms and antidotes are halfway measures. Specifically, it proposes:

- that the changes and the analyses that underlie attacks on bureaucracy grapple with hyper-organization at regional and national levels but fail to recognize the comparable organizational excess at local levels;
- that the local church structuring and national denominational ordering are in fact twins, both generated out of the organizational revolution;

- that recovery of Wesleyan connectionalism at the local level requires as much sustained criticism of "the local church" inertia and complexity as of distant bureaucracy;
- that such recovery or renewal is already well underway and pointing toward a new connectionalism normed on neither the corporate state nor congregationalism; and
- that a renewed connectionalism at the local level can help us reclaim some of the long-lost potential of our polity and our ecclesiology.

The Local Mission: A Retrospective

Early American Methodism knew what congregations and parishes were. The one epitomized church for New England Puritanism, the other typified southern Anglicanism and much of western Christendom. Methodism opposed both, took a different form, and committed itself constitutionally to a more radical vision of church. It had no congregations. And certainly no parishes. To be sure, it built or purchased preaching houses from its earliest days. But they were just that, houses for preaching. Except in rare (urban) instances, these small chapels did not center the movement at the local level; circumscribe the range of Methodist life, service, and mission; or command the services of a single preacher, even for his tenure in that locale. Preaching houses were just that, houses for preaching. And they had no monopoly on that.

Much of Methodist life, including the preaching, went on in houses for living. In homes, Methodists baptized, prayed, met, married, educated, and conducted funerals. Much of the early preaching as well went on in the houses in which converts lived. And the chapels not only resembled the houses amongst which they nestled but often took their name from the family chiefly responsible for erecting them—as Asbury's notation of their names indicates. When the crowd exceeded what a home or chapel would hold, preachers took the assemblage outside or to another denomination's facilities or to a public building. Such large gatherings—akin to today's Sunday worship—occurred infrequently, typically for quarterly meetings or camp meetings, which were often one and the same. On those occasions, presiding elders, preachers, local preachers, and exhorters would conduct the business of the circuit, hold love feasts, preach frequently, celebrate the Lord's Supper, and sometimes conduct memorial services. Methodist life did not center itself in its little buildings but rather was decentered and diffused across the Methodist landscape and was temporally rather than spatially centered in the weekly class, regular preaching, and liturgically rich quarterly conferences.

If Methodism did not locate itself in its buildings, it also did not confine itself in congregations or societies. The basic local unit of

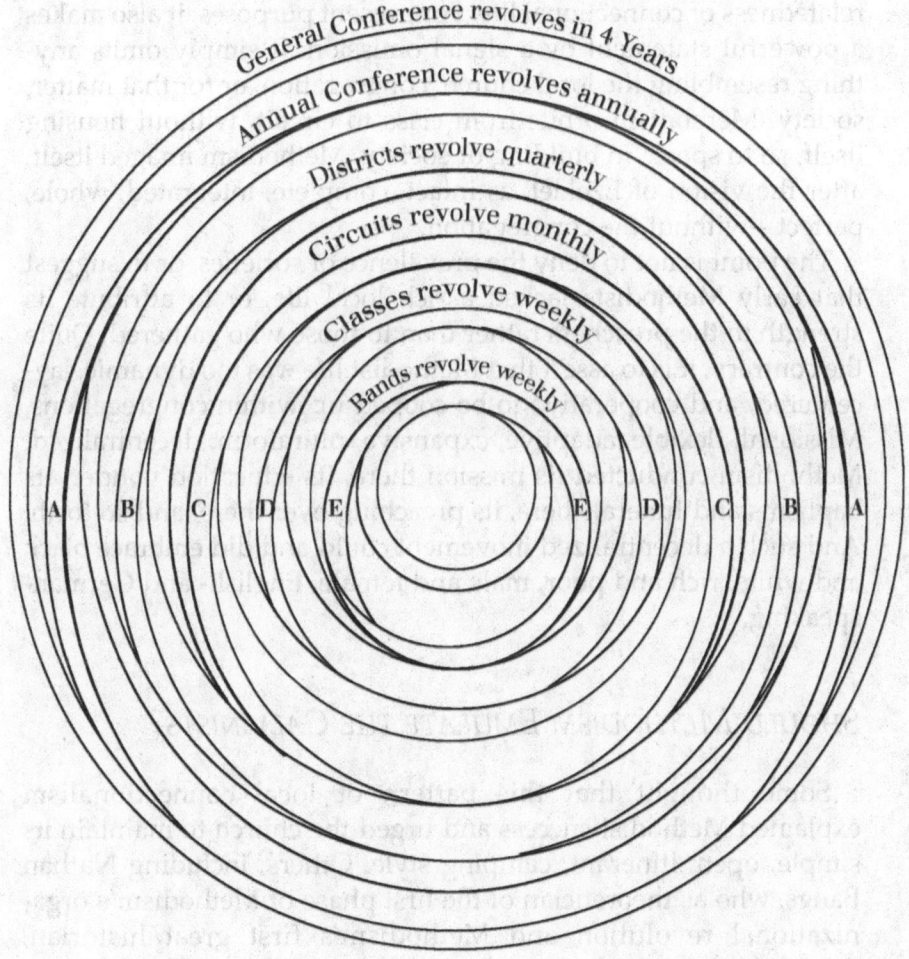

Methodist life, the unit to which one belonged, was not the society but the class. And the next recognized unit of Methodist life, recognized by the *Discipline*, was not the society but the quarterly conference. To be sure, classes might, indeed did, associate into societies, but the unit most closely resembling the official definition of church—where the Word was preached, sacraments administered, and discipline exercised—was the quarterly conference, a regional affair, typically embracing multiple societies.

The reproduced above chart from the 1820s depicts Methodism as an array of orbits within orbits, the spin of one affecting and being affected by that of all others.[2] The picture displays the interrelatedness of connectional life. For present purposes, it also makes a powerful statement by a signal omission. It simply omits anything resembling the local church, congregation, or for that matter, society. Methodism orbits from class to circuit, without housing itself, so to speak, in building or society. Methodism imaged itself, after the vision of Ezekiel, as intact, complete, integrated, whole, perfect—without the congregation.

The point is not to deny the prevalence of societies, or to suggest that early Methodists lacked a rich local life, or to attribute its strength to the preachers rather than to those who gathered. Quite the contrary, it is to assert that Methodist life was too dynamic, lay-centered, and cooperative to be cooped up within congregations. Missional, flexible, adaptive, expansive, pluraform, decentralized, Methodism conducted its mission there, its education yonder, its baptisms and funerals here, its preaching over there, and so forth. And such a decentralized movement could and did embrace black and white, rich and poor, male and female, English- and German-speaking.

SHOULD METHODISM EMULATE THE CALVINISTS?

Some thought that this pattern of local connectionalism explained Methodist success and urged the church to maintain its simple, open, itinerant, camping style. Others, including Nathan Bangs, who as theoretician of the first phase of Methodism's organizational revolution and Methodism's first great historian, thought that Methodism ought to build churches so as "to occupy the young and thriving villages that were rising into being by the hand of industry." He asserted:

> In these countries the Methodist preachers were the gospel pioneers, and for many years, in various places, the people had no other preachers who "cared for their souls." They were accustomed to go among them in their lonely retreats, preach in their log huts, hold their quarterly meetings in barns or in the woods, and they seemed to have been so long accustomed to this mode of preaching and living, that they almost forgot, in many instances, to provide themselves with better accommodations; and before they were aware of it, other denominations came, took possession of the villages, erected houses of worship, and thus drew the weightier part of population around them.[3]

Following Bangs's counsel, Methodism did increasingly orient itself toward the weightier and wealthier. In towns and cities it abandoned what Kenneth Rowe has termed its *side street* chapels for proper *main street* churches.[4] In the period before and after the Civil War, Methodism erected elegant, often Gothic, cathedrals. Such ventures lay beyond the capacity of the simpler, cellular class structure of earlier Methodism and were the expression of a new "congregational" style. Real *congregations* emerged, claimed the growing numbers of Methodists "on the make," demanded and got a stationed, more educated clergy, and kept clergy longer. And a stationed clergy increasingly took over the roles previously played by the class leaders and local preachers. Neither disappeared overnight but throughout the middle decades of the nineteenth century various appeals to reclaim the class system document its peril. Some of the advocates of that older Methodism—a Methodism of class and quarterly meeting and camp meeting and perfection—raised the holiness banner and took a separatist course. The mainstream of Methodism, however, moved, gradually at first, then more rapidly, to constitute itself like its competition—in congregations.

NATIONAL STRUCTURES

Consolidation into congregations not only meant de-emphasizing Wesleyan classes. It also entailed coming to terms with voluntary societies. Bangs had led Methodism into creating missionary societies and an effective communication system through *Advocates*, the *Methodist Quarterly Review*, and more sophisticated employment of Sunday schools. At the local level, the missionary and reform societies—men's and women's—and the Sunday schools offered new roles for the laity and an array of purposive gatherings not well integrated into the local connectional system. With such institutions and roles, as with the class, the settled pastor and the stable congregation experienced problems—of accountability, control, authority. Such problems and issues derived from the fact that the new dynamic entities did not mesh with or report to the existing authority structure and from the fact that the existing authority structure remained the old quarterly meeting. In 1852 the MEC dealt with part of the problem by providing a seat for "male superintendents of our Sunday schools . . . in the Quarterly Conferences . . . with the right to speak and vote on questions relating to Sunday schools, and on such questions only."[5] In 1864, the northern church made the superintendent a full member and granted the Quarterly Conference "supervision of all the Sunday-schools and Sunday-school societies within its bounds."[6]

Such problems in accountability ran up and down the connectional structure, and in 1872 the MEC moved to attack them at a national level by bringing its five major benevolent societies—the Missionary Society, the Church Extension Society, the Board of Education, the Sunday-School Union, and the Tract Society—"under the control of the General Conference." It did so by seeking necessary legal and legislative measures that would change each entity's charter and provide for General Conference election of its trustees or managers. This was the key maneuver in the organizational revolution by which Methodism achieved modern boards and agencies.[7] Three General Conferences later, the church effected the comparable revolution at the local level. It authorized quarterly conferences to "organize, and continue during its pleasure, an Official Board, to be composed of all the members of the Quarterly Conference," to be "presided over by the preacher in charge," to discharge many of the duties of the Leaders and Stewards's Meeting, and to "keep a record of its proceedings."[8] The creation of the official board brought to the local church what incorporation, consolidation, efficiency, bureaucratization, and professionalization brought to the church as a whole and, indeed, to American society, that is, corporate principles of finance, procedure, order, integration, governance, and cohesion. Bureaucratization at the top and business efficiency in the local church went together. Indeed, they were twins.

INSTITUTIONAL CHURCHES

The fruits of this development at the local level emerged a decade later during the late nineteenth-, early twentieth-century Social Gospel epoch in what were termed *institutional churches* (and were called *central halls* in Britain). These large-scale church complexes resembled the typical suburban or urban congregation of today, with sanctuary, educational wing, community service accommodations, kitchens, childcare facilities, and the like, and with a strong weekday as well as weekend program. Methodist life had fully moved from houses for living into houses for worship. Here was "the local church" we know today:

- a complex religious matrix incorporated or recognized as a single entity;
- functioning with a parishlike orientation to its geographical surroundings;
- channeling through its life the local mission efforts of the denomination;
- covering with its umbrella and governing structures a great variety of groups, missionary associations, benevolent causes, and educational endeavors (especially Sunday school);
- featuring one or more assemblies for weekly worship;
- owning or holding effective control over a building or buildings capable of housing the variety of weekly gatherings for worship, educational, service, and outreach ministries;
- understanding itself as a corporate religious body capable of, perhaps charged with, exercising communal leadership;
- channeling through its budget(s) the monies raised locally for its own purposes and services and those of denominational and ecumenical boards;

- all under the guidance of lay and clergy leaders who share accountability for these local efforts under Methodist mandate.

The turn-of-the-century "institutional church" consolidated and incorporated the distinguishable, diverse, sometimes discrete expressions of local religion. And the prevalence of this form of the church today, reinforced by the American predilection for local rule and by principled congregationalism, makes the congregation as intellectual construct seem to be *the*, and *the only*, modality of local religiosity. Today, it just seems natural that local religious functions will center in a single "congregation."

UNEASE IN ZION

All during this period of developing congregationalism, bishops and other leaders complained of the compromise of itinerancy and the appointive system. In 1912, for instance, in their episcopal address the bishops noted how congregational interests distorted the Methodist understanding of ministry. They argued, "The Christian ministry is not a profession," and therefore (it) should not be upheld "on the secular basis of compensation," that is, salary.

> Methodist preachers are "supported," not hired. The difference is vital. A "support" is the sum estimated, *for a pastor already appointed*, by an authorized committee after consultation with the pastor, as sufficient to furnish himself and family a comfortable livelihood. Under this plan consecration is not compromised, and the preacher's message may weigh its full gospel value. "Salary," on the other hand, implies a stated stipend proposed as compensation for services to be rendered, fixed before the service begins and as a condition to its beginning at all.

The "contract is not with the Official Board or Quarterly Conference. It is an altar covenant with God alone." They complained of "negotiations," asked, "What yet remains of the system?" and denounced the commercialization of pulpit service:

> Thus is pulpit service commercialized, and thus in time every prominent preacher is practically appraised, and not always by the gospel standard of success. His 'rank' or appoint availability in cabinet is determined—himself, alas! too often consenting, by lay valuation in dollars and prospects.[9]

The bishops concerned themselves with the terms of the contract, the monetary assessment of clergy, rather than the structural reality—the congregationalism—that interposed a contracting entity into the Methodism economy. Congregationalism and the official board rather than the contracting spirit might have been a more effective target.

Instead, the bishops accepted "the local church" and the power thereof as part of Methodist parlance and as much a given as its twin, the national boards and agencies, with which they also contended. The term *local church* crept into Methodist talk and became a touchstone for judging Methodist work, integrity, purpose. Nowhere was its new value better expressed than in the 1928 episcopal address (MEC). The bishops recognized the new norm for Methodism—the local church—by organizing their speech around it. They entitled the first long section "The Local Church and What It May Ask of General Methodism." They affirmed:

> The local church is taken as the unit in our study of denominational progress, for it is there that we are to test the value of our organization and polity. It is the point of Methodism's contact with humanity. It is our recruiting office for the King's service. It is for us the institute of religious technology, our workshop, our training camp, our spiritual hospital, our home.[10]

Here, rhetorically and theologically, the bishops completed the long process of redefining local Methodism. Methodism would be at home not with its people and in their homes but "at home" in its buildings, its congregations, its fortresses. Fittingly, they employed military language to describe local Methodism's institutionalization—"training camp," "recruiting office," "point of contact," "service,"—and these nuanced the other terms—"hospital," "workshop," "technology"—with military force.

The bishops devoted major subsections to the church building, members (of all ages), finances, the office, the pastor and pastoral office, laity and educational institutions (within which they discussed the whole range of Methodist schools and colleges, not just local or intra-church education). In the next major section, the bishops explored "What the Local Church Owes to General Methodism," only then turning to "What World-Wide Methodism Asks of the World" and "What World-Wide Methodism Owes to the World." In the first two sections, the bishops had embraced Methodism within the local church; in the latter two, the bishops revisited major issues in relation to national bureaucracy. Rhetorically, the bishops had recognized the twins of the organizational revolution.

ADJUSTING THE DISCIPLINE

Such episcopal statements played a vital role in the long process of obliterating the connectional principle that had once knit Methodism into a series of gatherings—band, class, quarterly conference, annual conference, general conference—and replacing it with a series of corporate structures—local church, district office, conference staff and agencies, (jurisdictional staff?), and national boards and agencies. The *Discipline* gradually recognized the linguistic changes and institutional realities. For instance, in 1920 the church quietly endowed the quarterly conference with a constitutional amendment changing "Quarterly" to "Local."[11] And in 1940, as one of the first acts of the newly jurisdictioned and united Methodism, the general conference authorized the incorporation into one section of the *Discipline* all the various references to local Methodism that had been described under the many rubrics and aspects of Methodism's work: "Motion of Alfred F. Hughes (West Wisconsin), duly seconded, prevailed that the Editors of the *Discipline* be instructed to bring together in one Section of the *Discipline* legislation referring specifically to the Organization and Administration of the local Church."

A subsequent motion (referred to the Committee on Publishing Interests) asked the editors to "consider publishing an inexpensive edition of said *Discipline* containing only those assembled Sections referring to the Local Church."[12]

The church achieved such salience for that part of the *Discipline* without dropping everything else out. With the 1944 *Discipline*, "The Local Church" became Part II, following immediately after "The Constitution" and preceding Part III, "The Ministry" and Part IV, "The Conferences." In the 1968 *Discipline*, "The Local Church" stood first, embracing even calendar, thus incorporating Methodist time into a congregational orbit. And in the 1976 *Discipline* that section expanded to include the discussion of ministry, a symbolical reframing of Wesleyan horizons; Wesley had spoken of the world as his parish; now Methodism indeed made parish its world. Was this the end to which Wesley intended itinerancy or just the end of itinerancy?

The church appropriately recognizes the new norm—congregationalism—by construing local church as *the* primary form of ministry and construing anything and everything else with a new, now technical, phrase, "Appointments beyond the local church." This trend produced the episcopal pastoral, *Vital Congregations, Faithful Disciples*. It culminates in the recent proposals to give the local church control over apportionments and appointments, effectively collapsing the connection into the congregation.

IMPLICATIONS

It would be in the spirit of the recent proposals concerning the local church to move in the next General Conference (1) that the local church rather than the annual conference constitutes the basic unit of the church; and (2) with a rephrasing of the motion of 1944: "That we publishing as the . . . *Discipline* . . . only those . . . Sections referring to the Local Church." Such motions would complete, constitutionally, the collapse of connectionalism into institutionalized congregationalism. This would be a mistake, as, I believe, are a variety of equally congregational but less dramatic recent proposals.

Methodism deserves better, both for its local mission and its wider witness. The question is not what is to be done at the local level, nor really where money might be spent. The issue has to do with agency, control, limits, horizon, permission, expansiveness. Fundamental is housing. Where will Methodism be "at home"?

Will it be at home only in its buildings, under corporate management, controlled by pastors, programmed only from one center, hemmed in by local bureaucratic procedure, preoccupied with accountability? Or will Methodism reenter the homes of its people, and more important, the people who need to hear its message? Will it move out of its buildings into its neighborhoods? Will it become again too dynamic, lay-centered, and cooperative to be cooped up within a congregation? Will it reclaim its missional, flexible, adaptive, expansive, pluraform, decentralized ecclesial principle?

Fortunately, we see signs that the answer is yes. That Wesleyan spirit we can see clearly at work in a variety of new efforts that work vitally at local levels but reconnect us nationally in new dynamic forms of gathering and witness. Such reconceiving and reanchoring the connection can be seen in the DISCIPLE Bible study, Emmaus Walk, Covenant Discipleship, the Academy for Spiritual Formation, Chrysalis, Volunteers in Mission, Good News and the several caucuses, Reconciling Congregations, and a variety of efforts, particularly in urban ministry, some specifically Methodist, others ecumenical. Many would think of these as essentially local. Each has connectional leadership as well as powerful local expression. Each moves beyond the walls of our buildings to find "new homes" for religious expression. Each draws in and equips fresh leadership. Each beckons the whole of Methodism to a new spirit and to renewal.

A Methodism that moves out of "the local church" will, I believe, recover its reforming and evangelistic style. The local church "killed" one of our main engines of evangelism and outreach, the local preacher. It "killed" the office by bottling up within the congregation and making accountable to a congregational "official board" an office and persons that had been deployed locally, on the circuit, and regionally. Thereafter the church recreated the local preacher as the non-seminary-Course-of-Study-trained pastor. Ironically, now it is the Southern Baptists who are rediscovering the office (now termed bivocationality), who are creating house churches and putting ministers on circuit to apartment gatherings. Methodism can also reclaim its evangelical heritage, if it also revisits its proper, Wesleyan notion of home and connection. Doing so does not mean abandoning existing buildings or congregations. Far from it. These constitute resources for local mission. The question is whether we will ask about that local mission, about where it calls us to be, about what it calls us to do. Will we put the same hard questions to "the local church" that we are now putting to boards and agencies? They are, after all, twins.

PART 4
CHURCH AND SACRAMENT

CHAPTER 13

METHODISM'S *PRACTICED* ECCLESIOLOGY

United Methodism defines itself and exhibits its ecclesial sensibilities with four books. Two of these, the Bible and *Hymnal*, one finds in the pew and in the homes of the Methodist faithful. The other two, *The Book of Discipline* and *The Book of Worship*, one finds in the studies of ministers or in church libraries.[1] Each characterizes or shapes the church, albeit in a distinct way. All are important. Each works for and works itself into the drama of the church's daily life.[2] The *Discipline* and *Book of Worship* function offstage, so to speak, but determine how the play unfolds, who acts, and what instructions to follow.

Bible and *Hymnal* script Methodist life together. The latter provides rituals from birth to death, norms Sunday morning worship, structures the weekly praise of God, specifies the Psalms to read and the hymns to sing. The former—studied downstairs by all ages in Sunday school, always read upstairs and now frequently fulsomely in accordance with the uniform lections—scripts life lived in Christ.

The four books, Scripture, *Hymnal*, *Discipline*, and *Book of Worship*, define how United Methodists do church.[3] In "practicing" church, Methodists have in their own way lived out what the church more generally has held to be important ecclesial understandings. I shall attempt to take note of those at first mention with *italicized bolding*, marking key Wesleyan or Methodist ecclesial notions in the same manner with **bolding**, thereby identifying how and where Methodism imbeds its ecclesiology in its practices and as guided by these books. The chapter endeavors to show the congruence, albeit in a few pages, of distinctive Methodist practices with classic doctrines (including the "marks" or "notes" of the church—one, holy, catholic, and apostolic) and with traditional forms (sacraments, the threefold ministry). Since the exposition must be compressed, a little guidance about directions:

Contents

I. FOUNDATIONS
    Wesley's Transmittal
    The Books and their Ecclesial Import
II. TRANSFORMATIONS
    The Quadrilateral: A Literary Evolution?
    Bible, *Discipline*, *Hymnal*
III. UNITED METHODISM
    A New Church
    United Methodism's Four Books
    Counterpoint
IV. MISSIONAL ECCLESIOLOGY
    The Official Stance
    Discipline: Catholic Spirit
    Discipline: Missional Commitment
CONCLUSION

I. FOUNDATIONS

Wesley's Transmittal

Each of these books John Wesley conveyed to the little North American Methodist movement and conveyed at the point of the movement's becoming church. His "Large Minutes," the governing instrument of the British movement, constituted the basis of the first *Discipline*.[4] Compiled out of the decisions of the "governing" conferences of Wesley with his preachers, the "Large Minutes" and the American versions thereof, the *Discipline*, provided quasi-constitution for the reformist Methodist movement, specified its distinctive practices and gatherings, and outlined its ministerial tasks and duties. Appended to the *Discipline* (in its first, 1785 edition) was *A Collection of Psalms and Hymns for the Lord's Day*.[5] *A Pocket Hymnbook* appeared the next year, one in a long series of hymnbooks for the Methodist people. The Wesleys had selected verse from Charles and structured and organized the collection to guide the faithful in the way of salvation.[6] Rich in scriptural citation and allusion,[7] it put biblical motif and Wesleyan doctrine on Methodist lips. It began with hymns entreating the sinner to turn to God and followed with several sections posing the consequences of one's action, either with God in heaven or in death and hell. A second part contrasted formal and inward religion. In a third part, the Wesleys located hymns evocative of repentance, conviction, conversion, and perseverance. Part four, the longest with ten sections, exhibited 261 hymns for Christians struggling toward perfection. The final part featured hymns for Methodist societies and classes.

The *Book of Common Prayer* (BCP) was dear to the Wesleys, and John had edited and digested it into the *Sunday Service of the Methodists in North America*. Despite the latter's apparently restrictive title, it provided a full set of rituals—morning prayer, evening prayer, weekday litany, Sunday service, eucharist, two baptismal rites, marriage, and orders for communion of the sick, burial, and ordination services for deacons, elders, and superintendents. It also included a brief lectionary and twenty-four Articles of Religion, excerpted from Anglicanism's Thirty-nine.[8]

A letter from Wesley conveyed these documents and authorized the establishment of the new church. Addressed to the two bishop-(superintendent-) designees and their brethren, "To Dr. COKE, Mr. ASBURY, and our Brethren in NORTH AMERICA," it instructed the young church: "They are now at full liberty, simply to follow the Scriptures and the Primitive Church."[9] The injunction to follow Scripture was hardly needed but it did effectively found the new church with the fourth book.

With Scripture, hymnbook, discipline, and book of worship, Wesley made provision for the movement that would call itself The Methodist Episcopal Church. By reference, inclusion, and allusion these books pointed to other standards: Twenty-five Articles of Religion (adapted from the Thirty-nine and one added to the twenty-four that Wesley had isolated); Wesley's *Sermons*; his *Notes upon the New Testament*; and the "General Rules" (a set of injunctions and disciplines by which Methodists might hold themselves and one another accountable for the ethical life and chart their way toward the knowledge and love of God—practices largely echoed in the *Discipline*). These standards also figured (and figure) in the definition of Methodism and of the Methodist way of life, but they tended to be less the day-to-day, week-to-week, traveling companions for Methodists in their pilgrim's progress. Scripture, hymnbook, discipline, and book of worship were made to travel.

The Books and Their Ecclesial Import

Two points about these books and their ecclesiological import should be registered. First, one can draw a rough correspondence between the four and the putative Wesleyan quadrilateral—*Scripture, experience, reason*, and *tradition*.[10] To be sure, we might rightly connect each of the books with all parts of the quadrilateral, as we will illustrate in the paragraph immediately below. But each book had, as well, a special force with respect to one of these Methodist epistemological impulses. Second, the four pulled early American Methodism in ecclesially different directions, one might say, in one of two opposing ecclesiological directions. Each book, its primary quadrilateral association, and its early ecclesial significance deserve remark.

The hymnal normed *experience*, providing poetic scripts for the Methodists to follow toward perfection. Its phrasing, images, themes, and organization captured and charted the ups and downs of the pilgrim's progress from the first stirrings of grace in the sinful soul through to the blessing of **holiness**. Though the hymnal featured the "evangelical doctrines," its verse comprehended the range of Christian experience, the whole task of the church, and the full catholic creedal witness. Rich in scriptural citation and allusion, offering the tradition's doctrinal consensus, and ordering the Christian walk in a rational though poetic style, the hymnal, like the other books, could be and should be recognized as evidencing all parts of the quadrilateral.[11] Most Methodists would have missed the hymnal's epistemological or methodological quadrilateral complexity.[12] For them it fed experience—the quiet private devotion and the fervid communal song. And it did so with exacting attention to Arminian doctrines predicated upon **free grace**, the goal of **holiness**, and the resources of Wesleyan spirituality or, as Methodists would have then put it, **piety** and discipline.

The *Discipline*, and the various authoritative texts that it included or referenced, gathered Methodist experience and belief, individual and collective, into *reason*ed order. If the *Discipline* can be said to have exhibited the *reason* aspect of the quadrilateral, it did so in a peculiarly Wesleyan fashion, indeed in an American Wesleyan fashion. The *Discipline* offered a practical reason; an ordered rule of life—individual and corporate; a set of regimens or "**disciplines**" for life in the kingdom; and the structures, offices, polices, and procedures by which to follow those dictates.[13] This was not reason in the mode of John Locke and his Age of Reason colleagues, nor that of Thomas Aquinas and the great tradition of scholasticism, nor even that of John Wesley himself, who could address *An Earnest Appeal to Men of Reason and Religion* and *A Farther Appeal to Men of Reason and Religion*. No, this was a practical reason that American Methodists referenced when in 1787 they refashioned their version of the "Large Minutes," now termed *A Form of Discipline . . . Arranged under proper Heads, and Methodized in a more acceptable and easy Manner*. The "rationality" of the *Discipline* would only increase over time, in no small part, the product of Methodism's rapid growth, consequent structural complexity, problem-solving, and missional diversification.

The *Discipline*, like the "Large Minutes," set forth the ordered life for the people, including what Wesley specified as the instituted **means of grace: prayer, searching the scriptures, the Lord's Supper, fasting,** and **Christian conference.** By the latter, he meant conversation about the good life, not the structures of governance. The *Discipline*, however, supplied the latter as well, outlining the responsibilities and prerogatives of each of the connectional level, and of several ministerial, offices: *bishops*, **presiding elders, traveling** *elders*, **traveling** *deacons*, **local preachers, exhorters, stewards,** and **class leaders.** Here was the threefold ministry augmented by the distinctively Wesleyan offices all **connected** as essential cogs in a missional system. The first four offices itinerated broadly, the latter four more locally.

These two books, *Hymnal* and *Discipline*, one for the believer's purse, the other for the preacher's saddlebag, pulled toward a discrete Wesleyan identity, perhaps one might say, inward or more accurately "**connectionally.**" They provided Methodists a Wesleyan grammar for the Christian life, a Wesleyan **missional** ecclesiology.[14] The 1787 *Discipline* made that missional ecclesial assertion explicitly, in defining Methodist **purpose:**

Of the Rise of Methodism (so called) in Europe and America.

Quest. 1. What was the Rise of Methodism, so called, in Europe?

Answ. In 1729, two young Men, reading the Bible, saw they could not be saved without Holiness, followed after it, and incited others so to do. In 1737, they saw likewise, that Men are justified before they are sanctified: but still Holiness was their Object. God then thrust them out, to raise an holy People. . . .

Quest. 3. What may we reasonably believe to be God's Design, in raising up the Preachers called Methodists?

Answ. To reform the Continent, and spread scripture Holiness over these Lands. As a Proof hereof, we have seen in the Course of fifteen Years a great a glorious Work of God, from New-York through the Jersies, Pennsylvania, Maryland, Virginia, North and South Carolina, even to Georgia.[15]

"**To reform the continent and spread scripture holiness over these lands**" refined John Wesley's purposive formulation for the American context. This mantra, despite its inward pull, did not yield a sectarian spirit—though such claims have occasionally been made—but instead an **evangelical or missionary connectionalism** or **denominationalism**. No sectarians, Methodists did not withdraw from a sinful world but sought to transform it. They would transform it revivalistically, by bringing in the sheaves and in witnessing against sins, individual and social. And what would they transform? Note their ambitions, hardly those of a sect but instead quite impressive territorial or geographical ambitions, indicated above in the church's commitment to reform the entire continent. They began, moreover, with a passion to take on what has been the most intractable American dilemma, that of race. They began with a commitment to African Americans and their freedom.[16]

Methodists undertook such transformative endeavor with Wesley's methods—the class-quarterly meeting-conference structure; exacting disciplines for both members and preachers; an elaborate schema of local and **itinerant ministries**; and Wesley-like **itinerant general superintendents (bishops)** with powers to appoint preachers to circuits or stations.[17] These practices, sung about in Wesleyan verse and performed in the directives of the *Discipline*, implicitly carried an ecclesiology, a **missionary** and **con-**

nectional conception of the church. It was, as Bishops Thomas Coke and Francis Asbury understood it and as we note below, the *apostolic* form of the church, a traveling order like that of the first apostles, particularly Paul.

However, as practices, as practical or experimental divinity, Methodism's gatherings, rituals, offices, and strategies did not yield very clear and concise theory.[18] Methodists became better at doing church than articulating an ecclesiology. Here and there one can find statements or discussions out of which a more formal **missionary** and **connectional** ecclesiology might have developed. (Only in recent years have Methodists pursued that project.)

• • •

If *Hymnal* and *Discipline* produced an implicit expansive missional denominationalism, Bible (*Scripture*) and *Sunday Service* (*tradition*) claimed Wesley's Anglican heritage and proclaimed Methodism's **catholic identity**, the church's *oneness*, and Methodist participation in that unity. These two books pulled outward, ecumenically. Although early Methodists may have been insecure in and frequently unclear about this ecumenical identity, it nevertheless defined the movement. It was there by received tradition and by continued practice.

The *Sunday Service* provided the Methodist Episcopal Church with the rights and rites for their middle name. Instructing the Americans of its dependence on the BCP, Wesley asserted in the preface to the *Sunday Service*: "I believe there is no LITURGY in the World, either in ancient or modern language, which breathes more of a solid scriptural, rational Piety, than the COMMON PRAYER of the CHURCH of ENGLAND."

Wesley conceded that he had shortened the Supper, omitted a few sentences from Baptism and Burial, and dropped some holy days and psalms.[19] But far more impressive than the abridgements and omissions was Wesley's preservation of the substance and structure of the BCP.[20]

Appropriately, those gathered in 1784 at the organizing Christmas Conference decided to call their new ecclesial entity the Methodist *Episcopal* Church, a name that they patented before the Protestant Episcopals did. They communed to Cranmerian cadences for *eucharist* and *baptized* with the Triune formula. They ordained *deacons, elders, and bishops* with ritual little altered from the BCP and lived into Anglicanism's *threefold ministry*. Although they could not claim apostolic succession and early and often found themselves defending the legitimacy of their orders, Methodist Episcopals nevertheless sustained *an orderly laying-on of hands* from John Wesley onwards. Methodists did diverge from Anglicanism in positing that bishops were **not a third order**, a stance occasioned if not necessitated by John Wesley's extraordinary venture in ordaining Thomas Coke who then ordained Asbury. Asbury's refusal to accept elevation to the episcopacy solely on Wesley's appointment and insistence that the American preachers be invited to assent, established the principle that **bishops be elected in conference**.[21]

Methodist formal definitions of the church and sacraments remained those in the BCP, the (Anglican) *articles*, and the *creeds*. The church manifested itself in *faithful congregations where the pure Word was preached and the Sacraments administered according to Christ's ordinance*. The church defined itself with the classic "notes" or "marks"—*one, holy, catholic, and apostolic*. Church by the book! So, in providing this book, these books, Wesley intended to anchor the American branch of his movement liturgically in the church to which he remained loyal. This was, to reiterate, a church that deserved its middle name. It sustained its continuity with the *tradition* of its birth.

To be sure, Methodists did not exhibit much of what later would be deemed Anglican practice and polity. However, their patterns were rather more in accord with what had been the actual practice of those colonial Anglicans who, with the Wesleys, had worried about the ethical and spiritual estate of the land and who had, in many instances, found common cause with the Methodist preachers up until 1784. Indeed, those like Devereux Jarratt experienced Methodist organization as a separate church as a violation of what had been, they thought, a Wesleyan covenant to work together for the reformation of the Church.[22]

• • •

The American Methodists sustained John Wesley's immersion in Scripture, aided in the understanding thereof by his *Explanatory Notes upon the New Testament*, an American edition of which they published as early as 1791.[23] Wesley had instructed the American Methodists in 1783: "Let all of you be determined to abide by the

Methodist doctrine and discipline, published in the four volumes of *Sermons* and the *Notes upon the New Testament*, together with the Large Minutes of conference."[24]

The Americans, particularly the preachers, were perhaps even more than Wesley himself *homo unius libri*, people of one book.[25] They lived with it, inscribed it on their hearts, guided their lives by its examples, teaching, and precepts. The preachers preached from it, frequently multiple times a day, often leaving in their journals little more than the notation of the text used. When for reasons of distance or weather they wanted for a congregation and opportunity to expound the Word, they would note that as a "dumb day."

And they understood their movement, their ministry, their ecclesial order as biblically scripted. They were and remained particularly conscious of the grounding of itinerancy in Scripture. It was, they believed, the pattern of Jesus himself and of the apostles. To that theme, Bishop Asbury returned again and again, insisting that both Methodist bishops and preachers adhered to the **apostolic, itinerant plan of ministry.** In parting instructions to his junior bishop, William McKendree, Asbury insisted that they, like the apostles of the Bible, were "apostolic bishops" for, like they, "we have both planted and watered, and do water still." He explained that it was the Methodists who had recovered the apostolic plan of ministry:

> This leads me to conclude that there were no local bishops until the second century; that the apostles, in service, were bishops, and that those who were ordained in the second century mistook their calling when they became local and should have followed those bright examples in the apostolic age. . . .
>
> It is my confirmed opinion that the apostles acted both as bishops and traveling superintendents in planting and watering, ruling and ordering the whole connection; and that they did not ordain any local bishops, . . .
>
> My dear bishop, it is the traveling apostolic order and ministry that is found in our very constitution. No man among us can locate without order or forfeit his official standing. No preacher is stationary more than two years; no presiding elder more than four years, and the constitution will remove them; and all are moveable at the pleasure of the superintendent whenever he may find it necessary for the good of the cause.[26]

Methodism's immersion in Scripture did not distinguish it from other Pietist movements and its appreciation thereof did not distinguish it from Protestants generally. Indeed, Methodists knew themselves to be a movement united in common endeavor with all who lived and loved Scripture. This unitive impulse, in its earliest North American expression, one might term *evangelical* rather than *catholic*. Among the groups with whom Methodists experienced the greatest commonality were the United Brethren and Evangelical Association, two groups with roots in Reformed-Mennonite and Lutheran Pietism, respectively, with their own distinctive evangelical-Reformation ecclesiology and with a strong confessional orientation. They shared much with the Methodists, including a unitive spirit, and over time grew even closer, eventually combining with one another and later with the Methodists to form United Methodism. That union, as we will note below, connected the new church with the major branches of the Protestant Reformation, with its diverse ecclesial principles, and with a confession of faith, occasionally updated, with a clear articulation of the classic "notes" of the church.

• • •

The two unitive commitments, one Anglican, the other Pietist, tugged the Methodist Episcopal Church in different directions—either back toward their English roots or forward into the Protestant endeavor to Christianize America—though the difference in the two options would become more marked as one of the two referents or poles itself moved (as the Protestant Episcopal Church gravitated away from the shared evangelicalism). Initially both Scripture and *Sunday Service* situated the distinctive Wesleyan ecclesial patterns and the energetic, competitive Methodist itinerant ministries within shared Protestant visions of the church.[27]

II. TRANSFORMATIONS

The Quadrilateral: A Literary Evolution?

Over the course of two centuries, Methodism's four books, Methodist ecclesial sensibilities, and the service thereunto that the several books rendered underwent interesting and significant shifts. Tradition suffered in the rough and tumble of evangelistic, frontier-oriented, camp-meeting-dominated Methodism. That trend surfaced early, in the Methodist decision to abandon its book of worship, the *Sunday Service of the Methodists in North America.* Jesse Lee explained why in his early, first person narrative of the American church, *A Short History of the Methodists.*

> The prayer book, as revised by Mr. Wesley, was introduced among us; and in the large towns, and in some country places, our preachers read prayers on the Lord's day: and in some cases the preachers read part of the morning service on Wednesdays and Fridays. But some of the preachers who had been long accustomed to pray extempore, were unwilling to adopt this new plan. Being fully satisfied that they could pray better, and with more devotion while their eyes were shut, than they could with their eyes open. After a few years the prayer book was laid aside, and has never been used since in public worship.[28]

As Lee noted, revivalistic evangelicalism trumped the prayer book. At times and in places, Methodism behaved like a continuous camp meeting. And the camp meeting did suit Methodist polity—Methodist practice of church—quite nicely. Routinely in the nineteenth century, Methodists placed in a camp meeting their warm weather quarterly meeting.[29] By locating in a camp meeting the circuit's—the local church unit's—official or business meeting, Methodists embraced albeit informally a revivalistic modality of being church. Experience, conversion, revivalism thus upstaged tradition.

However, Methodist Episcopals did not, could not, give up rituals for the Supper, Baptism, ordination, marriage. Indeed, though the *Sunday Service,* as book for pocket and pew, did not define Methodism's devotional life, the several services, typically and as appropriate, would be enacted at the high point of the church's worship calendar, the two-day quarterly meeting. And when camp meetings emerged, as I have already noted, Methodists located the quarterly meeting there, the Lord's Supper being one of its high-water marks.[30] Whether two days in colder weather or elongated into a week or more in a summer camp meeting, the **quarterly meeting** functioned as an enacted or dramatized BCP for Methodists. There the entire array of officers would gather, including the bishops if they were anyway nearby. There the circuit did its business. It exercised discipline, including conducting trials if necessary. It collected "quarterage" to supply the common salary for all the traveling ministers. It licensed or renewed licenses to preach, made recommendations about ordination, and filled local offices. That was Saturday agenda. Sunday wedded rituals of the BCP to distinctive Methodist practices. The day opened with a **love feast**, restricted to members, followed by preaching, the Lord's Supper, more preaching, baptisms if indicated, memorials when required. In the quarterly meeting Methodism was most fully church, offering to those gathered the preached word, the sacraments, and discipline or order.

Over the course of the nineteenth century, Methodism freed stations from its circuits, appointed educated preachers to those congregations, built substantial churches to house the middle class populations that filled its urban pews, and increasingly edged its way into the Protestant establishment. Such "improvements" spawned protests, various movements that hoisted a holiness banner or defended the camp meeting to recall Methodism back to its commitment to the marginalized. Schisms took some of the protesters out of the church but others remained to voice complaints as Methodism gained in respectability and in its interest in more formalized worship.

Methodists tracked Anglican reforms and kept up-to-date versions of the ritual available to preachers in the quadrennially produced *Discipline*.[31] On the popular level and over the course of the nineteenth century, Methodists gradually reclaimed traditions that had been important to the Wesleys, including liturgical practices and entire services that could hardly be managed without a published order in congregants' hands, much less with preacher's eyes shut. This reclamation went on more in the urban and upscale congregations than in rural areas but was modeled for all preachers in annual conferences. In 1905 the Methodist Episcopal Church and the Methodist Episcopal Church, South formalized that trend by including both an "Order of Worship" and a Psalter in the jointly published *Methodist Hymnal*.[32] And in 1945, the new Methodist Church (uniting in 1939 the MEC, the MECS and the MPC), revisited Wesley's recrafting or remodeling of the BCP. *The Book of Worship for Church and Home* provided a BCP-like full set of services. A sequel *Book of Worship* appeared in 1965 and *The United Methodist Book of Worship* in 1992.[33] With each of these successive liturgical efforts, save this most recent, Methodism reasserted its connection to the BCP and enriched its sense of tradition as mediated through Anglicanism.

Bible, Discipline, Hymnal

Scripture, reason and experience—and their literary expressions of Bible, *Discipline*, and *Hymnal*—found an easier path into the life of the young Methodist movement and into its ecclesial sensibilities. Wesley had exhorted his preachers and people to read and had made ample provision for their reading in his many publications. The American Methodists carried on that program, even under frontier conditions. They created a surrogate Wesley, in the person and office of Book Agent, who took responsibility for an aggressive publishing and distributing campaign of popular literature and eventually serials. Preachers functioned as regional sales representatives for the publishing enterprise. Colporteurs they were, with responsibilities to push the product, handle sales, collect and forward receipts, and in every way cultivate the reading and buying habit.[34] They kept a percentage of the profit, in some instances, substantially augmenting what was otherwise a meager annual salary.[35] Available records indicate significant sales of catechisms, pious memoirs, spiritual guides, Bibles, hymnals, and *Discipline*s and much more modest sales of weightier items, whether by Wesley or his theological successors. In one particularly profitable year (1814), Benjamin Lakin sold 1314 items. Hymnals constituted 413 of that total, *Discipline*s 505.[36] So the Methodist movement put pocket hymnals and mass-produced Bibles into the laps of the people. The preachers, if not all the laity, had carried a third book, the *Discipline*. Their saddlebags reputedly came with Bible, *Hymnal*, and *Discipline*.

The canon of Scripture, of course, did not change nor, one might argue, has Methodism's effort to be faithful to it. The modes of that fidelity have evolved, taken on complexity, found institutional niches, but nevertheless sustained the twofold commitments inherited from Wesley. He wanted his people and preachers to be students of the Bible. From the laity he expected daily reading; weekly participation in the small group (class) for study, prayer, and hymn-singing; attentiveness to the (perhaps) biweekly preaching that guided biblical understanding; and personal witness, including testimony in the quarterly love feast. He expected the same from the preachers, but also careful study of his commentary, *Notes on the New Testament*, one of the several formally identified Methodist touchstones of orthodoxy and drawn from what he regarded as the best scholarship of the day.

On the popular level, today's United Methodists have DISCIPLE Bible study plus an incredible array of other adult biblical resources from the United Methodist Publishing House (Cokesbury and Abingdon). Cokesbury makes similar provision for all other age groups. The clergy typically own the *Interpreter's Bible* and are acquiring the *New Interpreter's Bible*. Or if the IB and NIB are not to taste, Abingdon features several other commentaries itself and its distributing arm, Cokesbury, offers series from other publishers as well. The digitally inclined can discover the incredible array of United Methodist biblical resources through the Publishing House and other denominational agencies—biblical guides, commentaries, and devotional materials. Between the days of class meeting and *Notes upon the New Testament* and today's DISCIPLE Bible Study and *New Interpreter's Bible* lie almost two centuries of Methodist leadership in the Sunday School as a medium for popular instruction and of Methodist endeavor to stay current with biblical scholarship. Over that period Methodists had lived into the ecumenical promise of Scripture, becoming a denomination that spanned the center of American Protestantism from moderate evangelicalism to progressive liberalism.

Both hymnals and *Discipline*s have undergone dramatic changes since leaving John Wesley's hand. Initially, the *Discipline*,[37] titled to reflect "The Large Minutes" from which it derived—"Minutes of Several Conversations between The Rev. Thomas Coke, LL.D., The Rev. Francis Asbury, and Others . . . Composing a Form of Discipline For the Ministers, Preachers, and Other Members of the Methodist Episcopal Church in America"—functioned as a guide to corporate Christian life. It served the gathered community as the *Hymnal* served the individual believer, as rules for the pilgrim's progress. It really did discipline. Though addressed to the preachers, through them it instructed the faithful as well concerning dress, behavior, intermarriage, slavery, distilled beverages, means of grace, devotional practices, life together, and belief—in short, the way of salvation. Initially an action pamphlet, the *Discipline* grew gradually as Methodist expansion required enhancements to the simple missional imperatives inherited from Wesley and as the church saw reason to specify more clearly its belief, structures, authority, and governance. In 1788, 1789, and 1790, the church annexed to the *Discipline* "some other useful Pieces," Arminian essays by Wesley against Calvinist doctrines of predestination and unconditional perseverance and others explaining Christian perfection and baptism. In 1792, Methodists signaled the purpose the *Discipline* played in setting forth reasoned belief by retitling it *The Doctrines and Discipline of the Methodist Episcopal Church*.

Over time much of the explicitly doctrinal content of the *Discipline* eroded, or, to be more precise, was "outsourced," specified as authoritative but separately published. This change in Methodism's BOOK, sometimes interpreted as the church's loss of theological fiber, might better be construed as the consequence of ecclesial maturation. Ecclesial maturation led to a sharper constitutional awareness, most notably in the General Conference of 1808, which passed **"Restrictive Rules"** protecting Methodist **doctrine, conference structure, episcopacy, and "General Rules."**[38] Ecclesial maturation led to the rapid growth of a publication empire that produced or reproduced theological as well as devotional, historical, and instructional materials in abundance. Ecclesial maturation led to ever greater organizational complexity and therefore required much greater Disciplinary specificity and precision.[39]

For a variety of reasons, then, the *Discipline*, over time, kept doctrine to a minimum and let polity flourish. In 1972, as we will note below, consequent to the uniting of the Evangelical United Brethren and the Methodists and the challenge of putting together confessional and doctrinal traditions that drew on the Anglican, Calvinist, Lutheran, and Anabaptist Reformations, a Theological Commission brought in and General Conference adopted a rich theological apparatus. Revised in 1988 (and referenced below), this Disciplinary apparatus now plays a decisive role in orienting the church, and particularly those undergoing the ordination process, toward United Methodist doctrine and theology as witness to the church's apostolic and catholic faith.[40]

American Methodists began with a hymnal filled with Charles Wesley's verse, a poetic guide to the *via salutis*, the way of salvation. In the latest *Hymnal*, that of 1989, only 7 percent of the hymns come from Charles (52 of 734). Successive hymnals have seen a steady erosion of Wesley's hymns. Or to put it more constructively, successive hymnals have made increasing space for hymns expressive of the religious impulses of the day or the larger Christian witness. However, almost from the start, American Methodist leaders, like their British counterparts, struggled to keep the faithful faithfully signing Charles's hymns. The first American-generated hymnbook, the *Pocket Hymn Book* of 1786, drew on hymnals by Robert Spence as well as by the Wesleys.[41] Soon music reflecting the African American experience, camp meetings and revivals, singing schools and the Sunday school competed with that bearing the Wesleyan imprimatur. Hymnals capturing these religious impulses appeared quickly. As early as 1801, *A Collection of Hymns and Spiritual Songs Selected from Various Authors by Richard Allen, African Minister* appeared. Camp meeting hymnals appeared soon and thereafter the official or authorized hymnals, which appeared regularly (for the MEC: 1786, 1802, 1808, 1821, 1836, 1849, 1878, 1905) contended with a variety of popular alternatives.[42] Worship wars are hardly new.[43]

III. UNITED METHODISM

A New Church

In 1968, The United Methodist Church was created, bringing together The Evangelical United Brethren Church and The Methodist Church, and uniting into one the heritage and traditions that had informed the EA, the UBC, the MPC, the MEC, and the MECS. The first two of these had united with one another in 1946, the latter three with each other in 1939.[44] The 1968 union connected the new church with the major branches of and diverse ecclesial **principles of the Protestant Reformation**; through the UB with the Anabaptist and Reformed, through the EA with the Lutheran, through the Methodists with the Anglican reformations. The larger question of how the new church brought into harmony the practices, policies, and polity of these several denominational impulses lies beyond the scope of this enquiry. Here we do need to take note of the doctrinal, specifically ecclesiological, challenge represented in this union. In 1968 the uniting conference and UMC *Discipline* cared for the challenge by positing the congruence of doctrine of the two predecessor churches and of the most terse expressions thereof, the EUB **"Confession of Faith"** and the Methodist **"Articles of Religion."** Not content to leave it there, General Conference established a "Theological Study Commission" with a broad mandate, including the possibility of "a contemporary formulation of doctrine and belief."[45]

The Commission chose not to craft a new confession, creed, or set of articles but instead to embrace the EUB Confession and Methodist Articles within a long Disciplinary doctrinal-theological disquisition. Revised in 1988, this section now constitutes Part II of the *Discipline*, "Doctrinal Standards and Our Theological Task." Accordingly, Part I of the *Discipline*, the Constitution, continues both Articles and Confession (¶3, Article III) and revises the "Restrictive Rules" to protect both statements of belief. The Constitution also includes important ecclesial and ecumenical affirmations, as we note below. However, it is this Part II, which governs the reception and interpretation of these two standards, the General Rules, and Wesley's *Sermons* and *Notes on the New Testament*, which figures most prominently in United Methodist ecclesial understanding. One section, ¶101, treats "Our Doctrinal Heritage," covering "Our Common Heritage as Christians," "Basic Christian Affirmations," "Our Distinctive Heritage as United Methodists," "Distinctive Wesleyan Emphases," "Doctrine and Discipline in the Christian Life," and "General Rules and Social Principles." The following section, ¶102, attends to "Our Doctrinal History." Then follow the standards, Articles, Confession, and General Rules, reproduced in full, and declaratory statements indicating where the authoritative *Sermons* and *Notes* may be acquired. Having identified and ordered Methodist doctrine, the *Discipline* in a fourth section, ¶104, "Our Theological Task," sets forth guidelines for drawing on doctrine in the church's efforts to think theologically. Important now in Methodism's practice of theology and especially in ordination processes, this section posits a distinction between doctrine and theology, sets forth characteristics of United

Methodism's theological task, describes the quadrilateral and its hermeneutics, identifies challenges to theology, and concludes with a discussion of the church's ecumenical commitment.[46]

United Methodism's Four Books

"Doctrinal Standards and Our Theological Task," a feature of *Disciplines* since 1972, sets forth distinctively Methodist and Wesleyan belief vigorously and clearly. It does so within an explicitly ecclesiological, indeed an ecclesiologically ecumenical, framework, a point we exhibit in some detail in a separate section below. This conjoining of the Wesleyan and the ecumenical represents an important development, not a surprising development perhaps, but nevertheless an important development. Not surprising given Methodism's investment in the ecumenical enterprise nor because as we have noted, the other specifically Methodist books, *Hymnal* and *Book of Worship*, in addition to *Discipline*,[47] have also shifted in that ecumenical direction.

The current *Hymnal* gathers the best of the church's praise, whether recent or ancient. Supplementary volumes have followed so as to capture the *The Faith We Sing* and *Global Praise* of the church, the best of its music, the best of its verse. The *Hymnal* also features the liturgies used commonly in congregational life, reflecting, as we note below, the ecumenical liturgical consensus. In addition, United Methodists understand the two sacraments, Baptism and the Lord's Supper, as rites for the whole church—Baptism, inherently ecumenical, and the Eucharist, so now nuanced, often with the Wesleyan gloss that it is a converting ordinance.[48]

The two books, then, that had once looked inward and toward a distinctively Wesleyan identity—the *Discipline* and *Hymnal*—now sustain that identity within a clearly catholic context. Insofar as these two books retain their function as the quadrilateral principles of reason and experience, respectively, they point now, as do Scripture and tradition, toward Wesleyan or Methodist belief as within the faith confessed commonly across Christianity.

The *United Methodist Book of Worship* also repositions its witness to Methodism's tradition(s) within an ecumenical context. Eucharist can still be celebrated with the beautiful phrases of Archbishop Cranmer, but that liturgy, setting IV, now functions as an alternative in the *Book of Worship* (and in the *Hymnal*), as also in BCP. The *Book of Worship* no longer orients Methodism exclusively toward its Anglican past but rather more broadly to the catholic tradition generally, or perhaps one might say to the Anglican-Methodist reception of the catholic tradition. From beginning to end, from its initial setting out of "The Basic Pattern of Worship" to its concluding rites for missionaries and deaconesses, the *Book of Worship* draws into United Methodist life the best liturgical wisdom and practices of the twentieth century liturgical and ecumenical movements. The witness of the BCP remains, but now surrounded by worship patterns reflective of the great tradition of the church and its global expression today.

The *Book of Worship* does still function as an indicator of the place of tradition, in its widest sense, in United Methodist life. Some areas of the denomination and some congregations have become liturgically self-conscious to a remarkable extent. In such places worship draws significantly and imaginatively on the *Book of Worship*. There congregations experience the church year, the lectionary, the rich array of special services, a high degree of liturgical self-awareness, and albs and stoles. The trend is sufficiently prominent as to have worried Thomas Langford, who complained that a once preaching church had become a liturgical church.[49] Still, large sectors of United Methodism function out of lower church paradigms, in some cases now reenergized with the so-called contemporary styles of worship and music and a church-growth ecclesiology. The *Book of Worship* continues, therefore, as ecclesial touchstone and provides one clue to United Methodism's ecclesial self-understanding. Its use signals orientation toward ecclesial self-understanding and catholicity predicated on the long Christian tradition. Its nonuse often signals investment rather in more evangelical, missional, and present-oriented forms of Christian unity.

Scripture functions, one might argue, in Methodist/Wesleyan understanding, to orient believers toward the common witness of the church and the unity realized and promised in Christ. And such an affirmation and a direction clearly inform United Methodist scholarly and devotional attention to the Bible. The clear commitment, within sectors of United Methodism, to hold together critical scholarship and piety—nicely epitomized in DISCIPLE and

The New Interpreter's Bible, both products of The United Methodist Publishing House—orients this fundamental or primary epistemological criterion, one might insist, toward the other three aspects of the quadrilateral, a point that the *Discipline* itself makes explicitly.[50]

Counterpoint

However, the ecumenical convergence represented in current versions of Methodism's four books does not command the loyalty and adherence of the entire church. The culture wars ignited within North American society generally blaze as well across United Methodism. They blaze especially brightly over Scripture and its relation to other authorities. A conservative or evangelical wing of Methodism—actually comprising diverse religious impulses but achieving some unity through allegiances to a single seminary, an alternative missionary society, separate presses, collaborative media and websites, distinctive funding mechanisms, an entity that behaves like the congregation for the propagation of the faith, and a common insistence on a closed creed as well as closed canon—reads the Bible as yielding quite fixed doctrines.[51] Scripture, this sector of Methodism seems to suggest, speaks univocally and once-and-for-all-times. So Scripture and Scripture alone should settle matters deemed doctrinal, like abortion and homosexuality, insist spokespersons in this camp.

Experience, reason, and tradition thereby lose their capacity to function interactively and transmissively with respect to Scripture, and to bear forth and address the inspired Word to specific times and contexts. Only Scripture can be inspired. Some in this wing of United Methodism, not surprisingly, have little use of the notion of a quadrilateral, even in its post-1988 version with the guarantees of the primacy of Scripture: "Scripture is the primary source and criterion for Christian doctrine." This camp tends to pit Scripture against other authorities. It offers a new modality of Wesleyan inwardness, a loyalty to the Wesley of one book, the Bible. And it permits, if not actually encourages, a disuse of the other books. Particularly where energized by church growth or megachurch doctrine, it prefers contemporary worship that is electronically projected over the *Book of Worship,* the praise chorus over the *Hymnal,* and congregational prerogative over the connectional structures and processes that the *Discipline* describes and prescribes. The *Discipline* as a law book, however, this wing of United Methodism finds still serviceable, indeed, vital in the war they wage for Methodism's soul. Still, one could say, this wing pits the one book, the Bible, over against the other three.

One detects in this conservative-evangelical Methodist stance a somewhat different ecclesiology from that represented in the current versions of the four books, different from that I am positing as ecumenical Methodism, different from that outlined immediately below. This wing of the church certainly claims the Wesleyan missional emphasis; indeed, it makes mission, understood as disciple making, the primary, even sole, task and purpose of the church, a conviction recently legislated into the *Discipline*. It leavens mission not with the "Christ the transformer of culture" spirit that has been a hallmark of American Methodism but with a combative "Christ against culture" style, the external face of a "Christ of culture" nature. It undertakes its campaign in the conviction that, in so doing, it, rather than ecumenical United Methodism, is the more faithful to Wesley. Accordingly it launches a critique, sometimes quite harsh, against the agencies and leadership of United Methodism. And it does so convinced that "the missional" rather than "the catholic" requires the church's energy and focus in today's world. Its spirit is noncatholic and its style nonconnectional. Or, to be more generous, it reserves its catholicity for counterpart conservative wings of other denominations and in concert with them builds its own connectional structures. And, like the larger evangelicalism so suffused with Calvinist practice, it has begun to put a premium on the creedal and confessional shibboleths.

IV. MISSIONAL ECCLESIOLOGY

The Official Stance

In Methodism's official stance, its four books continue, in their own way, to sustain indebtedness to John Wesley—the Wesleyan commitment perhaps more salient post-1968 than before—but the important yet diverse heritages mediated through the EUB have helped reduce the distance or tension between that Wesleyan ecclesial self-understanding and that oriented toward the larger Christian witness. And in lessening that tension or achieving the new balance, the four books function, where they are all used, with some degree of harmony. Their harmony owes to the long-term developments to which we have alluded, rather than the formal enunciation of a quadrilateral hermeneutic or epistemology. Nevertheless, the quadrilateral, tersely described in *Disciplines* since 1972, provides United Methodists a language with which to grasp and explain this common focus. And, in various ways, the *Discipline* has become more explicit about Methodism's doctrinal commitments.

Discipline: *Catholic Spirit*

After 1968 and especially after 1972, the new church embedded within the *Discipline* expressions of a catholic spirit and pointers toward an ecumenical ecclesiology, understanding the bringing together of traditions representing the major strands of the Protestant Reformation as opportunity for still greater unity. That ecumenical, unitive, or catholic commitment defines United Methodism—in its structure, policy, and program, indeed, in its very Constitution—in the following ways.

- The Preamble to the Constitution (Part I) situates the newly constituted church within the universal church.
- Article III of the Constitution incorporates and Articles I and II of the Restrictive Rules protect the Articles of Religion (John Wesley's adaptation of the Thirty-nine Articles) and the Confession of Faith from the Evangelical United Brethren Church, thereby defining the church in classic Reformation terms (Articles) and claiming its classic marks or notes, "one, holy, apostolic and catholic" (Confession).
- Article IV of the Constitution on the "Inclusiveness of the Church" proclaims The United Methodist Church "a part of the church universal" and commits it to overcoming all those forces and factors that divide the human family.

- Article VI of the Constitution on "Ecumenical Relations" affirms "As part of the church universal, The United Methodist Church believes the Lord of the church is calling Christians everywhere to strive toward unity."

The ecumenical, unitive, or catholic commitment United Methodism also builds into its structure, policy, and program elsewhere in the *Discipline*—in particular:

- "Our Doctrinal Heritage" in Part II locates United Methodism within the "common heritage with Christians of every age and nation" and sets out "Basic Christian Affirmations" that United Methodists confess with all Christians.
- This statement concludes that "with other Christians, we declare the essential oneness of the church in Christ Jesus." It illustrates that ground of and commitment to unity, affirming, "This rich heritage of shared Christian belief finds expression in our hymnody and liturgies. Our unity is affirmed in the historic creeds as we confess one holy, catholic, and apostolic church. It is also experienced in joint ventures of ministry and in various forms of ecumenical cooperation. . . . Our avowed ecumenical commitment as United Methodists is to gather our own doctrinal emphases into the larger Christian unity, there to be made more meaningful in a richer whole."
- "Our Doctrinal History" begins by insisting that the church's constitutive traditions "understood themselves as standing in the central stream of Christian spirituality and doctrine," characterizes the church's vocation as "catholic spirit," and concludes by positing the recovery, updating, and reinvigorating of "our distinctive doctrinal heritage—catholic, evangelical, and reformed—as essential" to both evangelism and ecumenical dialogue.
- "Our Theological Task" ends with a section on "Ecumenical Commitment" insisting that "Christian unity is not an option" but is mandated theologically, biblically, and practically as "a gift to be received and expressed."

- "The Ministry of All Christians," Part III of the *Discipline*, evokes the ecumenical consensus of Vatican II, the Consultation on Church Union (COCU), and *Baptism, Eucharist and Ministry* that all baptized are called to ministry. Appropriately it situates important United Methodist rubrics—the Journey of a Connectional People, Servant Ministry, Servant Leadership, Called to Inclusiveness, and the Fulfillment of Ministry through The United Methodist Church—within the narration of the longer and larger story of God's covenantal initiatives and of the Church's mission.
- Part V, Chapter One, "The Local Church," in framing the church's global mission, makes provision for cooperative parishes and ecumenical shared ministries.
- The rubric on "Church Membership," ¶214, states "The United Methodist Church is a part of the holy catholic (universal) church, as we confess in the Apostles Creed." The next paragraph affirms "A member of any local United Methodist church is a member of the denomination and the catholic (universal) church."
- The episcopal or superintending office is assigned a number of tasks, among them, "to seek and be a sign of the unity of the faith" and "to exercise the discipline of the whole Church" (¶404) and specifically "To provide liaison and leadership in the quest for Christian unity in ministry, mission, and structure and in the search for strengthened relationships with other living faith communities" (¶414).
- The General Commission on Christian Unity and Interreligious Concerns, and its corresponding boards or officers on jurisdictional, conference, district, and congregational levels, are charged explicitly to exercise "ecumenical leadership" toward Christian unity and dialogue with others' faiths, cultures, and ideologies.
- The *Discipline* acknowledges UMC membership explicitly in several "Interdenominational Agencies"—World Methodist Council, COCU, the National Council of Churches, the World Council of Churches, the Commission on Pan-Methodist Cooperation, and the

American Bible Society—and assigns UMC leadership therein to the bishops and GCCUIC leadership (¶2401).

United Methodism's formal commitments to unity and catholicity set impressive standards and directions and accord with the role United Methodism and its predecessor denominations have exercised within the ecumenical movement. Methodism has been a major ecumenical player. At this writing, Methodists head both the National and World Council of Churches and the American Bible Society. In the past, Methodists have played leadership roles in COCU/CUIC, indeed, in many unitive efforts at regional, national, and global levels. Over recent decades, United Methodism has invested much in bilateral dialogues, as for instance, the one for which this chapter was originally crafted.[52] The catholic language of the *Discipline*, the prominence of Methodists in ecumenical endeavor, and the clear commitment of the church's leadership to dialogue give the appearance of ecclesiological single-mindedness and coherence.

In actual practice, the various kinds of unities—including those among the evangelical and progressive wings of the church and those that pull Methodists into the American civil religion—compete as much as or more than they cohere. Each beckons the church. United Methodists work on different fronts. The genuine laborers for unity and catholicity remain few. The church at all levels voices more commitment than it proves willing to honor. Some within the denomination express open hostility to ecumenical efforts. Many remain absolutely oblivious to longstanding Wesleyan catholic investments. And particularly now as we have seen and note further below, the important tension with which the denomination began, a tension lived out by John and Charles Wesley—the ecclesiological tension between the church's catholic and its missional self-understanding—remains present, though now politicized and potentially divisive. That original, constructive tension can therefore sometimes be obscured, forgotten, neglected, overlooked in ecumenical conversation in Methodist self-representation—in efforts to mirror our conversational partners or as a stratagem toward unity. The ecclesiological tension should not be obscured. It constitutes a gift of Methodism to the larger church but only when sustained as a real tension. A church badly divided within has difficulty in presenting its gifts. Our books, however, witness to our better nature.

Discipline: Missional Commitment

The missional understanding of the church remains prominent in the two books where it has been most salient from the start, in *Discipline* and *Hymnal*. Both nicely exhibit the tension, now both sides of the tension, within which United Methodism does church. The unitive side of this tension we have described above. The missional is equally prominent.

The *Discipline* devotes four paragraphs of the "Preamble" to the church's unity but affirms in a fifth, "The church of Jesus Christ exists in and for the world, and its very dividedness is a hindrance to its mission in that world." The "Restrictive Rules" continue the protection to Methodism's distinctive, missional understanding of episcopacy or superintendency, as itinerant and general in character. Several articles within the Constitution delineate the nature and tasks of the conferences of United Methodism and ¶31 identifies the annual conference as "the basic body in the Church." In so defining the church connectionally and at that level that admits into ordained ministry, at which ordination occurs and from which ministries proceed and ministers are sent, United Methodism sustains Wesley's missional ecclesiology. The *Discipline* treats the understanding and tasks of ministry that flow from this ecclesiology later. But from this definition flow Methodism's distinctive itinerant and appointive commitments. Part II on "Doctrinal Standards and Our Theological Task," as we have noted, accent Wesleyan practical, soteriological, and missional emphases within the shared catholic heritage.

The missional understanding becomes more marked in Part III, "The Ministry of All Christians," subtitled "The Mission and Ministry of the Church." ¶120. *The Mission* proclaims "The mission of the Church is to make disciples of Jesus Christ. Local churches provide the most significant arena through which disciple-making occurs." The "Rationale for our Mission," immediately following, begins: "The mission of the Church is to make disciples of Jesus Christ by proclaiming the good news of God's grace and thus seeking the fulfillment of God's reign and realm in the world. The fulfillment of God's reign and realm in the world is the vision Scripture holds before us."

The phrasing attempts to hold justification and justice, evangelism and social transformation, in tension, but the adequate development of the latter missional emphasis really is to be found in the next major Disciplinary section, Part IV.[53] Part III does set the mood by reference to and exegesis of Matthew 28:19-20. As of the 1996 *Discipline*, Part III also enunciates a theme of servant ministry and servant leadership. That calling figures prominently in the office of the permanent deacon but belongs also to the laity and is added as well to that of the elder and therefore of bishops. The full implications of and an adequate theology for servanthood need to be more fully developed, especially since the church made this missional addition, a fourth, to the traditional three—word, sacrament, and order.[54]

Another section in III, ¶138, declares the church to be "Called to Inclusiveness." That mission of the church, to be agent and anticipatory of the kingdom and of the redemption of the world, the *Discipline* develops quite fully in Part IV, "Social Principles"[55] This long treatise recalls early Methodism's social witness (including antislavery), notes the 1908 elaboration and adoption by the MEC of a social creed (other predecessor denominations following later) and develops United Methodism's contemporary social commitments under six rubrics, "The Natural World," "The Nurturing Community," "The Social Community," "The Economic Community," "The Political Community," and "The World Community." The principles are to guide United Methodist attitudes and practices with respect to the world outside the church. They also apply within, touching matters of marriage, divorce, sexuality, family violence, sexual harassment, abortion, care at the end of life, and suicide. More fully developed stances on both internal and external concerns, General Conference has chosen to locate in a now huge, quadrennially produced tome, *The Book of Resolutions*. One might wish that this could be added as a fifth book defining United Methodism and exhibiting its ecclesial sensibilities. However, despite its official status, United Methodist laity and clergy seemingly make little use of it. Fortunately, they are more likely to heed the injunction that appears with the "Social Creed" in the *Discipline* that the creed be available to the people and used in Sunday worship. A variant of the creed appears in the *Hymnal* to be used as an affirmation of faith.

The *Discipline* continues efforts to balance evangelism and social concern, mission and catholicity in the balance of what has now become a long book. Part V on "Organization and Administration," for instance, begins the treatment on "The Local Church" with successive paragraphs, the first of which affirms definitionally, "The **local church** provides the most significant arena through which disciple-making occurs." The next paragraph, treating the local church's function, declares, "The church of Jesus Christ exists in and for the world. It is primarily at the level of the local church that the church encounters the world."

The United Methodist Hymnal achieves the same balance, the balance at least in part explaining its wildly successful introduction and congregational adoption. It retains the favorites derived from Methodism's revivalistic and holiness past, like Fanny Crosby's "Pass Me Not, O Gentle Savior," "Blessed Assurance," "I Am Thine, O Lord," and "Rescue the Perishing." It includes social gospel hymns by Harry Emerson Fosdick and Frank Mason North, civil rights songs, and verse from across the world. Alongside Methodism's missional anthems can be found chants ancient and modern, from the Community of Taizé or Byzantium.[56] Like the *Discipline*, the *Hymnal* invites United Methodists to claim their distinctive voice but to sound it loudly for the church catholic.

CONCLUSION

United Methodism's four books define it and exhibit its ecclesial sensibilities. To only two of them, the Bible and *Hymnal*, would most United Methodists have ready access. The other two, *The Book of Discipline* and *The Book of Worship*, some Methodists would have never seen. Nevertheless, each can and I think should work for and work itself into the drama of the church's daily life. The *Discipline* and *Book of Worship* function offstage determining how the play unfolds, who acts, and what instructions to follow. Bible and *Hymnbook* script Methodist life together.

For present life together, especially life in congregations, the four books, where effectively used, orient Methodists toward the

Word, mediate United Methodism's traditions, including particularly its Wesleyan heritage, offer experiential expressions of the faith once delivered, and order belief and practice accordingly. The books evidence United Methodism's actual use of quadrilateral ways of knowing Christ and being Christlike. They also show, in their convergence, a convergence clearer now than in earlier days, how the fourfold epistemology or hermeneutic yields a common focus. And the common focus in the four books orients United Methodism to the classic marks or notes of the church—its *oneness*, its *holiness*, its *catholicity*, and its *apostolicity*. Methodism nuances those marks in its own distinctive fashion as connectional, disciplined, ecumenical, and missional. Its books claim those Wesleyan nuances or understandings but point as well toward the received ecclesiological doctrines of catholic Christianity.

In these four books, the catholic and missional, the high liturgical and fervid evangelical that the Wesleys held so curiously together come again into tension. The four books beckon United Methodists who press to one extreme or the other to reclaim balance and live our distinctive witness. Scripture, *Hymnal*, *Discipline*, and *Book of Worship* define how United Methodists do church. Ecclesiology in its most familiar doctrinal form this may not be. But in structure and practice, in office and program, United Methodists nevertheless live faithfully into the ecumenical ecclesial consensus, adding thereunto what they affirm to be an apostolic commitment to mission. Methodists offer a **via salutis** to augment the tradition's *ordo salutis* and an ecclesiological **via** to augment the tradition's ecclesiological **ordo**.[57]

APPENDIX TO CHAPTER 4

SECTION V.

Of the Presiding Elders, and of their Duty.[1]

Quest. 1. By whom are the presiding elders to be chosen?
Answ. By the bishop.
Quest. 2. What are the duties of a presiding elder?
Answ. 1. To travel through his appointed district.
2. In the absence of a bishop, to take charge of all the elders, deacons, travelling and local preachers, and exhorters in his district.
3. To change, receive, or suspend preachers in his district during the intervals of the conferences, and in the absence of the bishop.
4. In the absence of a bishop, to preside in the conference.
5. To be present, as far as practicable, at all the quarterly meetings: and to call together at each quarterly meeting all the travelling and local preachers, exhorters, stewards, and leaders of the circuit, to hear complaints, and to receive appeals.
6. To oversee the spiritual and temporal business of the societies in his district.
7. To take care that every part of our discipline be enforced in his district.
8. To attend the bishop when present in his district; and to give him when absent all necessary information, by letters of the state of his district.

Appendix to Chapter 4

Quest. 3. By whom are the presiding elders to be stationed and changed?

Answ. By the bishop.

Quest. 4. How long may the bishop allow an elder to preside in the same district?

Answ. For any term not exceeding four years successively.

Quest. 5. How shall the presiding elders be supported.

Answ. If there be a surplus of the public money, in one or more circuits in his district, he shall receive such surplus, provided he do not receive more than his annual salary. In case of a deficiency in his salary, after such surplus is paid him, or if there be no surplus, he shall share with the preachers of his district, in proportion with what they have respectively received, so that he receive no more than the amount of his salary upon the whole.

NOTES [by Asbury and Coke].

... However, there are some fundamental principles and general data afforded us in the New Testament (to which alone we can have recourse on this subject) on which we may build according to the circumstances in which we are placed. In the present instance, we have texts which indubitably prove that there were *presiding*, *superintending*, or *ruling* elders (the words bear the same meaning) in the church in the apostolic age, and that this office is fully warranted by the Word of God. Thus we read in Acts xx. 17-28. "From Miletus he [Paul] sent to Ephesus, and called the *elders* of the church. And, when they were come to him, he said unto them, Take heed—unto yourselves, and to all the flock over the which the Holy Ghost hath made you OVERSEERS," &c. The word *overseers* in this place signifies, as it does every where, persons who had a considerable degree of superintendency over the work in which they were employed. Again, in 1 Tim. v. 17, we read, "Let the elders that *rule well* be counted worthy of double honour," &c. Every person who understands the original or even our own language, well knows that there is no difference at all in the sense between the words *presiding* and *ruling*, and that one might be substituted for the other. Once more, St. Peter, in his 1st Epistle, v. 1-3, observes "The elders which are among you, I exhort 'Feed the flock of God which is among you, taking the *oversight* thereof, not by constraint, but willingly; not for filthy lucre, but of a ready mind, neither as being *lords* over God's heritage, but being ensamples to the flock.'" Here we also see, that there were *elders* who had the *oversight* or *superintendence* (for so the word signifies) of *the flock of God:* nor could St. Peter have cautioned these against *lording it* over God's heritage, if they had not had some authority in the church, which they might abuse. And we must desire our readers to remember, that we are not speaking here or in our observations concerning the episcopacy, of the powers which the apostles themselves exercised, but of those with which they invested others, or which the churches conferred upon their ministers respectively.

On the principles or data above-mentioned, all the episcopal churches in the world have, in some measure, formed their church-government. And we believe we can venture to assert, that there never has been an episcopal church of any great extent, which has not had *ruling* or *presiding* elders, either expressly *by name* as in the apostolic churches, or otherwise in *effect*. On this account it is, that all the modern episcopal churches have had their *presiding* or *ruling* elders under the names of grand vicars, archdeacons, rural deans, &c. The Moravians have presiding elders, who are invested with very considerable authority, though we believe they are simply termed elders. And we beg leave to repeat, that we are confident, we could, if need were, shew that all the episcopal churches ancient and modern, *of any great extent*, have had an order or set of ministers corresponding, more or less, to our presiding or ruling elders, all of whom were, more or less, invested with the superintendence of other ministers.

Mr. Wesley informs us in his works, that the whole plan of Methodism was introduced, step by step, by the interference and openings of divine Providence. This was the case in the present instance. When Mr. Wesley drew up a plan of government for our church in America, he desired that no more elders should be ordained in the first instance than were absolutely necessary, and that the work on the continent should be divided between them, in respect to the duties of their office. The general conference accordingly elected twelve elders for the above purposes. Bishop Asbury and the district conferences afterwards found that this order of men was so necessary, that they agreed to enlarge the number, and give them *the name* by which they are at present called, and which is perfectly scriptural, though not *the word* used in our translation: and this proceeding afterwards received the approbation of Mr. Wesley.

In 1792 the general conference, equally conscious of the necessity of having such an office among us, not only confirmed everything that bishop Asbury and the district conferences had done, but also drew up or agreed to the present section for the explanation of the nature and duties of the office. The conference clearly saw that the bishops wanted assistants; that it was impossible for one or two bishops so to superintend the vast work on this continent as to keep everything in order in the intervals of the conference, without other official men to act under them and assist them: and as these would only be the agents of the bishops in every respect, the authority of appointing them, and of changing them, ought, from the nature of things, to be in the episcopacy. If the presiding or ruling elders were not men in whom the bishops could fully confide, or on the loss of confidence, could exchange for others, the utmost confusion would ensue. This also renders the authority invested in the bishops of fixing the extent of each district, highly expedient. They must be supposed to be the best judges of the abilities of the presiding elders whom they themselves choose: and it is a grand part of their duty, to make the districts and the talents of the presiding elders who act for them, suit and agree with each other, as far as possible: for it cannot be expected, that a sufficient number of them can at any time be found, *of equal talents*, and, therefore, the extent of their field of action must be proportioned to their gifts.

From all that has been advanced, and from those other ideas which will present themselves to the reader's mind on this subject, it will appear that the presiding elders must, of course, be appointed, directed, and changed by the episcopacy. And yet their power is so considerable, that it would by no means be sufficient for them to be responsible to the bishops *only* for their conduct in their office. They are as responsible in this respect, and in every other, to the *yearly* conference to which they belong, as any other preacher; and may be censured, suspended or expelled from the connection, if the conference see it proper: nor have the bishops any authority to over-rule, suspend, or

Appendix to Chapter 4

meliorate in any degree, the censures, suspensions, or expulsions of the conference.

Many and great are the advantages arising from this institution. 1. It is a great help and blessing to the quarterly meetings respectively, through the connection, to have a man at their head, who is experienced not only in the ways of God, but in men and manners, and in all things appertaining to the order of our church. Appeals may be brought before the quarterly meeting from the judgment of the preacher who has the oversight of the circuit, who certainly would not be, in such cases, so proper to preside as the ruling elder. Nor would any local preacher, leader, or steward be a suitable president of the meeting, is his parent, his child, his brother, sister, or friend, might be more or less interested in the appeals which came before him: besides his *local* situation would lead him almost unavoidably to *prejudge* the case, and, perhaps, to enter warmly into the interests of one or other of the parties, previously to the appeal. It is, therefore, indisputably evident, that the *ruling elder* is most likely to be impartial, and, consequently, the most proper person to preside.

2. Another advantage of this office arises from the necessity of changing preachers from circuit to circuit in the intervals of the yearly conferences. Many of the preachers are young in years and gifts; and this must always be the case, more or less, or a fresh supply of travelling preachers in proportion to the necessities of the work could not be procured. These young men, in general, are exceedingly zealous. Their grand *forte* is to awaken souls; and in this view they are highly necessary for the spreading of the gospel. But for some time their gifts cannot be expected to be *various*; and, therefore, half a year at a time, or sometimes even a quarter, may be sufficient for them labour in one circuit: to change them, therefore, from circuit to circuit, in the intervals of the yearly conference, is highly necessary in many instances. Again, the preachers themselves, for family reasons or on other accounts, may desire, and have reason to expect, a change. But who can make it in the absence of the bishops; unless there be a presiding elder appointed for the district? A recent instance proves the justice of this remark. A large district was lately without a presiding elder for a year. Many of the preachers, sensible to the necessity of a change in the course of a year, met together, and settled every preliminary for the

purpose. Accordingly, when the time fixed upon for the change arrived, several of them came to their new appointments according to agreement, but, behold, the others had changed their minds, and the former were obliged to return to their old circuits, feeling not a little disgrace on account of their treatment. And this would be continually the case, and all would be confusion, *if there were no persons invested with the powers of ruling elders, by whatever name they might be called*; as it would be impossible for the bishops to be present every where, and enter *into the details* of all the circuits.

3. Who is able properly to supply the vacancies in circuits on the *deaths* of preachers, or on their *withdrawing* from the travelling connection? Who can have a thorough knowledge of the state of the district, and of its resources for filling up such vacancies, except the presiding elder who travels through the whole district? And shall circuits be often neglected for months together, and the flocks, during those times, be, more or less, without shepherds, and many of them, perhaps, perish for want of food, merely that one of the most scriptural and useful offices among us may be abolished? Shall we not rather support it, notwithstanding every thing which may be subtilly urged by our enemies under the cry of tyranny, which is the common cry of restless spirits even against the best governments, in order that they may throw every thing into confusion, and then ride in the whirlwind and direct the storm.

4. When a bishop visits a district, he ought to have one to accompany him, in whom he can fully confide; one, who can inform him of the whole work in a complete and comprehensive view; and, therefore, one who has travelled *through the whole*, and, by being present at all the quarterly meetings, can give all the information, concerning every circuit in particular, and the district in general, which the bishop can desire. Nor is the advantage small that the bishops, when at the greatest distance, may receive from the presiding elders a full account of their respective districts, and may thereby be continually in possession of a more comprehensive knowledge of the whole work, than they could possibly procure by any other means.

5. The only branch of the presiding elder's office, the importance and usefulness of which is not so obvious to some persons, but which is, at the same time, perhaps the most expedient of all, is *the suspending power*, for the preservation of *the purity* of our ministry,

Appendix to Chapter 4

and that our people may never be burdened with preachers of insufficient gifts. Here we must not forget, that the presiding agent acts as agent to the bishops; and that the bishops are, the greatest part of their time, at a vast distance from him; he must, therefore, exercise episcopal authority (ordination excepted) or he cannot act as their agent. All power may be abused. The only way which can be devised to prevent the abuse of it, if we will have a good and effective government, is to make the executive governors completely responsible, and their responsibility within the reach of the aggrieved. And, in the present instance, not only the general conference may expel the presiding elder—not only the episcopacy may suspend him from the exercise of his office—but the yearly conference may also impeach him, try him, and expel him: and such a threefold guard must be allowed, by every candid mind, to be as full a check to the abuse of his power, as, perhaps, human wisdom can devise.

But is it not strange, that any of *the people* should complain either of *this* or of the *episcopal* office? *These offices* in the church are peculiarly designed to meliorate the severity of Christian discipline, as far as they respect *the people*. In them the people have a refuge, an asylum to which they may fly upon all occasions. To them they may appeal, and before them they may lay all their complaints and grievances. The persons who bear these offices are their fathers in the gospel, ever open of access, ever ready to relieve them under every oppression. And we believe we can venture to assert, that the people have never had even a *plausible* pretence to complain of the authority either of the bishops or the presiding elders.

6. We may add, as was just hinted above, that the bishops ought not to enter into *small details*. It is not their calling. To select the proper men who are to act as their agents—to preserve in order and in motion the wheels of the vast machine—to keep a constant and watchful eye upon the whole—and to *think deeply* for the general good—form their peculiar and important avocation. All of which shews the necessity of the office now under consideration.

The objection brought by some, that many of the most useful preachers are taken out of the circuits for this purpose, whose preaching-talents are thereby lost to the connection, will by no means bear examination. Even if this was the case, the vast advantage arising from a complete and effective superintendence of the work would, we believe, far over-balance this consideration. But the objection is destitute of weight. Their preaching abilities are, we believe, abundantly more useful. Though all the preachers of matured talents and experience cannot be employed as presiding elders, yet those who are employed as such, generally answer this character. They are qualified to build up believers on their most holy faith, and to remove scruples and answer cases of conscience, more than the younger preachers in general. In many circuits, some parts of the society might suffer much in respect to the divine life, for want of those gifts peculiarly necessary for *them* were it not for this additional help; whilst the junction of the talents of the presiding elder with those of the circuit-preachers will, in general, make the whole complete. And as the presiding elder is, or ought to be, always present at the quarterly meetings, he will have opportunities of delivering his whole mind to a very considerable part of the people: nor is there any reasonable ground to fear that he will ever wear out his talents, if we consider the extent of a district, and the obligation the episcopacy is under to remove him, at farthest, on the expiration of four years.

To these observations we may add, that the calling of district conferences, on the immorality of travelling preachers, on their deaths, the necessity of removals, etc. would be attended with the most pernicious consequences to the circuits on this vast continent, where the districts are so large, and the absence of the preachers would be necessarily so long upon every such occasion. And we will venture to assert, that if any effective government ought to exist at all in the connection, during the intervals of the yearly and general conferences, there is *no alternative* between the authority of the bishops and their agents, the presiding elders, on the one hand, and the holding of district conferences on the other hand.

We will conclude our notes on this section with observing, that there is no ground to believe that the work of God has been injured, or the numbers of the society diminished, by the institution of this order, but just the contrary. In the year 1784, when the presiding eldership did, *in fact*, though not in *name*, commence, there were about 14,000 in society on this continent; and now the numbers amount to upwards of 56,000: so that the society is, at present, four times as large as it was twelve or thirteen years ago. We do not believe that the office now under consideration was the *principal cause* of this great revival, but the Spirit and grace of God, and the consequent zeal of the preachers in general. Yet we have no doubt, but the full organization of our body, and giving to the whole a complete and effective executive government, of which the presiding eldership makes a very capital branch, has, under God, been a grand means of preserving the peace and union of our connection and the purity of our ministry, and, therefore, *in its consequences*, has been a *chief instrument*, under the grace of God, of this great revival.

---

[1]MEC, *Doctrines and Discipline* (1798), 46–53.

APPENDIX TO CHAPTER 6

The 2004 General Conference of The United Methodist Church directed the Council of Bishops to convene a task force to study all aspects of the episcopacy. This task force developed a proposal (of which I was the principal writer and from which the foregoing derives), that was presented for consideration to the 2008 General Conference, under the sponsorship of the General Board of Higher Education and Ministry. Among its recommendations, the proposal calls for replacing ¶402 and ¶404 in the 2004 UMC *Discipline*, eliminating the first paragraph and adopting the following for ¶404.

¶404. The Role of Bishops and District Superintendents— Bishops and superintendents are elders in full connection.

1. Bishops are elected from the elders and set apart for a ministry of leadership, general oversight and supervision. As followers of Jesus Christ, bishops are authorized to guard the faith, order, liturgy, doctrine, and discipline of the Church. The role and calling forth of the bishop, as a follower of Jesus Christ, is to exercise oversight of the Church in its mission of making disciples of Jesus Christ for the transformation of the world. The basis of such discipleship of leadership (*episkopé*) lies in discipline and a disciplined life. The bishops lead therefore through the following disciplines:

    a) A vital and renewing spirit. The role of the bishop is to faithfully practice, model and lead the spiritual disciplines of our faith and to call and inspire the clergy and laity within the Church to practice the Christian disciplines in their individual lives through the tradition of personal holiness. The bishop is to lead in public worship, in the celebration of the sacraments and in the commendation of our faith.

b) An enquiring mind and a commitment to the teaching office. The role of the bishop is to continue to learn and to teach how to make disciples and lead faithful and fruitful congregations using scripture, spiritual disciplines, our Wesleyan heritage, and the history and doctrines of the Church.

c) A vision for the Church. The role of bishop is to lead the whole Church in claiming its mission of making disciples of Jesus Christ for the transformation of the world. The bishop leads by discerning, inspiring, strategizing, equipping, implementing, and evaluating the fulfillment of the mission of the Church. Working in partnership with the Council of Bishops, the cabinet and lay and clergy leadership of the annual conference, and the professing members of the Church, the bishop urges the whole church to move toward the vision of sharing Christ with the world in fulfillment of our mission, faithful discipleship and a "more excellent way" of being Christ's people in the world.

d) A prophetic commitment for the transformation of the church and the world. The role of the bishop is to be a prophetic voice for justice in a suffering and conflicted world through the tradition of social holiness. The bishop encourages and models the mission of witness and service in the world through proclamation of the gospel and alleviation of human suffering.

e) A passion for the unity of the church. The role of the bishop is to be the shepherd of the whole flock who thereby provides leadership toward the goal of understanding, reconciliation and unity within the church.

f) The ministry of administration. The role of the bishop is to uphold the discipline and order of the Church by consecrating, ordaining, commissioning, supervising and appointing persons in ministry to the church and the world. As the presiding officer of the annual conference, the resident bishop provides order and leads in new opportunities for ministry within the annual conference. The bishop shares with other bishops the oversight of the whole Church through the Council of Bishops and is held accountable through the Council of Bishops in collaboration with conference and jurisdictional committees on episcopacy.

APPENDIX TO CHAPTER 10

DICKINS'S BOOKLIST (1791)

The following Books are published by JOHN DICKINS, No. 182, Race Street, near Sixth Street, Philadelphia; for the use of the Methodist Societies in the United States of America; and the profits thereof applied for the general benefit of the said Societies. Sold by the publisher, and the Ministers and Preachers in the several Circuits.

The Arminian Magazine, Vol, 1st and 2d at 12ʃ, [Shillings] per volume.

The Rev. Mr. Wesley's Notes on the New Testament in 3 vols. Well bound 17 ʃ

The same lettered 18 ʃ 6d [pence].

Thomas a Kempis, bound 2 ʃ

Primitive Physic, bound 3 ʃ

The Form of Discipline for the Methodist Church, with Treatises on Predestination, Perseverance, Christian Perfection, Baptism, &c. All bound together 3, 6d.

The Experiences of about twenty British Methodist Preachers, well bound and lettered 5ʃ, 7d 1-2

The Experience and Travels of Mr. Freeborn Garrettson, well bound 3 ʃ

A Pocket Hymn-Book, containing three hundred Hymns well bound and lettered 3ʃ 9d.

The Excellent works of the Rev. Mr. John Fletcher, published one volume at a time; the whole will contain about six volumes: the 1st

APPENDIX TO CHAPTER 10

and 2d vols. Now published, well bound and lettered at 5 ʃ 7d 1-2 per volume.

An Extract on Infant Baptism, stitched 9d.

Children's Instructions, stitched 6d.

An Abridgment of Mrs. Rowe's Devout Thoughts, bound 1ʃ 10d 1-2.

A Funeral Discourse on the death of that great Divine, the Rev. John Wesley, stitched 1.1d.

The Saints Everlasting Rest will be republished some time in Dec. 1791; well bound 5 ʃ 7d 1-2.

Minutes of the Methodist Conferences, 4d.

As the profits of these books are for the general benefit of the Methodist Societies, it is humbly recommended to the Members of the said Societies, that they will purchase no books which we publish, of any other person than the aforesaid JOHN DICKINS, or the Methodist Ministers and Preachers in the several Circuits, or such persons as sell them by their consent.

NOTES

INTRODUCTION: DOCTRINE IN EXPERIENCE

1. Mark A. Noll, *America's God: From Jonathan Edwards to Abraham Lincoln* (New York: Oxford University Press, 2002); E. Brooks Holifield, *Theology in America: Christian Thought from the Age of the Puritans to the Civil War* (New Haven and London: Yale University Press, 2003).
2. See the several works by Henry Warner Bowden: *Church History in the Age of Science: Historiographical Patterns in the United States, 1876–1918* (Chapel Hill: University of North Carolina Press, 1971); *A Century of Church History: The Legacy of Philip Schaff*, ed. H. W. Bowden (Carbondale: Southern Illinois University Press, 1988); and *Church History in an Age of Uncertainty: Historiographical Patterns in the United States, 1906–1990* (Carbondale: Southern Illinois University Press, 1991).
3. Russell E. Richey, *The Methodist Conference in America: A History* (Nashville: Kingswood Books, 1996).
4. Russell E. Richey, *Early American Methodism* (Bloomington: Indiana University Press, 1991).
5. Nathan Bangs, *A History of the Methodist Episcopal Church*, 12th ed., 4 vols. (New York: Carlton & Porter, 1860).
6. *The Errors of Hopkinsianism Detected and Refuted* (New York, 1815); *The Reformer Reformed: or A Second Part of the Errors of Hopkinsianism Detected and Refuted* (New York, 1816); *An Examination of the Doctrine of Predestination* (New York, 1817); *A Vindication of Methodist Episcopacy* (New York, 1820).
7. See Thomas A. Langford, *Practical Divinity: Theology in the Wesleyan Tradition* (Nashville: Abingdon, 1983), 78–86.
8. Russell E. Richey and Thomas Edward Frank, *Episcopacy in the Methodist Tradition: Perspectives and Proposals* (Nashville: Abingdon, 2004).
9. *Marks of Methodism: Theology in Ecclesial Practice* (Nashville: Abingdon, 2005) is the fifth volume in the series "United Methodism and American Culture," Russell E. Richey, Dennis M. Campbell, and William B. Lawrence, editors and coauthors. Also see other volumes in this series: *Connectionalism: Ecclesiology, Mission, and Identity*, UMAC I (Nashville: Abingdon, 1997); *The People(s) Called Methodist: Forms and Reforms of Their Life*, UMAC II (Nashville: Abingdon, 1998); *Doctrines and Discipline*, UMAC III (Nashville: Abingdon, 1999); and *Questions for the Twenty-First Century Church*, UMAC IV (Nashville: Abingdon, 1999).

1. Four Languages of Methodist Self-Understanding

1. Minton Thrift, *Memoir of the Rev. Jesse Lee. With Extracts from his Journals* (New York: N. Bangs and T. Mason, 1823), 208–9. As the first great American-born leader of the movement, Lee gave voice to American Methodism. Note particularly the language: melting, weeping, singing, trembling, crying, revive. This strongly biblical and vernacular rhetoric typifies Methodist journals. It is a biblical vernacular, a biblical pietist vernacular, a biblical Wesleyan vernacular.
2. Jesse Lee gave some indication of his understanding of and commitment to this loud Methodist voice in Fairfield, "August 13th [1789] . . . After meeting was over, a man came to me and said the women complained that I preached so loud that it made their heads ache, and they wished me to speak a little lower the next time I came: but I hope God will help me to speak hereafter, so as to make their hearts ache" (ibid., 120).
3. Lee, of course, took Methodism into the Calvinist stronghold of New England. An entry of 1795 (ibid., 215–16) typifies his stance: "At night, I preached at doctor Hind's, on Rom. ix.22. Here I endeavoured to show the unreasonableness of predestination; and how the people had fitted themselves for destruction; and yet, God had much long-suffering towards them. I further told them, a minister ought to pray the people, in Christ's stead, to be reconciled to God, warn them of their danger, and weep over them, and let them know that the Lord was not willing that they should be damned; but that they should come to the knowledge of the truth and be saved. I also endeavoured to show how unreasonable it was for a minister to say that God was willing to send his hearers to hell; and that they should bless God for sending them there. I had a comfortable meeting, and freedom in speaking. Just as I was going to leave the house, the minister came in, and abundance of people flocked into the room, expecting to hear us dispute, but after asking him a few questions *civilly*, we parted."
4. The finding of the voice was often traumatic. Lee reported the following concerning his first effort at preaching: "On the 17th of November, 1779, I preached for the first time in my life, at a place called the Old Barn." He preached several times soon thereafter, "and found much of the Divine Presence with me in public, yet I was so sensible of my own weakness and insufficiency, that after I had preached, I would retire to the woods and prostrate myself on the ground, and weep before the Lord, and pray that he would pardon the imperfections of my preaching, and give me strength to declare his whole counsel in purity" (ibid., 22).
5. Harry S. Stout in *The New England Soul: Preaching and Religious Culture in Colonial New England* (New York: Oxford University Press, 1986) argues that the Great Awakening wrought a revolution in American discourse and this rhetorical revolution made possible the political revolution.
6. The people responded in kind. They also shouted, or as in this case with Lee in 1799, they roared: "Sunday, 10th [February 1799]. At Charlotte meeting-house, Mr. Asbury preached, and after an intermission of fifteen minutes, I preached. God was in the midst of us. Several young converts were present; and they, with others, were deeply melted into tears; some of them could hardly refrain from roaring aloud. Glory be to God in the highest, for this meeting." Thrift, *Memoir of Jesse Lee*, 247.
7. The term *language* in this paper obviously overstates the separateness and incompatibility of what might more judiciously be described as paradigm, frame of reference, meaning system. However, *language* does underscore problems of translation, mutual intelligibility, multiple reference, divergent meanings that this paper argues did haunt Methodist terminology. The use here is heuristic.
8. In *The Garden of American Methodism: The Delmarva Peninsula, 1769–1820* (Wilmington, DE: Scholarly Resources, 1984), William H. Williams suggests that Methodism's viability as a second English church was one source of its attractiveness (89–120).
9. The literature on republicanism is immense. See the helpful discussions thereof by Robert E. Shalhope, "Republicanism and Early American Historiography," *William and*

Mary Quarterly 39 (1982): 334–56; and "Toward a Republican Synthesis: The Emergency of an Understanding of Republicanism in American Historiography," *William and Mary Quarterly* 29 (1972): 49–80. See also Isaac Kramnick, "Republican Revisionism Revisited," *American Historical Review* 87 (1982): 629–64.

10. One could certainly illustrate these four languages with texts from most years after 1800. The choice of 1798 is somewhat arbitrary. As we shall see, it does afford us one of the earliest clear expressions of Methodism's adoption of republican ideas and a very powerful illustration of Methodism's episcopal self-understanding. Popular and Wesleyan language abound at all times. One virtue of such an early year is that we can see these several voices of Methodism in relatively pure form. For these reasons, the choice of 1798 seemed apt.

11. Thrift, *Memoir of Jesse Lee*, 236.

12. Ibid., 202, 203, 204, 205. Lee traveled then in New England.

13. For the roles of Dickins and Cooper in the Methodist book enterprise and the publications over which they exercised oversight, consult James Penn Pilkington, *The Methodist Publishing House: A History* (Nashville: Abingdon, 1968), 1:63–148.

14. Eventually, American Methodist serials would lend themselves to the popular idiom. *The Methodist Magazine, for the Year 1798* carried a subtitle that suggested such a purpose: "Containing Original Sermons, Experiences, Letters, and Other Religious Pieces; Together with Instructive and Useful Extracts from Different Authors." This was American Methodism's second effort at a serious magazine and the second (and final) year of the experiment. It could have passed as a British publication, for it carried virtually nothing American and was heavily dominated by Wesley's sermons, writings, and collected material. As such, it transmitted the Wesleyan idiom.

15. Methodist Episcopal Church, *The Doctrines and Discipline of the Methodist Episcopal Church in America, with Explanatory Notes, by Thomas Coke and Francis Asbury* (Philadelphia, 1798); facsimile edition, ed. Frederick A. Norwood (Rutland, VT: Academy Books, 1979), 70. The 1796 General Conference had authorized the publication of *The Methodist Magazine* with this notation: "N.B. The propagation of religious knowledge by the means of the press, is next in importance to the preaching of the gospel. To supply the people therefore with the most pious and useful books, in order that they may fill up their leisure hours in the most profitable ways, is an object worthy the deepest attention of their pastors." *Minutes of the General Conference of the Methodist Episcopal Church . . . 1796* (Baltimore, 1796), 15.

16. Methodist Episcopal Church, *The Doctrines and Discipline of the Methodist Episcopal Church in America, with Explanatory Notes, by Thomas Coke and Francis Asbury* (Philadelphia, 1798); facsimile edition, ed. Frederick A. Norwood (Rutland, VT: Academy Books, 1979), iv, Advertisement to the Reader: "The last General Conference desired the Bishops to draw up Annotations on the Form of the Discipline." In his "Introduction," Frederick Norwood argues that O'Kelly's movement motivated these annotations.

17. Ibid., 6. The italics appeared in the original.

18. Neither, however, made clear reference to the actual service to be used (ibid., 118–20).

19. On the character of colonial Anglicanism see Frederick V. Mills, Sr., *Bishops by Ballot* (New York: Oxford University Press, 1978) and Henry F. May, *The Enlightenment in America* (New York: Oxford University Press, 1976).

20. *Doctrines and Discipline* (1798), 40.

21. On O'Kelly and these events, see *The History of American Methodism*, ed. Emory S. Bucke (New York: Abingdon, 1964), 1:429–52.

22. William Warren Sweet acknowledged losses to the MEC in 1795–96 of almost 10,000 but attributed some of that to other causes; *Methodism in American History*, rev. ed. (New York: Abingdon, 1953), 134.

23. James O'Kelly, *The Author's Apology for Protesting Against the Methodist Episcopal Government* (Richmond: John Dixon, 1798).

24. Ibid., 4, 9, 21, 38.

25. For historiographical treatment of this tradition, see note 9 above. Classic treatment can be found in Caroline Robbins, *The Eighteenth-Century Commonwealthman* (Cambridge,

MA: Harvard University Press, 1959); Bernard Bailyn, *The Ideological Origins of the American Revolution* (Cambridge, MA: Harvard University Press, 1967); and Gordon S. Wood, *The Creation of the American Republic* (New York: W. W. Norton, 1972).
26. On the prevalence of conspiratorial visions and the underlying causes thereof, see the brilliant exposition by Gordon S. Wood, "Conspiracy and the Paranoid Style: Causality and Deceit in the Eighteenth Century," *William and Mary Quarterly*, 3rd Ser. 39 (1982): 401–41.
27. Nathan O. Hatch examines this preaching and the longer political experience that gave shape to it in *The Sacred Cause of Liberty* (New Haven: Yale University Press, 1977), 139–75.
28. These developments are treated in a variety of works. See especially Fred J. Hood, *Reformed America* (Tuscaloosa: University of Alabama Press, 1980); Robert T. Handy, *A Christian America. Protestant Hopes and Historical Realities*, 2nd ed. (New York: Oxford University Press, 1984); John F. Wilson, *Public Religion in American Culture* (Philadelphia: Temple University Press, 1979); and Martin E. Marty, *Religion and Republic* (Boston: Beacon Press, 1987).
29. This point is worked out in greater detail in chapter 2, "History as a Bearer of Denominational Identity."
30. "Minutes Taken at the Several Annual Conferences of the Methodist Episcopal Church, for the year 1798," in *Minutes of the Methodist Conferences, Annually Held in America; From 1773 to 1813, Inclusive* (New York: Published by Daniel Hitt and Thomas Ware, for the Methodist Connexion in the United States, 1813), 200–15.
31. Ibid., 201–4.
32. There is some question as to whether Methodism ever fully integrated those two, though it brought them into sufficient coherence for the polity to work.
33. The line from Dickins appeared in italics in the original. *Minutes of the Methodist Conferences, . . . 1773 to 1813*, 205.
34. Thrift, *Memoir of Jesse Lee*, 230–40.
35. Conception here refers to both the coming to understanding and the coming into being. For discussion of the variety of tensions in Methodist understanding of ministry, see Dennis M. Campbell's excellent volume, *The Yoke of Obedience: The Meaning of Ordination in Methodism* (Nashville: Abingdon, 1988), especially 72–97.
36. The literary fare for the Methodist faithful constituted an impressive and meaty diet. In the year 1798, for instance, Dickins placed this advertisement in the rear of the *Pocket Hymn Book* (Philadelphia: Henry Tuckniss, 1798):

The Following Books are Published by John Dickins . . . For the Use of the Methodist Societies in the United States of America . . . Sold by the Publisher, and the Ministers and Preachers in the several Circuits.
    The Arminian Magazine
    Thomas a Kempis
    The Form of Discipline . . . with Treatises on Predestination, Perseverance, Christian Perfection, &c.
    The Form of Discipline . . . with Explanatory Notes
    The Experience and Travel of Mr. Freeborn Garrettson
    An Extract on Infant Baptism
    Children's Instructions
    An Abridgement of Mrs. Rowe's Devout Exercises of the Heart
    The excellent Works of the Rev. Mr. John Fletcher, complete, in six volumes
    A Funeral Discourse on the Death of . . . John Wesley
    The Saints' Everlasting Rest
    The 1st volume of Mr. Francis Asbury's Journal
    A Tract on Slavery
    The Rev. John Wesley's Journal, vol. 1st.
    The Family Adviser and primitive Physic
    The Rev. John Wesley's Life
    Spiritual Letters, &c. by the Rev. John Fletcher

Sermons by the Rev. John Wesley . . . 1st and 2nd vols.
Doddridge's Sermons to Young People
A Scriptural Catechism
Minutes of the Methodist Conferences . . . 1773 to 1794 inclusive
The same, for several late years, separately
The Life of Monsieur De Renty
Jane Cooper's Life and Letters
Nicodemus, a Treatise on the Fear of Man
Defense of Methodism
Manners of the Ancient Christians
Dr. Coke's four Sermons
The Methodist Magazine

37. Thomas Coke, *The Substance of a Sermon, Preached at Baltimore . . . Before the General Conference of the Methodist Episcopal Church, on the 27th of December, 1784, at the Ordination of the Rev. Francis Asbury to the Office of a Superintendent* (London: J. Paramore, 1785).
38. Francis Asbury, *The Journals and Letters of Francis Asbury*, ed. Elmer T. Clark (London: Epworth Press; Nashville: Abingdon, 1958), 3:475–92. This statement was an oral publication.
39. For the controversies that elicited these defenses, see Lawrence O. Kline, "Anti-Methodist Publications (American)," in *The Encyclopedia of World Methodism*, ed. Nolan B. Harmon (Nashville: United Methodist Publishing House, 1974), 1:115–19.
40. *Minutes of the Methodist Conferences, . . . 1773 to 1813*, 162–64.
41. These were the questions Wesley posed at the first conference, questions that, over time, generated the structure and emphases of the Methodist "Large Minutes" and *Discipline*. See "Minutes of Some Late Conversations between the Rev. Mr. Wesley and Others," *Works* (Jackson), 8:275.
42. *Doctrines and Discipline* (1798), 18.
43. Asbury, *Journals*, 2:46. The entry is March 30, 1795.
44. This point is rather fully treated in Richey, "Conference as a Means of Grace," *Early American Methodism* (Bloomington: Indiana University Press, 1991), 65–81.
45. This point is elaborated in Richey, "Views of the Nation: 'A Glass to the Heart,'" (ibid., 33–46).
46. That phrase, from G. K. Chesterton, forms the title and motif of Sidney E. Mead, *The Nation with the Soul of a Church* (New York: Harper & Row, 1975).
47. The other points in this litany have been, at least, hinted out. Although the subject deserves more attention than can be given here, we should note that the several languages did conceive and invoke authority in distinctive fashion. That can be illustrated by reference to what has recently been regarded as a distinctively Wesleyan or Methodist (also distinctively Anglican and Catholic) conception of authority. Wesley and Methodists purportedly appeal to a fourfold scheme of authority, the so-called Wesleyan quadrilateral—Scripture, tradition, reason, and experience. On one cut through these languages, we might associate the elements of the quadrilateral respectively with popular, episcopal, republican, and Wesleyan languages. There is, in fact, some correspondence here: popular (Scripture), episcopal (tradition), republican (reason), and Wesleyan (experience).

At a deeper level of analysis, we would need to recognize each of the languages as possessing its own notion of the four elements that constitute the quadrilateral. For instance, the republican language had its own hermeneutic for reading Scripture, a very covenantal one, much commented upon in historical and literary studies of Puritanism (see, for instance, the work of Sacvan Bercovitch). The republican sense of tradition, of history as the struggle between liberty and tyranny, and of golden ages of republican government, we have already noted. For republicanism, reason seemed, at times, a virtual idol. To be sure, what Republicans meant by "reason" changed. Reason had strongly empirical, Lockean overtones until those were recast by the Scottish Common

Sense philosophers. Common sense became powerful among Methodists as among other Protestants. At that point, the line between reason and experience grew indistinct. Republican views of experience were affected by this shift in epistemology. Increasingly in the nineteenth century, experience was construed as common sense. Appeal to American experience, to American common sense also became common.

It would be easy to show that the other languages had their conceptions of the elements of this quadrilateral. The point of this excursus is to underscore the integrity of these languages and the divergent ways in which they pulled.

2. HISTORY AS BEARER OF METHODIST IDENTITY

1. Halford E. Luccock and Paul Hutchinson, *The Story of Methodism* (New York: Methodist Book Concern, 1926), 270.
2. Methodism's nineteenth-century historians, as we shall see, gave these propositions expressive form. M. L. Scudder gave particularly striking renditions of these four notions. See Scudder, *American Methodism* (Hartford: S. S. Scranton, 1868), pp. 270, 363 on (1), p. 521 on (2), p. 524 on (3), and p. 569 on (4).
3. This paper works on the propositional level, that is, with what Methodists affirmed about themselves. Those affirmations are derived from Methodist histories. The paper will endeavor to show how historians initially conceived Methodism's propositions, how they altered those propositions into the above form as nation and church changed, and how they struggled to make sense of the Methodist saga when the propositions no longer made sense. For reasons of control, the paper will focus upon The Methodist Episcopal Church; its successor, The Methodist Church; and its successor, The United Methodist Church. For the most part, the generalizations apply, but with important variations, to the experience of The Methodist Protestant Church, The Methodist Episcopal Church, South, the United Brethren in Christ, and The Evangelical Association as well as to members of the Wesleyan family of denominations not contributory to United Methodism.
4. Robert T. Handy, *A Christian America. Protestant Hopes and Historical Realities*, 2nd ed. (New York: Oxford University Press, 1984), 159–84.
5. See *The Book of Discipline of the United Methodist Church* (Nashville: United Methodist Publishing House, 1988), 40–60.
6. Russell E. Richey, "History in The Discipline," *Quarterly Review* 10 (Winter 1989): 3–20.
7. Beginning in 1816, candidates for the ministry in the MEC followed a prescribed course of study, a reading list initially elaborated and supervised on the regional "annual conference" level, which eventually operated as a kind of national college. Methodist History was a prominent part of this course of study from the beginning. L. Dale Patterson has carefully identified the literature of the course and the years each item was used in "The Ministerial Mind of American Methodism: The Course of Study for the Ministry of the Methodist Episcopal Church, the Methodist Episcopal Church, South and the Methodist Protestant Church, 1876–1920" (PhD diss., Drew University, 1984).
8. With the exceptions of Jesse Lee and James M. Buckley, whose histories claimed pre-eminence on other grounds, the individuals given attention here figured prominently in the MEC course of study, constituting an important formative influence on successive generations of Methodist ministers. In most cases, the individual histories enjoyed a long life on the course. Abel Stevens's *History of the Methodist Episcopal Church* appeared on the course in 1864, 1868, 1880, 1886, 1890 and then again in 1932; his compressed version, *A Compendious History of American Methodism*, remained on from 1872 to 1908, with only a curious gap of 1900, when another of his works took its place. Lee wrote the first Methodist history and in many ways set the terms for the genre. Buckley's effort appeared in the prestigious American Society of Church History series.
9. Jno. J. Tigert, *A Constitutional History of American Episcopal Methodism*, 3rd ed., rev. (Nashville: Publishing House of the MECS, 1908), 532–602.

10. *A Form of Discipline, For the Ministers, Preachers and Members of the Methodist Episcopal Church in America* (New York: W. Ross, 1787), 3–4.
11. Jesse Lee, *A Short History of the Methodists* (Baltimore: Magill and Clime, 1810; facsimile ed., Rutland, VT: Academy Books, 1974).
12. Minton Thrift, *Memoir of the Rev. Jesse Lee. With Extracts from his Journals* (New York: N. Bangs and T. Mason, 1823), 67ff.
13. William Warren Sweet, *Methodism in American History*, rev. ed. (New York: Abingdon, 1953), 176.
14. Cf. Bangs, *History*, 2:322–23; Asbury, *Journals*, 2:640–41; and Leroy M. Lee, *The Life and Times of The Rev. Jesse Lee* (Charleston: John Early, 1848), 466.
15. Lee, *Short History*, 139–40.
16. See R. Laurence Moore, *Religious Outsiders and the Making of Americans* (New York: Oxford University Press, 1986).
17. Lee, *Short History*, 60.
18. That saga, and particularly the declaration of independence by a group of the "southern" preachers through presbyterial ordination, thereby splitting the American movement, has been typically written from the Asbury side of the split, a side that sought to remain loyal to Wesley and not separate from him or the Church of England. Here as elsewhere Lee's handling of the story evidences his eagerness to show the American contours of the Methodist story. In so doing, however, he did not formally link church to nation.
19. Nathan Bangs, *A History of the Methodist Episcopal Church*, 12th ed., 4 vols. (New York: Carlton & Porter, 1860), 1:356–59.
20. Ibid., 4:436.
21. Richard E. Hermann, "Nathan Bangs: Apologist for American Methodism" (PhD diss., Emory University, 1973).
22. James Penn Pilkington, *The Methodist Publishing House: A History* (Nashville: Abingdon, 1968), 169–219.
23. Bangs, *History*, 1:11.
24. Bangs prefaced his four-volume work with a discussion of his sources. Among them, he acknowledged George Bancroft's *History of the Colonization of the United States* for his initial discussion. He defended his decision to make "Bishop Asbury the principal hero of the narrative" (1:6). He also indicated his respect for Jesse Lee and dependence upon Lee's *Short History* (1:7).
25. See respectively, ibid., 1:22, 26, 30.
26. Ibid., 1:46.
27. Cf. Mark A. Noll, *One Nation Under God?* (San Francisco: Harper & Row, 1988), 35–43; and Shalhope, "Republicanism."
28. Bangs, *History*, 2:146–48.
29. Ibid., 2:150.
30. "In addition to the direct influence which Christian principles were thus brought to exert on the heart and life, the itinerating mode of preaching had a tendency in the natural order of cause and effect, to cement the hearts of our citizens together in one great brotherhood. . . . What more calculated to soften these asperities [state and sectional rivalries], and to allay petty jealousies and animosities, than a Church bound together by one system of doctrine, under the government of the same discipline, accustomed to the same usages, and a ministry possessing a homogeneousness of character, aiming at one and the same end—the salvation of their fellow-men by means of the same gospel, preached and enforced by the same method—and these ministers continually interchanging from north to south, from east to west, everywhere striving to bring all men under the influence of the same 'bond of perfectness'? Did not these things tend to bind the great American family together by producing a sameness of character, feelings, and views?" (ibid., 2:148–49)

    Bangs noted that the church in its General Conference recognized that "a general itinerating superintendency [episcopacy] would 'prevent local interests and jealousies from springing up, and tend most effectually to preserve that homogeneousness of character and reciprocity of brotherly feeling by which Methodism had been and should be ever distinguished'" (ibid., 3:54–55).

This is a point that Donald Mathews has elaborated into a general theory concerning the second Awakening and C. C. Goen into a theory of the cause of the Civil War. Cf. Donald G. Mathews, "The Second Great Awakening as an Organizing Process, 1780–1830," *American Quarterly* 21 (1969): 23–43; and C. C. Goen, *Broken Churches, Broken Nation. Denominational Schisms and the Coming of the American Civil War* (Macon: Mercer University Press, 1985).

31. Abel Stevens, *A Compendious History of American Methodism* (New York: Eaton & Mains, 1868), 17. Most frequent reference in what follows will be to this condensed version (608 pp.) of Stevens's various accounts. This version appeared on the Course of Study for the quadrenniums of 1872 to 1908 with the sole exception of 1900. That year his *Supplementary History of American Methodism* (New York: Eaton & Mains, 1899), which had just appeared, took its place. The course also featured Stevens's four-volume *History of The Methodist Episcopal Church* (New York: Carlton & Porter, 1864–67) in 1864, 1868, 1880, 1896, 1900, and again interestingly in 1932. His work covering the whole Wesleyan tradition, *History of the Religious Movement of the Eighteenth Century Called Methodism* (New York: Philips & Hunt, 1858–61), enjoyed the longest, most sustained tenure on the course, continuously from 1860 to 1928, with the sole exception of 1884. The combined 72-year reign, 1860 to 1932, attests the great influence enjoyed by Stevens.

32. Stevens's four-volume *History* began with the same scene but lacks the chapter title. His *Religious Movement* gave only incidental attention to American developments and so did not lend itself to this vignette. Stevens achieved the same point there, the providential fitting of Methodism for America, with different staging and assertion (see 2:434–37).

33. Stevens, *Compendious History*, 19.

34. Ibid., 18–24.

35. Ibid., 176.

36. We noticed (note 2) M. L. Scudder's enunciation of these axioms. The viewpoints become a staple of Northern Methodist belief during and after the Civil War.

Matthew Simpson's *A Hundred Years of Methodism* (New York: Nelson & Phillips, 1876) is the first history featuring such views that figured on the Course of Study. It did not displace Stevens but was put on a different segment of the Course, the reading list for local preachers. It first appeared there in 1876 and remained for three more quadrennia (1876, 1880, 1884, 1888).

37. George R. Crooks, *The Life of Bishop Matthew Simpson* (New York: Harper & Brothers, 1891), 397–403.

38. For an even more striking public theology, see Jesse T. Peck, *The History of The Great Republic, Considered from a Christian Standpoint* (New York: Broughton and Wyman, 1869), 2, 693, 707.

39. Matthew Simpson, *A Hundred Years of Methodism* (New York: Nelson & Phillips, 1876), 41.

40. Ibid., 68.

41. Compare C. C. Goss, *Statistical History of the First Century of American Methodism* (New York: Carlton & Porter, 1866), 159: "The moral influence of Methodism is at least commensurate with its numerical strength. In no department of Christian effort are Methodists behind their sister denominations." Such affirmations abound.

42. Simpson, *Hundred Years*, 345.

43. Ibid., 156–57.

44. Mead, *Nation with the Soul of a Church*.

45. Simpson, *Hundred Years*, 209.

46. James M. Buckley, *A History of Methodists in the United States*, 4th ed. (New York: Charles Scribner's Sons, 1900).

47. Ibid., 685–86.

48. Sacvan Bercovitch, *The American Jeremiad* (Madison: University of Wisconsin Press, 1978).

49. The editor was Philip Schaff, who argued strenuously that it was the church historian's office and responsibility to discern the activity of God in human affairs. Schaff was a

major, perhaps the major, figure in the emergence of the discipline of church history. The inclusion of Buckley's volume in his series gave it great prominence. It was certainly frequently reprinted or republished; twelve times according to Kenneth E. Rowe, *Methodist Union Catalog: Pre-1976 Imprints* (Metuchen: Scarecrow Press, 1975–), 2:209–10. First published in 1896, Buckley's history went through six editions as a part of the ASCH series, the 6th appearing in 1907. Another version was reprinted in a 3rd edition in 1909. The first edition was again reprinted in 1973. It is because of the importance of this series and of Buckley's inclusion in it, that we include Buckley in this study. His work apparently did not appear on the Course of Study.

50. Buckley, *History*, 217.
51. Ibid., 220.
52. Ibid., 220–21.
53. For example, see Buckley, *History*, 170–71, 173, 176–77, 179, 203, 205, 248.
54. See, for instance, a volume contemporaneous to Buckley's, Henry Wheeler, *One Thousand Questions and Answers concerning the Methodist Episcopal Church* (New York: Eaton & Mains, 1898), especially questions 1 and 66 (pp. 1, 16).
55. Buckley, *History*, xviii.
56. Ibid., 1–2, 40–72.
57. Luccock and Hutchinson, *Story of Methodism* appeared on the Course of Study from 1932 to 1956. For all of those quadrennia except 1944, it was collateral reading. In 1944, it was required for admission on trial.
58. Illustrative are various providential/pneumatological claims that they make about Wesley or early Methodism. Of his field preaching they affirmed, "Clearly the hand of God was in this " as the unchurched heard "a word that was again proving its ancient power." They spoke of John Wesley's undertaking "his great task in England at the moment when the movement of world forces had marked that 'tight little island' for a spiritual shaking." Of the sending of missionaries to America, they affirmed, "It was a prophetic moment." In recognition of the small successes of Wesley's early missionaries to the colonies, they noted, "Methodism did not spring to life in America without long years of preparation. There is always a background for spiritual marvels, even when it is least apparent." Of the events of 1784, they proclaimed, "The ordinations of Methodism are entirely outside the mechanical realm. They derive their authority from the fact that their originator, John Wesley, was a man whose ministry was evidently approved of God."

Making a comparison of the shadows of two men on horseback, Napoleon Bonaparte, on Europe and Francis Asbury, on America, they asserted, "It is still easy to trace in the affairs of the United States the influence of this single man, Francis Asbury—Methodism's man on horseback. God send us such another!" (Luccock and Hutchinson, *Story of Methodism*, 19, 73, 142, 158, 172, 232).
59. Their predecessors, even Lee, attempted to be scholarly according to the expectations of the day. Luccock and Hutchinson made no such effort. The volume footnoted only where cited material was protected by copyright. (See, for instance, their references to Ezra Squier Tipple's *Francis Asbury, The Prophet of the Long Road* [New York: Methodist Book Concern, 1916] on pp. 236, 241, 242.) They also offered no bibliography.
60. Luccock and Hutchinson, *Story of Methodism*, 28.
61. Ibid., 34.
62. Ibid., 213–17.
63. Ibid., 217–300.
64. Ibid., 333–34, 494–95.
65. Ibid., 264.
66. Ibid., 440–42.
67. Ibid., 486–87.
68. Ibid., 494–95.
69. Handy, *Christian America*, 161–64.
70. Luccock and Hutchinson, *Story of Methodism*, 487–88.
71. William Warren Sweet, *Methodism in American History* (New York: The Methodist Book Concern, 1933 orig.) appeared on the Course of Study for the quadrennia beginning

1932, 1936, 1940, and 1944; for the first three as a requirement for admission on trial and for the last as collateral reading.
72. Sweet, *Methodism in American History*, Revision of 1953 (Nashville: Abingdon Press [1954]), 27.
73. Ibid., 143.
74. Ibid.
75. Ibid., 143–53.
76. Sweet employed this, in a more generalized form, as his organizing principle in *Religion in the Development of American Culture, 1765–1840* (New York: Charles Scribner's Sons, 1952).
77. Sweet, *Methodism*, 8, 336.
78. Frederick A. Norwood, *The Story of American Methodism* (Nashville: Abingdon, 1974).
79. Ibid., 15–17.
80. *Book of Discipline of the United Methodist Church* (1788), 7–15.

3. EVOLVING PATTERNS OF METHODIST MINISTRY

1. It is only in the last several decades that we have come to appreciate the elitism and presumption of writing the history of the church—of Methodism in this instance—with primary attention to the ministry. Women's history, Black history, the "academic" study of religion, and the new social history have served to open up the wider history of the people of God and called into question the easy equation of ministerial perspective, records, and accomplishment with the history of the church. During this period in which church history has recognized its myopic clericalism and sought to be more embracive, a new investigation of the history of ministry—now undertaken as an enterprise in its own right—has emerged. Among the several contributions to this endeavor are David D. Hall, *The Faithful Shepherd: A History of the New England Ministry in the Seventeenth Century* (Chapel Hill: University of North Carolina Press, 1972); Emory Elliot, *Power and the Pulpit in Puritan New England* (Princeton University Press, 1975); J. William T. Youngs, Jr., *God's Messengers: Religious Leadership in Colonial New England, 1700–1750* (Baltimore: Johns Hopkins University Press, 1976); Donald M. Scott, *From Office to Profession: The New England Ministry, 1750–1850* (Philadelphia: University of Pennsylvania Press, 1978); Ann Douglas, *The Feminization of American Culture* (New York: Knopf, 1977); and E. Brooks Holifield, *The Gentlemen Theologians* (Durham: Duke University Press, 1978). Following the New England bias typical of so much of American church history, these histories of ministry (except the last) have focused on Puritan and Congregational ministry. The major historical effort on Methodist ministry of which I am aware is the dissertation by James Lynn, "The Concept of the Ministry in the Methodist Episcopal Church, 1784–1844" (Princeton Theological Seminary, 1973). What distinguishes this work from older histories of ministry is the self-conscious endeavor to reflect on status, roles, self-understandings, authority, work of ministers, and the evolution of these over time. I shall attempt to pursue some of these issues in relation to Methodist ministry. Such a perspective does not replace but rather supplements that provided in older treatments of ministry, as for instance in H. Richard Niebuhr and Daniel D. Williams, eds., *The Ministry in Historical Perspectives* (New York: Harper & Row, 1956); and James Gustafson, "The Clergy in the United States," *Daedalus* (1963): 724–44. For comparative purposes see also Jacob Neusner, ed., *Understanding American Judaism*, 2 vols. (New York: Ktav, 1975); John Tracy Ellis, ed. *The Catholic Priest in the United States* (Collegeville, MN: St. John's University Press, 1971); and Charles V. Hamilton, *The Black Preacher in America* (New York: Morrow, 1972).
2. See William R. Cannon, "The Meaning of the Ministry in Methodism," *Methodist History* 8 (October 1969): 3–19; Gerald Kennedy, "The Methodist Ministry," in *The Methodist Way of Life* (Englewood Cliffs: Prentice-Hall, 1958), 109–21; Frederick A. Norwood, "The Shaping of Methodist Ministry," *Religion in Life* 43 (1974): 337–51; E. Dale Dunlap, "The

United Methodist System of Itinerant Ministry: Its Nature and Future," *Occasional Papers*, No. 30 (1980) (United Methodist Board of Higher Education and Ministry); Daniel L. Marsh, "The Ministry in the Methodist Church," in *Approaches Toward Unity* (Nashville: Parthenon, 1952), 75–85; and Gerald O. McCulloh, ed., *The Ministry in the Methodist Heritage* (Nashville: Abingdon, 1960); Dennis M. Campbell, *The Yoke of Obedience* (Nashville: Abingdon, 1988); William H. Willimon, *Pastor: The Theology and Practice of Ordained Ministry* (Nashville: Abingdon, 2002); Thomas E. Frank, *Polity, Practice, and the Mission of The United Methodist Church* (Nashville: Abingdon, 2006); and Beth Barton Schweiger, *The Gospel Working Up: Progress and the Pulpit in Nineteenth-Century Virginia* (New York: Oxford University Press, 2000).
3. See Robert H. Pope, "New England Versus the New England Mind: The Myth of Declension," *Journal of Social History* 3 (1969): 95–108.
4. Nathan Bangs, *The Present State, Prospects, and Responsibilities of the Methodist Episcopal Church* (New York: Lane & Scott, 1850), 72.
5. On croakers see especially John H. Wigger, *Taking Heaven by Storm: Methodism and the Rise of Popular Christianity in America* (New York: Oxford University Press, 1998), 180–90.
6. This typology derives from the literature on the history of ministry, some of which is cited in note 1 above.
7. The formulation is from Kenneth A. Lockridge, *A New England Town, The First Hundred Years* (New York: Norton, 1970), 16.
8. There is a considerable literature now on the relation of the Great Awakening to the Revolution. See Harry S. Stout, "Religion, Communications, and the Ideological Origins of the American Revolution," *William and Mary Quarterly* 34 (1977): 519–41. Mark Noll summarized the arguments in *Christians in the American Revolution* (Grand Rapids: Christian University Press, 1977).
9. On the American as booster see Daniel J. Boorstin, *The Americans: The National Experience* (New York: Random House, 1965), 113ff.
10. I have been aided in my analysis by L. Dale Patterson, "The Ministerial Mind of American Methodism: The Course of Study for the Ministry of the Methodist Episcopal Church, the Methodist Episcopal Church, South and the Methodist Protestant Church, 1876–1920" (PhD diss., Drew University, 1984).
11. Adam Clarke, *The Preacher's Manual: Including Clavis Biblica, or a Compendium of Scriptural Knowledge; and his Letter to a Methodist Preacher on His Entrance into the Work of Ministry; and also Dr. Coke's Four Discourses on the Duties of a Minster of the Gospel* (New York: Bangs & Mason, 1821), 132–33.
12. Matthew Simpson, *Lectures on Preaching* (New York: Phillips & Hunt, 1879), 271–72.
13. Nolan B. Harmon, *Ministerial Ethics and Etiquette* (Nashville: Cokesbury, 1928); Seward Hiltner, *Preface to Pastoral Theology* (New York: Abingdon, 1958); John R. Spann, ed., *The Ministry* (New York: Abingdon-Cokesbury, 1949).
14. Jno. J. Tigert, *A Constitutional History of American Episcopal Methodism*, 3rd ed., rev. (Nashville: Publishing House of the MECS, 1908), Appendix VII (pp. 532–602) reproduces the 1785 *Discipline* and "The Large Minutes of 1780" in parallel columns, showing thereby the near total reliance of the American on the Wesleyan model.
15. *A Form of Discipline, For the Ministers, Preachers and Member(s?) of the Methodist Episcopal Church in America* (New York: W. Ross, 1787), 12–13.
16. The combination of these two publications in a single volume seems to be an American venture. See Kenneth E. Rowe, *Methodist Union Catalog: Pre-1976 Imprints* (Metuchen: Scarecrow Press, 1975–), 3:86–87 for its numerous printings. Both items went through a number of editions and enjoyed several American printings. Clarke's *A Letter to a Preacher* was printed in London in 1800 and went through five British editions, and was published in America in 1816, 1819, and 1820. Thereafter it appeared in America as part of *The Preacher's Manual*. Coke's *Four Discourses on the Duties of a Ministry of the Gospel* was published in both London and Philadelphia in 1798, and again in London in 1820.
17. Clark, *Preacher's Manual*, 76.
18. Ibid., 106–8.
19. Ibid., 172.

20. Ibid., 175.
21. Ibid., 141.
22. Ibid., 142.
23. Ibid., 172.
24. Nathan Bangs, *An Original Church of Christ* (New York: Mason & Lane, 1837), 366.
25. Nathan Bangs, *The Present State, Prospects, and Responsibilities of the Methodist Episcopal Church* (New York: Lane & Scott, 1850), 72–73.
26. Ibid., 75.
27. Ibid., 76.
28. Randolph S. Foster, *A Treatise on the Need of the M. E. Church with Respect to Her Ministry* (New York: Carlton & Phillips, 1855), 22.
29. Ibid., 22–24, 26.
30. Alfred Brunson, *The Gospel Ministry: Its Characteristics and Qualifications* (New York: for the author, 1856), 26–27.
31. Ibid., 28.
32. See Howard A. Snyder, *Populist Saints: B. T. and Ellen Roberts and the First Free Methodists* (Grand Rapids: Eerdmans, 2006).
33. Simpson, *Lectures*, 11.
34. William A. Quayle, *The Pastor-Preacher* (New York: Eaton & Mains, 1910), 9–11.
35. Ibid., 12.
36. Ibid., 35.
37. Ibid., 61.
38. Lynn Harold Hough, *The Theology of a Preacher* (New York: Eaton & Mains, 1912), 12–13.
39. Washington Gladden, *The Christian Pastor and The Working Church* (New York: Charles Scribner's Sons, 1898).
40. Francis John McConnell, *The Preacher and the People* (New York: Abingdon, 1922).
41. James A. Beebe, *The Pastoral Office: An Introduction to the Work of a Pastor* (New York: Methodist Book Concern, 1923), 184.
42. G. Bromley Oxnam, *Preaching and the Social Crisis* (New York: Abingdon, 1933); and *Preaching in a Revolutionary Age* (New York: Abingdon-Cokesbury, 1944).
43. Beebe, *Pastoral Office*, 136.
44. H. Richard Niebuhr, *The Purpose of the Church and Its Ministry* (New York: Harper, 1956).
45. Ibid., 58.
46. Gibson Winter, *The Suburban Captivity of the Church* (Garden City, NY: Doubleday, 1961).

4. DISTRICT SUPERINTENDENCY: A RECONSIDERATION

1. On the notion of *episkopé* as oversight, see "The Nature and Purpose of the Church: A Stage on the Way to a Common Statement," *Faith and Order Paper No. 181* (World Council of Churches, November 1998), http://www.oikoumene.org/?id=2638.

Oversight: Communal, Personal and Collegial

The Church as the body of Christ and the eschatological people of God is built up by the Holy Spirit through a diversity of gifts or ministries. Among these gifts a ministry of *episkopé* (oversight) serves to express and promote the visible unity of the body. Every church needs this ministry of unity in some form.

The 17 paragraphs that follow develop the various dimensions of episcopal oversight. See also section III, "The Forms of the Ordained Ministry," *Baptism, Eucharist and Ministry* (Faith and Order Paper No. 111; World Council of Churches, 1982), http://www.oikoumene.org/?id=2638.

2. John and Charles Wesley, *Hymns and Sacred Poems* (Bristol: Farley, 1742), 283–84. available online at: http://www.divinity.duke.edu/wesleyan/texts/cw_published_verse.html.
3. Gil Rendle, "Finding the Path in the Wilderness: Middle Judicatory Case Studies and Learnings" (Bethesda, MD: The Alban Institute, 2001), 11. Rendle quotes a Presbyterian synod executive as saying, "the governing mission of synods is now to enhance the ministries of presbyteries and their congregations as the places where real ministry takes place" (p. 5).
4. On this point, see Russell E. Richey, *The Methodist Conference in America: A History* (Nashville: Kingswood Books, 1996), particularly 159–68; and Richey et al., "Are the Local Church and Denominational Bureaucracy 'Twins'?" in *Questions for the Twenty-First Century Church* (Nashville: Abingdon, 1999), 232–41. Another chapter in the same volume, "Are Extension Ministries an Opportunity to Reclaim a Wesleyan Understanding of Mission," 175–85, pertains to the argument of this chapter as a whole. On the localizing trend in Methodism, see also Thomas Edward Frank, *Polity, Practice and the Mission of The United Methodist Church* (Nashville: Abingdon, 2006).
5. See the discussion below and also Richey, *Methodist Conference*, 39–42, 59–61; and Richey, *Early American Methodism*, 21–32; see also Lester Ruth, *A Little Heaven Below: Worship at Early American Methodist Quarterly Meetings* (Nashville: Kingswood Books, 2000); and Karen B. Westerfield Tucker, *American Methodist Worship* (New York: Oxford University Press, 2001).
6. Richey, *Methodist Conference*.
7. The Council of Bishops of The United Methodist Church, *Vital Congregations, Faithful Disciples: Vision for the Church* (Nashville: General Board of Discipleship, 1990).
8. *Church, Identity, and Change: Theology and Denominational Structures in Unsettled Times*, ed. David A. Roozen and James Nieman (Grand Rapids: Eerdmans, 2005). Online: http://www.religion-research.org/UMR/mainHTML/Introduction.html
9. "Leadership and Servanthood: Episcopacy and District Superintendency in The United Methodist Church," Report, Recommendations, and Proposed Legislation of the 1972–76 Quadrennial Commission for the Study of the Offices of Bishop and District Superintendent, The United Methodist Church, *Daily Christian Advocate*, Advance Edition F, vol. IV, April 27, 1976, pp. F-1 to F-61.
10. Gerald Moede, *The Office of Bishop in Methodism: Its History and Development* (Zürich: Gotthelf, 1964; New York: Abingdon, 1965); Murray H. Leiffer, *The District Superintendent in the United Methodist Church* (Evanston: Garrett Theological Seminary, 1971); and Leiffer, *What District Superintendents Say—About Their Office and the Issues Confronting Them* (Evanston: Garrett Theological Seminary, 1972). Also underlying the quadrennial study was the work of a prior quadrennium, "The Study of the General Superintendency of the Methodist Church," which issued a three-volume preliminary report in 1963 and reported to General Conference in 1964. Part III of the 1963 draft attended to the "Relation of the Episcopacy to the District Superintendency."
11. Egon W. Gerdes, *Informed Ministry: Theological Reflections on the Practice of Ministry in Methodism* (Zürich: Publishing House of the UMC, 1976).
12. Emora Thomas Brannan, "The Presiding Elder Question: Its Critical Nature in American Methodism, 1820–1824 and its Impact upon Ecclesiastical Institutions" (PhD diss., Duke University, 1974); and Fred W. Price, "The Role of the Presiding Elder in the Growth of the Methodist Episcopal Church, 1784–1832" (PhD diss., Drew University, 1984).
13. In addition to the two volumes cited in note 10 above, see Murray H. Leiffer, *The Role of the District Superintendent in the Methodist Church* (Evanston, IL: Garrett Theological Seminary, 1960).
14. Leiffer, *What District Superintendents Say*, 52–58.
15. Methodist Episcopal Church, *The Doctrines and Discipline of the Methodist Episcopal Church in America, with Explanatory Notes, by Thomas Coke and Francis Asbury* (Philadelphia, 1798); facsimile edition, ed. Frederick A. Norwood (Rutland, VT: Academy Books, 1979), (1798), 46–47.
16. Ibid., 53. See the Appendix to this chapter for the full text of this *Disciplinary* section and of the commentary thereon by Coke and Asbury.

17. Peter Cartwright, *Autobiography of Peter Cartwright, the Backwoods Preacher*, ed. William Peter Strickland (New York: Methodist Book Concern, 1856); and Cartwright, *Fifty Years as a Presiding Elder*, ed. W. S. Hooper (New York: Phillips & Hunt, 1871).
18. Price, "Role of the Presiding Elder."
19. *The Doctrines and Discipline of the Methodist Episcopal Church*, Published by John Wilson and Daniel Hitt for the Methodist Connection (New York: Printed by J. C. Totten, 1808), 15.
20. But see Dennis M. Campbell, *Who Will Go for Us?: An Invitation to Ordained Ministry* (Nashville: Abingdon, 1994); and Campbell, *Yoke of Obedience* (Nashville: Abingdon, 1988).
21. For insights into the episcopal office, see Russell E. Richey and Thomas Edward Frank, *Episcopacy in the Methodist Tradition: Perspectives and Proposals* (Nashville: Abingdon, 2004); James K. Mathews and William B. Oden, eds., *Vision and Supervision: A Sourcebook of Significant Documents of the Council of Bishops of The United Methodist Church* (Nashville: Abingdon, 2003); James E. Kirby, *The Episcopacy in American Methodism* (Nashville: Kingswood Books, 2000); the various United Methodist essays in *Episcopacy: Lutheran-United Methodist Dialogue II*, ed. Jack M. Tuell and Roger W. Fjeld (Minneapolis: Augsburg, 1991); James K. Mathews, *Set Apart to Serve: The Meaning and Role of Episcopacy in the Wesleyan Tradition* (Nashville: Abingdon, 1985); Roy H. Short, *History of The Council of Bishops of The United Methodist Church, 1939–1979* (Nashville: Abingdon, 1980); and Norman Woods Spellman, "The General Superintendency in American Methodism, 1784–1870" (PhD diss., Yale University, 1961).
22. Price, "Role of the Presiding Elder," 280–306; summarized 314–19.
23. William Colbert, "A Journal of the Travels of William Colbert, Methodist Preacher: thro' parts of Maryland, Pennsylvania, New York, Delaware and Virginia in 1790 to 1838," 10 vols., typescript, held in the collection of Drew University.
24. See MEC, *Minutes . . . From 1773 to 1813*, 262, 279, for this circuit and also the district onto which Colbert was appointed PE.
25. Colbert, "Journal," 4:67–68.
26. Ibid., 4:88ff.
27. Ibid., 4:97–98.
28. Ibid., 4:115–16.
29. For a similar effort to grasp the theological meaning of episcopacy in terms of Word, Sacrament, Order (and Service), see Richey and Frank, *Episcopacy*.
30. For a brief discussion accenting the first two, but not the third, see Hilary T. Hudson, *The Methodist Armor; or A Popular Exposition of the Doctrines, Peculiar Usages, and Ecclesiastical Machinery of the Methodist Episcopal Church, South*, revised and enlarged (Nashville: for the author, 1892). This volume went through multiple editions.
31. *The Book of Discipline of the United Methodist Church* (Nashville: United Methodist Publishing House, 2004), ¶303; see also ¶¶301–2; 136; 137.
32. Paul Dietterich and Donald Arthur, *The District Superintendent, Key to District Revitalization* (Naperville, IL: The Center for Parish Development, 1974).

5. THE TEACHING OFFICE

1. MEC, *Minutes of the Methodist Conferences, Annually Held in America: From 1773 to 1813 Inclusive* (New York, 1813; Magnolia Press, Reprint Edition, 1983), "Minutes for 1773," 5.
2. *The Doctrines and Discipline of the Methodist Episcopal Church* (New York: Wilson and Hitt, 1808), 14–15.
3. *The Book of Discipline of The United Methodist Church* (Nashville: United Methodist Publishing House, 2004), "The Constitution," 25–27.

4. Ibid., ¶509, p. 317. ¶509.2 continues: "Any individual member called to testify before a legislative body to represent The United Methodist Church shall be allowed to do so only by reading, without elaboration, the resolutions and positions adopted by the General Conference of The United Methodist Church."
5. Nolan B. Harmon, *Understanding the United Methodist Church* (Nashville: Abingdon, 1977), 96.
6. Thomas A. Langford, "Conciliar Theology: A Report," in *Doctrine and Theology in The United Methodist Church*, ed. T. A. Langford (Nashville: Kingswood Books, 1991), 176–85.
7. This essay was given in lecture form, initially at "The John Wesley Theological Institute" (Illinois), later for the United Methodist Historical Society, and it benefits from the suggestions and criticisms made at those gatherings. It also profits from suggestions made by William B. Lawrence and my father McMurry S. Richey, now deceased. This study limits its concerns to one stream of the Methodist tradition, exploring tensions around general conference authority in the MEC, MC, and UMC.
8. On the latter see especially, Kenneth E. Rowe, "Pastorals for the People: Pastorals in the Methodist Tradition," in *Scholarship, Sacraments and Service. Historical Studies in the Protestant Tradition*, ed. Daniel B. Clendenin and W. David Buschart (Lewiston, NY: Edwin Mellen, 1990), 123–46.
9. For a careful delineation of the doctrine of the magisterium, see the article of that title by Karl Rahner in *Encyclopedia of Theology*, ed. Karl Rahner (New York: Seabury Press, 1975), 871–80. See also *Lumen Gentium*, The Dogmatic Constitution on the Church, of Vatican II on the web at: http://www.vatican.va/archive/hist_councils/ii_vatican_council/documents/vat-ii_const_19641121_lumen-gentium_en.html or in collections of Vatican II documents as for instance The documents of Vatican II. Introductions and commentaries by Catholic bishops and experts. Responses by Protestant and Orthodox scholars. Walter M. Abbott, general editor. Joseph Gallagher, translation editor. New York : Guild Press [1966].
10. Note that the emphasis does fall on the exercise of the teaching office. A related and interesting investigation would examine the national or centralizing principle in Methodism. What is it that *functions* to effect or make connectionalism? Here too we would look at a succession of agents: conference, bishop(s) and elders, bishop(s), General Conference, the book agents or editors, the seminaries, the boards and agencies, the caucuses, and then again the bishops.
11. See Richard P. Heitzenrater, *Mirror and Memory: Reflections on Early Methodism* (Nashville: Kingswood Books, 1989); and *Wesley and the People Called Methodists* (Nashville: Abingdon, 1993).
12. See especially Richard P. Heitzenrater, "At Full Liberty: Doctrinal Standards in Early American Methodism," *Quarterly Review* 5 (Fall 1985): 6–27; and Thomas C. Oden's response, "What Are 'Established Standards of Doctrine'? A Response to Richard Heitzenrater," *Quarterly Review* 7 (Spring 1987): 42–62 [these two are reprinted together in Langford, *Doctrine and Theology*, 109–42]. See also Oden's further elaboration in *Doctrinal Standards in the Wesleyan Tradition* (Grand Rapids: Zondervan, 1988). Also pertinent is Robert E. Cushman, *John Wesley's Experimental Divinity: Studies in Methodist Doctrinal Standards* (Nashville: Kingswood Books, 1989); W. Stephen Gunter et al., *Wesley and the Quadrilateral: Renewing the Conversation* (Nashville: Abingdon, 1998); and Richey et al., *Doctrines and Discipline*.
13. Thomas B. Neely, *A History of the Origin and Development of the Governing Conference in Methodism* (Cincinnati: Curts & Jennings, 1892), 9–10.
14. The disciplinary discussion itself, though it focuses on what Wesley left us rather than on the manner and fact of his leaving it, by its repeated evocation of Wesley clearly registers his teaching function.
15. For an able assessment of Coke's leadership intentions and ambitions, see Warren Thomas Smith, "Thomas Coke's Contribution to the Christmas Conference: A Study in Ecclesiology," in *Rethinking Methodist History*, ed. Russell E. Richey and Kenneth E. Rowe (Nashville: Kingswood Books, 1985), 37–47. The definitive treatment is John Vickers, *Thomas Coke: Apostle of Methodism* (Nashville: Abingdon, 1969).

16. MEC, *Minutes* (1785); reproduced in Jno. J. Tigert, *A Constitutional History of American Episcopal Methodism*, 3rd ed., rev. (Nashville: Publishing House of the MECS, 1908), 534.
17. MEC, *Minutes . . . From 1773 to 1813*, "Minutes for 1787," 62.

    In reflecting on the actions of Wesley (and of Coke who actually summoned the preachers to a place different from that earlier announced), Thomas Ware observed:

    > Mr. Wesley had been in the habit of calling his preachers together, not to legislate, but to confer . . . but the right to *decide* all questions he reserved to himself. This he deemed the more excellent way; and as we had volunteered and pledged ourselves to obey, he instructed the doctor, conformably to his own usage, to put as few questions to vote as possible, saying, "If you, brother Asbury, and brother Whatcoat are agreed, it is enough." To place the power of deciding all questions discussed, or nearly all, in the hands of the superintendents, was what could never be introduced among us.

    War, *Sketches of the Life and Travels of Rev. Thomas Ware* (New York: Lane & Sandford, 1842), 130.
18. See "Index of Sermon Texts," in Francis Asbury, *The Journals and Letters of Francis Asbury*, ed. Elmer T. Clark (London: Epworth Press; Nashville: Abingdon, 1958), 3:818–24. It is worth remarking that Asbury preached on the whole Bible.
19. Asbury, *Journals*, 2:332–33 (for April 5, 1802). Asbury complained that he did not get a chance to edit and correct the copy before it was printed.
20. Ibid., 3:426 (a letter to Nelson Reed, dated March 22, 1810). Asbury noted that he had spent five or six days reviewing and correcting 1000 pages of his journal. "Every thing personal, geographical, and prolix will go out, the most spiritual and historical parts will be reserved."
21. Ibid., 2:153 (for Feb. 6, 1798).
22. Ibid., 3:323 (letter to Ezekiel Cooper, July 26, 1805).
23. See James Penn Pilkington, *The Methodist Publishing House: A History* (Nashville: Abingdon, 1968), 1:51–154.
24. Asbury, *Journals*, 3:232–33 (letter to Ezekiel Cooper, the book agent, dated Dec. 31, 1801). There he spoke about his several publishing ventures. The preface to the hymnal appears in ibid., 3:397–98. For Asbury's personal efforts in its creation, see entries in 2:554 (for Aug. 1807); 2:558 (for Oct. 25, 1807); and 2:559 (for Nov. 4, 6, 1807).
25. Francis Asbury, *The Causes, Evils, and Cures of Heart and Church Divisions, Extracted from the Works of Mr. Jeremiah Burroughs and Mr. Richard Baxter* (Philadelphia: Parry Hall, 1792; republished in 1817 and 1849).
26. Methodist Episcopal Church, *The Doctrines and Discipline of the Methodist Episcopal Church in America, with Explanatory Notes, by Thomas Coke and Francis Asbury* Philadelphia, 1798); facsimile edition, ed. Frederick A. Norwood (Rutland, VT: Academy Books, 1979).
27. Asbury, *Journals*, 3:199 (letter to George Roberts, Feb. 4, 1801). Compare a letter two days later to Thomas Morrell (3:202): "You will favour me with a letter to Norfolk, the last of March. If the presiding elders, in the cities and towns and country would give once a year circumstantial accounts of the work. I would [an unreadable defaced line occurs here] annually of Methodism, like Prince's History for a select collection of original papers."
28. [Francis Asbury,] *Extracts of Letters Containing Some Account of the Work of God Since the Year 1800* (New York: Cooper & Wilson, 1805). The subtitle read "Written by the Preachers and Members of the Methodist Episcopal Church to their Bishops."
29. See Asbury, *Journals*, 2:739–40 (Aug. 1, 1813), 3:475–92 (Aug. 5, 1813), 2:744 (Oct. 29, 1813); 3:532–43 (Jan. 8, 1816); and *Methodist History* 1 (1962): 56–58, for Sept. 29, 1815.
30. For ready access to the bishops' intellectual leadership, see Roy H. Short, *Chosen to Be Consecrated: The Bishops of The Methodist Church, 1784–1968* (Lake Junaluska: Commission on Archives and History, 1976), particularly chapters entitled "The Church Lawyers," "The Educators," and "The Scholars."
31. See Pilkington, *Methodist Publishing House*, 1:19–168.

32. The full title was *The Mutual Rights of the Ministers and Members of the Methodist Episcopal Church*. The concerns voiced in this vehicle—lay representation, the rights of local preachers, election of presiding elders, abusive power of the episcopacy—found considerable support. The reform efforts eventually divided the church and eventuated in the MPC.
33. Particularly notable were William Nast's *Der Christliche Apologete* of the MEC, the *Religious Telescope* of the UBC, *Der Christliche Botschafter* and *Evangelical Messenger* of the EA. On the role of the latter two see J. Bruce Behney and Paul H. Eller, *The History of the Evangelical United Brethren Church* (Nashville: Abingdon, 1979), and particularly the subsections entitled "Publications" in chapters 5 and following.
34. Bledsoe's *Southern Review* was not an official magazine of the MECS but nevertheless functioned in lieu of one.
35. For their place and roles in Methodist theological development, see Thomas A. Langford, *Practical Divinity* (Nashville: Abingdon, 1983), chapters 4 and 5. Striking is the absence of such a powerhouse at the helm of the *Methodist Protestant* during this period.
36. On the importance of this journal see Melvin E. Dieter, *The Holiness Revival of the Nineteenth Century* (Metuchen: Scarecrow Press, 1980).
37. See Dale L. Patterson, "The Ministerial Mind: The Course of Study for the Ministry of the Methodist Episcopal Church, the Methodist Episcopal Church, South and the Methodist Protestant Church, 1876–1920" (PhD diss., Drew University, 1984).
38. See Robert E. Chiles, *Theological Transition in American Methodism, 1790–1935* (Nashville: Abingdon, 1965), especially 32–36.
39. On these developments see Gerald O. McCulloh, *Ministerial Education in the American Methodist Movement* (Nashville: United Methodist Board of Higher Education and Ministry, 1980).
40. At present, there seems to be a disposition to rethink this, a disposition registered in the Commissions to Study the Ministry and in conversations (formal and informal) among those who worry whether in years ahead we will have sufficient numbers of clergy and/or whether smaller congregations, communities, and circuits can continue to afford seminary-trained professionals.
41. Garber's statement was an oral one. Whatever the truth of his remark at the time, I am happy to report that in the last few years the seminaries have labored mightily to pay deliberate attention to the church.
42. In their several books, Paul Mickey, Will Willimon, and the late Robert Wilson have offered penetrating criticisms of United Methodist bureaucracy.
43. This is reflected in the tendency to think of ministry in parish terms, a long popular perception of both laity and clergy, now codified in the *Discipline*'s handling of those once termed "special" as "appointments beyond the local church." Wesley's "the world is my parish" becomes, as the quip puts it, "my parish is the world." A congregational impression of the church may also be gathered from the bishops' 1990 statement, *Vital Congregations, Faithful Disciples: Vision for the Church*, though that would doubtless not have been their intention.
44. The person who has most effectively demonstrated this is William McGuire King. See his "The Role of Auxiliary Ministries in Late Nineteenth-Century Methodism," in Richey and Rowe, *Rethinking Methodist History*, 167–72; and "Denominational Modernization and Religious Identity: The Case of the Methodist Episcopal Church," *Methodist History* 20 (January 1982), 75–89.
45. The most powerful expression of its complex inner structure is to be found in the four-volume study executed by faculty from Boston University School of Theology on behalf of the Board of Social and Economic Relations of The Methodist Church. The volumes of this "Methodism and Society" project—MESTA, "The Methodist Church in Social Thought and Action"—(Nashville: Abingdon, 1961–62) were entitled: *Methodism and Society in Historical Perspective; Methodism and Society in the Twentieth Century; Methodism and Society in Theological Perspective;* and *Methodism and Society: Guidelines for Strategy*. Georgia Harkness compressed the four into a one-volume paperback, *The Methodist Church in Social Thought and Action—A Summary* (New York and Nashville: Abingdon, 1964).

46. See the listing in *The 1993 United Methodist Directory and Index of Resources* (Nashville: Cokesbury, 1993), 85–86. Included are *Newscope, Quarterly Review,* and *Circuit Rider,* which reach the ministers; *New World Outlook* and *Response,* which cover missions; *The Interpreter,* which treats program and resources for church leadership at all levels; several Spanish-language items, others aimed at age levels, still others covering special interests in worship, social action, spirituality, rural ministries, and so forth.
47. Robert Wuthnow, *The Struggle for America's Soul: Evangelicals, Liberals, and Secularism* (Grand Rapids: Eerdman's, 1989).
48. UMC, Council of Bishops, *In Defense of Creation: The Nuclear Crisis and a Just Peace* (Nashville: Graded Press, 1986).
49. UMC, Council of Bishops, *Vital Congregations, Faithful Disciples: Vision for the Church* (Nashville: Graded Press, 1990).
50. Portions of these several initiatives, along with various internal and public statements expressive of the Council of Bishops' teaching office, are gathered in James K. Mathews and William B. Oden, eds. *Vision and Supervision: A Sourcebook of Significant Documents of the Council of Bishops of The United Methodist Church* (Nashville: Abingdon, 2003).
51. In addition to several committees that now guide the Council, the bishops draw on the theological expertise of one general agency, the General Commission on Christian Unity and Interreligious Concerns. For illustration of how the bishops have used that expertise, see John Deschner, "United Methodism's Basic Ecumenical Policy," in *Ecumenical and Interreligious Perspectives: Globalization in Theological Education* (Nashville: QR Books, 1992), 45–57.
52. See note 13.
53. On these two processes, see Langford, *Doctrine and Theology*—particularly Albert C. Outler, "Introduction to the Report of the 1968–72 Theological Study Commission," 20–25; and Richard P. Heitzenrater, "In Search of Continuity and Consensus: The Road to the 1988 Doctrinal Statement," 93–108.
54. The processes that yielded *The United Methodist Hymnal* and *The United Methodist Book of Worship,* though similar and clearly also functioning to teach, seem to belong somewhat less completely to General Conference and so are not discussed here.
55. While I credit the work of this committee to General Conference, I do recognize that it was appointed by the Council of Bishops and hence might be construed as, in some sense, a dimension of that body's teaching authority.
56. See Heitzenrater, "In Search of Continuity"; and Thomas W. Ogletree, "In Quest of a Common Faith: The Theological Task of United Methodists," *Quarterly Review* 8 (Spring 1988): 43–53 (reprinted in Langford, *Doctrine and Theology*, 168–75).
57. On that process, see Langford, "Conciliar Theology," in *Doctrine and Theology*, 176–85.
58. *The Book of Discipline* (1988), 78.
59. In reviewing and critiquing an earlier draft of this chapter, William Lawrence noted in the margin that "Prospects for the Council may be more promising since the Council can refine, disseminate and otherwise control the teaching product that it generates. The General Conference Commissions, on the other hand, could labor in open forums, respond to political pressures, then fail in General Conference itself to carry their hard work to successful adoption."

6. Itinerant General Superintendency

1. Methodist Episcopal Church, *The Doctrines and Discipline of the Methodist Episcopal Church in America, with Explanatory Notes,* by Thomas Coke and Francis Asbury (Philadelphia, 1798); facsimile edition, ed. Frederick A. Norwood (Rutland, VT: Academy Books, 1979), 40.
2. Ibid., 42.
3. *The Doctrines and Discipline of the Methodist Episcopal Church* (New York: Wilson and Hitt, 1808), 15.

4. See the Appendix to this chapter for the proposed change to the current Disciplinary language being presented to the 2008 UMC General Conference from the Task Force to Study the Episcopacy created by the 2004 General Conference. As its writer, I presented much of this essay to the Task Force and benefitted from its criticisms and suggestions.
5. In this section, which covers the sweep of the Methodist and EUB experience, "United Methodist" is used when the reference is to the post-1968 or contemporary church and "Methodist" is allowed to stand for the composite experience (UBC, EA, MEC, MPC, MECS, UMC).
6. All following references are to the UMC, *Discipline* (2004), unless otherwise noted.
7. See Russell E. Richey and Thomas Edward Frank, *Episcopacy in the Methodist Tradition: Perspectives and Proposals* (Nashville: Abingdon, 2004), 43–88.
8. In addition to Richey and Frank, *Episcopacy in the Methodist Tradition*, other survey treatments and collections of resource materials include: James E. Kirby, *The Episcopacy in American Methodism* (Nashville: Kingswood Books, 2000); James K. Mathews and William B. Oden, eds., *Vision and Supervision: A Sourcebook of Significant Documents of the Council of Bishops of The United Methodist Church* (Nashville: Abingdon, 2003); James K. Mathews, *Set Apart to Serve: The Meaning and Role of Episcopacy in the Wesleyan Tradition* (Nashville: Abingdon, 1985); Gerald F. Moede, *The Office of Bishop in the Methodist Church* (Zürich: Publishing House of the Methodist Church, 1964); Gerald F. Moede, "Bishops in the Methodist Tradition: Historical Perspectives," in *Episcopacy: Lutheran-United Methodist Dialogue* II, ed. Jack M. Tuell and Roger W. Fjeld (Minneapolis: Augsburg, 1991), 52–69; Roy Hunter Short, *Chosen to be Consecrate: The Bishops of The Methodist Church, 1784–1968* (Lake Junaluska: Commission on Archives and History for the Council of Bishops, 1976); and Norman Woods Spellman, "The General Superintendency in American Methodism, 1784–1870" (Ph.D. diss., Yale University, 1961).
9. In *An Introduction to World Methodism*, Kenneth Cracknell and Susan J. White argue persuasively, and despite Wesleyanism's fragmentation, that the Methodist experience in British and American contexts establishes "two quite distinct traditions" (New York: Cambridge University Press, 2005): vii.
10. For a sense of the debate on this latter matter, the global nature of The United Methodist Church, see Bruce W. Robbins, *A World Parish? Hopes and Challenges of The United Methodist Church* (Nashville: Abingdon, 2004); Patrick Streiff, "The Global Nature of The United Methodist Church: What Future for the Branch Outside the United States," *Quarterly Review* 24.2 (2004): 181–93; and Patrick Streiff and David J. Lawson, "Is The United Methodist Church a Global Church Yet?" *Quarterly Review* 25.1 (2005): 83–88.
11. See chapter 4 for my initial efforts in this regard.
12. See chapter 5.
13. *Baptism, Eucharist and Ministry*, Faith and Order Paper No. 111 (Geneva: WCC, 1982), abbreviated *BEM*. Online: http://www.oikoumene.org/?id=2638. The references are to the paragraph number of the Ministry section.
14. See *Make Us One with Christ: The Study Guide Version*, Prepared by the Office of Ecumenical and Interfaith Relations of the Episcopal Church in the USA and the General Commission on Christian Unity and Interreligious Concerns of The United Methodist Church (2006); online: http://www.episcopalchurch.org/documents/MUOCFINAL.pdf
15. The Commission on Pan-Methodist Cooperation and Union brings together the AME, AMEZ, CME, UAME, and UMC. Online: http://www.gccuic-umc.org/panmeth/
16. See in this regard particularly "Consultation on Episcopé," *Call to Unity/Resourcing the Church for Ecumenical Ministry* 7 (December 2006); and the earlier *Churches in Covenant Communion* (Princeton, NJ: Consultation on Church Union, 1989).
17. *Confessing Our Faith Together* (ELCA– UMC Dialogue Team, 2005). ¶62. Online: http://gccuic-umc.org/web/webpdf/confessing-faith-f_color_2.pdf. See also *Episcopacy: A Lutheran-United Methodist Common Statement to the Church* (1988); and *Episcopacy: Lutheran-United Methodist Dialogue II*, ed. Jack M. Tuell and Roger W. Fjeld (Minneapolis: Augsburg, 1991).

7. Ministerial Formation

1. Edward Farley, *Theologia: The Fragmentation and Unity of Theological Education* (Philadelphia: Fortress Press, 1983), chapter 2; and *The Fragility of Knowledge: Theological Education in the Church and the University* (Philadelphia: Fortress, 1988), part II.
2. This chapter will endeavor to make that point, limiting attention to the several ways in which Methodists did undertake to prepare persons for itinerant ministry, for full membership in the Methodist connection, for ordination as elder.
3. For a good illustration of this perspective, see *The Methodist Centennial Year-Book for 1884*, ed. W. H. De Puy (New York: Phillips & Hunt, 1883), 172–98. Note the statement, predicated on that perspective but questioning its viability, by Marjorie H. Suchocki, "A Learned Ministry?" *Quarterly Review* 13 (Summer, 1993): 3–17.
4. "Autobiography of Rev. William Burke," in James B. Finley, *Sketches of Western Methodism: Biographical, Historical, and Miscellaneous*, ed. W. P. Strickland (Cincinnati: Methodist Book Concern, 1854), 58. He continued, "When the preachers met from their different and distant fields of labor, they had a feast of love and friendship; and when they parted, they wept and embraced each other as brothers beloved. Such was the spirit of primitive Methodist preachers."
5. Ibid., 27. Burke registered his expectation for and value of companionship when later he lacked it: "I traveled this year alone, and had not the pleasure of seeing the face of a traveling preacher through the entire year" (ibid., 52). Of course, the image of the lonely itinerant drew from reality as well. Here it is captured by local preacher, Thomas S. Hinde, writing as "Theophilus Arminius" in *The Methodist Magazine* 5 (1822): 393.

> That the preachers suffered much in forming these new Circuits is unquestionable; having often to swim the deep and large Creeks on their horses, and to ride from twenty to thirty miles through the wilderness from one settlement to another, and not infrequently had to take up their lodgings in the woods, amidst the howling wolves and screaming panthers. It was not uncommon occurrence for the scattered members of Society, on hearing of a preacher, to travel ten or twenty miles through the woods to invite him to come and preach at their cabin, and to mark for him a way by blazing the trees.

6. "The early Methodist itinerant system functioned as a 'School of the Prophets'. Young ministers 'On Trial' were always yoked with an older and more experienced brother on one of the two-preacher, twenty-four preaching place appointments. They were required to be literate in order to be accepted, and their habits of reading, study, and personal devotions were kept under Conference oversight and guidance throughout the four years during which they qualified for Elder's ordination." Wallace Guy Smeltzer, *The History of United Methodism in Western Pennsylvania* (Nashville: Parthenon Press, 1975), 148.
7. Ibid.
8. See Glenn T. Miller, *Piety and Intellect. The Aims and Purposes of Ante-Bellum Theological Education* (Atlanta: Scholar's Press, 1990), especially 403–4. Miller portrays this period on trial in a different fashion than what is suggested here. He accents its individualistic, trial-by-error, self-knowledge, self-disciplined character and distinguishes it explicitly from genuine "apprenticeships" or from modern internships (406).
9. Worth Marion Tippy, *Frontier Bishop. The Life and Times of Robert Richford Roberts* (New York: Abingdon, 1958), 32.
10. John F. Wright, *Sketches of the Life and Labors of James Quinn* (Cincinnati: Methodist Book Concern, 1851), 51, 57, 67–68.
11. Ibid., 73.
12. Ibid., 263.
13. Ibid., 191–92. For similar patterns among German "Methodists," see R. Yeakel, "Life and Labors of John Dreisbach, Evangelical Minister and the First Presiding Elder in the Evangelical Association," *Jacob Albright and His Co-Laborers* (Cleveland: Publishing House of the Evangelical Association, 1883), 185, 190, 283, 284–85, 294–95.

14. S. R. Beggs, *Pages from the Early History of the West and Northwest* (Cincinnati: Methodist Book Concern, 1868), 15.
15. Joseph M. Trimble, *Semi-centennial Address . . . Before the Ohio Conference of the Methodist Episcopal Church* (Columbus: Gazetter Steam Printing House, 1878), 11.
16. *Minutes of the New England Conference of the Methodist Episcopal Church . . . 1766 to . . . 1845*, 2 vols. (Typescript prepared by George Whitaker for New England Methodist Historical Society, 1912), 1815: 215.
17. Nathan Bangs, *A History of the Methodist Episcopal Church*, 12th ed., 4 vols. (New York: Carlton & Porter, 1860), 3:43–47. Bangs reproduced the report of the "committee of *ways and means*, appointed to provide a more ample support of the ministry among us, to prevent locations, and the admission of improper persons into the itinerancy." All three factors bore, the committee indicated, on the intellectual caliber of the itinerancy. Inadequate salary led many of the most able to "locate" and thus necessitated the admission of those insufficiently gifted or prepared.
18. Ibid., 47. Bangs observed: "From that time forth a regular course of study has been prescribed by the bishops for those on trial in the annual conferences, to which the candidates must attend, and give satisfactory evidence of their attainments, especially in theological science, before they can be admitted into full membership as itinerant ministers" (48).
19. See Patterson, "The Ministerial Mind: The Course of Study for the Ministry of the Methodist Episcopal Church, the Methodist Episcopal Church, South and the Methodist Protestant Church, 1876–1920" (PhD diss., Drew University, 1984).
20. Baltimore Conference Journal, Ms., 1817, 99–100; quoted by William J. E. Apsley, "The Educational Concerns, 1816–61," in *Those Incredible Methodists. A History of the Baltimore Conference of the United Methodist Church*, ed. Gordon Pratt Baker (Baltimore: Commission on Archives and History, Baltimore Conference, 1972), 132–33.
21. The examination process and review of characters was carried out carefully by category, according to Disciplinary question. Here, for instance, were the actions of the 1832 Indiana Conference:
    admitting on trial 91
    examining those on trial 91
    examining the character of the deacons 92
    election of elders
    examination of characters of elders 93–94
    cases heard of individuals who had withdrawn 92–93
    quasi-trial of suspended preacher 100
    The numbers refer to the pages on which each process of examination begins in the republished version of that journal; William Warren Sweet, *Circuit-Rider Days in Indiana* (Indianapolis: W. K. Stewart, 1916).
22. "Geo. Pickering, E. Hedding, & M. Ruter appointed a Committee to examine the candidates for full connexion." *Minutes of the New England Conference*, 271–72.
23. "The Journal of The Reverend Jacob Lanius. An Itinerant Preacher of the Missouri Conference of the Methodist Episcopal Church from 1831 A.D. to 1851 A.D.," ed. Elmer T. Clark, 1918 (manuscript in possession of his son, James A. Lanius, of Palmyra, Missouri).
24. Ibid., 8. Then Whepley's Compend of Natural History (Oct. 14, 24, 1833); a grammar (Nov. 20, 1833); A. Campbell on the New Birth (Nov. 26, 1833); "I closed the examination of Paley's evidence which I very much admired and which I think is sufficient . . . to authoriticate the Holy Scripture" (Nov. 27, 1833); pp. 10, 12, 17, and 18, respectively.
25. Ibid., 28. In Feb. 1834, confined by weather he noted: "During my confinement I was employed in reading Mr. Watson's View of the 'Deity of Jesus Christ'" (38).
26. Ibid., 89. These entries followed:

    [Dec. 27, 1834] "I have just closed the perusal of Dr. Young's 'Night Thoughts' in which I found some sublime sentiments and Ideals" (100).

    [Jan. 12, 1835] "After spending the morning in conversation and reading at Father B's" (109).

The next day he employed an account of a death published in the Christian Advocate and Journal in a sermon.

[Jan. 16, 1835] "I spent the night in reading the Public Religious news, conversation and balmy sleep" (112).

27. Ibid., 143.
28. Ibid., 165.
29. Ibid., 276. On Dec. 25, 1836, he engaged in a disquisition on dating of Christ's birth, expressed doubts on the 25th and made reference to Dr. Lightfoot. Effectively, the references to reading stop at Sept. 1835, when he was ordained elder.
30. "As the Circuit System declined the pastoral oversight of the 'junior preacher' by the senior Circuit Rider was supplanted by a strengthening of the requirements of the Course of Study." Smeltzer, *History*, 150. A contemporary estimated this change as revolutionary:

About a generation ago a great change occurred in the practical working of our ecclesiastical system. Through all the older and more settled portions of the Church the circuit system was generally abandoned. The gravity of this change has seldom, if ever, been duly estimated. Measured by its effects upon the whole Church, it is entitled to be designated a radical revolution.

The first and most serious result of this revolution was the practical paralysis of our whole system of ministerial training. The great theological seminary of Methodism was not indeed closed, but it received a blow equivalent to that which would be dealt to a college by abolishing its working faculty....

It effectively deprived our candidates and junior ministry of the instruction, drill, and personal influence which they had been wont to receive from their senior associates upon the district and the circuit. It robbed them of the stimulus and profit of contact with superior minds, the advantages of living models, the blessed contagion of maturer character. William F. Warren, "Ministerial Education in Our Church," *Methodist Quarterly Review* 54 (1872): 246–67, 253.

31. MECS, North Carolina Conference, "Minutes of The North Carolina Annual Conference, 1838–85," 2 vols. (xerox copy of original handwritten minutes; special collections, Duke University), 1:55b (1840/41).
32. See J. Bruce Behney and Paul H. Eller, *The History of the Evangelical United Brethren Church* (Nashville: Abingdon, 1979), 158–59, 192–93; and Gerald O. McCulloh, *Ministerial Education in the American Methodist Movement* (Nashville: UMC Board of Higher Education and Ministry, 1980), 11–15.
33. John O. Gross, "The Field of Education, 1865–1939," in *History of American Methodism*, 3 vols., ed. Emory S. Bucke (New York: Abingdon, 1964), 3:201–49, 244.
34. Sweet, *Circuit-Rider Days*, 133.
35. Stephen Olin, "Christian Education," *The Works of Stephen Olin, D.D., LL.D., Late President of the Wesleyan University* (New York: Harper & Brothers, 1852), 2:240–53, p. 249.
36. Ibid., 251.
37. Ibid., 252.
38. See especially Miller, *Piety and Intellect*; McCulloh, *Ministerial Education*; and A. W. Cummings, *The Early Schools of Methodism* (New York: Phillips & Hunt, 1886). Miller asserts in contradiction to the point being made here: "Methodist colleges did have one unusual feature: they did not self-consciously intend to educate candidates for the denomination's ministry.... For Calvinists, the college was a means to reform both church *and* nation; for the Methodists, the college was primarily a way to reform the nation. The church was already reformed" (421).

Miller then concedes that the college network stimulated the church's aspirations for a better trained ministry in a variety of ways. In arguing that Methodists typically did not erect colleges for the purpose of ministerial preparation or structure curriculum to that end, Miller may well be correct. Nevertheless, as the colleges for the church, they did receive persons who would end up in ministry and so *de facto* found themselves playing that role. Appreciation for and substantiation of such a formative role for Wesleyan University is made, from close range, by James Mudge, in *History of the New England Conference of the Methodist Episcopal Church, 1796–1916* (Boston: Published by the Conference, 1910), 335–36. From his seat as longtime secretary of the New England Conference, Mudge noted that Wesleyan had trained much of the leadership, gradually conceding that role to Boston as the New England Conference focused more on the latter and Wesleyan gravitated more into the New York orbit.

39. Bangs, *History*, 3:106.
40. Ibid., 105–7.
41. James Edward Scanlon, *Randolph-Macon College: A Southern History, 1825–1967* (Charlottesville: University Press of Virginia, 1983), 15–22.
42. Ibid., 25.
43. Wesleyan made an overture to move to its campus the ministerial academy opened at Newbury, Vermont, but failed to carry through with an appointment and a theological department. See Cummings, *Early Schools*, 371–72.
44. See especially David B. Potts, *Wesleyan University, 1831–1910: Collegiate Enterprise in New England* (New Haven, CT: Yale University Press, 1992).
45. See ibid., 23ff. for the expansive "Christian America" language and metaphor of motivation and intentionality.
46. Scanlon, *Randolph-Macon College*, 86.
47. He says, "No other official statements of the number of Methodists seem to exist. Godbold states that 'Fifty out of one hundred students at Randolph-Macon College in 1836 were members of the Methodist Church' but gives no authority for the figure. It may be taken as an upper limit" (ibid.).
48. For a stronger and more persuasive case for the denominational and specifically Methodist ethos of such institutions, see Bradley J. Longfield, "'Denominational' Colleges in Antebellum America?: A Case Study of Presbyterians and Methodists in the South," *Reimagining Denominationalism*, ed. Robert Bruce Mullin and Russell E. Richey (New York and Oxford: Oxford University Press, 1994), 288–306.
49. Scanlon, *Randolph-Macon College*, 56ff.
50. This tone to the program is well documented in ibid., 25–34.
51. Wesleyan's fourth (third, if Nathan Bangs is not counted) president, Augustus Smith, was not a minister and Potts judges that he was as "a layman, poorly equipped to sustain the evangelical tone set for Wesleyan by his predecessors. Unable to use the pulpit he also lacked talent as a platform speaker" (ibid., 29).
52. Stephen Olin, *The Life and Letters of Stephen Olin*, 2 vols. (New York: Harper & Brothers, 1853), 1:153.
53. Ibid., 2:217.
54. Potts, *Wesleyan University*, 112, 107. Potts argues that Methodist schools became more denominationally self-consciousness in the latter part of the century and the denomination more intent upon and successful in imprinting itself on collegiate affairs. Earlier he suggests that colleges balanced community with denominational interest and influence.
55. Matthew Simpson, *Cyclopaedia of Methodism*, 5th rev. edition (Philadelphia: Louis H. Everts, 1883).
56. See pp. 70, 961, and 676, respectively.
57. Ibid., 556, 26, 339, 576, 928.
58. Sweet, *Circuit-Rider Days*, 132–34.
59. Ibid., 148–50.
60. "Minutes of The North Carolina Annual Conference," 1:7b, 8b, 9b–10a.
61. Ibid., 12a–13a.
62. See 1841–44, in ibid., 25a–26a.
63. Bangs, *History*, 3:107.
64. Olin, *Life and Letters*, 1:314.
65. Cf. ibid., 1:146.

66. See La Roy Sunderland, "Essay on Theological Education," *Methodist Magazine and Quarterly Review* 16 (1834): 423–37; and "Theological Education," 17 (1835): 204–21.
67. Miller, *Piety and Intellect*, 423–24.
68. Cummings, *Early Schools*, 369–72. See John Dempster, *A Discourse on the Ministerial Call* (Concord: Jones & Cogswell, 1854); and Dempster, *Lectures and Addresses*, ed. D. W. Clark (Cincinnati: Poe & Hitchcock, 1864).
69. Cummings, *Early Schools*, 375–95; McCulloh, *Ministerial Education*, 19–25.
70. Charles Wesley, "At the Opening of a School in Kingswood," st. 5, *Hymns for Children* (1763), 36.
71. De Puy, *Methodist Centennial*, 191, 198.
72. David Kelsey, *To Understand God Truly. What's Theological About a Theological School* (Louisville: Westminster/John Knox Press, 1992), 50–56. The quotation is from 56.
73. Comments made by Miller at the 1993 Wheaton (ISAE) Conference on Theological Education in the Evangelical Tradition.

8. METHODIST CONNECTIONALISM

1. See *The Dictionary of Religious Terms* by Donald T. Kauffman (Westwood: Fleming H. Revell Co., 1967).
2. Certainly one important exception is the United Church of Christ, which, on its Puritan or Congregational side, combined elements of the Radical and Magisterial Reformations in complex fashion. American Puritanism sought to be both congregational and established. Until well after the Revolution, the Congregational Churches were established in New England.
3. One would need to concede that these distinctions are handy and somewhat arbitrary. No church now behaves in a more centralized, coercive, connectional way than the Southern Baptist Convention. And all connectional churches have had to come to terms with localism and a congregationalist mentality, particularly within the flock.
4. The connectional background for the Evangelical and United Brethren traditions is more complex, showing some indebtedness to Wesley; having deeper roots in the Magisterial Reformation (Lutheran and Reformed, respectively); but betraying as well the critiques mounted by Pietism and Anabaptism.
5. In its original version, this chapter functioned as the Introduction to Russell E. Richey et al., eds., *Connectionalism: Ecclesiology, Mission, and Identity*, UMAC I (Nashville: Abingdon, 1997). See in this regard the articles in this volume by Richard Heitzenrater, Thomas Frank, and William Everett, Kenneth Rowe, Charles Zech, Penny Long Marler, and Kirk Hadaway, and Rob Sledge. The reader is invited to consult that volume and its Introduction for indications of how my points allude to or reinforce emphases made by the various essayists. Articles related to this chapter appear as well in other edited volumes in the United Methodism and American Culture series (see Bibliography under Richey et al.).
6. So titled they the minutes of the first conference: "Minutes of Some Conversations between the Preachers in Connexion with The Reverend Mr. John Wesley. Philadelphia, June, 1773," in MEC, *Minutes of the Methodist Conferences, Annually Held in America; From 1773 to 1813, Inclusive* (New York: Published by Daniel Hitt and Thomas Ware, for the Methodist Connexion in the United States, 1813), 5–6.
7. MEC, *Minutes of Several Conversations between the Rev. Thomas Coke, LL.D., the Rev. Francis Asbury, and Others . . . Composing a Form of Discipline for the Ministers, Preachers, and other Members of the Methodist Episcopal Church in America* (Philadelphia: Charles Cist, 1785), Q. 4.
8. Article XIII.—Of the Church, *The Book of Discipline of The United Methodist Church* (Nashville: United Methodist Publishing House, 2004), 62. Thankfully that is now buttressed by the richer and more Wesleyan article from "The Confession of Faith of the Evangelical United Brethren Church," Article V.—The Church (67–68), and by the other

Disciplinary renderings that bear on ecclesiology: "Historical Statement" (9–20), "Our Doctrinal Heritage" (40–50), "Our Doctrinal History" (50–59), "The General Rules" (72–74), "Our Theological Task" (74–86), "Mission Statement" (87–89), "The Ministry of All Christians" (89–94), and "Social Principles" (95–124). Given this rich theological array in the *Discipline*, we could and ought to recognize connectionalism for its ecclesiological force. The resources are at hand and readily combined.

9. John Miley, one of American Methodism's early systematic theologians, positioned his discussion of the church under soteriology, affirming: "As the Church is divinely constituted for the work of evangelization and the spiritual edification of believer, and also contains the divinely instituted means for the attainment of these ends, it may properly be treated in connection with soteriology." John Miley, *Systematic Theology* (New York: Hunt & Eaton, 1892), 2:385.
10. In Richey et al., *Connectionalism*, 221–42.
11. Ibid., 245–64.
12. For assessments of Methodism's working, see Nathan O. Hatch, *The Democratization of American Christianity* (New Haven, CT: Yale University Press, 1989); and Roger Finke and Rodney Stark, *The Churching of America, 1776–1990* (New Brunswick: Rutgers University Press, 1992). The latter measures Methodist success by the numbers, by membership statistics, a mode of assessment to which Methodists themselves inclined. A more appropriate gauge of the success or fidelity of connectionalism, we would suggest, would draw on each of these eight points. After all, the period of greatest and fastest Methodist growth came as it embraced slavery and was not expressive of Methodism's better self-understanding, mission, ideals, and commitment—a point made eloquently by William B. McClain in Richey et al., *Connectionalism*, 77–91.
13. A different statement of the argument of this paragraph can be found in chapter 5. The section as a whole depends on Richey's works: *The Methodist Conference in America: A History* (Nashville: Kingswood Books, 1996); and *Early American Methodism* (Bloomington: Indiana University Press, 1991).
14. For the levels of dependence upon and independence from the MEC pattern in the UBC and EA, see J. Bruce Behney and Paul H. Eller, *The History of the Evangelical United Brethren Church* (Nashville: Abingdon, 1979).
15. Minton Thrift, *Memoir of the Rev. Jesse Lee. With Extracts from his Journals* (New York: N. Bangs and T. Mason, 1823), 48–60. From the itinerant's angle, his own "liberty" keyed the process. Hence the constant assessment of whether the word was preached and heard:

> Sunday 7th of March, I preached at Robert Jones', to a serious congregation, and blessed be God, it was a happy time, and the Lord was among us of a truth. I continued to preach with much liberty.... Sunday 4th, I preached at Robert Jones', to a serious company of people, and had liberty among them (ibid., 59–60).

> [June] Sunday 20th, I preached at Coles, but the congregation was so large, that the house would not hold them, of course we had to look for another place; we got under the shade of some trees, where I spoke with great freedom, and with a heart drawn out in love to the souls of the people; and I felt a longing desire to be instrumental in bringing their souls to God. When I met the class, the friends wept greatly, while they heard each other tell of the goodness of God to their souls (ibid., 66–67).

16. The second edition of the *Discipline*, printed with *The Sunday Service of the Methodists in North America* (London: Frys & Couchman, 1786), ran to twenty-nine pages.
17. In Richey et al., *Connectionalism*, 41–73.
18. See the extended discussion and documentation in Richey, *Early American Methodism*.
19. MEC, *Minutes of the Methodist Conferences . . . 1773 to 1813*, 26.
20. John Firth, *The Experience and Gospel Labours of the Rev. Benjamin Abbott*, published by Ezekiel Cooper (Philadelphia: Solomon W. Conrad, 1802), 164–66.
21. George Coles, *My First Seven Years in America*, ed. D. P. Kidder (New York: Carlton & Phillips, 1852), 49–52.

22. George Peck, ed., *Sketches & Incidents; or A Budget from the Saddle-Bags of a Superannuated Itinerant* (New York: Lane & Sandford, 1844–45), 101. Compare another retrospective, also reported by Peck:

> His quarterly meeting was on Lycoming circuit. It was held in a barn, and the meeting was highly favored of the Lord. In those days there was seldom a quarterly meeting held where there were not souls converted. The Methodists would attend from every part of the circuit. Twenty, or thirty, and even fifty miles was not so far off but they would make an effort to attend, and look upon it as a great privilege to go to quarterly meeting. They would come on horseback through the woods, and from the settlements and towns in their great old-fashioned wagons, drawn by oxen very often, and crowded full; sometimes they would come down the river in canoes. They came with hearts alive to God, and every one was ambitious of excelling in getting nearest to, and in doing most for God and truth. Consequently many sinners were converted before the meeting closed. Such exhortations and prayers, such shouting, for old-fashioned Methodists would shout. Their thorough enjoyment, their genuine tokens of holy delight, their ready responses, always expressed in a hearty manner, bore the preacher onward to success. To preach tamely before such an audience would be an impossibility. No Christian could slumber in such a vivifying atmosphere, no aspirations became weary, no ardor grow cold.

Peck, *Early Methodism Within the Bounds of the Old Genesee Conference from 1788 to 1828* (New York: Carlton & Porter, 1860), 419–20. This account was for a quarterly meeting in 1814 at Painted Post, on the northern Pennsylvania border, for George Harmon, presiding elder on Susquehanna District, and was rendered by his daughter.

23. The representative, delegative, republican, political style of connection might well be introduced and developed here. It clearly has early origins, indeed, roots in typically American patterns of political behavior that Methodists began drawing into their religious life from the 1760s onward. I choose to focus on this style of conference not in this early "republican" stage, nor during the formative phases of the Methodist Protestant movement, but in the twentieth century. A good case can be made, I concede, for introducing what Frank and Everett term the *federal* style at this point.

24. Nathan Bangs, *An Original Church of Christ: Or A Spiritual Vindication of the Orders and Powers of the Ministry of the Methodist Episcopal Church* (New York: Mason and Lane, 1837), 348–51. Bangs continued: "This is a general outline of the system, the different parts of which have grown out of the exigencies of the times, suiting itself to the mental, moral, and spiritual wants of men, and expanding itself so as to embrace the largest possible number of individuals as objects of its benevolence. I may well be suspected of partiality to a system, to the benign operation of which I am so much indebted, and which has exerted such a beneficial influence upon the best interests of mankind; but I cannot avoid thinking that I see in it that 'perfection of beauty, out of which God hath shined,' and that emanation of divine truth and light, which is destined, unless it should unhappily degenerate from its primitive beauty and simplicity 'into a plant of a strange vine,' and thus lose its original energy of character, to do its full share in enlightening and converting the world." (350-51)

25. A. J. Kynett, "Report of the Board of Church Extension," MEC, *Journals of General Conference*, 1876, 602–4.

26. "Report of Committee on Benevolent Societies," MEC, *Journals of General Conference*, 1872, 295.

27. Ibid., 298.

28. In recent years, the Council of Bishops has begun to take important leadership initiatives as a council—that is, collectively.

29. See Richey, *Methodist Conference in America*, 145–74.

30. In Richey et al., *Connectionalism*, 137–75.

31. Ibid., 179–202.

32. Ibid., 95–113.
33. For discussion of changes in denominational life see Milton J Coalter, John M. Mulder, and Louis B. Weeks, *The Re-forming Tradition: Presbyterians and Mainstream Protestantism* (Louisville: Westminster/John Knox, 1992); and Robert Bruce Mullin and Russell E. Richey, eds., *Reimagining Denominationalism: Interpretive Essays* (New York: Oxford University Press, 1994), especially Richey, "Denominations and Denominationalism: An American Morphology."

9. METHODIST CREATION OF THE DENOMINATION

1. George G. Cookman, *Speeches Delivered on Various Occasions* (New York: George Lane, 1840), 135–37.
2. Abel Stevens, *History of the Methodist Episcopal Church in the United States*, 4 vols. (New York: Carlton & Porter, 1864–67), 1:25–28.
3. J. R. Graves, *The Great Iron Wheel: or, Republicanism Backwards and Christianity Reversed*, 12th ed. (Nashville: Graves, Marks and Rutland, 1856), 157, 162, 169.
4. H. Richard Niebuhr's *The Social Sources of Denominationalism* (New York: Meridian Books, 1957) is generally acknowledged as the standard statement on denominationalism. Some of what is said here is directed against Niebuhr's treatment of denominationalism. It should be noted, however, that this chapter is concerned with issues that are really implicit in Niebuhr's analysis and that his basic arguments are not under review. Niebuhr's theologically-informed sociology, despite the title, does not seem to concern itself with denominationalism as a form of the church. Rather he seems to be concerned with the divisions in Protestantism and the factors of caste and class that explain their origin and perpetuation. He assumes the Weber-Troeltsch church-sect typology and the sect-to-church (denomination) movement. His concern is to bring into view the less-than-ideal dynamics that are productive of the ideal types. This work, widely admired by historians, is more useful for its explanation of specific denominations and their social sources than for the perspective provided on denominationalism per se.
5. Robert Baird, *Religion in America—A Critical Abridgment with Introduction by Henry Warner Bowden* (New York: Harper & Row, 1970; orig., 1844), 124. This volume, with Philip Schaff's *America* (New York: Scribners, 1855), remains one of the most penetrating analyses of voluntarism and denominationalism.
6. For another study conceived along these lines see William G. McLoughlin, *New England Dissent 1630–1883*, 2 vols. (Cambridge: Harvard University Press, 1971). See also Anson Phelps Stokes, *Church and State in the United States*, 3 vols. (New York: Harper and Brothers, 1950).
7. See, in particular, Alexis de Tocqueville, *Democracy in America*, ed. Phillips Bradley, 2 vols. (New York: Vintage Books, 1945), 2:123–28; and William E. Channing, "Remarks on Associations," *The Works of William E. Channing* (Boston: Houghton Mifflin, 1892), 237–70.
8. Sidney E. Mead, *The Lively Experiment* (New York: Harper & Row, 1963), 103–4.
9. Ibid., 108–33.
10. Winthrop Hudson, "Denominationalism as a Basis for Ecumenicity: A Seventeenth Century Conception," *Church History* 24 (1955): 32–50, p. 32. Compare Winthrop Hudson, *American Protestantism* (Chicago: University of Chicago Press, 1961), 34.
11. Hudson, "Denominationalism," 39–47.
12. Baird, *Religion in America*; H. Richard Niebuhr, *The Kingdom of God in America* (New York: Harper & Brothers, 1937); James F. Maclear, "'The True American Union' of Church and State: The Reconstruction of the Theocratic Tradition," *Church History* 28 (1959): 41–62; Elwyn A. Smith, "The Voluntary Establishment of Religion," in *The Religion of the Republic*, ed. Elwyn A. Smith (Philadelphia: Fortress Press, 1971), 154–82; Martin E. Marty, *Righteous Empire* (New York: Dial, 1970); and Robert T. Handy, *A Christian America* (New York: Oxford University Press, 1971). The very important essay by D. A. Martin, "The Denomination," *British Journal of Sociology* 13 (March, 1962): 1–14,

presents a similar portrayal of the denomination. Martin does not, however, relate the pragmatism or instrumentalism of the denomination to the end that legitimized the pragmatism, namely, the building of the kingdom. Since the end of the kingdom was what kept the tendencies to relativism, politicization, divisiveness, and other human exploitations of religion in bounds, this omission is significant. To no small degree, it would seem to me, does the cynicism about the compromises of the denomination found in sociological literature derive from this oversight. To no small degree also do present difficulties in the denominations derive from their loss of the higher purpose and larger unity that once defined them and made them more than bureaucracies.

13. Niebuhr, *Kingdom of God*, ix–xiv, 11–12, 44, 164–84, and esp. 177–78.
14. For discussion of this issue see Alan W. Eister, "H. Richard Niebuhr and The Paradox of Religious Organization: A Radical Critique," in *Beyond the Classics?* Ed. Charles Y. Glock and Phillip E. Hammond (New York: Harper & Row, 1973), 355–408; and Benton Johnson, "Church and Sect Revisited," *Journal for the Scientific Study of Religion* 10 (1971): 124–51.
15. For the substantial literature on the Wesleys see Betty M. Jarboe, *John and Charles Wesley: A Bibliography* (Metuchen, NJ: Scarecrow Press, 1987).
16. Frank Baker, *John Wesley and the Church of England* (Nashville: Abingdon, 1970).
17. Albert C. Outler, ed., *John Wesley* (New York: Oxford University Press, 1964), vii–viii.
18. Colin W. Williams, *John Wesley's Theology Today* (New York: Abingdon, 1960), 13–22.
19. Wesley, "Reasons against a Separation from the Church of England," I.12, *Works*, 9:336.
20. Ibid., III.1, *Works*, 9:337. Wesley charged his people: "Ye are a new phenomenon in the earth—a body of people who, being of no sect or party, are friends to all parties, and endeavour to forward all in heart-religion, in the knowledge and love of God and man. Ye yourselves were at first called in the Church of England; and though ye have and will have a thousand temptations to leave it, and set up for yourselves, regard them not; be Church-of-England men still; do not cast away the peculiar glory which God hath put upon you, and frustrate the design of Providence, the very end for which God raised you up." Wesley, Sermon 121, "Prophets and Priests," §18, *Works*, 4:82–83.
21. Wesley, "The Character of a Methodist," Pref. & §3, *Works*, 9:32, 34.
22. Ibid., §18, *Works*, 9:42.
23. Wesley, "Letter to 'John Smith'" (25 June 1746), §10, *Works*, 25:206.
24. Wesley, *A Plain Account of the People Called Methodists*, Pref., §2, *Works*, 9:254. Compare his *Journal* entry (6 August 1788): "One of the most important points considered at this Conference was that of leaving the church. The sum of a long conversation was (1) that in a course of fifty years we had neither premeditatedly nor willingly varied from it in one article, either of doctrine or discipline; (2) that we were not yet conscious of varying from it in any point of doctrine; (3) that we have in a course of years, out of necessity not choice, slowly and warily varied in some points of discipline by preaching in the fields, by extemporary prayer, by employing lay preachers, by forming and regulating societies, and by holding yearly Conferences. But we did none of these things till we were convinced we could no longer omit them but at the peril of our souls" (*Works*, 24:104).
25. Cf. Frank Baker, "The People Called Methodists—3. Polity," in *A History of the Methodist Church in Great Britain*, vol. 1, ed. Rupert Davies & Gordon Rupp (London: Epworth, 1975), 211–55, p. 213; John Lawson, "The People Called Methodists—2. Our Discipline," in ibid., 181–209; and Wesley, *A Plain Account of the People Called Methodists*, *Works*, 9:254–80.
26. "Large Minutes," Q. 3, in Wesley, *Works* (Jackson), 8:299.
27. Richard P. Heitzenrater, *Wesley and the People Called Methodists* (Nashville: Abingdon, 1995).
28. Both varieties of Baptists were somewhat exceptional in that they did by organization, belief, practice, and class mark themselves off from all paedo-Baptists, other Dissenters included. See Russell E. Richey, "English Baptists and Eighteenth-Century Dissent," *Foundations* 16 (October–December, 1973): 347–54.
29. The argument in this paragraph is worked out in more detail in Russell E. Richey, "Did the English Presbyterians become Unitarian?" *Church History* 42 (1973), 58–72. See also Mark A. Noll, *The Rise of Evangelicalism: The Age of Edwards, Whitefield and the Wesleys*

(Downers Grove, IL: InterVarsity Press, 2003); David W. Bebbington, *The Dominance of Evangelicalism: The Age of Spurgeon and Moody* (Downers Grove, IL: InterVarsity Press, 2005); Michael R. Watts, *The Dissenters: From the Reformation to the French Revolution* (Oxford: Clarendon Press, 1978); R. Tudor Jones, *Congregationalism in England, 1662–1962* (London: Independent Press, Ltd., 1962); A. H. Drysdale, *History of the Presbyterians in England* (London: Publication Committee of the Presbyterian Church of England, 1889); H. W. Clark, *A History of English Nonconformity*, 2 vols. (New York: Russell & Russell, 1965; ori., 1913); Walter Lloyd, *The Story of Protestant Dissent and English Unitarianism* (London: Philip Green, 1899); C. G. Bolam et al., *The English Presbyterians* (London: George Allan & Unwin Ltd., 1968); Joseph Ivimey, *A History of the English Baptists*, 4 vols. (London, 1811–20); A. C. Underwood, *A History of the English Baptists* (London: Kingsgate Press, 1947); and W. T. Whitley, *A History of the British Baptists*, 2nd ed. (London: Kingsgate Press, 1932).
30. Marty, *Righteous Empire*, 67–72.
31. William Warren Sweet, *The Story of Religion in America* (New York: Harper & Brothers, 1939), 280. Sweet says: "The first American religious body to form a national organization was the Methodists and their priority in this respect is due to the fact that their national organization was largely worked out for them by Mr. Wesley." Again, in *Methodism in American History* (p. 100), Sweet affirms that the Methodists were the first "to work out an independent and national organization."
32. See Hatch, *Democratization of American Christianity*; A. Gregory Schneider, *The Way of the Cross Leads Home: The Domestication of American Methodism* (Bloomington: Indiana University Press, 1993); Christine Leigh Heyrman, *Southern Cross: The Beginnings of the Bible Belt* (New York: Knopf, 1997); John H. Wigger, *Taking Heaven by Storm: Methodism and the Rise of Popular Christianity in America* (New York: Oxford University Press, 1998); Cynthia Lynn Lyerly, *Methodism and the Southern Mind, 1770–1810* (New York: Oxford University Press, 1998); Dee E. Andrews, *Religion and the Revolution: The Rise of the Methodists in the Greater Middle Atlantic, 1760–1800* (Princeton: Princeton University Press, 1999); Donald G. Mathews, *Religion in the Old South* (Chicago: University of Chicago Press, 1977); H. Shelton Smith, *In His Image, But . . . : Racism in Southern Religion, 1780–1910* (Durham: Duke University Press, 1972); and Richey, *Early American Methodism*. For an earlier and critical discussion of this designation see Winthrop S. Hudson, "The Methodist Age in America," *Methodist History* 12 (April 1974): 3–15. See also Jaroslav J. Pelikan, "Methodism's Contribution to America," in *The History of American Methodism*, 3 vols, ed. Emory S. Bucke (New York: Abingdon, 1964), 3:596–614; Robert T. Handy, "Methodism's Contributions to American Life," *Christian Advocate*, 10 (April 7, 1966): 7–8; C.C. Goen, "The 'Methodist Age' in American Church History," *Religion in Life* 34 (1965): 562–72; Douglas R. Chandler, "Towards the Americanizing of Methodism," *Methodist History*, 13 (October 1974): 3–16; and Frank Baker, "The Americanization of Methodism," *Methodist History* 13 (April 1975): 5–20.
33. See John Kewley, *An Enquiry into the Validity of Methodist Episcopacy* (Wilmington: Joseph Jones, 1807), 4; Kewley repeatedly calls Methodism a "new plan." For discussion of the range of anti-Methodist ideas see Lawrence O. Kline, "Anti-Methodist Publications (American)," in Harmon, *Encyclopedia*, 115–99; and Frank Baker, "Anti-Methodist Publications (British)," ibid., 119–22.
34. Graves, *Great Iron Wheel*, 34–35.
35. Wesley, "Letter to 'Our Brethren in America'" (10 September 1784), *Letters* (Telford), 7: 239.
36. Norwood, *Story of American Methodism*, 61–69.
37. Ibid., 101.

10. CONNECTING THROUGH EDUCATION

1. For treatment of this concept, see chapter 8; Russell E. Richey et al., *Connectionalism: Ecclesiology, Mission, and Identity*, UMAC I (Nashville: Abingdon, 1997); Thomas Edward

Frank, *Polity, Practice and the Mission of The United Methodist Church* (Nashville: Abingdon, 2006); and Richey, *The Methodist Conference in America: A History* (Nashville: Kingswood Books, 1996).

2. Beth Adams Bowser, *Living the Vision: The University Senate of the Methodist Episcopal Church, the Methodist Church, and the United Methodist Church, 1892–1991* (Nashville: Board of Higher Education and Ministry of The United Methodist Church, 1992), i. Bowser observes that the Senate "was the first body in the United States to establish and apply standards for educational institutions on a nationwide basis," a fact appreciated, she notes, by neither the regional accrediting associations nor other denominations (i). See also Myron F. Wicke, *A Brief History of the University Senate of the Methodist Church* (Nashville: Dept. of Public Relations and Finance, Division of Educational Institutions, Board of Education, The Methodist Church, 1956).

3. The controversy today over what constitutes standards makes it clear how important his clarity on the point was. For details on this controversy, see above, chapter 5, note 13.

4. On this point see chapters 5 and 8.

5. See A. W. Cummings, *Early Schools of Methodism* (New York: Phillips & Hunt, 1886); Francis I. Moats, "The Educational Policy of The Methodist Episcopal Church Prior to 1860" (PhD diss., University of Iowa 1926), 38–56; and Slyvanus M. Duvall, *The Methodist Episcopal Church and Education up to 1869* (New York: Bureau of Publications, Teachers College, 1928).

6. For an able assessment of Coke's leadership intentions and ambitions, see Warren Thomas Smith, "Thomas Coke's Contribution to the Christmas Conference," in *Rethinking Methodist History*, ed. Russell E. Richey and Kenneth E. Rowe (Nashville: Kingswood Books, 1985), 37–47. The definitive treatment is John Vickers, *Thomas Coke: Apostle of Methodism* (Nashville: Abingdon, 1969).

7. This discussion distills treatment of Asbury in Russell E. Richey, "Legacy of Francis Asbury: The Teaching Office in Episcopal Methodism," *Quarterly Review* 15 (Summer 1995).

8. Francis Asbury, *The Journals and Letters of Francis Asbury*, 3 vols., ed. Elmer T. Clark (London: Epworth; Nashville: Abingdon, 1958), 3:323 (letter to Ezekiel Cooper, July 26, 1805).

9. See James Penn Pilkington, *The Methodist Publishing House: A History*, vol. 1, Beginnings to 1870 (Nashville: Abingdon, 1968), 1:51–154.

10. Asbury, *Journals*, 3:232–33 (letter to Ezekiel Cooper, the book agent, dated Dec. 31, 1801). There he spoke about his several publishing ventures. The preface to the hymnal appears in ibid., 3:397–98. For Asbury's personal efforts in its creation, see entries in 2:554 (for Aug. 1807), 2:558 (for Oct. 25, 1807); and 2:559 (for Nov. 4, 6, 1807).

11. *The Causes, Evils, and Cures . . . Jeremiah Burroughs and Mr. Richard Baxter* (Philadelphia: Parry Hall, 1792; republished in 1817 and 1849).

12. *Extracts of Letters . . . the Year 1800* (New York: Cooper & Wilson, 1805). The subtitle read "Written by the Preachers and Members of the Methodist Episcopal Church to their Bishops."

13. Methodist Episcopal Church, *The Doctrines and Discipline of the Methodist Episcopal Church in America, with Explanatory Notes, by Thomas Coke and Francis Asbury* (Philadelphia, 1798); facsimile edition, ed. Frederick A. Norwood (Rutland, VT: Academy Books, 1979).

14. See Asbury, *Journals*, 2:739–40 (Aug. 1, 1813), 3:475–92 (Aug. 5, 1813), 2:744 (Oct. 29, 1813); 3:532–43 (Jan. 8, 1816); and *Methodist History* 1 (1962): 56–58, for Sept. 29, 1815.

15. See "Index of Sermon Texts," in Asbury, *Journals*, 3:818–24. It is worth remarking that Asbury preached on the whole Bible.

16. Samuel Luttrell Akers, *The First Hundred Years of Wesleyan College, 1836–1936* (Macon, GA: Wesleyan College, 1976). "Greensboro College . . . was chartered by the Methodist Church in 1838 as a women's college." *Handbook of United Methodist-Related Schools, Colleges, Universities and Theological Schools* (Nashville: GBHEM/UMC, 1996), 89.

17. Donald G. Tewksbury, *The Founding of American Colleges and Universities Before the Civil War* (New York: Arno Press, 1969), 103–11. By contrast, Tewksbury estimates the Presbyterians founded forty-nine (102).

18. Bowser, *Living the Vision*, vi-viii.
19. On this point see James E. Kirby, Russell E. Richey, and Kenneth E. Rowe, *The Methodists* (Westport, CT: Greenwood Press, 1996), 24–42.
20. For further information on Durbin, see the entry in ibid., 291–92; also the estimates of him by John A. Roche, *The Life of John Price Durbin* (New York: Phillips & Hunt, 1889); and Roche, "John Price Durbin," *Methodist Quarterly Review* 69 (May 1887): 329–54.
21. *Minutes of the Philadelphia Conference of the Methodist Episcopal Church*, 1835 (Typescript version of apparently printed minutes), unpaginated, but p. 10. On his presidency see James Henry Morgan, *Dickinson College: The History of One Hundred Fifty Years, 1783–1933* (Carlisle: Dickinson College, 1933); and Charles Coleman Sellers, *Dickinson College: A History* (Middletown: Wesleyan University Press, 1973).
22. J. P. Durbin was, for instance, listed first as delegate to the 1844 General Conference. *Minutes of the Philadelphia Conference of the Methodist Episcopal Church*, 1844, 10.
23. *Minutes of the Philadelphia Conference of the Methodist Episcopal Church*, 1845, 12.
24. *Minutes of the Philadelphia Conference of the Methodist Episcopal Church*, 1846, 14.
25. *Minutes of the Philadelphia Conference of the Methodist Episcopal Church*, 1849, 5. This office is now known as the District Superintendent. By that time the *Minutes* listed a North German Mission in N. Phila. District and South German Mission in S. Phila. District *Minutes of the Philadelphia Conference of the Methodist Episcopal Church*, 1849, 5–6.
26. Francis H. Tees et al., *Pioneering in Penn's Woods. Philadelphia Methodist Episcopal Annual Conference Through One Hundred Fifty Years* (Philadelphia Conference Tract Society of the Methodist Episcopal Church, 1937), 117–19.
27. Morgan, *Dickinson College*, 248–72 and 283–94; Sellers, *Dickinson College*, 195–229.
28. For more on this point, see chapter 7.
29. Stephen Olin, *The Works of Stephen Olin, D. D., LL.D., Late President of the Wesleyan University* (New York: Harper & Brothers, 1852), 2:249.
30. Ibid., 2:251.
31. Joseph Holdich, *The Life of Willbur Fisk, D. D., First President of The Wesleyan University* (New York: Harper & Brothers, 1842), 218.
32. These figures, from the Society of the Alumni, are reported in James Edward Scanlon, *Randolph-Macon College: A Southern History, 1825–1967* (Charlottesville: University Press of Virginia, 1983), 56ff.
33. Duvall, *Methodist Episcopal Church and Education*, 39–40.
34. Sellers, *Dickinson College*, 195–99.
35. Scanlon, *Randolph-Macon College*; and David B. Potts, *Wesleyan University, 1831–1910: Collegiate Enterprise in New England* (New Haven, CT: Yale University Press, 1992). Compare the estimate of John O. Gross: "While both Wesleyan and Randolph-Macon were under the control of the Methodist Church, neither required religious tenets for the admission of students. . . . The religious life of these first two, like that of all early Methodist colleges, took on the character of the supporting church. . . . There was no conflict between evangelism and education. The religious aim of the college was to evoke a creative response to God, to instill faith and to inspire devotion. This furnished the students with the motivating power needed for living." John O. Gross, *Methodist Beginnings in Higher Education* (Nashville: Board of Education, The Methodist Church, 1959), 39.
36. Glenn T. Miller, *Piety and Intellect: The Aims and Purposes of Ante-Bellum Theological Education* (Atlanta: Scholar's Press, 1990), 127–39.
37. Potts, *Wesleyan University*, 72.
38. Cited in ibid., 76, 73.
39. See Quentin Charles Lansman, *Higher Education in the Evangelical United Brethren Church: 1800–1954* (Nashville: Division of Higher Education/UMC, 1972).
40. MEC, *Journals of General Conference*, 1872, 295–99. For a discussion of the import of this change, see the "Report of the Board of Church Extension," an explanation made after the change to the General Conference of 1876, by A. J. Kynett (ibid., 1876, 602–4). Kynett noted that previously: "Although organized by order of the General Conference, the corporate body was, by the terms of its Constitution and Charter, a 'Society' composed of such members and friends of the Church as might contribute to

its funds the sum of one dollar per annum, or twenty dollars at one time. These had the legal right to elect its managers; but only such as could be present at the annual meetings in Philadelphia could share in the exercise of this right. It was, therefore, clearly beyond the reach of the Church government, and equally beyond the reach of all contributors to its funds, except only a portion of those who resided in the city of Philadelphia."

41. MEC, *Journals of General Conference*, 1872, 300–2. The adopting resolution described the Freedmen's Aid Society "as a regular constituted Society of the Methodist Episcopal Church" (300).
42. "Report of the Committee on Education appointed by the General Conference of 1860," MEC, *Journals of General Conference*, 1864, 390, 391.
43. Cited by Potts, *Wesleyan University*, 63.
44. See ibid., chapters 3 and 4.
45. See Bowser, *Living the Vision*, 7–43.
46. This estimate comes from Samuel Plantz, *The History of Education in the Methodist Episcopal Church, 1892 to 1917* (New York: The Board of Education of The Methodist Episcopal Church, 1918), 3–4.
47. "Report of the Freedmen's Aid and Southern Education Society," MEC, *Journals of General Conference*, 1892, 692–704; and "On Freedmen's Aid and Southern Education Society," ibid., 479–81. The statements, including the heading, are from 696–97. See William Wilson, "The Methodist Episcopal Church in Her Relation to the Negro in the South," *Methodist Review* 76 (1894): 713–23.
48. MEC, *Journals of General Conference*, 1892, 480–81, 703. The General Committee included the bishops, the officers and agents, representatives from each general conference district ("appointed by the General Conference") and "a number equal to the district representatives, to be appointed by the Board of Managers."
49. Ibid., 481.
50. Ibid., 694, 701. "Of these 22 are among colored people, 1 being theological, 10 collegiate; and 11 academic in grade. Among white people there are 3 of collegiate and 17 of academic grade. The number of students of all schools in attendance the past year was 9,495." 692–93.
51. Ibid., 693, 699. Emphasis in the original. A different total of students was reported on the same page, namely 9,495. Of interest are the gender proportions: male teachers 184, female 150; male students 4,696, female 4,614.
52. Ibid., 697.
53. A nice indicator of its ongoing character is Robert H. Conn, *A Handbook for Higher Education and Campus Ministry in the Annual Conference* (Nashville: Division of Higher Education/GBHEM, 1989), which takes ten chapters to summarize conference responsibilities. For a longer view with respect to one conference, see Carl H. King, *Historical Highlights of The Educational Ministry: Western North Carolina Conference Seventy-five Years, 1890-1965* (np, 1965).
54. See the treatment in Robert H. Conn with Michael Nickerson, *United Methodists and Their Colleges*, foreword by F. Thomas Trotter (Nashville: United Methodist Board of Higher Education and Ministry, 1989), especially chapter 5.
55. This is not the twentieth century development that looms largest in treatments of religion and higher education. Instead, the themes that predominate are secularization, the increasing role of the Federal government, the dominance in higher education generally of the research university and its values, the consequent displacement of the liberal arts ideal as an integrative principle and the effective marginalization of religion (in religious studies, student groups, chaplaincies, and the Christian college). See the trilogy of 1994 items: Merrimon Cuninggim, *Uneasy Partners: The College and the Church* (Nashville: Abingdon, 1994); George M. Marsden, *The Soul of the American University: From Protestant Establishment to Established Nonbelief* (New York: Oxford University Press, 1994); and Douglas Sloan, *Faith and Knowledge: Mainline Protestantism and American Higher Education* (Louisville: Westminster John Knox, 1994). Also pertinent is Conrad Cherry, *Hurrying Toward Zion: Universities, Divinity Schools, and American Protestantism* (Bloomington: Indiana University Press, 1995).

56. These processes began early. Note, for instance, this 1911 Philadelphia action:

> RESOLUTION ON MINIMUM SALARY OF $800.—On Motion of J. Watchorn, the following was adopted: "Resolved, That a committee of fifteen, including the five District Superintendents, five ministers, one from each district, and five laymen, one from each district, be appointed to prepare an equitable plan to raise the minimum salary of all effective members of the Conference and members on trial to $800, and to report the same at the next Annual Conference." Official Journal and Year Book of the Philadelphia Annual Conference of the Methodist Episcopal Church, 1911, 86.

57. See, for instance, the attention to group life insurance by the Philadelphia Annual Conference in 1924, *Official Journal and Year Book of the Philadelphia Annual Conference of the Methodist Episcopal Church*, 1925, 837–40; similarly the following year, ibid., 1926, 44; and in ibid., 1930, 295.
58. The 1928 Philadelphia Conference passed a resolution for General Conference asking that any changes in the pension system "assure adequate and full protection to all the approved claims of the present members of the Conference, and that no plan be approved that proposes apportionments above the present rate, or the raising of additional funds, without the consideration and consent of the Annual Conference" (*Official Journal and Year Book of the Philadelphia Annual Conference of the Methodist Episcopal Church*, 1928, 762). The same conference urged a commission "to study the matter of pastors' salaries, so that a minimum salary of living support shall be given to every member of each Annual Conference" (p. 774).
59. Marsden, *Soul of the American University*; Sloan, *Faith and Knowledge*.
60. See also George M. Marsden and Bradley J. Longfield, eds., *The Secularization of the Academy* (New York: Oxford University Press, 1992), especially 3–45 and 170–94.
61. A good place to discover these networks is through the latest *United Methodist Directory and Index of Resources*, especially the section entitled "Programs and Resources" that identifies contact persons.
62. See Robert Wuthnow, *The Restructuring of American Religion* (Princeton: Princeton University Press, 1988); and Wuthnow, *Struggle for America's Soul* (Grand Rapids: Eerdmans, 1989). The fault lines created by the struggle, especially between armies that line up left and right, led Wuthnow in the 1980s to wonder about the future of denominations.
63. "Are Extension Ministries an Opportunity to Reclaim a Wesleyan Understanding of Mission?" in Russell E. Richey et al., *Questions for the Twenty-first Century Church*, UMAC IV (Nashville: Abingdon, 1999, 175–85); and Richey, *Extension Ministers: Mr. Wesley's True Heirs* (forthcoming from GBHEM).

11. METHODIST CULTURE WARS

1. On the mainline problematic, see Milton J. Coalter, John M. Mulder, and Louis B. Weeks, *The Reforming Tradition: Presbyterians and Mainstream Protestantism* (Louisville: Westminster/John Knox, 1992), the seventh culminating, synthetic volume in the series, The Presbyterian Presence: The Twentieth Century Experience.
2. On the timing of "dis-establishment" and its consequences, see William R. Hutchison, *Between the Times: The Travail of the Protestant Establishment in America, 1900–1960* (New York: Cambridge University Press, 1989).
3. This contrast is used in Robert Wuthnow, *The Restructuring of American Religion* (Princeton: Princeton University Press, 1988); and Wuthnow, *The Struggle for America's Soul* (Grand Rapids: Eerdmans, 1989).
4. Commentators employing "liberal and evangelical" as rubrics include Richard J. Coleman, *Issues of Theological Conflict: Evangelicals and Liberals* (Grand Rapids: Eerdmans, 1972); James Davison Hunter, *American Evangelicalism: Conservative Religion and the*

Quandary of Modernity (New Brunswick: Rutgers University Press, 1983); Richard Quebedeaux, *The Worldly Evangelicals* (San Francisco: Harper & Row, 1978); and R. Stephen Warner, *New Wine in Old Wineskins: Evangelicals and Liberals in a Small-Town Church* (Berkeley: University of California Press, 1988).

5. The contrast that James Davison Hunter employs in *Culture Wars* (New York: Basic Books, 1991) is "progressive and orthodox." The "public and private" formulation of the two-party division for twentieth century Protestantism was by Jean Miller Schmidt, accessible now in the published version of her dissertation, *Souls or the Social Order: The Two-Party System in American Protestantism* (Brooklyn: Carlson, 1991); and by Martin E. Marty in *Righteous Empire* (New York: Dial Press, 1970). See also Dean R. Hoge, *Division in the Protestant House* (Philadelphia, Westminster Press, 1976). A contrast of this worldly and otherworldly is drawn by David A. Roozen, William McKinney, and Jackson W. Carroll in *Varieties of Religious Presence* (New York: Pilgrim Press, 1984). Richard J. Mouw, "New Alignments: Hartford and the Future of Evangelicalism," in Peter L. Berger and Richard John Neuhaus, eds., *Against the World For the World* (New York: The Seabury Press, 1976) contrasts the two parties as "ecumenical and evangelical."

6. On the end to denominationalism, see Wuthnow, *Restructuring*; and especially Wuthnow *Struggle*, 72–94. See also Wade Clark Roof and William McKinney, *American Mainline Religion* (New Brunswick: Rutgers University Press, 1987).

7. H. Richard Niebuhr, *The Social Sources of Denominationalism* (New York: Meridian, 1957), 25. Niebuhr had earlier affirmed: "The evil of denominationalism lies in the conditions which makes the rise of sects desirable and necessary: in the failure of the churches to transcend the social conditions which fashion them into caste-organizations, to sublimate their loyalties to standards and institutions only remotely relevant if not contrary to the Christian ideal, to resist the temptation of making their own self-preservation and extension the primary object of their endeavor" (21).

8. See, for instance, *Yearbook of American and Canadian Churches 1966*, ed. Kenneth B. Bedell (Nashville: Abingdon, 1996).

9. Robert Handy, "The American Religious Depression, 1925–35," *Church History* 29 (1960): 3–16.

10. To speak as though denominationalism were a living creature is only to grant the religious historian the license of the economist who treats the market in similar fashion. The analogy, I would suggest, is a close one.

11. Richard P. Heitzenrater, *Wesley and the People Called Methodists* (Nashville: Abingdon, 1995), especially 207–8, 218–19, 232–33, 237, 256, 269, 284, 293–96, 304–5.

12. Minutes of a Conference held at Roger Thomson's in Fluvanna County, Va, May 18, 1779, in "Minutes of Conference from the year 1774 to the year 1779," *Western Christian Advocate* 4/5 (May 26, 1837), 18–19. This published version was from minutes kept by Philip Gatch.

13. "*Quest. 8. Why was the Delaware conference held?* Ans. For the convenience of the preachers in the northern stations, that we all might have an opportunity of meeting in conference; it being unadvisable for brother Asbury and brother Ruff, with some others, to attend in Virginia; it is considered also as preparatory to the conference in Virginia." Methodist Episcopal Church, *Minutes of the Methodist Conferences . . . 1773 to 1813 Inclusive* (New York: Published by Daniel Hitt and Thomas Ware, for the Methodist Connexion in the United States, 1813), 19.

14. Ibid.

15. Ibid., 25–26.

16. MEC, *Minutes of Several Conversations between the Rev. Thomas Coke, LL.D., the Rev. Francis Asbury, and Others begun in Baltimore, in the state of Maryland, on Monday, the 27th of December, in the year 1784. Composing a Form of Discipline for the Ministers, Preachers, and other Members of the Methodist Episcopal Church in America*. Philadelphia: Charles Cist, 1785, Q. 2 (p. 3). Convenient access to the first *Discipline* can be had in Tigert, *Constitutional History*, 534.

17. See J. Gordon Melton, *A Will to Choose: The Origins of African American Methodism* (Lanham: Rowman & Littlefield, 2007); Carol V. R. George, *Segregated Sabbaths*. Richard

Allen and the Rise of Independent Black Churches, 1760–1840. (New York: Oxford University Press, 1973); *The Life Experience and Gospel Labors of the Rt. Rev. Richard Allen*, 2nd ed. (New York: Abingdon, 1960); and Will B. Gravely, "African Methodisms and the Rise of Black Denominationalism," in Russell E. Richey and Kenneth E. Rowe, eds., *Rethinking Methodist History* (Nashville: Kingswood Books, 1985), 111–24.
18. For a firsthand treatment, see Jesse Lee, *A Short History of the Methodists* (Baltimore: Magill and Clime, 1810; facsimile edition, Rutland, VT: Academy Books, 1974), 178–80.
19. See on the latter Neil Semple, *The Lord's Dominion: The History of Canadian Methodism* (Montreal: McGill-Queen's University Press, 1996).
20. See Melvin E. Dieter, *The Holiness Revival of the Nineteenth Century* (Metuchen, N.J.: Scarecrow Press, 1980).
21. See C. C. Goen, *Broken Churches, Broken Nation. Denominational Schisms and the Coming of the Civil War* (Macon: Mercer University Press, 1985).
22. Reginald F. Hildebrand, *The Times Were Strange and Stirring: Methodist Preachers and the Crisis of Emancipation* (Durham: Duke University Press, 1995); Katharine L. Dvorak, *An African-American Exodus: The Segregation of the Southern Churches* (Brooklyn: Carlson Publishing, 1991); and Melton, *Will to Choose*.
23. See Clarence E. Walker, *A Rock in a Weary Land: The African Methodist Episcopal Church During the Civil War and Reconstruction* (Baton Rouge: Louisiana State University Press, 1982); and Melton, *Will to Choose*.

12. ARE THE LOCAL CHURCH AND THE DENOMINATIONAL BUREAUCRACY "TWINS"?

1. *The Book of Discipline of The United Methodist Church* (Nashville: United Methodist Publishing House, 2004), ¶¶243–44, ¶¶901–7.
2. The original of the "Methodist Itinerant System," New York: John C. Totten, [ca.1822] is a single-sheet broadside. Kenneth Rowe dated it as "about 1822" from internal evidence: 12 conferences, 70 districts and 545 circuits and from the fact that John C. Totten was principal New York printer for the MEC from 1804 to 1826.
3. Nathan Bangs, *A History of the Methodist Episcopal Church*, 12th ed., 4 vols. (New York: Carlton & Porter, 1860), 2:293–94.
4. A formulation that Rowe has used frequently in lectures.
5. MEC, *Journals of the General Conference of the Methodist Episcopal Church*, 1852, 116.
6. MEC, *Journals*, 1864, 261, 404–5.
7. MEC, *Journals*, 1872, 295–98.
8. MEC, *Journals*, 1884, 337.
9. *Journal of the . . . Delegated General Conference of the Methodist Episcopal Church*, 1912, 178–82.
10. *Journal of the . . . Delegated General Conference of the Methodist Episcopal Church*, 1928, 152–74.
11. *Journal of the . . . Delegated General Conference of the Methodist Episcopal Church* 1920, 424–25, 1457. The action amended Division III, Chapter, I, Article II, ¶35 to read, "A Local Conference shall be organized in each Pastoral Charge, and be composed of such persons and have such powers as the General Conference may direct." In the floor action and debate, the original language of the legislation, which had spoken of "Church conference," was so amended. The MECS had, of course, recognized "Church Conferences" from 1870.
12. *Journal of the . . . General Conference of the Methodist Church* (Nashville: Methodist Publishing House, 1940), 236–38.

13. Methodism's Practiced Ecclesiology

1. The full titles are *The Book of Discipline of the United Methodist Church, 2004* (Nashville: The United Methodist Publishing House, 2004); *The United Methodist Book of Worship* (Nashville: The United Methodist Publishing House, 1992); and *The United Methodist Hymnal* (Nashville: The United Methodist Publishing House, 1989). The first is revised and a new version published after each General Conference, typically quadrennially.
2. See Karen B. Westerfield Tucker, *American Methodist Worship* (New York: Oxford University Press, 2001).
3. For an effort to set out standards of United Methodist doctrine by their official level of authority, see Scott J. Jones, *United Methodist Doctrine: The Extreme Center* (Nashville: Abingdon, 2002), 43–56. Jones distinguishes ten texts that fall into three levels. First are the constitutional standards, which include items embraced in the *Discipline* (Constitution, Articles, Confession and General Rules) plus infrequently used but official standards, Wesley's "Standard Sermons" and *Explanatory Notes Upon the New Testament*. At a second level he places contemporary statements, namely, other parts of the *Discipline* and the wonderful but rarely used *Book of Resolutions*. At the third level he locates the *Hymnal* and *Book of Worship*, which he terms *liturgy*. In his formulations, he recognizes the degrees of authority represented but draws on all three levels. For a simpler schema, compare Ted A. Campbell, *Methodist Doctrine: The Essentials* (Nashville: Abingdon, 1999), "Appendix 2," 116–22. See also Thomas C. Oden, *Doctrinal Standards in the Wesleyan Tradition* (Grand Rapids: Zondervan, 1988). The discussion that follows addresses the issues they raise.
4. MEC, *Minutes . . . Composing a Form of Discipline* (1785). For the text of the first *Discipline* in parallel columns with the "Large Minutes," see Jno. J. Tigert, *A Constitutional History of American Episcopal Methodism*, 3rd ed., rev. (Nashville: Publishing House of the Methodist Episcopal Church, South, 1908), 532–602.
5. See Carlton R. Young, *Companion to The United Methodist Hymnal* (Nashville: Abingdon, 1993), 94–95.
6. See *A Collection of Hymns for the Use of the People Called Methodists* (1781), which is vol. 7 of Wesley, *Works*.
7. To some extent, it would function for Methodists as the *Book of Common Prayer* (BCP) did and does for Anglicans.
8. *John Wesley's Sunday Service of the Methodists in North America*, with an introduction by James F. White (Nashville: *Quarterly Review*, 1984).
9. Wesley, "Letter to 'Our Brethren in America'" (10 September 1784), *Letters* (Telford), 7: 239.
10. See Ted A. Campbell, "The 'Wesleyan Quadrilateral': The Story of a Modern Methodist Myth," and Albert C. Outler, "The Wesleyan Quadrilateral—In John Wesley," in Thomas A. Langford, ed., *Doctrine and Theology in The United Methodist Church* (Nashville: Kingswood Books, 1991), 154–61 and 75–88; W. Stephen Gunter et al., *Wesley and the Quadrilateral: Renewing the Conversation* (Nashville: Abingdon, 1997); Scott J. Jones, *John Wesley's Conception and Use of Scripture* (Nashville: Kingswood Books, 1995); Jones, *United Methodist Doctrine*; and Walter Klaiber and Manfred Marquardt, *Living Grace: An Outline of United Methodist Theology* (Nashville: Abingdon, 2001), 17–92.
11. See the scriptural annotations, the rubrics and indexes, and the theological acuity clearly evident in *Works*, vol. 7.
12. The quadrilateral as a construct does not come into Methodist usage until the late twentieth century.
13. I owe this formulation to my colleague Thomas Frank.
14. For an overview of Wesley's theology and theological development accenting its missional and salvific character, see Kenneth J. Collins, *John Wesley: A Theological Journal* (Nashville: Abingdon, 2003).
15. MEC, *Discipline* (1787), 3. Compare the earlier (1784) formulation, lacking the second assertion, actually lacking points (2) and (3) of Methodist purpose, in the first *Discipline*, in Tigert, *Constitutional History*, 535.

16. On early Methodism's antislavery witness and the retreat therefrom, see A. Gregory Schneider, *The Way of the Cross Leads Home: The Domestication of American Methodism* (Bloomington: Indiana University Press, 1993); Christine Leigh Heyrman, *Southern Cross: The Beginnings of the Bible Belt* (New York: Knopf, 1997); John H. Wigger, *Taking Heaven by Storm: Methodism and the Rise of Popular Christianity in America* (New York: Oxford University Press, 1998); Cynthia Lynn Lyerly, *Methodism and the Southern Mind, 1770–1810* (New York: Oxford University Press, 1998); Dee E. Andrews, *Religion and the Revolution: The Rise of the Methodists in the Greater Middle Atlantic, 1760–1800* (Princeton: Princeton University Press, 1999); Donald G. Mathews, *Religion in the Old South* (Chicago: University of Chicago Press, 1977); H. Shelton Smith, *In His Image, But . . . Racism in Southern Religion, 1780-1910* (Durham: Duke University Press, 1972); and Russell E. Richey, *Early American Methodism* (Bloomington: Indiana University Press, 1991).
17. One gets a nice overview of the Methodist missionary system through the day-to-day activities, the scenes described, and the instructions of its itinerant apostle and chief bishop, Francis Asbury. For the day-to-dayness of missionary itinerancy, see all three volumes of Asbury, *Journal*. For a recent review of Asbury at the center of Methodism's missionary system, see Darius L. Salter, *America's Bishop: The Life of Francis Asbury* (Nappanee, IN: Evangel, 2003).
18. On this dimension to Wesleyan theology, see Robert E. Cushman, *John Wesley's Experimental Divinity: Studies in Methodist Doctrinal Standards* (Nashville: Kingswood Books, 1989); Langford, *Practical Divinity*; Jones, *United Methodist Doctrine*, 61, 71–77, 241–97; and Kenneth J. Collins, *A Real Christian: The Life of John Wesley* (Nashville: Abingdon, 1999).
19. *Sunday Service*, p. A 1. White's "Introduction" and "Notes" provide more extensive documentation of Wesley's changes to the BCP.
20. One may most easily visualize the changes and yet the integrity of the liturgies in Nolan B. Harmon, *The Rites and Ritual of Episcopal Methodism* (Nashville: MECS Publishing, 1926). In separate sections on the Eucharist, Infant Baptism, Adult Baptism, Matrimony, Burial, and the Ordinal, Harmon puts into six parallel columns across two pages: Ancient Sources, The 1661 Prayer Book, Wesley's Sunday Service, 1844 ME Ritual, 1922 MECS Ritual, and 1924 ME Ritual.
21. For the first sustained defense of Methodist ecclesiology, ministry, and episcopacy, see the annotated *Discipline* produced by bishops Thomas Coke and Francis Asbury: MEC, *Doctrines and Discipline* (798). "Wesley's ministry laid the essential foundation of what became the Methodist style of episcopacy, and in many ways that foundation has remained intact in America," ed. Gerald F. Moede, "Bishops in the Methodist Tradition: Historical Perspectives," in *Episcopacy: Lutheran-United Methodist Dialogue II*, ed. Jack M. Tuel and Roger W. Fjeld (Minneapolis: Augsburg, 1991), 52–69, 58. For an overview and assessment of the office, see James E. Kirby, *The Episcopacy in American Methodism* (Nashville: Kingswood Books, 2000); Thomas Edward Frank, *Polity, Practice and the Mission of The United Methodist Church* (Nashville: Abingdon, 2006), 229–53; Norman Woods Spellmann, "The General Superintendency in American Methodism, 1784–1870" (PhD diss., Yale University 1961); and chapter 6.
22. See *The Life of the Reverend Devereux Jarratt*, foreword by David L. Holmes (Cleveland: Pilgrim Press, 1995; ori., 1806), especially Letter II, penned in 1794 (47–78 and particularly 61–70).
23. The first American edition of John Wesley's *Explanatory Notes upon the New Testament* was published in 1791 (Philadelphia: Printed by Joseph Crukshank, sold by John Dickins, No. 43, Fourth Street, near the corner of Race Street). At least twenty-five reprints or new editions were issued over the nineteenth century.
24. Wesley, "Letter to the Preachers in America" (3 October 1783), *Letters* (Telford), 7: 191. Cf. Bangs, *History*, 1:148. For the case for the continued authority of the *Notes*, see Oden, *Doctrinal Standards*, 15–68. The sales of the *Notes* must have been primarily to the preachers as they were minuscule in comparison to the movement of other Methodist books, particularly the hymnals. See midwestern sales records in William Warren Sweet, ed., *The Methodists: A Collection of Source Materials* (Chicago: University of Chicago Press, 1946), 698–706.

25. For Wesley's self-identification, see Preface to *Sermons on Several Occasions*, §5, *Works*, 1:105; and Sermon 107, "On God's Vineyard," I.1, *Works*, 3:504. On Wesley's understanding and use of Scripture, see Jones, *Wesley's Conception and Use of Scripture*.
26. Asbury, "A Valedictory Address to William McKendree" (August 5, 1813), in *Journal*, 3:475-92, 475, 480. Several pages into the address, Asbury began to appeal by extensive citation to Thomas Haweis's *History of the Church of Christ*, on the basis of which he posited the apostolic character of Methodist episcopacy.
27. For recent efforts to review Methodist ecclesiology, typically with reference to its Wesleyan foundations and their catholic import, see Campbell, *Methodist Doctrine*, 64–79; Jones, *United Methodist Doctrine*, 241–74; Klaiber and Marquardt, *Living Grace*, 311–417; and Theodore Runyon, *The New Creation: John Wesley's Theology Today* (Nashville: Abingdon, 1998).
28. Jesse Lee, *A Short History of the Methodists* (Baltimore: Magill and Clime, 1810; facsimile edition, Rutland, VT: Academy Books, 1974), 340.
29. The placement of camp meeting in quarterly meeting can be seen in the quarterly meeting records reproduced in Sweet, ed., *The Methodists*. I have explored the relation between camp meeting and quarterly meeting in *Methodist Conference* and *Early American Methodism*.
30. See Russell E. Richey, *The Methodist Conference in America: A History*. (Nashville: Kingswood Books, 1996); Richey, *Early American Methodism*; and Lester Ruth, *A Little Heaven Below: Worship at Early American Methodist Quarterly Meetings* (Nashville: Kingswood Books, 2000).
31. See Tucker, *American Methodist Worship*.
32. Young, *Companion to Hymnal*, 112–13.
33. See Tucker, *American Methodist Worship*, 3–30.
34. See James Penn Pilkington and Walter Newton Vernon, Jr., *The United Methodist Publishing House: A History*, 2 vols. (Nashville: Abingdon, 1968 and 1989).
35. For an illustration of this point and documents that sustain the argument of this paragraph, see Sweet, *The Methodists*, 709, 680–709.
36. Ibid., 706.
37. See Tigert, *Constitutional History*, 463, 533. Tigert examined the titles and contents of the early *Disciplines* in Appendix I, 463–76.
38. MEC, *Doctrines and Discipline* (1808), 15.
39. Richey, *Methodist Conference*, traces this evolution.
40. For exploration of the 1972 statement and its 1988 revision, see Langford, *Doctrine and Theology*.
41. Young, *Companion to Hymnal*, 97 108.
42. For the stemma of MEC, MECS, MPC, and MC hymnals, see ibid., 94–95; for EUB, 81–82.
43. See Thomas G. Long, *Beyond the Worship Wars: Building Vital and Faithful Worship* (Alban Institute, 2001).
44. For the terse, official narrative of this union and the histories behind it, see UMC, *Discipline* (2004), 9–20, 50–59.
45. See Albert C. Outler, "Introduction to the Report of the 1968–72 Theological Study Commission," in Langford, *Doctrine and Theology*, 20–25. The entire volume, on which this discussion draws, attends to the 1972 Commission and 1988 Committee and the resultant doctrinal-theological disciplinary sections. See also Frank, *Polity*, 141–57.
46. See the final section below on the ecclesiological and ecumenically ecclesiological import of the *Discipline*.
47. UMC, *Discipline* (2004); *The United Methodist Book of Worship*, 1992; and *The United Methodist Hymnal*, 1989.
48. United Methodists divide as to whether the "open table" extends universally or to the baptized. See E. Byron Anderson, *The Meaning of Holy Communion in The United Methodist Church* (Nashville: Discipleship Resources, 2000); Gayle Carlton Felton, *This Gift of Water: The Practice and Theology of Baptism among Methodists in America* (Nashville: Abingdon, 1992); Felton, *By Water and the Spirit: Making Connections for Identity and Ministry* (Nashville: Discipleship Resources, 2003); Felton, *This Holy Mystery: A United*

Methodist Understanding of Holy Communion (Nashville: Discipleship Resources, 2005); and Lester Ruth, *A Little Heaven Below*.
49. Langford enunciated such claims several times in conversation or discussion.
50. UMC, *Discipline* (2004), 78–79.
51. See Riley Case, *Evangelical and Methodist, A Popular History* (Nashville: Abingdon Press, 2004) and Leon Howell, *United Methodism @ Risk: A Wake-up Call* (Kingston, NY: Information Project for United Methodists, 2003).
52. On Methodist participation in the various ecumenical conversations, see Geoffrey Wainwright, *Methodists in Dialog* (Nashville: Kingswood Books, 1995).
53. However, as the "Counterpoint" discussion indicates, not all United Methodists hold these two aspects together. The more progressive wing of the church believes that the conservatives slight justice and social transformation. The conservative wing believes that the progressives slight justification and evangelism.
54. On issues and problems related to this concept, see Frank, *Polity*, 162–68; and chapter 6.
55. UMC, *Discipline* (2004), 95–124.
56. Young, *Companion to Hymnal*.
57. See Jones, *United Methodist Doctrine*, 246–70; and Campbell, *Methodist Doctrine*, 64–79.

BIBLIOGRAPHY OF FREQUENTLY CITED TITLES

Asbury, Francis. *The Journals and Letters of Francis Asbury*. Edited by Elmer T. Clark. 3 vols. London: Epworth; Nashville: Abingdon, 1958.
Bangs, Nathan. *A History of the Methodist Episcopal Church*. 12th ed. 4 vols. New York: Carlton & Porter, 1860.
———. *An Original Church of Christ: Or A Spiritual Vindication of the Orders and Powers of the Ministry of the Methodist Episcopal Church*. New York: Mason and Lane, 1837.
———. *The Present State, Prospects, and Responsibilities of the Methodist Episcopal Church*. New York: Lane & Scott, 1850.
Behney, J. Bruce and Paul H. Eller. *The History of the Evangelical United Brethren Church*. Nashville: Abingdon, 1979.
Bercovitch, Sacvan. *The American Jeremiad*. Madison: University of Wisconsin Press, 1978.
Bucke, Emory S., ed. *The History of American Methodism*. 3 vols. New York: Abingdon, 1964.
Buckley, James M. *A History of Methodists in the United States*. 4th ed. New York: Charles Scribner's Sons, 1900.
Campbell, Dennis M. *The Yoke of Obedience*. Nashville: Abingdon, 1988.
Clarke, Adam. *The Preacher's Manual: Including Clavis Biblica, or a Compendium of Scriptural Knowledge; and his Letter to a Methodist Preacher on His Entrance into the Work of Ministry; and also Dr. Coke's Four Discourses on the Duties of a Minster of the Gospel*. New York: Bangs & Mason, 1821.
Colbert, William. "A Journal of the Travels of William Colbert, Methodist Preacher: thro' parts of Maryland, Pennsylvania, New York, Delaware and Virginia in 1790 to 1838." 10 vols. Typescript. Held in Drew University Library.
Cummings, A. W. *The Early Schools of Methodism*. New York: Phillips & Hunt, 1886.
De Puy, W. H., ed. *The Methodist Centennial Year-Book for 1884*. New York: Phillips & Hunt, 1883.
Duvall, Slyvanus M. *The Methodist Episcopal Church and Education up to 1869*. New York: Bureau of Publications, Teachers College, 1928.

Bibliography of Frequently Cited Titles

Frank, Thomas Edward. *Polity, Practice and the Mission of The United Methodist Church*. Nashville: Abingdon, 2006.

Handy, Robert T. *A Christian America. Protestant Hopes and Historical Realities*. 2nd ed. New York: Oxford University Press, 1984.

Harmon, Nolan B., ed. *The Encyclopedia of World Methodism*. 2 vols. Nashville: United Methodist Publishing House, 1974.

Hatch, Nathan O. *The Democratization of American Christianity*. New Haven, CT: Yale University Press, 1989.

Heitzenrater, Richard P. *Wesley and the People Called Methodists*. Nashville: Abingdon, 1995.

Hiltner, Seward. *Preface to Pastoral Theology*. New York: Abingdon, 1958.

Jones, Scott J. *United Methodist Doctrine: The Extreme Center*. Nashville: Abingdon, 2002.

Kirby, James E. *The Episcopacy in American Methodism*. Nashville: Kingswood Books, 2000.

Langford, Thomas A. *Practical Divinity*. Nashville: Abingdon, 1983.

———, ed. *Doctrine and Theology in The United Methodist Church*. Nashville: Kingswood Books, 1991.

Lee, Jesse. *A Short History of the Methodists*. Baltimore: Magill and Clime, 1810; facsimile edition, Rutland, VT: Academy Books, 1974.

Luccock, Halford E. and Paul Hutchinson. *The Story of Methodism*. New York: Methodist Book Concern, 1926.

Mathews, James K. and William B. Oden, ed., *Vision and Supervision: A Sourcebook of Significant Documents of the Council of Bishops of The United Methodist Church*. Nashville: Abingdon, 2003.

McCulloh, Gerald O. *Ministerial Education in the American Methodist Movement*. Nashville: UMC Board of Higher Education and Ministry, 1980.

Mead, Sidney E. *The Nation with the Soul of a Church*. New York: Harper & Row, 1975.

Methodist Episcopal Church. *The Doctrines and Discipline of the Methodist Episcopal Church in America, with Explanatory Notes, by Thomas Coke and Francis Asbury*. Philadelphia, 1798 (facsimile edition, edited by Frederick A. Norwood, Rutland, VT: Academy Books, 1979).

———. *The Doctrines and Discipline of the Methodist Episcopal Church*. New York: Wilson and Hitt, 1808.

———. *A Form of Discipline, For the Ministers, Preachers, and Member(s?) of the Methodist Episcopal Church in America*. New York: W. Ross, 1787.

———. *Journal of the . . . Delegated General Conference of the Methodist Episcopal Church*. New York: Eaton & Mains, 1904–1936.

———. *Journals of the General Conference of the Methodist Episcopal Church*. 16 vols. New York: Carlton & Porter, 1796–1900.

———. *Minutes of Several Conversations between the Rev. Thomas Coke, LL.D., the Rev. Francis Asbury, and Others begun in Baltimore, in the state of Maryland, on Monday, the 27th of December, in the year 1784. Composing a Form of Discipline for the Ministers, Preachers, and other Members of the Methodist Episcopal Church in America*. Philadelphia: Charles Cist, 1785.

———. *Minutes of the Methodist Conferences, Annually Held in America; From 1773 to 1813, Inclusive.* New York: Published by Daniel Hitt and Thomas Ware, for the Methodist Connexion in the United States, 1813.

Miller, Glenn T. *Piety and Intellect. The Aims and Purposes of Ante-Bellum Theological Education.* Atlanta: Scholar's Press, 1990.

Moede, Gerald F. *The Office of Bishop in the Methodist Church.* Zürich: Publishing House of the Methodist Church, 1964.

Niebuhr, H. Richard. *The Social Sources of Denominationalism.* New York: Meridian, 1957.

Norwood, Frederick A. *The Story of American Methodism.* Nashville: Abingdon, 1974.

Olin, Stephen. *The Works of Stephen Olin, D. D., LL.D., Late President of the Wesleyan University.* New York: Harper & Brothers, 1852.

Patterson, L. Dale. "The Ministerial Mind of American Methodism: The Course of Study for the Ministry of the Methodist Episcopal Church, the Methodist Episcopal Church, South and the Methodist Protestant Church, 1876–1920." PhD diss., Drew University, 1984.

Pilkington, James Penn. *The Methodist Publishing House: A History.* vol. 1 (Beginnings to 1870). Nashville: Abingdon, 1968.

Potts, David B. *Wesleyan University, 1831–1910: Collegiate Enterprise in New England.* New Haven, CT: Yale University Press, 1992.

Richey, Russell E. *Early American Methodism.* Bloomington: Indiana University Press, 1991.

———. "The Legacy of Francis Asbury: The Teaching Office in Episcopal Methodism," *Quarterly Review* 15 (Summer 1995): 145–74.

———. *The Methodist Conference in America: A History.* Nashville: Kingswood Books, 1996.

Richey, Russell E. and Thomas Edward Frank. *Episcopacy in the Methodist Tradition: Perspectives and Proposals.* Nashville: Abingdon, 2004.

Richey, Russell E. and Kenneth E. Rowe, eds. *Rethinking Methodist History.* Nashville: Kingswood Books, 1985.

Richey, Russell E., William B. Lawrence, and Dennis M. Campbell, eds. *Connectionalism: Ecclesiology, Mission, and Identity.* United Methodism in American Culture, Vol. 1. Nashville: Abingdon, 1997.

———, eds. *The People(s) Called Methodist: Forms and Reforms of Their Life.* United Methodism in American Culture, Vol. 2. Nashville: Abingdon, 1998.

———, eds. *Doctrines and Discipline.* United Methodism in American Culture, Vol. 3. Nashville: Abingdon, 1999.

———, eds. *Questions for the Twenty-first Century Church.* United Methodism in American Culture, Vol. 4. Nashville: Abingdon, 1999.

———, eds. *Marks of Methodism: Practices of Ecclesiology.* United Methodism in American Culture, Vol. 5. Nashville: Abingdon, 2005.

Rowe, Kenneth E. *Methodist Union Catalog: Pre–1976 Imprints.* Multivolume series, in process. Metuchen, N.J.: Scarecrow, 1975–.

Ruth, Lester. *A Little Heaven Below: Worship at Early American Methodist Quarterly Meetings.* Nashville: Kingswood Books, 2000.

Bibliography of Frequently Cited Titles

Scanlon, James Edward. *Randolph-Macon College. A Southern History, 1825–1967*. Charlottesville: University Press of Virginia, 1983.

Shalhope, Robert E. "Republicanism and Early American Historiography." *William and Mary Quarterly* 39 (April 1982): 334–56.

Short, Roy Hunter. *Chosen to be Consecrated: The Bishops of The Methodist Church, 1784–1968*. Lake Junaluska: Commission on Archives and History for the Council of Bishops, 1976.

Simpson, Matthew. *Lectures on Preaching*. New York: Phillips & Hunt, 1879.

Smeltzer, Wallace Guy. *The History of United Methodism in Western Pennsylvania*. Nashville: Parthenon, 1975.

Spann, John R., ed., *The Ministry*. New York: Abingdon-Cokesbury, 1949.

Spellman, Norman Woods. "The General Superintendency in American Methodism, 1784–1870." PhD diss., Yale University, 1961.

Stevens, Abel. *A Compendious History of American Methodism*. New York: Eaton & Mains, 1868.

Sweet, William Warren. *Circuit-Rider Days in Indiana*. Indianapolis: W. K. Stewart Co., 1916.

———. *Methodism in American History*. Revised edition. New York: Abingdon, 1953.

———, ed. *The Methodists: A Collection of Source Materials*. Chicago: University of Chicago Press, 1946.

Thrift, Minton. *Memoir of the Rev. Jesse Lee. With Extracts from his Journals*. New York: Bangs and Mason, 1823.

Tigert, Jno. J. *A Constitutional History of American Episcopal Methodism*. 3rd ed., rev. Nashville: Publishing House of the Methodist Episcopal Church, South, 1908.

Tucker, Karen B. Westerfield. *American Methodist Worship*. New York: Oxford University Press, 2001.

United Methodist Church. *The Book of Discipline of The United Methodist Church*. Nashville: United Methodist Publishing House, 1988.

———. *The Book of Discipline of The United Methodist Church*. Nashville: United Methodist Publishing House, 2004.

Vernon, Walter Newton, Jr., *The United Methodist Publishing House: A History*, vol. 2 (Nashville: Abingdon Press, 1989).

Vickers, John. *Thomas Coke: Apostle of Methodism*. Nashville: Abingdon, 1969.

Wuthnow, Robert. *The Restructuring of American Religion*. Princeton: Princeton University Press, 1988.

———. *The Struggle for America's Soul*. Grand Rapids: Eerdmans, 1989.

Young, Carlton R. *Companion to The United Methodist Hymnal*. Nashville: Abingdon, 1993.

www.ingramcontent.com/pod-product-compliance
Lightning Source LLC
Chambersburg PA
CBHW011710290426
44111CB00019B/2927